PENGUIN BOOK

THE SUN IN THE M[...]

M. M. Kaye was born in India and spent most of her childhood and much of her early married life in that country. Her ties with India are strong: her grandfather, father, brother and husband all served the Raj, and her grandfather's first cousin, Sir John Kaye, wrote the standard accounts of the Indian Mutiny and the first Afghan War. When India achieved independence her husband joined the British Army, and for the next nineteen years she followed the drum to all sorts of exciting places she would not otherwise have seen, including Kenya, Zanzibar, Egypt, Cyprus and Berlin. M. M. Kaye is known world-wide for her bestselling historical novels *The Far Pavilions* and *The Shadow of the Moon* (both of which are published in Penguin), and *Trade Wind*; and for her detective novels *Death in Berlin*, *Death in Kenya* and *Death in Cyprus*, and *Death in Zanzibar*, *Death in Kashmir* and *Death in the Andamans* (which are published together in Penguin as *House of Shade*). Penguin also publishes *Golden Afternoon*, the second volume of her autobiography. M. M. Kaye has also written a children's story, *The Ordinary Princess* (1991).

M. M. KAYE

THE SUN IN THE MORNING

BEING THE FIRST PART OF
SHARE OF SUMMER,
HER AUTOBIOGRAPHY

PENGUIN BOOKS

PENGUIN BOOKS

Published by the Penguin Group
Penguin Books Ltd, 27 Wrights Lane, London W8 5TZ, England
Penguin Putnam Inc., 375 Hudson Street, New York, New York 10014, USA
Penguin Books Australia Ltd, Ringwood, Victoria, Australia
Penguin Books Canada Ltd, 10 Alcorn Avenue, Toronto, Ontario, Canada M4V 3B2
Penguin Books (NZ) Ltd, Private Bag 102902, NSMC, Auckland, New Zealand

Penguin Books Ltd, Registered Offices: Harmondsworth, Middlesex, England

First published by Viking 1990
Published in Penguin Books 1992
13 15 17 19 20 18 16 14 12

Printed in England by Clays Ltd, St Ives plc

To

TACKLOW

and the India that he knew
and loved so much

Portrait of my father, Sir Cecil Kaye CSI, CIE, CBE,
to whom this book is dedicated.

List of Illustrations

Contents

Foreword

Beyond the wheat and harvest
of fruit upon the bough,
I recognize old Autumn
riding on a plough.
The year has passed its zenith
and now it must decline;
Earth's had her share of summer
As I have had of mine.

J.H.B.

It was still high summer with me when those few lines of verse in a monthly magazine, now long defunct, caught my attention by suggesting an appropriate title for something I had long promised myself that I would write in the autumn of my days: an autobiography that would tell my children and I hoped my grandchildren, something of the lavish, sun-splashed share of summer that has fallen to my lot. However, since at that time I was not yet ready to give much thought to autumn, I contented myself with copying out that little verse,* and having pasted it for safe keeping inside the cover of an old copy of Kipling's *Kim*, I pushed the whole idea of an autobiography into a cupboard in the back of my mind labelled '*Some day when I am old and grey . . .*'.

Millions of people, I am told, are not only convinced that they could write an autobiography, but equally certain that it would sell like potato-crisps if they did. And when one realizes how many people do write one — and how very many readers (my husband among them) prefer true stories to fiction — who is to say they are wrong? Any number of autobiographies and biographies pour off the presses every

---

*I have been unable to trace the author of these lines. No one seems to know any longer who J.H.B. is — or was. But I am more than grateful to him or her.

1

year, and since even the dullest of them are, if nothing else, small fragments of History, they should be valued as such even if the authors or their subjects cannot claim to be famous or notorious figures in their own right. 'Mr Pooter' is a shining example to us all.

My decision to write my own some day was made as far back as 1947; the year in which that brief period that has come to be known as 'the Raj'* came to an end and the British packed up and left India: for witnessing a once great Empire crumble and dissolve like a child's sandcastle when the tide comes in, and watching, appalled, the Pax Britannica snap like a thread of cotton, I felt that I must one day write about all the people and places and things I had seen and known, before it was too late. Not for my own sake, because as far as I am concerned it is all safely in my head where it will stay until I die — and perhaps after that. Not even, really, for my children; because they like myself were born in India and I intended to tell them all I could about the past that I had known. But for my children's children and their children, whose lives are going to be so very different from my own. No one else will ever again live the kind of life that I have lived. Or see what I saw. That world has vanished for ever — blown away by the wind which as the Chinese proverb says 'cannot read'.

A few years ago my younger daughter, who was with a touring company that was booked to play in a dozen exotic cities starting in the Far East and ending in Cairo, wrote home to say she was afraid that she had seen them all a good ten years too late, because every city they had played was exactly like the last. The hotels were all 'Eastern-Hilton' style; while shops, offices, flats and public buildings were all exactly like the last. To which I replied sadly that she had not been ten years too late, but thirty at the very least.

I, however, had not been too late. It has been my great good fortune to see India when that once fabulously beautiful land was as lovely, and to a great extent as peaceful and unspoiled, as Eden before the Fall. To live for two years in Peking in an old Chinese house, once the property of a Manchu Prince, at a time when the citizens of that country still wore their national costumes instead of dressing up —

---

* In my time the term was Sikār, which means 'Government', rather than 'Rule'. But since the media and the public have taken to using Raj as shorthand for the time that the British governed India, I may as well do the same.

or down! — in dull, anonymous, Russian-style 'uniforms'. To have visited Japan before war, the Bomb and the American occupation altered it beyond recognition, when the sight of a Japanese woman in European dress was unusual enough to make you turn and stare, feeling startled and more than a little shocked; and when there was only one major tourist hotel in beautiful Nikko, and no railway desecrated the lovely road that leads up through the mountain gorges to Lake Chuzenji . . .

I have lived in Persia; in Khorramshahr on the banks of the Shatt-al-Arab. Bought silks and brocades in the Covered Bazaar in Basra; known Egypt in the days when that country and its capital city looked much as it did when Walter Tyndale painted it, and been privileged to see so much of this wonderful world in the last sunset blaze of its infinite charm and variety, before the nations involved in the Second World War drenched it in blood and destruction, and then replaced the beauty they had destroyed with a jungle of ferro-concrete, vast glass matchboxes and instant council-houses — together with the weed-like growth of class warfare, quangos, racism and Government interference; — not to mention envy, hatred, malice and all unchari-tableness! For which reason my share of summer is going to concern itself as little as possible with politics.

Too many people have already written, or are engaged in writing, 'committed', politically slanted or fashionable books for me to try adding to their number. Yes, there was poverty, squalor and starvation; drought and famine; epidemics and corruption. There still is. Yes, mistakes were made — some of them terrible. And yes, of course there were demonstrations and riots and reprisals — just as there are now. Anyone who was not aware of that would have had to be blind, deaf or half-witted. I knew all right, and I saw. But if I do not choose to write much about such things it is because I know I can safely leave that to the legions who can — and are only too eager to do so!

The years had begun to pass with ever increasing speed, but while my decision to write about my own prodigal share of summer remained firm, I felt no sense of urgency; there was still plenty of time — and so many other things to do. Too many things. The autobiography could wait. Then one day, not for the first time, I returned to India again.

On this occasion I went back with my sister to Jaipur in Rajasthan to watch my novel *The Far Pavilions* being filmed for a TV serial. And one evening while the two of us were having tea on the verandah of what had once been the British Residency but was now the Raj Mahal Hotel, which the film company had taken over as its administrative headquarters, someone from the costume department dumped two or three sackfuls of discarded scraps and off-cuts of material on the floor near our table.

The sacks were large and unwieldy and presently one toppled over, spilling a cascade of assorted bits and pieces onto the cool marble. And as we sat looking down at it and idly identifying the various fragments, it occurred to me that the contents of that rag-bag could be an allegory of my life. Those exotic, shimmering remnants of gold and silver tissue, shot-silk, brocade, embroidered velvet and sequin-sewn satin in every imaginable tint and colour, together with off-cuts from darker, thicker and more sombre materials in black, brown and grey and the plain, coarse white cotton cloth that is worn in India for mourning ... it was all there.

That thought was followed by a much more disturbing one. All those multicoloured shreds and patches were destined for a rubbish-heap or a bonfire! It brought me up with a jolt, for it seemed like a timely reminder that the sooner I started work on that autobiography the better. Quite suddenly, there was no blinking the fact that by now my year was well past its zenith and it was no longer a case of 'old autumn on a plough', but winter that I could see ahead. My summer was over; and by now my autumn was almost over too; that miraculous, golden autumn that had been transformed for me into a totally unexpected Indian Summer by the success of *The Far Pavilions*.

The events of that astonishing Indian Summer had kept me too busy to spare either time or thought for writing my autobiography. And now that I have at last got round to it I am worried for fear that I have, after all, left it too late. Because, let's face it, my memory, which except in the matter of a perennially weak spot, names, has never let me down, is beginning to fail me. And as most of the earlier family records and photographs that could have helped me out with facts, dates and names were tragically destroyed in a warehouse fire a year or two after my father's death — together with all his books, my mother's photograph-albums and most of our family possessions — I have lost an invaluable source of reference.

Readers will therefore have to forgive me if my recollections are as varied and as scrappy as that rag-bag of off-cuts from the lovely costumes of *The Far Pavilions*. And if I occasionally make mistakes over dates or in chronology, I do most sincerely regret it. Perhaps I should have called this book 'If Memory Serves'? (except that someone else has already used that for his own autobiography). If there are places where mine has not served me well enough, I apologize. But this is how I remember it now — those lovely, glittering scraps sewn with sequins and gold thread, and those drab brown, grey and black ones, without which no life and no rag-bag would be complete.

Among them you will also find various snippets of historical information that I have thrown in because my father so infected me, at an early age, with his own love of history, that to me the tale of times past, and the thought that great events took place centuries ago on the very ground where I am standing, has always added an extra dimension to my enjoyment of the present ...

> *Ah, did you once see Shelley plain,*
> *And did he stop and speak to you*
> *And did you speak to him again?*
> *How strange it seems, and new!*

Here, then, in *The Sun in the Morning*, are the contents of the first rag-bag of my own lavish Share of Summer.

M. M. Kaye

begun at
Laggan House,
Morayshire

completed at
Northbrook,
Hampshire.

❊ I ❊

'Only yesterday — !'

Chapter 1

'O, call back yesterday, bid time return'

Shakespeare, *Richard II*

A nightjar called harshly from somewhere in the fields beyond the ugly brick-and-stucco house that Mother had rented for our school holidays; and hearing it she paused by an open window to look out into the lilac-coloured twilight of an English summer evening, and said in the abstracted voice of one who is speaking a thought aloud: 'I remember standing in the dusk by a window at Fairlawn, holding Bill in my arms and listening to the nightjars crying in the valley below ...'

The house that she had gone back to in memory lies on the other side of the world among the foothills of the Himalayas; a few miles beyond Simla (which in the days of the Raj was the summer capital of the Government of India) on a steep hillside below the road that leads to Kulu and Tibet — the same road that Kipling's fictional Sir Puran Dass, 'Prime Minister of no small State', took when he put on the orange-coloured robes of a *bairagi** and went into the mountains in search of peace and enlightenment. I do not know whom the house belonged to then; though my memory is that he was an Indian. But whoever he was, he must have been a close friend of my parents, because I remember spending many weekends there when I was a child. And if my brother Bill, who is older than I am, was still an infant-in-arms, Mother must have been speaking of something that happened well before I was born and when she herself was not yet twenty-one. Yet inexplicably, that memory had stayed clear-cut in her mind for all those years.

* A wandering holy man. (The story of Puran Baghat appears in Kipling's *Second Jungle Book*.)

Everyone must possess a store of similar trivial incidents in their minds: unimportant moments that for no particular reason seem to be charged with a special significance. But though the memory of that long-ago Indian twilight is not mine but my mother's, it has become mine; because I never hear a nightjar cry without seeing clearly, in my mind's eye, the girl who will be my mother standing by an open window with her first-born in her arms, looking down at the dusk gathering in a Himalayan valley and listening to the voices of the nightjars crying and calling among the shadows below. It is one of many reasons that make me believe that genes are not the only things that our forebears hand down to us —

The manner in which our parents and grandparents thought and behaved, as well as much of what they told us about themselves, must surely exert a sufficiently strong influence on us to make it seem as though we share some of their more vivid memories and have actually witnessed sights and events that happened well before we were born. I never saw anyone ride a 'penny-farthing' bicycle. But Mother did, and from hearing her describe it to me when I was small, I feel that I have seen it too. Just as I have seen Queen Victoria — a little, dumpy, frumpy old woman in black — riding in an open landau through cheering, adoring crowds to St Paul's Cathedral in the City of London to give thanks for sixty glorious years on the throne; because my father stood and cheered among the crowd on Constitution Hill on the day that she celebrated her Diamond Jubilee, and he described it to me graphically many years later.

A part of me, too, has stood beside my mother's father, Thomas Bryson, known to his children and many grandchildren as 'the Grand-Dadski' ('the Dadski' for short), on a bridge in Edinburgh far back in the nineteenth century when, as a young and up-and-coming architect, he was astounded to hear God telling him that he must become a missionary and go out to preach the Gospel to the heathen.

The Dadski is the only person I ever met who literally received the Word and His orders; he told me about it when I was around twelve years old and I demanded to know if God had spoken to him out loud and in English (or rather Scottish, since the Dadski himself was a dyed-in-the-wool Scot). If so, why hadn't the passers-by heard it too? The Voice, explained the Dadski, was inside his head; and painfully clear. Painfully, because he had no desire at all to be a missionary or preach the Gospel to anyone; he was doing fine in his chosen career as an architect. He therefore ignored the Voice and went home. The Voice, however, refused to be silent and continued to issue orders until finally the badgered young man took the problem to the experts and consulted the minister of his local kirk (he was Church of Scotland).

The minister was of the opinion that the Voice, if genuine, was not to be disobeyed; but that it might be advisable for the young architect to take a dose of Gregory's Powder and a course of iron tonic, followed by a short holiday involving plenty of fresh air and exercise. If, after that, the Voice still persisted in issuing instructions, then there was plainly nothing for it but to obey, and he suggested a visit to one or other of the many missionary societies.

To cut a long story short, the Dadski eventually presented himself at the headquarters of the London Missionary Society and offered his services. He seems to have had no preference as to which lot of 'heathens' he would prefer to try his hand at converting, and the Society apparently ran a careless finger down the list of countries in need of Enlightenment, found most of them fairly well provided with Spreaders-of-the-Word, and decided that there was a vacancy in China. Whereupon the Dadski bought several Chinese–English dictionaries and booked a passage on the sailing-ship, 'Silver Eagle', bound for Shanghai; a voyage that took just under five months, which in those days was well under par for the course: particularly when one takes into account that they rounded the Cape of Good Hope, battled through storms in which a number of sails were shredded by gale-force winds, and for ninety consecutive days did not catch so much as a glimpse of land. However, after all that they reached their destination in safety towards the end of January 1867.

Posted to Wuchang as its first resident missionary and only 'foreign devil', the Dadski wore Chinese dress and learned to speak the local dialect with such fluency that he was soon preaching on street corners and in markets and fields. I don't know how many converts he made there, but it was not until some considerable time later, when he was transferred up north to the raw new Treaty Port of Tientsin, that it became abundantly clear that God had known exactly what He was about when He told my grandfather to become a missionary. Tientsin was not in any particular need of another saver of souls, but it did need, urgently, a competent architect. The Dadski rolled up his sleeves and dealt with that problem: on the lay front as well as the secular. The old church that he built in the Mission Compound on the Taku Road vanished long ago, giving place to a wing of the MacKenzie Memorial Hospital. But the Tientsin Anglo-Chinese College and various other public buildings, which may or may not have survived into the 1980s, were still standing when he died in 1936 aged ninety-three. And I suspect that the Union Church, which eventually contained a charming chapel dedicated to the memory of the Rev. Thomas Bryson and his wife Mary Isabella, is by now plastered with Communist posters and slogans and calls itself a 'Hall of Youth and Culture' or something of the sort.

The Rev. Thomas married my grandmother in 1875 during his first home leave from China. I never saw her, but if the daguerreotypes taken of her at the time of her marriage are anything to go by, she was a very pretty creature indeed. Moreover, like Jo March in *Little Women*, she cherished dreams of becoming a writer. Like Jo, she wrote a story under a pen-name — in her case 'Isa Carr' in place of Isabella Carruthers — and her story was accepted for publication by one of the few women's weekly magazines of her day. When it appeared as a serial, Isabella, again like Jo, read it aloud to her family without disclosing that she was the author until she had finished reading them the final instalment. *Triumph!* Apparently they had all enjoyed it immensely. Though it is hard to know why, as I have to admit that it bored me rigid when in the 1920s I read, in a cherished bound volume, the relevant chapters removed from that forgotten mid-Victorian magazine. Its meek, virtuous and much persecuted heroine (Jane Eyre's 'Helen' diluted with pints of buttermilk) was so determinedly long-suffering that one felt she deserved everything she got.

As 'Isa Carr' my grandmother also wrote poetry; equally dire and only comparable to the poetical effusions of dear Wally Hamilton, a real-life character out of one of my historical novels, *The Far Pavilions*. But after her marriage to my grandfather, Isabella took to writing books for the China Inland Mission under her own name: beautifully bound volumes profusely illustrated with steel engravings, of which only one, *Child Life in Chinese Homes*, is worth reading. The rest are almost impossible to plough through because their themes are overloaded with pious and sugary Victorian platitudes. She was undoubtedly a good and truly Christian woman who was dearly loved by her husband and her eight children (nine, if one counts '*Little Lily, born at Wuchang on the Yang-tse-Kiang, died at Chepoo on the Yellow Sea*', to whose memory her mother dedicated that book about Chinese children). I would like to have met her, but I never did. She died in 1913 in North China; the land in which she spent the greater part of her life and where most of her children were born and one was buried.

Two of those children, my mother — who was christened Margaret Sarah but never called anything but 'Daisy' — and her twin brother Kenneth, were born on 26 August 1886, in the Mission House in Tientsin that had been built by their father the Dadski. Isabella's eight surviving children, Tom, Alec, Arnold, Alice, the twins Daisy and Ken, Dorothy and finally Lillian, were eventually taken back to England and to school by their mother, who brought her Chinese house-servant, Jen-Nan, with her and installed the family in a large rented house in Blackheath — in those days a green and rural spot on the outskirts of London where the London Missionary Society had a school for the children of missionaries; this was later attended by the young Eric Liddell, the 'Flying Scotsman' of Olympic fame, whose story was told in an award-winning film called *Chariots of Fire*.

Jen-Nan, who like Voltaire's Habakkuk appears to have been *capable de tout*, ran the house with the utmost efficiency, acting as cook and general factotum and, despite the fact that his English was limited to a few words of 'Pidgin', sallying out to do the household shopping pigtailed and wearing his customary grey or blue Chinese dress complete with black silk slippers and black skull-cap with a button on top; invariably accompanied by an interested crowd of local citizens which included almost every child in Blackheath, enthralled by their first sight of a slant-eyed, yellow-skinned son of the Celestial Kingdom. Mother says he thoroughly enjoyed the sensation he created among the 'Outer Barbarians'.

Jen-Nan went back to China with Isabella when she returned there to rejoin her husband, leaving her children with a distant kinswoman who lived in Bedford and was known as 'Aunt Lizzie': a childless little woman with a face like a frog's and a heart of gold and marshmallow, who was dearly loved by three generations: Isabella and her children and her children's children — for we in our turn would often spend the school holidays with Aunt Lizzie when our parents had to return to the East without us.

My mother and her brothers and sisters went to school first in Blackheath and then in Bedford, and when Isabella returned again (this time without Jen-Nan) they went back to Blackheath, where Mother acquired her first beau; a dashing young man called Owen Kentish. Apparently Alice, the eldest of the four Bryson sisters, had a *tendre* for the handsome Owen and was sadly cast down at overhearing him confide to a friend that 'the one *I'd* like to marry is Daisy — if she wasn't still much too young'! A remark which, repeated to her by some little pitcher with long ears, did wonders for Mother's morale, however much it may have lowered poor Alice's.

Mother is a very old lady now, and there are times when she thinks I am her sister Alice and that the two of us, wearing, I presume, high buttoned boots and frilly cotton petticoats under ankle-length summer frocks with eighteen-inch waistbands and leg-of-mutton sleeves, plus large flat hats, are walking up the steep road into Folkestone during a long-vanished seaside summer holiday to meet the Kentish boys. I am interested, and more than a little amused, to discover that she is not above twitting Alice (who has been dead for many years) on the subject of Owen's known preference for herself, and find it fascinating to discover myself cast in the role of a love-lorn seventeen-year-old back in early Edwardian England, being needled by a pretty chit of a younger sister who will grow up to be my mother.

Not long after this particular holiday Isabella, who had come home again for a furlough in England, returned once more to China taking some if not all of her children with her. Their ship put in at a great many ports during that long, exciting voyage; among them Bombay, where the family went ashore to see the sights and visit the Zoological Gardens. Almost a third of a century later — in the year, in fact, that the Second World War broke out — Mother and I spent an afternoon at the same zoo, and she paused before the entrance and looking up at the wide iron arch that spans the top of the gate proclaiming the Zoological Gardens, said thoughtfully that the last time she walked under that arch she had been fifteen years old and on her way out to China. I observed lightly that that must seem a very long time ago, and she sighed and shook her head and said, 'No; that's what is so frightening. It seems as though it was only yesterday.'

Perhaps because she had used the word 'frightening', it was then that I realized how paltry, in the face of the swift centuries, is the 'three score years and ten' that the Bible reckons as man's allotted span. For by then Mother had been a widow for several years, my brother and sister were both married and had children of their own, and our family circle had broken up. Yet that first visit to the Bombay Zoo in the dawn of the twentieth century, when she was still a schoolgirl who had not even put her hair up or met her future husband, still seemed to her as though it had happened 'only yesterday'.

I learned in that moment what all of us learn in the end: that on the inside most of us stay the same even though our outsides change so greatly, wrinkling, withering or growing stout and unwieldy; our hair turning grey and unattractive things happening to our chins. Yet within that ageing outer shell we remain very much the same as we did in our late teens and early twenties. Mother, for instance, became infuriated on being told that she could not accompany my sister Bets and myself to India when we flew there to watch part of my *Far Pavilions* being filmed in Jaipur. She wanted so much to come with us, and insisted that she was perfectly capable of doing so and that any number of her Indian friends would be only too delighted to see her again and put her up. Which, alas, was no longer true, since those friends are either dead or far too advanced in years to cope with a very frail old lady. *Eheu fugaces* indeed! But since I am writing about my parents, let us go back to the daybreak years of this century —

Victoria has died at long last and her eldest son, stout, jolly, bearded Edward VII (who once complained that he had got used to the idea of an everlasting father but considered it a bit hard to be saddled with an everlasting mother as well), has ushered in the rollicking and often scandalous Edwardian era. And young Daisy Bryson — having taken her first look at Imperial India and spent an enjoyable afternoon at the Bombay Zoo before travelling on to catch a glimpse of Colombo, Madras, Calcutta, Penang, Singapore, Hong Kong and Shanghai — has crossed the Taku Bar and sailed up the Wang Po River, to disembark at her birthplace, the North China treaty port of Tientsin.

In that part of the world, in those days, young unmarried European women were as rare as butterflies in December. This meant that when the steamer carrying Isabella Bryson and her brood drew into the dock, every male 'foreign devil' in that thriving port who could find an excuse to do so was there to watch it berth and to take a good look at Isabella's daughters. Among that watching crowd was a young businessman, Howard Payne, who, smitten to the heart by his first sight of Alice walking down the gangway in the wake of her mother, announced loudly and firmly: 'That's the girl I'm going to marry!' And marry her he did, though in the event it was Daisy who married first, with Alice as her chief bridesmaid. Which brings me to Father — who was seldom if ever called by that name, but for some forgotten reason, long lost sight of in the mists of childhood, I used to call 'Tacklow'. So Tacklow he will remain for the rest of this book.

According to my mother the first time he set eyes on me as a small, shawled bundle in a bassinette, barely two days old and newly washed and tidied up for what was — until a certain June morning over thirty years later — to be the most important meeting in my life, he took one look at me and said: 'This one's for me!' Unfortunately, my memory does not go back as far as that momentous occasion. But the attraction was mutual. I adored him from the start. He was mine; my own particular and special property. Perfection personified. No one ever had a better father, and my only complaint against Providence in this matter is that I saw far too little of him during the long years of school in England. He was much too conscientious to badger the Powers-that-Be for leave, and would send Mother home whenever he could afford to do so (which was not often, what with heavy school bills to pay and a perennial shortage of money), while he himself stayed at his desk, working and saving all the harder.

Any skill I may have with words I owe to Tacklow, who started reading to me almost before I had learned to talk. He never read me babyish books, or any of the innocuous wish-wash about jolly elves and bunnies on which future generations would be brought up. Instead, he started me on Kingsley's *Heroes*, which is full of lovely lines that can sound like poetry. I suspect him of occasionally paraphrasing for my benefit, because a sentence from the end of the story of Perseus sticks in my head to this day as: 'And Polydectes and his guests sit there still; a ring of cold grey stones upon the mountain side!' — which is not a strictly accurate quotation; as I was to discover years later when I spotted a battered copy of *The Heroes* on a second-hand bookstall in London's Fulham Road, and bought it for sixpence. He read me Kipling's *Jungle Books* and I remember crying my eyes out when

Mowgli has to leave the jungle and go down to the croplands to join his own kind — and laughing my head off at the tales in *Uncle Remus*; another book that I bought off a second-hand bookstall, only to find that I could not make head or tail of the dialect spoken by Uncle Remus, which Tacklow (who really should have been an actor) had read aloud to me with such fascinating fluency and effect.

I could discuss anything with my father. He treated me as an adult from the start and would talk to me by the hour, so that I came to know a lot more about him than I ever learned about Mother. So much, indeed, that he must have a chapter or two all to himself.

Chapter 2

~ぶだなぶ~

Let us now praise famous men,
And our fathers that begat us.

Ecclesiasticus XLIV.i.

He was born in 1868 in the early hours of Wednesday, 27 May: the
first surviving son of William Kaye, of the Indian Civil Service, and
his formidable wife, Jane, who had been Jane Beckett. It was Derby
Day, and his father, who had plunged heavily on a horse listed as
'Tom Bowline Colt' at odds of fifteen to one, had declared his intention
of naming the latest infant after the horse: provided of course that the
baby was a boy and the animal won. Thomas Bowline Colt Kaye ...
The mind boggles! But that was my grandfather all over.

Fortunately for the new arrival, though a sad blow for the family
bank balance, the Derby was won that year by the favourite, a horse
called Bluegown.* Which is why my beloved parent ended up being
christened 'Cecil' instead, a name that in those days was considered
distinctly cissy, being regarded as more a girl's name than a man's. It
was in fact bestowed upon him in compliment to his grandmother,
Mary Cecilia, a daughter of the Gibson-Craigs of Riccaton House,
near Edinburgh, from whom his parents may have cherished expectations on his behalf. (If so, they did not come to anything.)

When he was old enough to be sent to his public school (which for
some inexplicable British reason is the name we choose to apply to
our private ones), his Christian name was recorded in its rolls as
'Caecilius Kaye' because, by tradition, Winchester still inscribes the
names of its pupils in Latin. Despite this, he managed for a time to
give his classmates the impression that his name was Charles: a simple
ambition which was eventually thwarted by a doting maiden-aunt

* Owner, the then Prince of Wales, later King Edward VII.

18

who wrote to him addressing the envelope to 'Master Cecil Kaye'. Thereafter he was stuck with it. He seems on the whole to have enjoyed his schooldays, and in the course of them he made at least one lifelong friend: Reginald 'Cull' Brinton of Kidderminster, who like himself actually *enjoyed* Greek and Latin and was equally stage-struck.

I cannot remember his ever telling me how or why he should have become so fascinated by the theatre. Perhaps he did not know himself. But from the time that he was a small boy in a nankeen suit he had written, directed and sometimes acted in plays that were performed during the holidays before an audience of indulgent grown-ups, while many of his leisure hours were spent in poling his brothers and sisters around in a punt named 'The White Indian' on the upper lake at Tetworth Hall — a house in Bedfordshire then owned by his grand-parents — and dragooning them into being Red Indians on the warpath or early settlers in hostile territory. I still have a playbill that dates from his teens and advertises a single performance (matinée only) of a pantomime 'devised, written and directed by C. Kaye'.

His theatrical ambitions, however, were stamped on with the utmost firmness; Victoria's England believing to a man, and certainly to a woman, that the trap-door in the centre of every stage, out of which the Demon King would spring up during the pantomime season in scarlet tights and accompanied by a glare of red light and some effective pink smoke, did in fact lead straight down to Hell.

Winchester, which has the distinction of being the oldest public school in England, takes its name from the cathedral town in which it stands. It was founded in 1387 by a colourful character called William Wykeham who also founded New College, Oxford.

It is one of my regrets for an opportunity lost that I never visited Winchester with my father. I would have enjoyed a Tacklow-conducted tour round the College and the city, but it was one of those things that we were always going to do some day and for some reason or another never found the time to. Today there is a small tablet in the organ loft of the chapel to 'the memory of Sir Cecil Kaye, Kt, CSI, CIE, CBE, 21st Punjabis Indian Army, a Commoner of This College.'*
I saw Winchester for the first time when I went there to see the Bursar

---

* Paying pupils were called 'Commoners', while those who had won scholarships were known as 'Scholars'.

about the wording and positioning of the tablet. And again to see it dedicated. Later on I would sometimes go there to look at it and to walk through the cloisters and the various buildings that Tacklow had described so vividly that I felt as though I knew them. But I did not go very often, because there was nothing of him there: not even the shadow of a shadow. If his ghost walks anywhere it goes punting on the upper lake at Tetworth or fly-fishing in the glass-clear waters of the Test; or perhaps, sometimes, it sits on a low curved block of silvery, lichen-spotted stone that stands high above the winding Simla road on a spur of the foothills, looking out between the tall trunks of the pine trees at what he once described as 'one of the loveliest views in all India, if not in all the world'. From here, on a clear day, it really does seem as though one can see for ever and ever. To the right the foothills fall away to merge into the wide, golden vastness of the plains, while ahead and below, embedded among pine trees, lies the little Cantonment town of Dugshai, and on the left the rising ridges of the hills are backed by the long, long line of the high Himalayas, spanning the horizon with shimmering snow peaks that stand out like a jagged fringe of white satin against the limitless blue distance.

During the lengthy periods that my grandparents spent overseas, their children, in common with most children whose parents served in India, were either left behind in the care of home-based relatives or, like poor little Rudyard Kipling, to the less than tender mercies of professional child-minders. But Tacklow, when not at Tetworth, had the good fortune to spend a number of his school holidays with his maternal grandmother at Riccaton House near Edinburgh. Having learned the art of fly-fishing on the chalk streams near Winchester, he would go after salmon in the Scottish lochs and rivers, and became a skilful and dedicated fisherman.

In those days that great British institution, the country-house weekend, which had come into vogue in Georgian times, was still flourishing, and owners of stately homes either gave or attended these functions — which seem to have lasted from Friday afternoons to Monday mornings — as a matter of course. A popular form of after-dinner entertainment on these occasions was amateur theatricals, and it was at one of these house-parties — after a performance of *She Stoops to Conquer* by a group of lively and talented young amateurs — that a larger-than-life gentleman walked in on Tacklow while he was busy removing his make-up, and congratulated him warmly on his performance as Tony Lumpkin. It was, he said, the best he had ever seen, and should young Mr Kaye be interested in taking up acting as a profession, he, personally, would always be pleased to employ him. Here was his card. ... He handed it over with a flourish; as well he might, for the name engraved upon it is remembered to this day. It was Sir Henry Irving — the first Knight of the Theatre.

Hurrying back to Tetworth, Tacklow hopefully showed it to his parents and grandparents. But it failed to make the smallest impression. The chances are, of course, that none of them had ever even *heard* of Henry Irving ('An actor-fellow, for heaven's sake! What next?'). In any case, young Cecil was destined for service in India where the family links were strong, three of his father's first cousins having served in the East India Company; Charles Kaye in the Madras Civil Service and the other two, Sir John, the historian, as political secretary, India Office, and his brother Edward as a General in the Bengal Artillery. Then there was John's son Ernest, who was in the Bengal Police, and ... but why go on? The list is a long one. In any case it was the duty of the eldest son to follow his father into the ICS* and since my grandfather's views on the matter were fully endorsed by his formidable wife Jane — who was a Beckett and a tough character if ever there was one — there was nothing more to be said. One did not argue with Victorian parents. Tacklow abandoned the unequal struggle.

The elder of his two younger brothers, my Uncle Elliot, was graciously permitted to choose which service he would enter. Provided, of course, that it was an Indian one. Whereupon, apparently with the object of irritating his papa and mama rather than from any love of playing trains, he chose the Indian Railways, and, when forced to abandon this deliberate tease, stuck out for joining the Police. And did so. The youngest brother, Alec, a born black sheep if ever there was one, flouted tradition and refused to have anything whatever to do with India, or the forces of law and order either, and, metaphorically speaking, ran away to sea. In point of fact he set sail, steerage, for Canada, and was written off as a dead loss. Letters occasionally turned up from him, but only at long intervals. He seems to have worked for

* Indian Civil Service.

21

a time as a logger and then as a trapper (furs, one presumes?) and later, inevitably, taken part in the great California Gold Rush. He ended up as a mining engineer; at which he would appear to have been reasonably successful, for he acquired a house on Vancouver Island and a wife.

I don't know what happened to the house, but the wife was not a success. She seems to have been a confirmed hypochondriac who enjoyed ill-health to the hilt, and the last piece of information I ever heard on the subject of this unknown, shadowy, black-sheep uncle was a tale that when the wife of his bosom took to her bed he took over the cooking and the housework, and one day, while busy preparing the midday meal, he was interrupted by the appearance of the afflicted lady in the kitchen, announcing that she was about to die. To which my uncle replied firmly: 'Well you can't die here! I'm busy.' History does not relate what happened after that. Presumably she went back to bed while Alec finished basting the joint and making an apple pie. There were no children.

In addition to his brothers Elliot and Alec, Tacklow had a couple of sisters. One older and one younger than himself: my aunts Molly and Nan. I never met Nan, who died in India before I was born. And I regret this because according to Tacklow she was a darling and everybody loved her. When she came out to India to join her parents she was instantly besieged by suitors, and I remember him telling me that a snobbish acquaintance of his, who had been strongly critical of parents who brought pretty daughters out to India, declared that for his part he would never allow any sister of *his* to come out; why, the girl could easily marry a nobody — 'some dreadful fellow in the Railways'! To which Tacklow replied amiably that his sister Nan had done exactly that: married a 'fellow in the Railways'. The fellow in question was John Polwhele of Polwhele, whose name and manor are listed in Domesday Book. Sadly, there will be no more Polwheles of Polwhele, for her grandson, my cousin Reggie's only son, died in a road accident; so now the ancient manor-house in Cornwall, with its minstrels' gallery and its windows that had watched for the Armada, '*and a ghost on the stairs*', has been sold to strangers.

Nan's older sister, Aunt Molly, had already done her duty as a well-brought-up daughter by marrying Richard Ebb Hamblin of the Bengal Civil Service, and in 1886 she presented her parents with their first grandchild, a daughter. Her second child, another girl, born just over a year later, lived for less than eight weeks; to be followed by a third who did not even live as long as that. The wives of the British who served India paid a heavier price for that privilege than their critics realize. A fourth daughter, like the first, survived into old age, and my cousin Dick, the younger of their two brothers, died only very recently. The elder was killed in the First World War at the age of twenty-two.

Now that I am in my own 'sere and yellow leaf' and have learned a little more about life and what it can do to people, I realize that there was a lot to be said for Aunt Molly, and that much should be forgiven someone who in her early twenties had to endure the loss of two successive babies, and, in middle age, the death in action of a beloved son. But as I only learned all that after she herself was dead, I made no allowance for her. And I still regard her as a major battle-axe who, given half a chance, could have cut Napoleon down to size in two minutes flat and put the fear of God and Britannia into Ghengiz Khan and Attila the Hun. She also possessed an impressive moustache and no patience with children, and I disliked her so much that in later years I changed the spelling of my name from Molly to Mollie as a breakaway gesture: a small private form of UDI. Tacklow was scared to death of her, and when his father died he made no attempt to lay claim to any of the family possessions which should by rights have been handed down to the eldest son, but which she calmly appropriated. He did not even squeak when, without consulting him, she gave away the delightful portrait of Joseph Kaye (which now hangs in the Court Room of the Bank of England) solely because it turned out to be too large to fit into her new house! He was a quiet man, my father; one who disliked loud voices and any form of family discord.

Tacklow had been a house-prefect for two terms when he left Winchester in 1886 with the dutiful intention of following in his father's footsteps and entering the Indian Civil Service.

In those days it was customary for young men wishing to join the ICS and become what Anglo-India referred to, acidly, as 'the Heaven-Born', to attend a London crammers. In other words an establishment devoted to cramming young hopefuls with the brand of knowledge they would require in order to pass the rigorous examination for the Indian Civil Service. There were similar crammers who did the same service for would-be candidates for the Army; a task that schools of that period did not undertake — a rare exception being Kipling's school at Westward Ho!, Devon, which specialized in Army classes for the entrance examination into the Royal Military Academies of Sandhurst and Woolwich.

To a young man recently freed from the restricted life of a public school, Victorian London was a revelation: a glittering, gas-lit city full of theatres, music-halls and bars, and pretty ladies and their beaux — those bewhiskered 'swells', 'mashers' and 'stage-door johnnies' who drove around London in hansom cabs or open landaus, and could be seen of a morning riding in Rotten Row. Young Caecilius Kaye, up in the big City to acquire knowledge of a strictly academic kind, turned his back on cramming and spent his time instead in riotous living. It was probably the only time in his life that he really let go and in company with several like-minded friends enjoyed himself in a thoroughy uninhibited manner.

Together they worshipped at the shrine of such glittering stars as Nellie Farren, darling of the music-halls, and laughed and applauded that famous singer of comic songs, Corney Grayne. Brought up as a member of the Church of England with overtones of the Kirk of Scotland (a relic of those holidays spent at Riccaton?), he shocked his sternly Anglican landlady by attending service three Sundays out of every month at Westminster Cathedral in order to hear Santley sing — that well-known song-bird used to sing the solos — while on the fourth Sunday he would go to Brompton Oratory* in order to gaze at Mary Anderson, a stunningly beautiful American actress whose photograph, hand-painted on picture-postcards, sold by the thousand, and with whom every male in London, including my impressionable parent, was in love.

When his crammers closed for the holidays he went 'on the bummel' in Germany, enjoying walking tours in the Black Forest, downing steins of beer in ancient taverns, singing glees with students at Heidelberg and learning to speak German like a native. Once he and a friend were arrested and only just escaped being thrown into jail because the friend was accompanied by his dog, a dachshund named Bismarck (no quarantine laws in those days!). The local Polizei, who

* The Cathedral and the Oratory are both Roman Catholic places of worship.

appear to have lacked a sense of humour, took exception to the name on the grounds that it was an insult to the Great Man. However, their fury changed to smiles when Tacklow explained that since it was well known that 'the mad English' doted on dogs, the name bestowed on this particular one had naturally been most carefully chosen, and far from being an insult was the highest of compliments.

On another and much later occasion, long after the crammer days were over, he and an Army friend were on a walking tour and had stopped for a beer and a bite at an inn in Heidelberg which was patronized by one of that famous University's military clubs. They were placidly drinking beer when a young man entered and every other man in the place, with the exception of the two *Englanders,* sprang to his feet, clicked his heels together and bowed. The newcomer glared at the two, and marching over to their table inquired haughtily why they had remained seated instead of acknowledging the entry of a Captain? Tacklow rose courteously and explained that they happened to be strangers: Englishmen on a walking tour who were ignorant of local etiquette; adding that, incidentally, his companion happened to be a Major. The Captain bowed deeply, and turning to face the crowded room said: 'Gentlemen! this gentleman is a Major.' Whereupon the entire company leapt to their feet as before, clicked their heels together and bowed smartly to the Major before resuming their seats and getting on with the drinking. Tacklow said that he found the incident curiously disturbing and was not surprised when, just over a decade later, the First World War broke out. He had expected something of the sort to take off a good deal sooner.

Those earlier walking-tour holidays, together with the term-time frivolity in London in the bright morning of his life, were a part of his past that he was always to look back on with deep affection. And his description of that time was so vivid that I sometimes feel that I too knew and lived in Victorian London in the days before that magnificent weapon of destruction and din, the motor-car, was invented. In Caecilius's city of hansom cabs and horse-drawn buses, of pea-soup fogs and crossing-sweepers, lamp-lighters and muffin men, Sherlock Holmes and Oscar Wilde ... a London in which men wore 'toppers', 'Derbys' or cloth caps, and women's skirts and petticoats brushed the pavements while their hats soared skywards from vast platters that sprouted ostrich feathers or piles of fruit, flowers and tulle — the whole edifice skewered to their hair with fearsome-looking hatpins.

London provided him with so much fun that he neglected his work: imagining, as too many intelligent people have done before him, that when examination time arrived he was clever enough to play it off the cuff. But Nemesis overtook him and disaster struck. His name did not appear on the 'Pass' list. C. Kaye had failed the 'Indian Civil'. Well, as I have already mentioned, my grandfather was a Victorian parent. In other words, a martinet. He was also well aware that his eldest son could have passed that exam with ease and that there was no excuse for failure except idleness and riotous living.

Punishment was swift and, though possibly just, harsh in the extreme: both on Tacklow and the nation. He was not permitted to take the examination again. Since he had not cared enough to give his attention to passing it, he would enter the Army instead and see if he could make a career for himself in that! It was a horrifying prospect. And an unforgivable one, for if ever anyone was totally unfitted to be a soldier it was poor Tacklow.

There was no appeal. My deflated parent, fully aware that he had thrown away a career that would have suited him down to the ground, and had no excuses, said nothing. Because there was nothing to say. He returned sadly to London, this time to the Army crammers, and set to work. And it was not long before his new tutors realized that they had got hold of something really remarkable and backed him heavily for the Army Stakes in the betting book run by the various London-based crammers. Their entry romped home an easy first, leaving the remainder of the field far behind, and not only notching up higher marks than had ever been recorded before, but creating a record that can never be taken away from him: he was the first candidate to achieve five figures.

Not surprisingly, having made his point, Tacklow sat back and took little further interest in matters military. But his time at Sandhurst was not wasted, for it was during his final term there that the Government sent down a man from Army Intelligence (or whatever they called it in those days) to lecture the cadets of the Royal Military College on ciphers, with particular reference to the 'Playfair' which was at that time the only really safe one, since — and he explained why — it was insoluble. When the lecture ended, Tacklow's room-mate went up to the speaker and asked to be given a message in Playfair ·because, he said diffidently, he — er — thought that perhaps he had seen a way in which it could be solved. The lecturer was not amused. Had he *really* been wasting his valuable time explaining to these so-and-so young pups why the Playfair was insoluble, only in order to have one of the damned puppies calmly claiming to see a way in which it could be broken? The puppy in question stuck valiantly to his guns, and eventually the lecturer gave way and handed over a message in Playfair.

Tacklow, who had no interest whatever in ciphers, was pressed into service as a sort of Sorcerer's Apprentice. And though he did not understand what on earth the boy was driving at, he obligingly read off columns of numbers and/or letters in his free time for several days running, and was rewarded by his room-mate's yell of triumph when the thing suddenly came out and the Playfair was successfully broken. He never heard the result of that breakthrough, or knew what became of the boy who made it. The Playfair continued, for years, to be regarded as insoluble, and Tacklow told me he suspected that the fact that this was untrue had been hushed up: the Intelligence boffins hoping that the enemy would just toss it into their waste-paper baskets in the belief that as it could not be cracked, why waste time over it? He was also certain that his one-time room-mate must have died young, for otherwise he could not have failed to make a name for himself.

Chapter 3

~※◆※~

All animals are equal but some animals
are more equal than others.

Orwell, *Animal Farm*

Apart from the episode of the Playfair cipher, which was to have a
profound effect on Tacklow's future, only two other incidents of any
special interest happened to him during his time at Sandhurst. I am
not even certain that the first of these actually occurred at the College
itself; it could have happened at a ball given at some private house
during the holidays. But whether the setting was an end-of-term ball
at Sandhurst or one in some stately home, Tacklow, much to his
dismay, found himself put down to partner a young and very minor
German 'royal' for one of the dances — probably because he could
speak her language with great fluency.

She turned out to be a pretty young woman with a dazzling peaches-
and-cream complexion, a slim, hour-glass figure, the bluest eyes he
had ever seen and the golden hair that all proper Princesses should
have. She was also very shy: almost as shy as he was! But in his own
words, 'a darling'. He was very taken with her. Her name was Princess
May of Teck and he had every reason to remember her, for a year or
two later she became engaged to young 'Eddie', Duke of Clarence,
eldest son of the future Edward VII and Queen Alexandra. And when
less than a month after that poor Eddie died of pneumonia (fortunately,
it would seem, since he appears to have been a bad hat*), his grandmother, Victoria, who had arranged the match because she thought
that 'dear May' would make an admirable Queen of England — and
how right she was! — set about re-engaging her to Eddie's younger
brother, George, with whom, according to the press, she had been in

* He was once even suspected of being Jack the Ripper!

love all the time, though expediency and a strong-minded mother had forced her to accept the proposal of the late Duke of Clarence. The dutiful May accepted George and eventually became that much-loved and greatly admired character, Queen Mary, grandmother of Elizabeth II.

The second, and far more intriguing incident, was a curious and completely inexplicable affair that fascinates me to this day. The R M C* used to run a betting book on the Derby, and the cadet in charge of this operation asked Tacklow if he'd care to have a flutter? My parent, no betting man and totally uninterested in racing, hunting or horses in general, cast an eye down the list of runners and seeing no name that attracted his attention, declined. But that night he dreamt that he was at a race-meeting — something he never attended in his life. ...

He was standing among a dense crowd of jostling, peering people who were all looking in one direction, and he could hear a thunder of approaching hoof-beats that grew louder and louder until, over the heads of the crowd, he caught a brief glimpse of jockey caps flashing past and heard a roar of cheering. The race was obviously over and a man standing near him tapped him on the shoulder and said: 'So-and-so's won', mentioning the winning horse by name. Tacklow turned about and saw the numbers going up on a board and, at that point, woke up. Since his memory worked entirely by sight (as, to a large extent, does mine) he remembered the number next morning though he had completely forgotten the name. However, he hunted up the cadet with the betting book and said he had decided to put his all on number 16, or whatever; his all being £10, which was a *vast* sum in the days when a farthing (a quarter of an old penny) could still buy a stick of candy. But as the animal who bore the number was an outsider and the odds against it winning were in the region of 100 to 1, the cadet regretfully declined to accept the bet on the grounds that should the impossible happen, there would not be enough money in the kitty to pay out that amount. So Tacklow agreed to a reduction of the odds from 100 to 20, and won a staggering £200.

This story has a very curious sequel. Many years later when Victoria and her century were dead and gone and Tacklow was a Major serving on Kitchener's staff in Simla (Kitchener was then Commander-in-

* Royal Military College.

Chief, India), he told this tale at a dinner-party at the United Services Club and was urged by everyone present to do it again and dream another winner. But how on earth, demanded the indignant Tacklow, could anyone *make* themselves dream anything? Nevertheless, bowing to popular demand, he agreed to see what he could do about it, and thereafter set himself to try to dream about a race-meeting: though he had still never attended a real one. Every night, before he went to sleep, he would concentrate on horse-racing in the hope that it was just possible that one might dream about the last thing one had been thinking about before falling asleep. But no luck. Always, as sleep overtook him, his mind would wander off onto something else. Then suddenly, when he had given up trying, he dreamed the same dream. Once again he was standing among a crowd of racegoers. Once again he heard the same thunder of approaching hooves, caught the same flashing glimpse of jockeys' heads streaking past, heard the roar of cheering and was tapped on the shoulder by a man who said that so-and-so had won. He turned, as he had before, to see the numbers going up on the board. But by now he was a married man, and it was at this crucial point that Mother turned over in her sleep and woke him before he saw it.

As I have said, his memory worked by sight and had he seen the number he would have remembered it. But try as he might, he could not recall the name. All he could remember was that it had at least five syllables and began, he thought, with the letter 'C'. The members of the United Services Club and half Army Headquarters fell on the sports pages of *The Civil and Military Gazette, The Pioneer* and *The Statesman* — India's three main English-language newspapers — but no Derby runner had a name beginning with C. Or one of five syllables either!

Unfortunately, the Derby attracted a great many entrants and the Indian newspapers of that day did not bother to print the names of horses who were classed as 'also-rans' — the hopeless outsiders. And since wireless-telegraphy was still in its infancy and only used for more serious matters of State, it was not until the day after the race was run that India learnt that it had been won by a 100 to 1 outsider; a filly named 'Senorinetta' ... five syllables and beginning with the *sound* of C! I was told later, by several middle-aged and, by then, very senior gentlemen who remembered the occasion, that the Corridors of Power in Simla echoed to the sounds of lamentation and hair-tearing for at least a week afterwards.

Tacklow never again tried to dream a race to order. He told me that he had tried to 'dream true', though without success, after reading George du Maurier's haunting novel *Peter Ibbetson*. But that odd experience of his always intrigued me, and several years after his death I tried it myself: concentrating, as he had done, on race-meetings and horses before I fell asleep. Like him, I gave it up in disgust — and then suddenly dreamt I was at Epsom on Derby Day, standing against the rails at Tattenham Corner. Someone shouted: 'Here they come!' and the leading horses came sweeping round the bend. In the same moment a piece of waste paper, caught by the wind, flapped across the course in the path of the oncoming horses, and the leader jinked sharply sideways so that I saw the number — I think it was 6 — on its saddlecloth before it lost its place to those behind it. That was all. The dream ended there, and all I had learned from it was not to put any money on number 6. Which, not being a betting type, or a horsey one either, I was unlikely to do in any case; though I would certainly have bet my all on anything I had seen coming first past the winning-post. However, the story does not end there —

I was at that time in Ootacamund in southern India, and a few days later, on the day that the Derby was run, we were listening in to a running commentary on our radio. I have forgotten the name of number 6 — call it 'George's Joy' — but the commentator at Tattenham Corner knew it and announced excitedly that 'Here comes George's Joy! — rounding the corner a good length ahead of Mabel's Mum and Percy's Pottage' (or whatever). And in the next second, his voice rising to a frenzied shout, he informed us that George's Joy had shied wildly at a piece of paper blowing across the course and was now virtually out of the race. . . .

Well, how does one explain that? It did me no good and it seems odd, to say the least of it, that I should have been handed a piece of totally useless advance information well before it had occurred.

✳ Having passed top into Sandhurst, with record marks, Tacklow's exit was a lot less spectacular. He passed out at number 16, though with honours, and shortly afterwards embarked for India to join a British regiment, the First Battalion of the Devonshire Regiment which was stationed at that time at Dugshai in the Simla hills. Here Tacklow got down to studying for his language exams; it being standard practice, right up to the outbreak of the Second World War, that all candidates for the Indian Army must serve an attachment to a British regiment stationed in that country until such time as they were reasonably fluent in at least two of India's many major languages. Should they fail (I believe candidates were allowed three tries) they were sent back to England as unsuitable material for the armies of the Raj, and ended up in some British regiment instead.

That square-peg-in-a-round-hole, C. Kaye, who collected languages much as other young men collect birds' eggs or stamps, passed his preliminary examinations with flying colours and was eventually posted to the 21st Punjabis; a Frontier Force regiment that vanished from the Army List in 1922 during one of the periodic amalgamations of several regiments. Since the 21st had been part of the Kurram Valley Field Force which was commanded by General Sir Frederick Roberts — 'Bobs Bahadur' — during the second Afghan War, I managed to insert a reference to it in *The Far Pavilions* solely because it was once my father's regiment. And many years later, after the Raj had faded into history and legend and a large part of north-west India had become the new and independent country of Pakistan, I was shown his name, written in his own hand on the old Rolls of the Punjab Regiments, when I was invited to luncheon in the Regimental Centre by serving officers whose fathers had not even been born when that yellowed, faded ink was fresh.

The tales that Tacklow told me make up a sort of mental photograph-album-cum-diary, the pages of which bring him so clearly to mind that I might almost have known him in his youth. I can see him as a toddler because I have not only a photograph of him but an original water-colour sketch, painted by some doting aunt, which shows a small, fair-haired one-year-old in short socks and wearing a vast hat and a full-skirted white dress with puff sleeves and a blue sash that could have been worn equally well by a girl. Apparently the sexes in the nineteenth century were dressed exactly alike for the first few years of their lives.

I also have a clear mental picture of him, aged about six, and having been instructed by his autocratic mother — who was taking him to lunch with an elderly relative noted for her lavish hospitality — that he was to wait until he was asked before expressing a preference for any dish, surveying the selection on offer and announcing loudly: 'When I'm *asked,* I shall say Pie!' I can see him too as a schoolboy, fishing for trout in the chalk streams near Winchester or for salmon in the lochs and rivers of Scotland. One favourite inn, at Tummel Brig, used to serve a special kind of bap which as a boy he was particularly fond of; and revisiting the inn after a lapse of forty years he asked if they still made them. He was assured that they did, but when they were brought to the table in a covered dish, the waitress whispered in Tacklow's ear: 'Th' Cook's varra nairvous; she hopes ye won't be thinkin' she's the same cook!' There are no early photographs taken of him in Scotland, but there are a few of him in cricketing flannels and the traditional Wykehamist's straw hat, sitting with folded arms and a stern expression among the other members of his house eleven; looking extraordinarily like his son, my brother Bill.

Another ancient photograph, that still survives, always stood for as long as I can remember, on his dressing-table wherever we happened to be. I removed it from the last of these a few days after he died. It is a very small studio photograph, mounted on heavy card that is printed in gold with the photographer's name and town — Chas. Johnson, Gillingham — and it portrays an alert but otherwise undistinguished mongrel terrier. Foxy had been rescued by Tacklow only a few months after his arrival in India; starving, mangy, suspicious and forlorn, age unknown, but obviously once the property of a British Tommy who had abandoned the unfortunate creature when his regiment had been ordered home, for the dog answered instantly to a British voice and cringed away from an Indian one. Tacklow had a way with all animals. They seemed to know at once that here was someone they could trust, and all our family pets were never ours for more than a day or two at most; after that they attached themselves to him and were his and no one else's. I honestly believe that he could have attracted and tamed a tyrannosaurus or a sabre-toothed tiger.

Foxy's faith in humans must have been sorely strained when his original master left him, and he had very nearly reverted to the wild by the time Tacklow first befriended him. He was, it seems, a sorry sight; gaunt, ragged, dirty and inclined to snap and snarl or else cringe in expectation of a kick, he had been forced to live on his wits for some considerable time and the mongrel element in his ancestry was

33

very apparent. Tacklow had not really wanted a dog. Dogs were a liability in a country where the threat of hydrophobia and a hideous death was ever present, and where there was only one place in all India, Kasauli, where anti-rabies vaccine was obtainable — and to reach Kasauli in time to take the treatment was not always possible. There were also other hazards that faced dogs in India. Snakes for instance, in particular the little dust-coloured kraits whose bite is fatal; or leopards, who relish the flesh of dogs. All the same Tacklow decided to adopt this disgraceful waif, and within a month all the diamonds in Golconda would not have bought Foxy from him. They doted on each other; and for twelve long and happy years they were never apart for more than a few hours, except for a brief interval during Tacklow's first home leave. . . .

There being no quarantine regulations in those carefree days, Foxy had travelled home with him. But as I have already mentioned, my paternal grandmother, like her daughter my Aunt Molly, was a considerable battle-axe, and this formidable old despot (see photograph; the camera, in this case, does not lie!) gave one basilisk glare at the mongrel at her eldest son's heels and banished Foxy to the stables. On no account whatever would he be permitted to enter the house; let alone sleep in it! There was no appeal. During the next few days Tacklow and his faithful adorer spent as much time as possible in the garden or the countryside together, and their nights apart; and when, after a few days, Tacklow had to go up to London to report himself to the War Office (it was probably still called The Horse Guards in those days) Foxy was perforce left behind in the stables.

Two days later Tacklow returned — to find his faithful hound not only installed in the house but occupying, as by right, the most comfortable chair in the drawing-room. How Foxy had managed this was never fully explained, but he had obviously succeeded in charming the flinty heart out of my grandmother's solid, bombazine-and-lace-encased bosom. And from then until the end of that home leave and the departure of the two of them, hand in paw back to India, he remained a beloved and honoured guest and the apple of my grandmother's eye — in which, it seems, there was actually a tear when he left! Foxy's conquest of her is about the only interesting thing I know about my grandmother: apart from the fact that one of her family married the younger son of Scotland's favourite poet, the immortal

Robert Burns of 'Comin' through the Rye' and 'Auld Lang Syne'.

As for Foxy, he died very peacefully of old age, and Tacklow, who was not prone to tears, confessed that he wept buckets and missed him so sorely that he made a solemn vow never, never again 'to give his heart to a dog to tear', as Kipling puts it. That vow was never broken. There were other pets of course: cats, monkeys, mongooses (or should that be 'mongeese'?), squirrels, parrots and bulbuls; but never another dog. He never forgot Foxy. The little photograph that went with him everywhere right up to the day of his death is proof of that.

After Foxy, he acquired a pair of brown monkeys called Jacko and Jillo; an exhilarating but exhausting pair of pets, as anyone who has ever owned a monkey will know. The havoc that one small member of this tribe (let alone two) can cause in the space of sixty seconds has to be seen to be believed; I suppose it comes from having four hands instead of two, and excellent teeth. There was one occasion when the demon pair managed to capture a crow and were in the process of plucking out its feathers one by one when the shrieks of the victim alerted Tacklow, who rescued it, tailless, just in time; getting bitten in the process by Jillo and severely pecked by the ungrateful crow. The pair eventually joined forces with a troop of their wild brethren whom they had quite obviously invited in to share their owner's bungalow, and when after a period of chaos and anarchy the friends were successfully evicted, Jacko and Jillo elected to go with them and were last seen in their company eating stolen corn-cobs on the roof of a shop in the bazaar. Tacklow said that he missed them, but that life was a lot more peaceful after their departure.

His next pet was a mongoose that had somehow got into his bathroom, and finding itself shut in, behaved like a lunatic; racketing around the walls and upsetting tin water-cans, soap-dishes, razors and other movable objects in its frenzy. The noise, which was considerable, merely increased its panic, and drew Tacklow to investigate; and since he had always wanted a mongoose, he shut himself into the bathroom with it and sat down cross-legged on the floor, where he remained without moving for over an hour — I think that his ability to remain silent and immovable for long periods was probably the secret of the rapport he was able to establish with animals and birds. After some ten or fifteen minutes the mongoose ceased to dash wildly round the room and retreated behind the upturned tin bathtub. But as Kipling says, every mongoose is eaten up from nose to tail with curiosity and the motto of the mongoose family is 'Run and Find Out'. This one ran true to form. It could not resist peering round the side of the bath to discover what this strange human creature was doing, and after a time it began to creep forward, inch by inch, until at long last, having cautiously investigated Tacklow's shoes and then his ankles, it climbed up onto his knee, sniffed at his watch-chain and nibbled at a coat-button, and exhausted by its previous shenanigans, yawned and went to sleep. When, after a further hour, it woke up, it allowed itself to be stroked; and from then on they were the best of friends for two glorious years.

I once had a mongoose myself, and they are the most adorable and entertaining of creatures. Tacklow's Rikki (the name was new in those days — Kipling's *Jungle Book,* which contains the story of Rikki-Tikki-Tavi, having only recently been published) was the best of companions. He slept on Tacklow's pillow, went along with him to the office, and to the Mess where he shared his meals, sitting on his knee and occasionally venturing onto the table to take a drink of water from one of the finger-bowls. Like his famous namesake he kept the bunga-low and the surrounding compound free from snakes, and he would accompany Tacklow on his morning rides and evening walks; tearing along across the scrub-covered plains between the kikar trees or along the river banks, and sitting up and chittering loudly when he wished to be picked up and given a lift. Tacklow told me that he always came when called and learned, on those evening walks, to come to heel when danger threatened or caution demanded it. The only thing he objected to was crossing the vast open space of the sun-scorched Parade Ground, where there was no cover and he knew that he was vulnerable to kites and other birds of prey. When Tacklow did that, Rikki would run between his feet in the protection of his shadow; but otherwise he came and went as he pleased. As did my Rikki, years later.

Unfortunately, Tacklow did not know that one of Rikki's favourite hot-weather retreats, where he liked to take a nap when the temperature soared, was a culvert under the drive leading to the bungalow; and he was there one hot afternoon in mid-June when the first storm of the approaching monsoon swept down without warning and a flash-flood fell like a cataract out of the sky. Within seconds the whole Cantonment was awash, and Rikki, trapped by a deluge of water pouring in from both sides of the culvert, was drowned.

After that, Tacklow acquired cats and the occasional parrot. Not intentionally, as he had acquired Rikki, but because they attached themselves to him and he allowed them to stay. But no cat ever took the place of Foxy; or of Rikki either. And each in turn bore the same name because by tradition all Kaye cats were called 'Chips'.

All cats liked Tacklow. They would see him coming, and remarking to themselves in pleased surprise 'Ah! — a man who likes cats!', would rise to their paws and come to meet him, arching their backs, tails well up, and rubbing themselves against his ankles. A walk with him in any place where there were cats — Naples being a case in point! — closely resembled a 'royal' on walkabout. He would exchange a word or two with them and they would reply, presumably in Italian. But the creature that Tacklow would most have liked to own (failing a dog, of course) was an elephant. For it is true that they have a remarkably good memory, and since their life-span is a long one, with luck they could outlive you. They are also very intelligent and truly endearing. But unfortunately they need a lot of space and a great deal of care and attention, plus a vast amount of fodder. His pad-elephant, Pramekali, and her *mahout** were only hired by Tacklow for a few seasons during the tail-end of the 1890s; and then only when he was on shooting leave in the Terai. But he loved her dearly and never forgot her, and would often say wistfully that if only he were rich he would buy a large estate — a *zemindari* — somewhere on the edge of the Terai, and acquire a baby elephant of his own and just live there and grow old with it.

There were a great many elephants in India even in my day; and when my father was a young man their numbers must have been far larger, for in those days the Army used them to haul guns and carry tents, baggage, ammunition and stores. They were also the normal, everyday transport of forest officers and their families and assistants, as well as of countless Sahibs on shooting leave. They worked in logging camps, moving, lifting and stacking huge tree-trunks; and in

* The man who sits on the elephant's neck, knees clamped behind its leathery ears, and guides it.

timber yards all over India, handling the great balks of seasoned wood — the sleepers on which the railway tracks ran for thousands of miles, criss-crossing the subcontinent, and the logs and planks that were used for building houses, bridges and factories. They and their *mahouts* were used for keddahs: the driving of herds of wild elephants into huge stockades in the jungles of Assam and Mysore, where they were roped between two tame elephants and taken away to be trained to work. Princes and potentates, Maharajahs, Rajahs, Nawabs and Ranas, with their Queens and Princesses and Ministers, rode on them in processions at weddings or religious festivals and on state occasions. And so also, in those days, did Viceroys and Governors of Provinces.

Pramekali's *mahout* would come of an evening to the verandah of the forest hut in which my father stayed when shooting in the Terai, to smoke his hookah and gossip and tell enthralling stories about the elephant-folk and their ways. He told Tacklow that the *mahouts* speak to their elephants in a special language that is the last remnant of the language that was spoken in the days when the world was new and elephants were the masters and men their servants. He taught him some of that language, and Tacklow taught it to me when I was a child. But by now I can only remember two words of it, perhaps because I myself heard them used fairly often by other *mahouts* — though I am ashamed to say that I have forgotten which means what! The two words were 'Dutt' and 'Dug': one means 'Take a long step' and the other 'Push it down with your head'. And as Tacklow said, even the most intelligent dog would be hard put to tell the difference between those two very similar monosyllables. Yet an elephant never makes a mistake. He may be loafing across the countryside in the manner of one who has his hat over one eye and his hands in his pockets, paying no attention to the scenery, when his *mahout* taps him on the head and says 'Dutt!' (or it may be 'Dug') and without pausing he will lengthen his stride and pass safely over the yawning ditch, or alternatively, pause to push over a young tree that is obstructing the path; putting it down with his head if it is a large one, or using one foot if he judges that to be sufficient. Yet there are gaps in their intelligence: which is just as well. Because there was an occasion when Tacklow, on local leave down south, accepted an offer to cross the Bay of Bengal on a tramp steamer that was taking a consignment of elephants to Burma; and very nearly did not live to tell the tale. ...

The elephants were below decks tethered in two rows, each in a separate stall, and on the second day out, with the sea as flat as a skating rink, one of them decided to relieve the tedium by rocking gently from side to side. Presently another and then a third took it up, until the ship itself began to sway. The elephants found the movement delightful and soon they were all doing it. The steamer, which was not a large one, began to tip from port to starboard and back again like a canoe in a cross sea, and it became alarmingly clear that it was only a matter of time — and not much of it either! — before one gunwale or the other dipped below the water level and the sea rushed in and sent the entire ship to the bottom.

Seamen and *mahouts* together raced below to put a stop to this blissful but deadly game. But to no avail. Until at last, and only just in time, some genius suggested tethering every other animal the opposite way round. This was done with frantic haste. And it worked! The elephants, who had been enjoying themselves just as much as kids enjoy a swing or a see-saw, continued to rock from side to side, but could not work out that if number one swayed to the left his neighbour must now sway to the right. Fortunately, they never did work it out; for if they had, nothing could have stopped the steamer from sinking like a stone in that enormous, glassy sea. And since launching a lifeboat in those circumstances would have been out of the question and there was no wireless on board, the chances are that there would have been no survivors and the total disappearance of the steamer in a flat calm sea would have become another 'Unsolved Mystery of the Sea'.

Chapter 4

~※⚬٭⚬※~

Tyger, tyger, burning bright ...
Blake, 'The Tyger'

The reason why I know so much about my father's childhood and his
early years in India is because he used to reminisce to me about those
times. He had a fund of real-life stories that I treasure. As I treasure
the claw of his first tiger and the tale of how he came to shoot it. This
last took place somewhere in the Terai, which is (or was) a wide belt
of jungle and grassland that skirted the foothills of the Himalayan
range for almost two thirds of its length, but which at present is
shrinking rapidly before the encroachments of India's exploding and
rapacious population. The tiger's claw must by now be almost a
hundred years old; which I find difficult to believe, because I can
remember so clearly Tacklow telling how he acquired it; and the tale
is still so real to me that like Mother's first visit to the Bombay Zoo,
it seems as though it happened only yesterday. ...

Seated on the backs of a line of elephants, the shooting-party had
been waiting for what seemed like hours; rifles at the ready as they
listened to the noises of the jungle and the far-off sounds of the
approaching beaters. Tacklow, as the most junior member of the party,
was on the extreme left of the line; a spot from which it was highly
unlikely that he would get so much as a glimpse of a tiger, since
immediately in front of him, separating him from the jungle, lay a dry
ravine full of elephant-grass and thorn-scrub that the head *shikari*,*
who had planned the beat, judged would dissuade the tiger from
coming that way and ensure that it would make for the centre of the
line and the rifle of the Commissioner-Sahib for whose benefit the beat
had been laid on.

* Hunter.

Tacklow's position being little more than that of a stop, he was able to give his undivided attention to the varied and entertaining assortment of jungle wildlife that emerged from cover ahead of the beat to scud through the waiting line of elephants and vanish into the jungle behind them. The beaters were still a long way off when his eye was caught by what he took to be a jungle-cock — a bright flash of colour among the scrub in the ravine. He could see the vivid orange neck ruff and the white eye of the bird, but as he watched it idly, wondering how long it would be before it decided to run for it, the patch of colour between the grass stems and the thorn boughs seemed to cohere and become clearer: 'like a photographic print in a tray of developing solution' was the way he put it. And suddenly, he was looking at the face of a crouching tiger. It was staring directly at him and he lifted his rifle very, very slowly — hearing the whispered protest of his *shikari*, who had not seen it — and pulled the trigger.

The crack of the shot was not followed by any noticeable movement from the spot he had aimed at, and the orange and white patches were still there; though in a slightly different position. But everyone seemed to be shouting at him, and the Commissioner's elephant came trundling down the line with the Commissioner himself bellowing furiously from his *howdah*,* demanding to know what the devil young Kaye meant by loosing off like that and ruining the whole dam' shoot? 'Not at nothing, sir,' replied Tacklow politely. 'It was the tiger. And what's more, I think I must have got it.' And he had. Smack between the eyes. The Commissioner was not pleased: true, he had served for many years in India and had taken part in a great many tiger-shoots, but he had yet to bag his first tiger and this particular one had been specially marked down for him. It should by rights have emerged near the centre of the line, and the sportsmen on either side of him, who knew the form, would certainly have held their fire and let him have first shot. Instead of which the wretched animal had elected to sneak up at the far end of the line and get picked off by a scrubby little 'griffen' fresh out from home, whose sole function had been to act as a stop.

Tacklow, on the other hand, was delighted. People did not go around armed with loaded cameras in those far-off days, so there is no

---

* A seat to contain two or more persons, fitted with a railing (and, on occasions, a canopy), strapped onto the back of an elephant.

photograph of him posing with a foot on the King of the Jungle. But when the skin was cured he sent it to his school-friend, Cull Brinton, then working in the family firm of Brinton's Ltd in Kidderminster, where I saw it many years later — faded by time to a pale beigy-grey and denuded of most of its hair by reason of being walked on for so long. It still retained a claw or two, and Cull gave me one as a memento of his friend and my father's first tiger. That is the one I still have. Tacklow was not a keen *shikari*. Only one more tiger and, much later on, a single tigress, fell victim to his rifle. And I fancy those, like that first one, were lucky flukes, because he was the first to admit that as a marksman he was firmly on the wrong side of 'average'.

To any animal-lover-cum-conservationist who reads this and immediately suffers a rise of blood-pressure, I would like to point out that back in the last century — and right up to the day that the Raj ended — the tiger population of India was very large. Too large, according to the villagers who suffered most from their depredations. It was only after the British left and every peasant who could afford it bought a gun and a woodman's axe — using the former to kill any wild animal that preyed on his crops and his cattle, and the latter to hack down trees and decimate the jungle in order to increase his holding — that the number of tigers, together with their one-time habitat, began to shrink like a water-hole in a year of drought; almost to vanishing-point. And if anyone does not believe this, I would suggest that they write to the headquarters of the World Wildlife Association and ask for the actual figures: which will (I hope) shock them more than somewhat.

Among my favourite *shikar* stories were those that Tacklow told me about his pad-elephant, Pramekali, who when he was on shooting-leave in the Terai used to present herself daily at *chota-hazri** time before the verandah of whatever forest bungalow he happened to be staying in. Fruit is always served with *chota-hazri* and if there was one food that Pramekali really fancied above all others it was fresh fruit. When Tacklow gave her apples, oranges or bananas, or any ordinary-sized fruit, she would take it elegantly with the tip of her trunk and pop it into her mouth. But when he gave her something like a melon or a papaya (pawpaw, to you!) she would place it carefully on the

---

* Lit. 'small breakfast'. An Indian institution to this day, consisting of early-morning tea and fruit.

ground, and then lift up a foot like a trip hammer and bring it down so gently that instead of smashing the fruit to pulp she merely broke it into suitably-sized pieces.

He told me, too, of a day when the entire line of elephants, plodding in single file through the thick jungle, was brought to a halt by a single king cobra who reared up in the middle of the narrow, marshy track and weaved its spectacled hood and its small, wicked head from side to side in a menacing manner, daring the leading elephant to move one step further. The dare was not accepted and word passed back down the line to send up Pramekali who, being a lady of strong common-sense, took in the situation at a glance and dealt with it competently. She merely plucked a trunkful of the tall grass that formed a high, impenetrable wall on either side of the path, and brandished it in the cobra's face, simultaneously bombarding the creature with fids of wet mud kicked up with her forefeet. The cobra lowered its hood and departed at speed and Pramekali tossed away the grass and led the procession forward. Tacklow always swore he heard her sniff in a contemptuous manner.

Yet another of his Terai stories was about a tiger-shoot in which a half-circle of pad-elephants, each carrying a rough-and-ready *howdah* containing one or two Sahibs in addition to its *mahout*, were listening to the shouts and yells of the approaching beaters and waiting for the tiger to emerge into the clearing ahead, when a porcupine scuttled wildly out of the jungle scrub. Faced with a line of elephants it made straight for the nearest one who, being young and nervous, lost his nerve and attempted to kneel on it.

The porcupine fought back gamely, discarding quills in a manner that would have done credit to Robin Hood and his Merrie Men, until the elephant, realizing its mistake, scrambled to its feet and began to fling itself to and fro in an endeavour to rid itself of the quills; dislodging its *mahout*, who lost his grip and was catapulted into a clump of pampas grass while his three Sahibs and their *shikari* were thrown from side to side of the *howdah* like peas in a drum. The tiger, emerging suddenly from the jungle, took one shocked look at this disgraceful scene before streaking past the firing-line to disappear into the safety of the tall grass behind — closely followed by the hysterical elephant, the occupants of its *howdah*, the infuriated *mahout*, and the victorious porcupine; in that order. Not a single shot was fired, for the simple reason that the rest of the assembled company, Sahibs, *shikaris* and *mahouts* alike (and possibly the elephants as well), were so helpless with laughter that when a second tiger loped out of the jungle ahead of the beat, it too got off scot free. The hunt had to be called off and the rest of the day was spent pulling quills out of the elephant and applying arnica to the bruised and battered occupants of its *howdah*.

There were also other kinds of stories; four of which I put into my Mutiny novel, *Shadow of the Moon*, from which they were removed by an editor. So I put them into *The Far Pavilions* instead. There was the story of the Higher-standard Languages Examination that my hero, Ashton, fails; the one about the three drops of water on a biscuit-tin which he used to explain the Trinity; his verdict on the sepoy who shot at an unknown man riding a supposedly stolen horse; and lastly the death of an incautious Brass-hat who took an evening stroll on the Frontier.

It was Tacklow who failed that examination paper and whose *munshi** rushed to his Colonel, insisting that he get back the papers because there must be some mistake — Kaye-Sahib was the best pupil he had ever taught and it was not *possible* that he could have failed! The Colonel complied, and when the papers were returned they were found to have written across them in red ink: '*Flawless. This officer has obviously used a crib*'! Unlike my hero, my father sat the exam again, put in a few deliberate errors and passed with higher marks than anyone had ever achieved before; or since.

It was also Tacklow, not Ash, who, when asked to explain the Trinity by a group of his sepoys with whom he had been sitting round a campfire discussing theology (the regiment was out on Autumn Manoeuvres), picked up the lid of a biscuit-tin they had been using as a makeshift frying-pan, and after pouring a drop of water into each of three corners, tilted the lid to make the three separate drops run together, and said: 'Those three are now one, are they not? Yet all three are still there.' And it was a local missionary doctor who, riding homeward by moonlight on a grey pony, was challenged by a sepoy on sentry duty whose orders were to look out for a grey horse that had recently been stolen. The pony took fright and bolted without giving the doctor a chance to reply, whereupon the sentry, convinced

* Tutor.

that this must be the thief and that he was attempting to escape, fired at the rider and fortunately missed — but by such a narrow margin that the infuriated doctor laid a complaint and the sentry was duly brought up for judgment. The sentence delivered by the Colonel, and received with loud and appreciative applause by the rank-and-file, was three days' detention with loss of pay for having shot at a Sahib, and a further twenty for having missed him when he did.

I allowed Wally Hamilton, one of the real-life characters in *The Far Pavilions*, to tell how a red-coated and bemedalled General, who had ridden out from Peshawar to inspect a Frontier Force battalion on manoeuvres, had taken a stroll beyond the perimeter of the camp to admire the view, and been shot by one of the local tribesmen for no better reason than that his red coat presented such an alluring target in that waterless, treeless, dun-coloured region that the temptation to take a pot-shot at him had proved irresistible. That story too I had from Tacklow, who told me that the elders of the tribe had brought the marksman in for judgment, explaining that the General-Sahib had been greatly to blame for putting temptation in the way of a young man with a brand new *jezail*.* No harm, they urged, had been intended.

A conversation that I put into *Shadow of the Moon* in fact took place between Tacklow and his Pathan orderly in the 1890s. The orderly had just returned from the rifle range, and Tacklow, having asked him how he'd done at the butts and been told that he had scored a bullseye, two inners and two outers, said that he presumed they were in the opposite order: the outers first and the bullseye last, since the reverse would be poor shooting. 'Not so,' returned the Pathan grimly. 'In *my* country it is the first shot that counts; if you miss with that you may not get a chance to fire another!'

Senior Indian Army officers in those days were apt to be elderly and liverish grey-beards, and on one frontier campaign (the border was seldom at peace) Tacklow and his Subadar-Major and about a hundred *jawans*† of the 21st Punjabis, who were perched on a stony ridge overlooking tribal territory, were kept waiting for over an hour for the arrival of the Brigadier in charge of operations — that dignitary being so old and fat and infirm that the only way he could reach the

---

* The long-barrelled muzzle-loading guns that can still sometimes be seen on the Frontier to this day.

† Sepoys: Indian other-ranks.

ridge was with the help of three hefty young sepoys, two of whom towed him from in front while the third pushed hard from behind. When at last they made it, puffing and panting in the chill air of early dawn, the Subadar-Major turned to Tacklow and remarked acidly in Punjabi: 'Now that all the halt and lame have arrived, perhaps we may be permitted to begin the battle?'

Tacklow got on with Indians. All Indians; irrespective of religion, caste or kind. He felt completely at ease in their company, for being one of those fortunate individuals who can pick up languages as easily as other people pick up pebbles off a beach, he never had the slightest difficulty in communicating with them. He spoke and wrote nine major languages besides his own (eleven, if one counts Latin and Greek, which he himself would not have thought of including, since in his day anyone with a public school education was automatically expected to have a sound working knowledge of both). The nine were French, German, Italian, Spanish, Persian, Arabic, Hindustani (which included Hindi and Urdu), Pushtu and Chinese – Mandarin as well as Cantonese. In addition to these he spoke eighteen dialects; which by no means covers all those spoken in India and her border countries, but should do to go on with. As a consequence of this he acquired a great many lifelong friends in far-away places. Yet he was never any good at making friends among his own people. Partly, I suspect, because the attitude of some of the British in India irritated him, but largely because he was, at heart, a loner. He did not really *need* other people. ... Take, for instance, the case of the fort —

Somewhere in the vast area in which his regiment operated in the 1890s there was a small, isolated and almost forgotten fort which, at that time, it was the unpopular duty of the 21st Punjabis to garrison. This they did with a token force consisting of one junior British officer and a small detachment of *jawans* who faced the unenviable prospect of spending three months there before being relieved by the next batch; and so on. ... The assignment was dreaded by one and all, for the ancient fort lay in the middle of nowhere, surrounded by an endless sea of sand dotted with small islands of pampas grass and outcrops of rock, and in the opinion of the Punjabis a term of garrison duty there was the equivalent of three months' solitary in a particularly spartan jail. In the course of time it came to the turn of Second-Lieutenant C. Kaye to take over this unenviable chore, and accompanied by a reluctant but resigned platoon of Punjabis he set off into the wide and sandy yonder. Only to put in for an extension when the three months were up.

Such a thing had never happened before in the history of the regiment, but the astonished Adjutant (having first made sure that young Kaye had not gone off his head) agreed to his taking over the new platoon. And at the end of the next spell of duty received another request for a further extension. Tacklow eventually succeeded in spending nine months there — and would probably have been quite content to spend the rest of his life there had his seniors not decided that enough was enough. He told me that he enjoyed every minute of it because, apart from inventing a number of new and original ploys to keep the platoon interested and on their toes, it gave him time to think and read and write. And also, of course, because he quite literally did not know what it was like to be bored; which is a trait that I have been fortunate enough to inherit from him, and for which I have always been truly grateful.

He was deeply interested in languages, butterflies, astrology, history, cricket and stamps. And fly-fishing, of course. So he was never without something to think about or puzzle over, study, watch, make notes on or collect, and it is my belief that he could have recited Wisden* from memory — probably backwards as well as forwards! He had an outsize brain, but not a grain of common-sense; or of social sense either. Like the Cat That Walked By Himself, 'all places were alike to him', and he was perfectly content with his own company.

He liked peace and quiet. Especially the latter. And he would not have liked our present-day world at all. The noise! The squabbling; the recrimination. The whingeing and complaining. The *fuss*! I don't believe I ever saw Tacklow lose his temper or heard him raise his voice in anger. Which does not mean that he could not be angry. But never shouting-angry, or worse, cold, unpleasant, up-tight angry. And at no time did he ever let the sun go down on his wrath.

He was interested, too, in the strange workings of fate. For instance when he was in his twenties he became acquainted with a man who, many years previously, having fallen sick while on garrison duty in an isolated outpost on India's North-West Frontier, had been sent off to

* The bible of all cricket-lovers.

the nearest hospital in a *dooly** escorted by half-a-dozen sepoys only a few hours before the outpost was attacked and overrun, leaving no survivors. The *dooly* with its carriers and escort had been ambushed among the hills and met a similar fate — with one exception: the sick man, though badly wounded and left for dead, was found to be alive by the relief column that arrived too late to save the garrison of the outpost. He recovered and was sent home on sick leave; only to become, once again, the sole survivor of a tragedy when the transport in which he sailed went down in a great storm in the Indian Ocean. Later still, on another wild night of storm the hansom cab in which he had been driving to the station to catch a train was delayed by the gale, so that by the time he reached the station the guard had already blown his whistle and the train had begun to move. He sprinted down the platform in a frantic attempt to catch it, and only just failed to do so; thereby saving his life yet again, for the train happened to be the one that toppled into the black, icy, gale-whipped water in the terrible Tay Bridge disaster of 1879.

Tacklow was enormously intrigued by this story, for he, like the little Padre in Thornton Wilder's *Bridge of San Luis Rey*, was convinced that if there was any underlying pattern in individual human existence, it must show in a case such as this, and that anyone who had escaped death by the very narrowest of margins on four separate occasions *must* have been spared by God for a very special purpose. He believed, as I do, that nothing happens without a reason; even though the reason may not necessarily be a good one. One cannot believe in God and deny the existence of the Devil. Or in Good without accepting that there is Evil. I remember Tacklow reading *The Bridge of San Luis Rey* and saying: '*That's* what I mean. That's *exactly* what I mean!'

* Palanquin.

Chapter 5

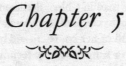

An' the dawn comes up like thunder outer China 'crost the Bay!

Kipling, 'Mandalay'

If there were any fairy-godmothers at the cradle of the twentieth century, their gifts, as far as those proud parents of the British Empire, John Bull and Britannia, were concerned, were far from good ones.

The new century was only six days old when the Boers besieged Ladysmith, a small town in South Africa. A few days later the British forces suffered defeat and severe losses at the battle of Spion Kop, and though news of the relief of another besieged and comparatively unimportant town, Mafeking, was greeted in Britain with as much hysterical enthusiasm as though it had been a glorious victory on the scale of Waterloo or Agincourt, the lamentable Boer War was to drag on for another year. . . .

On the other side of the world a band of militant and violently anti-Western Chinese, calling themselves 'The Harmonious Fists' (a name that the Westerners translated as 'The Boxers'), turned in fury on the 'strangers within their gates' and all those of their own race who had become Christians — plus any of their fellow countrymen with whom they happened to have fallen out! When the centre of their aggression became Peking, any 'foreign devil' who could do so took refuge in the walled compounds of the Legations; the majority of them in the British Legation where they were besieged for nearly nine weeks. The Dowager Empress, Tzu Hsi, widely known as 'the only man in China', while unwilling to get on the wrong side of the Boxers (whose aims she was inclined to sympathize with), was careful to send the beleaguered foreigners gifts of food, fresh fruit and vegetables. But apart from that she made no move to come to their support and kept cautiously — and barely — on the safe side of a very finely drawn line. Her Majesty was nothing if not wily.

The Boxer Rising fizzled out after a nasty, nerve-racking interval. And as the international army marching to the relief of the Legation neared Peking, 'the only man in China' fled from her capital disguised as a peasant woman in a covered cart such as country folk use; accompanied by a handful of her courtiers and her nephew, the youthful, reluctant and weeping Emperor, now technically ruler of all China though his masterful aunt continued to act as Regent. Tzu Hsi had paused only long enough to order his favourite concubine, who had had the temerity to urge him to stay and face the 'foreign devils', to be torn from his arms and thrown shrieking down a nearby well, before hastily quitting the Forbidden City by a back gate. The foreign troops marched into Peking and Siege of the Legations came to an end.

On 22 January 1901, Victoria, Queen and Empress, died at Osborne in the arms of her grandson, Kaiser Wilhelm of Germany. And in the following year Tacklow's regiment received orders to sail for North China and help clear up the ruinous mess left by those far-from-Harmonious Fists.

The 21st Punjabis embarked for Tientsin from Kidderpore Docks in Calcutta, and it was left to Tacklow, as the best linguist among the British officers, to explain to the rank-and-file what a long sea voyage would entail; or, for that matter, any sea voyage, since none of them had ever laid eyes on the sea before or had the haziest idea of geography. In fact it is doubtful if any of them, even the VCOs* or the non-commissioned Havildars and Havildar-Majors, had the remotest idea where China was or knew anything much about it. They listened attentively to everything that Tacklow had to say until he warned them about seasickness. *Seasickness?* — what sort of illness was that and why did he think they might suffer from it? What caused it? Tacklow explained that it was caused by the motion of the ship in windy weather; the pitching and tossing of the boat was apt to make landsmen feel ill, though such people as lascars (Indian seamen) and other seafaring men became immune to it. The men of the 21st Punjabis rejected the whole idea, declaring scornfully that they did not believe for a moment that the mere motion of a ship could make them feel ill. Foreigners and Sahib-log might do so, but not them! They were not

* Viceroy's Commissioned Officers.

sissies to fall sick because of a little jogging about. The Sahib would see!

The Sahib did. He said he had never seen anything like it. The first few days had been calm and hot and the sepoys laughed at him and pointed out that not one of them had suffered any of the ill-effects he had described. 'Wait until the wind rises,' said Tacklow. And sure enough, before long the ship ran into bad weather and within a matter of hours the entire battalion was laid flat on its collective stomach, vomiting its heart out. 'Never,' said Tacklow, 'had any regiment disintegrated so swiftly.' Every available inch of deck space, passageway or cabin was strewn with groaning bodies which the ship's company and those of their own officers who were not also laid low had to step over as they went about their duties, since they were wholly incapable of moving. Tacklow said it was just like one of Gustave Doré's illustrations of 'The Flood' — or Dante's 'Inferno'.

By the time they reached Singapore and ran out of the bad weather they had decided that perhaps they were not going to die after all. And as it was fortunately not the season for storms and typhoons on the China Seas, they arrived in Tientsin in excellent shape. But when, some three years later, they completed their tour of duty in North China and heard that they were about to return to India, a deputation headed by a Subadar lined up in front of the Colonel to ask if this was true. Were they indeed going home? 'Assuredly,' said the Colonel. 'By ship?' 'Certainly by ship.' Well in that case, said the Subadar, they had come to the unanimous conclusion that they would prefer to walk. They had been studying an atlas which clearly showed that it was possible to return to India without crossing the sea, and as they would not ask the Sikār to feed them, but would undertake to feed themselves during the journey, the Sikār would save a great deal of money not only on the price of their food but on their passages as well.

It took a long time to explain exactly how and why this generous offer must be rejected as impractical, and Tacklow said that he wasn't sure that they believed the Colonel in the end. But the fact that they were prepared to undertake a year-long trek on foot through trackless jungles, fording rivers, crossing swamps and mountain ranges, and fighting off hostile tribes *en route* — not to mention head-hunters! — shows what they thought of seasickness. They have all my sympathy. I'm a terrible sailor myself.

�֍ Tacklow fell in love with China at first sight, and his tour of 'China-side service' was probably the happiest period of his life. The fact that he already spoke Mandarin and Cantonese, and had passed the higher standard in both, may have had something to do with it; for languages being one of his hobbies he had added these two to his collection for fun and not because it had ever crossed his mind that he might be posted to China one day. In fact it was his firm opinion (and one that was only too frequently proved to be true) that any young Army officer who passed the higher standard in, say, Persian could be certain, on the grounds of his 'proficiency at languages', of being posted to Burma or Kathmandu; though never on any account to Persia. Tacklow said that one could safely bet on this, because that was how the official mind at Headquarters worked.

Being able to speak two of China's languages made a great difference to his feelings for that country, since it meant that he could always make himself understood without having to fall back on sign-language, or on Pidgin-English — that fascinating *lingua franca* of the China coast. Though he confessed that any ordinary Chinaman whom he met, whether in town or country, took it for granted, when addressed, that the 'foreign devil' would naturally be speaking in some strange barbaric tongue that would be unintelligible to him, and therefore made his mind a blank. The way out of this impasse was simple. One merely threatened the man with a stick and announced loudly and clearly: 'I AM SPEAKING CHINESE!' whereupon the amiable Son of Han would beam with intelligence, and from there on it was all plain sailing.

That magic formula has become a catchword in our family, and if there is anything one of us wishes to impress on another who shows signs of inattention, we say: '*I am speaking Chinese!*', which not only underlines its importance but invariably works like a charm, making the listener snap to attention. My sister and I use it to this day.

I heard innumerable stories from Tacklow about the years that the regiment spent in China. Stories about the looting of the Summer Palace, where the British troops ran riot and behaved like hooligans, destroying or vandalizing anything they could not carry away. One of these vandalized treasures was a wonderful red lacquer screen that, according to Tacklow, could only have been made *in situ* since it was far too large to be taken through any doorway. There were also the huge pair of lion-dogs, carved from jade-coloured marble, that stood guard on either side of a central pavilion at the top of the long flight of stone steps, and like the priceless lacquer screen were far too heavy to remove. They were simply smashed up; the superb lion-dogs being toppled from their pedestals and sent crashing down the stone stairway to end up in mutilated fragments; an example of crude and stupid yobbism that in Tacklow's opinion was enough to reduce any thinking person to tears of despair. But the orders were that since the Empress and not the Chinese people must be held responsible for the death and destruction caused by the Boxers, it was therefore only just and right that her personal property should suffer. It did.

The loot taken in Peking and its environs must have been fabulous. Tacklow bought one item of it, offered to him for a modest sum by a corporal in the French contingent of the International Force that had marched to the rescue of the Europeans in Peking. It was a Kossu scroll, meant to be hung on a wall, depicting a Chinese lady attended by a serving boy carrying a censer that is giving off a cloud of incense. Kossu is a hand-woven picture or design in which each separate colour is cunningly woven into the fabric; though in this one a number of small details and decorations have been superimposed with a paint-brush — which reduces its value considerably.

I have the scroll still. It was the only piece of loot — if you can call it that, since he paid for it — that Tacklow brought back from Peking. Others acquired far more valuable objects, and he told me about an acquaintance of his, the adjutant of one of the British regiments, whose men would bring him any item of bric-à-brac that they had looted, in the certainty that if he fancied it he would say 'All right — stand yourself a pint of beer on me at the canteen'; which was considered adequate payment and gratefully received. One day a private soldier brought him a necklace, describing it as 'this 'ere string o' glass beads, sir'. The adjutant, no expert, examined the gaudy thing carefully and had his doubts, so he decided to take a gamble and offered the man five pounds. The private, whose pay was a shilling a day, looked very taken aback at the vastness of the sum, but after mulling it over for a moment or two, said he'd changed his mind about selling it and took it back. The adjutant thought no more about it; but a long while later, happening to meet my father again, he told him the end of the story. . . .

He and his regiment had in due course returned to England, and one day, some five or six years later, while strolling down Regent Street in London he was accosted by a very smartly dressed man who said: 'Do you remember me, sir? — Private So-and-so.' The Adjutant, now a Colonel, said he did indeed, and shaking hands asked him how he was getting on; adding that he looked as though he was doing all right. 'I am that, sir,' agreed the ex-private. 'Do you remember that necklace of red glass beads I offered you in Peking? Well, if you'd told me to have a pint of beer on you at the canteen you could have 'ad 'em and welcome. But when you said you'd give me a fiver for them, it give me a bit of a shock and I thought I'd stick to 'em. I brought 'em 'ome with me and took 'em to a jeweller who said they wasn't glass at all; they was rubies and worth a mint of money. They was too — just about a fortune. So I buys my discharge, and a nice little business into the bargain that's doing so well that I'm a rich man. And I owes it all to you, sir, 'cause if you 'adn't offered me the five pounds I'd still be in the ranks!'

Another prize of war in those days was the Pekinese dog. Among the earliest of the breed to leave China had been a peke annexed by Lord John Hay during the sacking and destruction of the original Summer Palace at the end of the Taiping Rebellion, and subsequently presented to Queen Victoria; who does not seem to have appreciated the gift. These pampered creatures were regarded as royal, and known as 'lion-dogs' because though their frames were small they were lion-hearted; a fact that anyone who has ever owned a Pekinese will know well.

One unexpected result of the Boxer Rising was that for the first time many of these hitherto carefully guarded Palace-dogs found their way out into the streets and alleys of Peking, and it was not long before every masterless dog in the city (in India we called such dogs pariah dogs — 'pi-dogs' for short — and in China they are called 'wonks') had a dash of Pekinese blood. With the years the strain spread throughout the Celestial Kingdom, and the effects are distinctly odd. Dogs with the bodies of terriers or dachshunds but the flat pansy-faces and curling, chrysanthemum tails of Pekinese; others with the squat, silky-haired bodies of Pekinese but with the whippy tails of bull-terriers and the faces of various long-nosed, pointy-eared breeds. The variations appear to be endless, but the sections that hark back to the Imperial lion-dogs are unmistakable.

✼ North China winters are bitter, and the first winter that the 21st Punjabis spent there was a memorable one. With the arrival of the frost the sea froze for three miles outside Chingwentao, and every river and canal turned to solid ice. Tacklow and his fellow officers acquired skates, and on the first morning that they tried these out they became aware of a row of turban-crowned faces watching them wide-eyed with horror over the top of the canal bank; apparently the Punjabis thought that this was some form of evil magic and imagined that the water would open and swallow up the Sahib-log at any moment. Eventually, however, reassured by explanation and demonstration, the entire audience lined up in fours and marched resolutely down the bank and onto the ice. The result was a shambles, for as each rank reached it, four pairs of feet either shot up into the air or performed the splits as their owners fell sprawling and skidded every which way across the slippery surface; bodies piled up on bodies, arms and legs flailing wildly, while the frosty air turned blue with strange oaths. Tacklow assured me that no Keystone Cops comedy that he ever saw lived up to it, but that in no time at all the whole regiment had acquired skates and were performing complicated acrobatics on the ice.

There was ice-sailing too: a fast, furious and thrilling sport in which small flat-bottomed boats with matting sails skimmed before the wind across the flooded, frozen levels of the countryside at a terrifying speed; leaping dykes as a racehorse or a hunter leaps a fence, and turning and swerving like a flight of swallows. On windy days the speeds that the ice-boats could achieve were hair-raising, and much of the heavy traffic on the rivers and canals, where in winter the boats were poled along the ice, would raise lateen sails and make use of the wind to drive them forward.

That year when the first snow fell, the regimental post office received a number of bottles filled with snow and labelled to various addresses in the Punjab, with messages attached saying that this was the peculiar kind of rain that fell in this country. The senders had to be tactfully told that long before the bottles reached India this interesting stuff would look no different from the rain that fell anywhere else, and if left for an hour or so they would be able to witness this disappointing transformation for themselves.

Tacklow also told me of the occasion when, talking to a Manchu friend in the presence of a stranger wearing peasant dress, he noticed with interest that the stranger held his nose throughout the interview. When the man finally left, still holding his nose, Tacklow asked his friend the meaning of this curious behaviour. The Manchu, deeply embarrassed, apologized profusely; explaining that the man was from a small village in the interior that had not enjoyed the benefits of education, so he hoped that Tacklow would forgive such uncouth behaviour. Tacklow replied that he wouldn't give it another thought, but he would dearly like to know *why* the man had behaved like that? Well, it was this way, explained his friend: to the Chinese, all Western people smell unpleasant, though this did not of course justify bad manners! — people who knew how to behave bit on the bullet and politely ignored it. When pressed, he said he supposed that the unpleasant odour of Occidentals sprang from the food they ate, which included an inordinate amount of red meat and animal fat; plus the fact that they smoked a great deal of tobacco in pipes, cigars and cigarettes, used shaving-soap and strange-smelling mouthwashes and washed with strongly scented soaps.

This piece of information fascinated Tacklow, because of course Occidentals have often complained that Orientals, Asians and Africans, probably on account of their diet, have strongly individual body-odours which white races are apt to criticize and take exception to. It was therefore salutary, he said, to discover that other races thought that *we* were the ones who smelt unpleasant; and he was duly grateful to his Manchu friend for enduring it without complaint.

Another foreigner whom he made friends with in China was a convalescent Russian officer who was in Tientsin in the early months of 1905, recovering from the effects of starvation and a wound received during the siege of Port Arthur — a fortified town that Japan had ceded to Russia less than seven years earlier, and recently retaken. Port Arthur, in a day well before the age of aerial warfare, and when high-explosives had yet to be invented and no gun then made was heavy enough to breach its massive walls, had been considered impregnable. Nevertheless the Japanese took it by assault, after a prolonged siege and many days of ferocious fighting. Tacklow's Russian friend, telling him of it, said that it was like being opposed by a vast and inexhaustible army of killer-ants to whom death had no meaning whatsoever. He described to him how rank after rank of Japanese troops would rise from their entrenchments and race forward (their officers, sword in hand, always well to the fore), only to be mown down by the guns and rifle-fire of the defenders; how another line of officers would instantly leap up, raise their swords and shout the order to advance to the next rank — who would rise and run forward over the piled-up bodies of their dead and wounded, and falling in their turn, be trodden under by the next rank ... and then the next and the next —

The Russian said that it was not only uncanny but beyond belief, and that no one who had not seen it with their own eyes could believe it. They died, he said, in their thousands; yet there were always more of them. They kept coming and coming until in the end it broke the nerve of the garrison. He said, too, that the famous story of the Japanese officer who, not trusting to a fuse, used the tip of his cigarette to touch off the charge of explosive that relays of men had carried forward — the living picking it up from the hands of the dead to run on with it for the next few yards until at last it was put in place against the outer walls or one of the gates — was inaccurate. Not because it had not been done, but because it was *always* done. And not by just one officer, but by dozens of officers who took no chances but pressed the lighted tip of a cigarette against the charge, and shouting '*Banzai!*' were blown to pieces with it. This, and sheer numbers, was, according to the Russian, the reason why the 'impregnable' fortress fell to the descendants of the Samurai. The kamikaze pilots of the Second World War were only following the example of their fathers — or perhaps grandfathers — who died for their country before the walls of Port Arthur in the violent opening years of the twentieth century.

With the fall of the Boxers and the lifting of the siege of the Legations, peace was established in China and the Dowager Empress returned to Peking and was gracious to the 'foreign devils' and their wives. She gave a reception for them in the Forbidden City — several receptions in fact — and succeeded in charming the diplomats' women, who could not believe that this small, pleasant old lady could possibly have carried out any of the terrible deeds attributed to her. Tacklow, on temporary loan as ADC to some senior General, was privileged to see her once and he described her as looking rather like an Egyptian mummy; her face a yellow parchment-like mask, in which only the eyes were alive, under an elaborate Manchu head-dress; her hands hidden in the sleeves of a yellow satin robe that was stiff with embroidery.

He got the impression, he said, that if by saying a single word she could have doomed every one of them to the 'Death of a Thousand Cuts', she would have said it without a second's hesitation — and with relish!

Tzu Hsi was undoubtedly a wicked and murderous old woman. But she was also a great one and a ruler to be reckoned with. Even after that second ignominious retreat from Peking (she had run away once before and returned in triumph) she still retained her hold upon her subjects. She was still, to them, the 'Old Buddha'; and Tacklow told me that when a portrait of her, painted by an American artist, Miss Katherine Carl, was carried through the streets of Peking on its way to America and the St Louis Exhibition, the citizens treated it as though it had been the Empress herself, kowtowing to the ground as it passed; and that a special train was laid on to take it to Tientsin from where it was sent on by sea with royal honours.

She was very old when Tacklow saw her. But once she had been young and beautiful and burning with ambition. As the daughter of a petty Manchu official she was required, on reaching puberty, to present herself before the Empress Dowager, together with a number of other Manchu maidens of the same age, from among whom the Emperor's mother, assisted by a panel of eunuchs and elderly court ladies, would annually select those who were considered fit to become the Emperor's concubines. The young Tzu Hsi (then known by her clan name of Yehonala) passed the test and was sent to the women's quarters to apply herself to a rigorous course of tuition in manners, deportment and the art of pleasing a man. Each concubine had her name engraved on one side of a tablet of jade, and every night the Emperor would be presented with a selection of these tablets laid face downwards on a lacquer tray. He would turn one over at random, and the owner of the name thus disclosed would be bathed, rubbed with scented oil and parcelled up naked in a padded quilt of scarlet satin, to be carried into the bedroom of the Son of Heaven and unrolled on the floor at the foot of his bed.

Since this particular Emperor, Hsien Feng, was a sickly youth who suffered from headaches and had little or no interest in women, the wretched girl would generally spend the night flat on the floor in a humble kowtow with her forehead on the outspread quilt; shivering from a combination of cramp, cold, terror and pins-and-needles until dawn brought the eunuchs to re-wrap and remove her. Yehonala, however, was made of sterner stuff. She managed to charm or bribe one of the eunuchs into arranging that her tablet would be the one turned up, and when that happened she literally took her life in her hands, for instead of remaining on the floor she rose and sat boldly on the edge of the bed and began to talk to the boy; sympathizing with him, stroking his aching forehead and soothing him to sleep so that he passed the first comfortable night he had had in years. As a result, he demanded her presence on the following night. She became so necessary to him that neither his young wife nor any of the concubines ever visited him again, and soon there was a new Empress in the Forbidden City with the title of 'Empress of the West' — the first Empress now being known as the 'Empress of the East'. When Yehonala bore a son the poor Empress of the East ceased to be of any importance at all, and when the sickly Emperor died and her rival, as mother of the new Son of Heaven, was declared Regent during his minority and given the honorific title of Tzu Hsi (Motherly and Auspicious), she must have known that her days were numbered.

Since the new Emperor was only a little boy when his father died, Tzu Hsi had a long run for her money. But when the Regency ended and her son took possession of the Dragon Throne, she was reluctant to hand over power to him, and legend has it that he was disposed of, with her connivance, by means of one of those little steam-heated towels that nowadays air-hostesses offer to passengers on long flights, and which in his case had first been pressed to the ulcerated face of someone suffering from smallpox. The Emperor caught the infection and died, and his mother ignoring the fact that his widow was with child (who could well turn out to be a son), indulged in some spirited plotting that resulted in the election of a candidate of her own to succeed him — the four-year-old son of her youngest sister. The widowed Empress, her child still unborn, died mysteriously a short while later, and Tzu Hsi embarked triumphantly on a second Regency ...

It was this child, by then a youth, whose favourite concubine was thrown down a well before his 'Motherly and Auspicious' aunt fled from Peking during the Boxer Rising. And when he too died (in all probability hastened on his way by poison) his elderly aunt once again made certain of being Regent by selecting another infant to succeed him: this time the two-year-old grandson of the only man who, as far as anyone knows, she ever loved; the man to whom she had been once betrothed, and would certainly have married had she been rejected as an Imperial concubine all those years ago. His name was Jung Lu, and he had served her all his life — and saved hers on many occasions. When she died a few days later, it was Jung Lu's grandson who succeeded her: little Pu Yi, who was destined to become the last Emperor of China: the last, the very last Son of Heaven to occupy the Dragon Throne! His reign was a brief one. And though after China became a Republic the Japanese installed him as a puppet Emperor of Manchuria, that did not last very long either, and he ended up as an ordinary Chinese citizen, Comrade Pu Yi Aisin Giorro, who died only recently.

✳ The three short years that the 21st Punjabis spent in North China changed the whole course of Tacklow's life. For one thing, he met my mother there; and married her. And for another, he and a great friend of his, a Major Brownlow, attended a stag-party in Tientsin where over the port and cigars the conversation happened to turn to ciphers. When, inevitably, someone mentioned the unbreakable Playfair, Tacklow intervened to contradict him and ended by telling the company the story of his room-mate at Sandhurst. I am not too certain which one of these two events was the more important, but am putting Mother first — !

Tacklow was standing on the up-platform of Tientsin's railway station, seeing off a friend who was leaving for Peking, when his eye fell on what he later described to me as 'one of the prettiest girls I ever saw in my life'. He also noted, with a sense of outrage at the sheer waste of it, that this delectable creature was warmly embracing 'a grey-bearded fogey old enough to be her father'! The fact that it *was* her father was something he was to discover much later; but at that point the guard blew his whistle, the friend began to shout last messages, an eleventh-hour rush of baggage coolies and late arrivals swept Tacklow aside, and by the time the train pulled out in a cloud of steam the vision and her old fogey had vanished.

He had no idea who she was and though he looked hopefully for her at every party, accepting all the invitations that came his way in the hope of seeing her again, he drew a blank. There followed another extended tour of duty in Peking, but he did not forget her; and when at length he returned to Tientsin he still kept looking, just in case. He had almost given up hope when one day his friend Major Westhrop-White of the 74th Sikhs invited him to accompany the regiment on one of their morning constitutionals, that combined showing-the-flag with a bit of brisk exercise by marching the battalion through Tientsin. 'There's one street,' said Westhrop-White, 'in which we always play "Marching through Georgia", because the prettiest little missionary-girl you ever saw lives there. She teaches a class of Chinese kids and as soon as she hears that tune she comes flying down the path, with the whole kindergarten at her heels, to hang over the gate and listen to us as the band goes by.'

Tacklow accepted and rode beside the Major at the head of the column. And sure enough, when the regimental band swung into 'Marching through Georgia' a starry-eyed girl with a long plait of chestnut-brown hair as thick as his arm shot out of a doorway, and accompanied by a horde of Chinese tots came running down the path to see the Sikhs march past. It was, of course, Daisy Bryson; the girl he had seen at Tientsin's railway station. . . .

Years later, told by a friendly and admiring Head of Department to 'write your own letter recommending yourself for the job, and I'll sign it!', he was to list among his qualifications the fact that despite his belonging to what at that date was too often regarded as 'the brutal and licentious soldiery', he had not only managed to inveigle himself into the good graces of the family of a Scottish missionary, but had actually succeeded in marrying one of their daughters!

The claim was not entirely a frivolous one, for he always insisted that it had been the toughest assignment he had ever undertaken. And there is little doubt that initially he was regarded with the gravest suspicion by my mother's parents. But having found what he was looking for he had no intention of letting it go, and he persisted; though the first occasion on which he was actually invited to supper was not exactly a success, due to the home-made ice cream having somehow managed to get flavoured with raw onion. Tacklow, who as the guest was served first (and who detested the taste of raw onion), meekly ate a portion of the revolting stuff without flinching – an exhibition of good manners that did not go down at all well with the rest of the family who, loudly condemning the dish, thought he was incredibly silly to have eaten more than the first spoonful. However, he managed to live that down too. But it was a long courtship. And an expensive one, since the girl of his choice possessed three sisters and four brothers, and as he did not wish anyone to guess that he was only interested in one member of the family, he used to bring presents for all of them whenever presents were called for; which cost him a packet.

By 1904 he had become sufficiently friendly with the Brysons to be invited to spend Christmas Day with them, and when pulling a cracker with some fellow guest he found himself in possession of small trinket — a little silver ring with a flower-shaped boss that was not unlike a daisy — he handed it surreptitiously to Mother, whispering that he hoped she would allow him to exchange it one day for a real one. When that day eventually came she returned the cracker ring to him as fair exchange, and he wore it on his watch-chain to the day of his death. I have it now for safe keeping, because Mother is afraid she might lose it. Though I am not even sure that she would still recognize it; or even remember anything about it. But as long as someone remembers, that is really all that matters. For *'beauty vanishes; beauty passes; However rare — rare it be; And when I crumble, who will remember This lady of the West Country?'*.

When Tacklow finally decided that it was now safe (and also high time) to come out into the open and ask the Rev. Thomas Bryson's permission to marry his second daughter, the Dadski, not the most observant of men, was astounded. It seems that he had not had the faintest suspicion as to what Captain Kaye was after, let alone whom he was after. When he had recovered from the shock, all he would say was that he 'did not feel that he could part with the lassie today'. A dusty answer that was to be repeated again and again during the following months.

There used to be a popular song in those days called 'A Bicycle Made for Two', with a refrain that began *'Daisy, Daisy, give me your answer do!'* and Mother had had it sung to her for years and was by now heartily sick of it. But though her father prevaricated, she herself had already given Tacklow the answer he wanted. She had said 'yes'. Yet despite this, his Daisy, now aged eighteen, was remorselessly chaperoned, and had it not been for a sympathetic family friend, a Mrs Edkins who used to invite Mother to tea or out on a picnic and arrange for her swain to be present so that he could snatch a few words with her alone, he would probably never have got to first base. Not that her parents had anything against him. On the contrary, they approved of him; particularly on account of his age, which was exactly twice that of his intended bride. And if that sounds odd to us, it didn't to the Victorians. Or to the Edwardians either. They preferred mature husbands for their young daughters, being convinced that an older man would, in the approved fashion of the day, be a father-figure who could be trusted to take the greatest possible care of an innocent and inexperienced damsel who had only recently been given permission to put her hair up and let her skirts down. (In my day the process was reversed: hair being 'bobbed' or 'shingled' and skirts raised well above the knee.) My grandparents' objection to the marriage was merely a sentimental reluctance to face the fact that the family circle was bound to break up as their children grew into adults. Daisy's was the first defection. That was all. Tacklow was a very patient man; but there are limits, and eventually he told Mother that enough was enough and that he was going to buy her an engagement ring and then pay a call on her father to demand a straight — and shorter! — answer from him.

That crucial interview took place in the hall of the Brysons' house in Tientsin. And when the Rev. Thomas gave his usual answer, the lassie in question (who had been hanging anxiously over the banisters on the landing above, listening to every word) marched resolutely down the stairs and, putting her arms about her suitor's neck, kissed him soundly; whereupon he produced a little diamond ring from his pocket and put it on her finger. At this point her father threw in the towel; though he insisted on an engagement period of at least six months by which time 'the lassie' would have turned nineteen and Tacklow's regiment, their tour of China duty almost over, would be on the verge of embarking for India.

The marriage of Cecil Kaye, Captain 21st Punjabis, eldest surviving son of William and Jane Kaye, to Margaret Sarah (Daisy) Bryson, second daughter of the Rev. Thomas and Mrs Bryson, London Mission, took place not once but twice, on 5 September 1905, in Tientsin. The first ceremony being a civil one conducted in the British Consulate by His Britannic Majesty's Consul-General, Mr L. C. Hopkins, 'according to the provisions of the Foreign Marriages Act

1892'. Later that same day the conventional white wedding took place in the Union Church where the address was given by Mother's brother Arnold, who had like his father taken Holy Orders, and the closing prayer by her father, who had given her away. Major Westhrop-White, who had invited Tacklow to go with him on the fateful march through Tientsin, acted as his best man, and the band of the 47th Sikhs played 'suitable selections' — including, one hopes, 'Marching through Georgia' — at the wedding reception.

My uncles Tom, Alec, Arnold and Ken were ushers. My aunts Alice, Dorothy and Lillian, carrying baskets filled with marguerites and wearing hats the size of flying saucers made of net and trimmed with daisies, were bridesmaids. And my mother, who had set her heart on wearing a wedding veil so long that it would trail behind her down the aisle, wept bitterly when it arrived that morning (lent for the occasion, as wedding veils were very expensive) and she discovered that it was not much bigger than a pocket handkerchief! That veil was the one blot on an otherwise happy occasion, and accounts for the wooden expression with which she faced the cameras as she descended the Church steps on her bridegroom's arm under an arch of swords raised by his brother officers. Mother has always said that it was the bitterest disappointment of her life and that it ruined her wedding day . . .

A yellowed page from the *Peking & Tientsin Times* of 5 September 1905, which is still in existence, has three columns of print describing the whole festivity in detail and informing the reader that the bride was 'very becomingly dressed' in plain white silk made with a 'transparent yoke' (!!! *surely* not?) and that she wore 'a wreath of orange blossoms under a plain tulle veil'. The reporter adds that 'she looked remarkably sweet and pretty'. Not in the photographs she doesn't! She looks excessively po-faced, and she still insists that her nose was red and her eyes pink and swollen from crying and that 'it was all the fault of that horrid, mingy little veil with its wide, dowdy, hemmed edge — just like an outsized man's handkerchief, *ugh*!'. Hence the stuffed expression, I suppose. She never forgot the incident, and when years later my sister Bets married, compensated for it at one remove by buying Bets the longest, widest and flimsiest wedding veil you ever saw. And very pretty it looked too!

The ancient *Peking & Tientsin Times* that reported the Bryson–Kaye wedding also prints a short account of the speech given by Mr McLeish (described as 'one of the oldest Tientsin friends of the family') who proposed the health of the bride and bridegroom. In it he mentions the siege of the Legations and that some humorist in those days had predicted that one of the most striking results of the Boxer Rising would be that some of the 'soldier johnnies' would be walking off with some of the Tientsin girls. He also — wouldn't you know it? — expressed sympathy for Mr and Mrs Bryson who were seeing the first of their brood 'take flight from the nest'. That 'soldier johnnie', C. Kaye, gets barely a mention, but looks very smug and pleased with himself in the wedding photographs.

I still do not know why Mother married him. She was barely seventeen when she met him and he was not only bald on top — and had been since he turned twenty — but he was twice her age,* and no taller than she was (though he always claimed to be half an inch taller and said she cheated by wearing high heels and having so much hair!). Every young businessman in Tientsin was in love with her — with the exception of the faithful Howard Payne who married her sister Alice not long afterwards — and since they were all in Trade they must have been far better endowed with 'worldly goods' than a penniless Captain in an Indian infantry regiment. Yet she chose him, and never regretted it.

The sympathetic Mrs Edkins and her husband, whose daughter Effie had been a flower girl at the wedding, lent the honeymooners their house at Pei-tai-ho, a small town on the Yellow Sea that, in those days, was little more than a village.

Tacklow used to talk to me about that honeymoon as though it was an enchanted time in some dreamlike Shangri-La: the lonely house standing on low cliffs above a small, secluded beach that was screened on the south-west by a fantastic cluster of tall rocks; the shimmering expanse of the Yellow Sea stretching below. From their cliff-top, they would look out together across the flat lands that curved away eastward in a wide bay to where, on the far side of that bay, lay the small coastal

---

* She had wanted to add a year to her age on the marriage licence so that no one could say that her bridegroom was twice as old; but when her father refused to countenance this, she persuaded Tacklow to subtract a year from his. This he did, and that is why their marriage lines show her to be nineteen and he thirty-seven — not thirty-eight.

town of Chingwantao where the Great Wall of China ends in the sea. He told me of a day-long expedition by rickshaw to the Lotus Hills that lie to the west of Pei-tai-ho, where they had picnicked and wandered among the ancient temples that are a feature of those peaceful, pine-clad hills; returning in the cool of the evening by the pale light of a huge, apricot-coloured September moon to that quiet house on the cliff. And best of all, one unforgettable sight — the most beautiful, he said, that he had ever seen before or since — Mother, wading out naked ahead of him into a satin-smooth sea in the dawn, her hair hanging down loose to below her waist with the rising sun, shining through it, turning it to every colour in the world; red, green, blue and violet, glittering gold and burnished copper ... Venus Anadyomene, robed in a rainbow. That picture would remain with him for ever, indelibly printed on his memory by the camera of his eye, and he spoke of it as though Mother had been Eve herself bathing, new-made, in a lake in Eden in the radiant sunrise of the world's morning.

He never forgot it. Nor did he ever look at any other woman. I honestly do not think he ever noticed there were any others around! He cherished and spoilt her and loved her dearly, and when, years later, his knighthood appeared in the Honours List, a woman friend of hers rushed into the ladies room of the Old Delhi Club, brandishing the newspaper and shouting excitedly: 'Daisy's got her K!'

I have also seen the telegram, lovingly preserved by Tacklow, that she sent him on their Silver Wedding day to thank him for his gift — they were not together for the anniversary, for he had sent her to the cool of the hills and was tied himself by work in the scorching heat of the plains. The telegram, handed in at Srinagar in Kashmir on 5 September 1930 and delivered an hour later in Rajputana, begins: 'Happy Returns. Solomon one two ...' (Those who are interested can look that one up in the Bible — Song of Solomon, Chapter 1, Verse 2.)

Chapter 6

~✷✷✷~

Fate, Time, Occasion, Chance, and Change? To these
All things are subject ...

Shelley, *Prometheus Unbound*

Not long after they returned to Tientsin, Tacklow and his bride and
the 21st Punjabis said a sad farewell to North China and embarked on
the troopship that was to take them back down the Pei-ho River to
the Taku Bar. Once across the bar it was southward across the Yellow
Sea, past Shanghai and Formosa, Hong Kong and Hainan, into the
South China Sea. Then northwards at Singapore through the Straits
of Malacca and into the Indian Ocean, and southward again to Ceylon;
from where they would turn north once more into the Arabian Sea,
past Cochin, Calicut, Mahé, Goa, Bombay and the great peninsula of
Kathiawar, to Karachi. From here they travelled by river-boat up the
Indus to Jhelum, a garrison town on the borders of the North-West
Frontier Province where the 21st Punjabis had been posted, and where
it was discovered on arrival that owing to some official miscalculation
there was no Army quarter available for Captain and Mrs Kaye.

It did not worry them. They cheerfully agreed to make do with
two sparsely furnished rooms in the Dâk-bungalow* — a singularly
comfortless building that looked, when I last saw it, almost exactly as
it had done when it became Mother's first home as a married woman —
or so she assured me, and judging by her old and faded photographs
of it, she was right!

Dâk-bungalow or no, she enjoyed Jhelum and still looks back on
her time there with nostalgic affection. But she was not allowed to
spend the summer there because she was expecting her first baby, and

---

* Lit. post bungalow. A local rest-house in which travellers could obtain a bed and a meal
on payment of a small sum, and could normally put up for two or three days at most.

the heat being as near unbearable as makes no matter, Tacklow sent her up to the hills to Naini Tal and the care of his intimidating elder sister, Aunt Molly — the human battle-axe previously referred to. Here, on 3 August 1906, my brother William (originally called 'Willie' but eventually, thank goodness, shortened to 'Bill') was born to the proud nineteen-year-old Daisy, while his father sweated in Jhelum in a temperature that moved between 103 and 120 degrees Fahrenheit. Only when autumn came round and the weather turned cooler did he allow her to return to Jhelum with her son, and a few months later they were able to move into half a bungalow; the other half of which was occupied by a much older and more senior Army couple: a Colonel and Mrs something-or-other, with whose niece, or it may have been cousin? a Miss Beatrice Lewis, Mother had already made friends.

'Bee' Lewis had come out to India as a hopeful member of what Anglo-Indians* chose to call 'the Fishing Fleet'. Sadly, though, she became one of the equally cruelly named 'Returned-empties'. But during her stay in Jhelum she earned Mother's lasting gratitude by hotly supporting her when certain of the more hidebound ladies in the station were snootily critical of young Mrs Kaye's insistence on pushing her son's pram herself when she took him out on her morning and evening walks along the tree-shaded Cantonment roads, or across the mile-long iron bridge that spans the Indus, 'the Father of Rivers', at Jhelum. Such undignified behaviour, said these old pussies, demeaned the British and 'let the side down'. Pushing prams was 'servant's work', and they lectured Mother about it and told her she should let the ayah or a *chokra*† push it. Mother said that she greatly enjoyed pushing it herself and didn't see why she shouldn't; it was *her* baby! To the dismay of the disapproving Top Cats, Tacklow supported her. They considered that he should have known better. But since Tacklow was uninterested in their views, his Daisy continued to push her son's pram around Jhelum.

And now back to Major Brownlow and that stag-party in Tientsin ...

* In those days the term applied to the British who served in India, and not, as now, to people of mixed blood, who were known as Eurasians.

† Small boy.

✁ The story that Tacklow had told on that occasion about his Sandhurst room-mate who had broken the unbreakable Playfair cipher was, even at that date, an old one — the episode having occurred a good many years previously. Now, after several more had passed, Major Brownlow, the friend who had taken him to that dinner-party, happened to be dining at Flagstaff House in Peshawar with the GOC Peshawar District, General Smith-Dorrian, when, as in Tientsin, the conversation chanced to turn to ciphers and the General observed that at least there was one unbreakable cipher, the Playfair. Not so, said Major Brownlow; he knew a man who had actually broken it — and who was, what's more, at that moment stationed in Jhelum! (Either the Major's memory was hazy or else he had been paying over-much attention to the port, for all that he could remember was that Cecil Kaye had claimed that the Playfair was breakable; QED Cecil Kaye himself must have broken it.) General Smith-Dorrian didn't believe a word of it. The fellow must have been pulling their legs. Or else he was trying to show off. Well, he'd show him — !

The upshot was a large official envelope that arrived on Tacklow's desk some two days later. It contained a message written in Playfair, a sealed envelope, and a curt letter from the General himself that said in effect: 'I have been informed that you claim to have broken the Playfair. Well, let's see you do it! Here is a message in Playfair, and in case you can't solve it I have sent the code word in a sealed envelope. Yours, etc.'

This bolt from the blue arrived on a sultry morning in mid-April when the leaves were beginning to curl up and turn brown in the heat and the brain-fever bird had begun to sing its maddening hot-weather song. Tacklow read it with amazement and then, realizing what must have occurred, sat down and wrote an immediate reply. He said that the General's informant had got the wrong end of the stick, as he himself had no knowledge of ciphers. He merely claimed to have known someone who had deciphered this one. Also, the test message was unfair in that it was much too short; which made it twice as difficult to solve. However, as he still retained a vague memory of how his room-mate of more than twenty years ago had worked the trick, if the General would send him a slightly longer message he would dearly like to have a stab at cracking it.

A longer message duly arrived and Tacklow set to work. It took him the best part of a week — Mother says she can't remember exactly how long but that it seemed ages to her, because she helped him by making lists of paired letters and reading out lines of numbers. She never could understand the way in which a code could be cracked, for it was all miles above her head (mine too!). But she *does* remember the long hours he worked at it and his excitement, and hers, when at last it began to come out. The thing hinged on a key word that was chosen at random by whoever happened to be encoding the message; which I suppose was the reason it was considered to be unbreakable, since the key word was likely to be different every time — the choice of words being virtually endless. Tacklow returned the sealed envelope to Smith-Dorrian with the seal still unbroken and a letter that said: 'Your key-word is so-and-so; message reads as follows —'

I have a tape-recording of Mother telling me that story; though in such a muddled, wavering and croaky voice that one has to listen very carefully to catch what she is saying; and towards the end she goes off at a tangent on to quite another story: one that I never heard from Tacklow and that I have never been able to sort out. A tale about some officer who should have been on guard duty somewhere else and would be court-martialled for dereliction of duty if he failed to turn up on time — which, for some reason (an unacceptable one, obviously) he was not going to be able to do. Tacklow had apparently come to the rescue by offering to stand in for him, and did so by riding *ventre à terre* from Jhelum to wherever, all through the night like another Paul Revere, to save a fellow officer's bacon. Mother says on that tape that she always thought that was 'such a marvellous thing for him to have done'. But she can't recall anything more than him doing it; 'for a friend'. It certainly sounds a very dashing exploit for a man of forty who was never a particularly good horseman anyway.

A month or so before the Playfair episode, Tacklow, faced with the prospect of having to send his wife and baby to some hill station for the coming hot weather, had done a number of anxious sums on the backs of envelopes and decided that if he sold part of his cherished stamp collection (he was a keen philatelist and remained hooked on stamps to the end of his days), he could *just* afford to send them instead to North China to stay with the Brysons in a house that the Dadski had recently acquired at Pei-tai-ho, and let Mother show them their first grandchild. She could stay there for six months and he himself would join them there later, taking four months' leave, of which two would be spent on the outward and return voyages. This would allow him two with his wife and son at Pei-tai-ho and enable him to bring them back with him.

Mother had been wildly excited at the prospect of showing off 'Willie' to his grandparents and his bevy of uncles and aunts. Her only regret was that Tacklow would not be able to accompany them on the outward voyage. But then his leave did not begin until 1 June, and apart from May being the hottest and nastiest month of the hot weather, there were no electric fans, fridges or air-conditioning in those days; nor did any bungalow boast electric lights; it was oil lamps or candles. In the circumstances, Tacklow thought it best to get the long, dusty, sweltering train journey across India to Calcutta over before the temperature soared too high, so the stamps were sold and the passages booked for the middle of April. An 'experienced travelling ayah' was engaged to accompany Mother as far as Tientsin to help her look after her nine-month-old baby, and Tacklow obtained his Colonel's permission to go with them to see that 'Daisy and the little imp' got safely aboard ship.

On the evening before they left Jhelum the two of them took their 'little imp' for a last airing; but as she pushed the pram along the familiar Cantonment roads and they talked of the voyage that lay ahead and the fun they would have when he joined her at Pei-tai-ho, Mother was seized by a sudden premonition. 'You won't come!' she said, on the verge of tears. 'Something will happen to stop you coming. I *know* it will! I'm sure of it — you won't come!' Tacklow dried her eyes and told her not to be silly; of course he would come! His leave had been granted and his passage was booked, so there was no need for her to worry. But she could not shake off the conviction that he would not be able to join her in Pei-tai-ho after all, and in spite of anything he could say to the contrary she was still tearfully convinced that she was right when a week later she waved goodbye to him in Calcutta from the deck of the ship that was to take her to China.

This seems to have been the only time in her life when Mother experienced a definite foreknowledge of the future. For she was right. Tacklow, arriving back alone in Jhelum, tired and depressed after the heat and discomfort of the long return journey across India from Calcutta, walked into his bungalow and saw, lying on the hall table waiting for him, a telegram from Army Headquarters saying that he had been transferred to GHQ Simla with the rank of Major and would he please report there immediately.

It was that Playfair business, of course. Anyone who possessed an outstanding talent — even if it was only a wife who could sing! — was sooner or later summoned up to Simla, where they collected talent. For Simla, as any reader of Rudyard Kipling will know, was in those days the summer capital of India to which the Viceroy, the Commander-in-Chief and the Governor of the Punjab, together with their respective wives and families, staffs, attendants and hangers-on, retreated to escape from the rigours of the hot weather. And during those six months in which the plains lay scorching in the relentless heat, the entire subcontinent was virtually ruled from that one small town among the pines. Army Headquarters occupied large blocks of offices on the steep hillside below the Mall; there were clubs, shops and churches, a theatre and a racecourse, and any number of hotels and boarding-houses as well as innumerable gimcrack tin-roofed and wooden-walled dwellings that were either privately owned or else hired for the season by rich Indians, British officials or wives and children taking refuge from the heat. Grass-widows, mothers with marriageable daughters, and young men on leave, flocked to it just to have a good time. It was the best-known and most popular hill station in India, and to be posted there was the height of many a man's ambition, since it was regarded as the gateway to promotion.

The homes of the nobility and gentry, Indian and British, were dotted among the pines and deodars* on the heights, while the town itself poured down the hillside in a wide cataract of flimsy wooden walls and crowded roof-tops of corrugated tin. Kipling said that it climbed up; but since I saw it first from above, to me it always pours down. Here is the way he saw the purely Indian part of the city, known as the Lower Simla Bazaar, in 1887, the year that his *Plain Tales from the Hills* was published. And this is how he was to describe it many years later in that retrospective love-letter to India, *Kim*:

... the crowded rabbit-warren that climbs up from the valley to the Town Hall at an angle of forty-five. A man who knows his way there can defy all

---

* The Indian cedar.

the police of India's summer capital; so cunningly does verandah communicate with verandah, alley-way with alley-way, and bolt-hole with bolt-hole. Here live those who minister to the wants of the glad city — jhampanis to pull the pretty ladies' rickshaws by night and gamble till the dawn; grocers, oil-sellers, curio-vendors, firewood-dealers, priests, pickpockets and native employees of the Government. Here are discussed by courtesans the things which are supposed to be the profoundest secrets of the India Council; and here gather all the sub-sub-agents of half the Native States.

And here is his description of the Mall, in —

... the mysterious dusk, full of the noises of the city below the hillside, and the breath of a cool wind in deodar-crowned Jakko, shouldering the stars. The houselights, scattered on every level, made, as it were, a double firmament. Some were fixed. Others belonged to the rickshaws of the careless open-spoken English folk, going out to dinner.

That's Simla — that was. And probably still is! Though 'the careless open-spoken English folk' have gone long ago.

The Commander-in-Chief, India, at the time that my father deciphered the Playfair, was none other than Field Marshal Lord Kitchener of Khartoum, and an order from his Army Headquarters in Simla was not to be disobeyed. Or even questioned. Not that Tacklow would have considered doing either, for it meant an immediate step upward in rank and a consequent rise in pay, and he knew that Mother would love to spend a season or two in a hill station that had the reputation of being the gayest city in India (gay in the old-fashioned sense of that once delightful word, I hasten to add). How could he have guessed that his desire to try his hand at proving that the Playfair could and had been broken might lead to this? He ought to have known that he hadn't heard the last of it. But *Simla* — ! If only that telegram had arrived a few days earlier it would have solved all their problems. The three of them could have gone up together to the cool air of the hills and there would have been no need for him to ship Daisy and the 'little imp' off to China alone, for there would be proper accommodation for them in Simla — perhaps even a house of their own. And they would all have been together ...

Tacklow thought seriously of sending a cable to Penang, which would be their first port of call, telling Mother to come back. But then what if it should prove difficult to get a return passage to India for

73

herself and her son (not forgetting the 'experienced travelling ayah', who rejoiced in the unforgettable name of Sarah Nicodemus)? They might have to stay in Penang for days. Even weeks! Besides, her mother had not been too well of late and who knew, apart from God, when there would be another opportunity for Isabella to see her first grandchild, or her darling Daisy again? Perhaps not for years. He spent a sleepless night going over all the pros and cons of the problem and then decided to let Mother go on to China and spend the summer with her family in Pei-tai-ho. It proved to be the right decision, for had she left the ship at Penang she would never have seen her mother again. A year later Isabella suffered a stroke from which she never recovered, and though she lingered on for some years, she died before her Daisy had another chance to see her.

Tacklow packed up his belongings and left for Simla alone.

�֍ One of the things I still bitterly regret is that after he died, Mother put all our 'furniture and effects', which included Tacklow's many books, papers and family records (together with her own collection of photograph-albums that she had meticulously kept ever since she was in her early teens), into storage in a warehouse in London that was gutted by fire barely two years later. We lost so much of our past in that fire, and had it not been for the affection that the Brysons and their children, and later on, their grandchildren, had for dear Aunt Lizzie in Bedford, and hers for them, there would be no photographs at all of Mother's youth or her wedding or her children's early years. But luckily Mother had never stopped writing to Aunt Lizzie and sending her copies of family snapshots, and after the latter's death I found a drawer full of them, lovingly hoarded, and annexed them.

I owe the existence of almost all the early photographs of Mother and her three children to Aunt Lizzie's magpie-storing of old snapshots. But unfortunately she cannot have been sent a copy of a group photograph of Lord Kitchener and the officers of Army Headquarters, taken in Simla in, I think, about 1907. We must have had a copy of it once, but if so it was probably burnt in that warehouse fire. Nor do I know how the key to it managed to survive. Yet survive it did, for we still have it: a printed copy of a rough pen-and-ink drawing of the sitters in that old group photograph (only one row actually sitting, the remaining four rows standing). Each outline bears a number and there is a list of names below that can be matched with them. Number 9, among those seated in the front row, and drawn wearing that impressive and familiar moustache, is Lord Kitchener — his name followed by a whole alphabet of initials, starting with the GCB. The list of names includes two future Commanders-in-Chief, Lord Birdwood and Sir John Cassalls, and several future Generals; as well as the Colonel Malleson who married Wigram Battye's* only sister and, when my kinsman Sir John Kaye died leaving his contemporary *History of the Sepoy Rebellion* unfinished, completed it and had the full text published as Kaye and Malleson's *History of the Indian Mutiny*. (He was not, incidentally, nearly so good a writer as John Kaye!) At the right hand of row 3 and bearing the number 61 is Major C. Kaye, no less; standing shoulder-to-shoulder with a Captain G. C. E. Wylley, VC (and I wonder what happened to *him* and where and when he won that Victoria Cross?). This key-drawing gives no date, but I imagine that the original photograph must have been taken during the summer of 1907; about the same time as a charming snapshot of Mother and my brother Bill taken on the beach at Pei-tai-ho.

Mother says she wept buckets when she got Tacklow's letter telling her of his new posting and breaking the news that he would not be able to join her because his leave had been cancelled. Not that she was in the least surprised, because she had been quite sure that he would not come and that something was going to stop him. In fact she was, I think, rather pleased with herself over the accuracy of her prediction, while the news that she would not have to return to Jhelum, but would be going up to live in Simla instead, went a long way towards making up for her disappointment. She thoroughly enjoyed her summer in Pei-tai-ho, and when she returned to India in October, was enchanted by her first sight of Simla; even though, by the time she arrived there, it was already half empty and most of the houses were closed and shuttered. For by then the Government of India had moved down to the plains for the cold weather, leaving Simla to shiver under a deep quilt of snow that would cover it from the end of November to as late as the first week of March; sometimes even later.

A skeleton staff remained in Simla during the winter months, and this year Tacklow was among them. He had engaged rooms at the

* See *The Far Pavilions*.

Central Hotel, and that year the snow came late and the town enjoyed a prolonged and golden Indian Summer during which Mother walked and rode, painted pictures of wildflowers and went house-hunting for a suitable cottage for the next season. There were no cars in Simla in those days, or indeed right up to the end of the Raj. Even in the late 1930s only the Viceroy, the Commander-in-Chief and the Governor of the Punjab were allowed to own a car, for the roads were steep and narrow and never intended for motorized traffic: people walked or rode, or were conveyed in rickshaws. Mother no longer pushed the pram, for the grades were too steep, and Bill went for walks with his ayah or, at weekends, with his father, who took him along the road that leads over the Combermere Bridge and past the shop that had once belonged to Lurgan-Sahib — the 'Healer of Pearls' in Kipling's *Kim* — and up to the ridge, where Christ Church stood and where there was a bandstand in which the Viceroy's band would often play of an evening during the Simla season.

Tacklow was baffled by the fact that his first-born, holding tightly to his hand as they went walking together and talking of this and that, had a favourite question that he had no idea how to answer. Had it been 'What's that man doing?' he could have coped. But Bill was not in the least interested in what men, animals or birds were doing, because he could see for himself what they were up to. What he wanted to know was 'What's that tree doing?' or 'What's that house doing?'.

Tacklow had tried, 'Standing up'; to which Bill would reply a trifle impatiently: 'I know. But what's it *doing*?' 'Growing' or 'Sitting down' were equally unacceptable and were greeted with: 'Yes, but what's it *doing*?'. This question, asked again and again during their walks, defeated Tacklow because it was clear to him that his son was after something and was not just being silly-childish. He really *did* want to know. He wanted an answer; a proper answer. But how did one answer a question like that? In the end Tacklow took to dealing with this teaser in one of two ways: he would either reply 'Sliding down a coal-pit' or 'Climbing up a steeple'; whereupon Bill, who had enough sense to know that he was being trifled with, would throw his hand in.

He was four years old when his father woke him up one night and, lifting him out of his cot, wrapped him in a blanket and carried him out into the darkness to show him something; telling him again and again that he was to remember what he had seen. He has never forgotten this incident, though he could not remember what it was that he was shown. It was in fact Halley's Comet — trailing its gorgeous, glowing train across the unpolluted skies above the Simla hills; the comet that passes our planet every seventy-six years and is supposed to presage disaster. Tacklow wanted Bill to see it because not many people can claim to have seen it twice.

Poor Tacklow! And poor 'little imp'! They spent such a small part of his childhood together. Only six years. After that, like so many parents and children of the great Age of Empire, the service of the Raj was to separate them, and they never grew to know each other at all. That was sad for both of them; but it was part of the price of Empire — the heaviest part. And very many paid it.

Tacklow did not know it then, but Simla was to be home to him for six months of each year for the greater part of his working life. The other six months would be spent in Delhi, where the Government of India moved as soon as the leaves began to fall on the wooded slopes of Jakko, and the snow-line moved downwards on the long ramparts of the Himalayas that spanned our horizon to the north. He would never again return to regimental duty, and his work thereafter was of an ambiguous nature: something vaguely connected with ciphers, security, and intelligence matters, under the guise of one of the many humdrum jobs at Army Headquarters.

Kitchener sent for him soon after his arrival and asked him if, in addition to his other work, he would produce and edit a magazine for the Indian Army, to be entitled *Fauje Akbar*: 'You'll do it on the usual terms, of course; "Find your own time and no pay!"' Tacklow did it — on the usual terms. And, I am told, it is still being published. A friend of his once told me that my father's arrival in Simla caused a good deal of confusion, because whenever anyone mentioned that Kaye had said or done or written this or that, it was instantly assumed that the speaker was referring to or quoting Kitchener — there being only one 'K' in Simla in those days.

In due course 'K' left and was succeeded by another Commander-in-Chief. But Tacklow was to spend another twenty-four hot weathers there. Almost a quarter of a century . . .

2

The Silver Sails

Chapter 7

> And up from India glances
> The silver sails of dawn ...
>
> Housman, *Last Poems*

There was a popular song in the 1930s with a refrain that began: '*When I fall in love, it will be for ever. Or I'll never fall in love'*.... I don't know exactly when I fell in love with India, but it was certainly for ever and it must have happened at a very early age. About the same time that I began to talk, I imagine, for the first language that I spoke with any fluency was Hindustani* and all the earliest songs that I became familiar with were the old, old lullabies of India: '*Arre ko ko; jarre ko ko*'; '*Nautch kurro, Baloo*'; '*Ah'za dindah*'; '*Ninni, baba, ninni*', and many others. I loved the sounds of India. The myriad noises that seem weird or harsh, or merely 'foreign' to the ear of the average Westerner, will always spell 'home' to me. I loved the scent of India. The look of it. The colour of it. And most of all I loved its people.

To begin with it never occurred to me that I wasn't one of them. I merely thought of myself as belonging to a particular sect in a land that was chock-full of sects and castes and races speaking a wide variety of different languages and a bewildering number of dialects. It was as simple as that. And fortunately for me, neither of my parents would have known what you were talking about if you mentioned that modern and grossly overworked epithet 'racist'. To Tacklow, as with the early Greeks and Romans, and in their day the Venetians, all men were 'people' irrespective of race or colour: there were good people and bad ones, nice or nasty ones, clever or stupid ones, interesting or

---

* The lingua franca of the greater part of India. It developed under the Moguls (who invaded and conquered Hindustan but spoke Persian and Arabic) and is a mixture of Hindi with Urdu, which is a mixture of all three.

boring ones — plus all the degrees that range between those poles. But all the same. Just 'people'. His fellow men. As for Mother — born in China of devout missionary parents who believed that the Bible was an exact account of man's beginnings — she assumed that all men and women, no matter what country of the world they were born in, were descended from Adam and Eve; and that was that!

Mother had only been in Simla for a few weeks and was looking forward to enjoying some of the gaiety for which the town was famous, when she discovered that she was pregnant again. The prospect of my arrival was, in consequence, hardly a welcome one, and she told me that taking the advice of some of her married girl-friends, she went for gruelling walks and rides round Jakko and also jumped hopefully off the kitchen table several times! However, these amateur attempts at dislodging me proved useless, and she was forced to resign herself to the inevitable.

It wasn't that she did not want a large family, for she did: she came from one herself. But 'Major Kaye's pretty American wife' had already caused a mild stir in Simla's social circles, and invitations to parties, picnics and balls arrived daily. That 'American' story, which stuck to her for several seasons, was due to the 'Tientsin accent' she had acquired during her years there: a peculiar amalgam of half-a-dozen foreign accents, predominantly Scottish and American, that arose from Tientsin being full of missionaries and men of different nationalities engaged in trade with China. It was those clipped 'A's of the United States and Scotland that caught people's attention and made them certain that Mother must be an American; and it did her no harm. In fact, it added considerably to her attractions, for the Viceroy's wife, Lady Curzon, who had been Miss Mary ('Daisy') Leiter of Chicago, was such a beautiful and enchanting woman that every man in India seems to have fallen in love with her on sight. Tacklow was no exception: he told me that it was almost worth the boredom of having to attend Viceregal functions just to be able to sit and admire her! You can see what she was like in her photograph in this book: remembering that in those days 'ladies' did not use make-up — or if they did, so discreetly that the fact that they were doing so could not be noticed. Just think what a modern make-up expert would have done with that face and those marvellous eyes!

Mother has always adored parties and dancing and fun. She still does. Her eyes light up at the very word 'party' and her many friends have always insisted that if we throw one at her funeral she'll leap out of her coffin and join in the fun. The merry-go-round of social life in Simla was therefore very much to her taste, and she enjoyed every minute of it; aided and abetted by her like-minded girl-friends and a phalanx of male admirers — the latter headed by her very anti-social husband whose character does not seem to have contained one single grain of jealousy.

Tacklow would accompany her to the balls and fancy-dress dances for which Simla was famous, and, having waited to see that her dance programme was full, and arranged for someone to see her safely into her own rickshaw when the festivities ended, he would return home and go placidly to bed; happy in the knowledge that his youthful Daisy was having a lovely time dancing the night away. And in case you don't know what a dance programme is, they were a relic of the Victorian age that lasted in India to the very end of the Raj: little gilt-edged cards, folded in half like a book-cover, on one side of which were listed the dances and the tunes that accompanied them, while the opposite side bore dotted lines on which people could write down, with the aid of a tiny pencil attached by a thin silk cord, the names of the partners they were booked to dance with. I still have one; stuck in a 1940s photograph-album and affectionately preserved as a sentimental souvenir. But alas, minus its pencil, because the album would not shut properly if it was included, so I had to cut if off; and lost it of course.

Mother's singing voice was small but pretty, and as a member of the Simla Amateur Dramatic Society she appeared in the chorus of *The Quaker Girl*, *The Little Michus*, *The Dollar Princess* and other popular musical comedies of that era; shows for which Tacklow wrote the words for the inevitable topical songs, sung by the comic, that the Simla ADS liked to include. I sometimes wonder if my own and my sister's love for the theatre, and the fact that my younger daughter, Nicola, is an actress, could have anything to do with pre-natal influence, since Mother spent quite a sizeable portion of her time treading the boards of Simla's Gaiety Theatre while carrying me, and later on my sister. Though when I come to think of it, she herself knocked a large hole through that 'pre-natal influence' theory by deciding that she wanted her first-born to be an artist, and painting assiduously during the months of her pregnancy with a view to bringing this about. The experiment was a total flop, for Bill has never been able to draw a straight line; and by the time she was carrying me she was having far too much fun to waste any of it painting wildflowers or sketching the Himalayas. The same went for my sister: not a single painting accompanied her gestation — though there was plenty of music and dancing, and I have to admit that since she grew up to be good at both it may have worked for her. And possibly all that pre-natal painting that failed to work on my brother had a delayed-action effect on his sisters: which may account for the fact that both of us draw and paint.

After weeks of house-hunting, Mother at last found one that she liked, at a rent that Tacklow could afford. It was a small two-storey house called Chillingham on the road to Chota Simla, but since it would not be vacant until the autumn (when its occupants would be leaving) they decided to keep their hotel rooms for another season and move into the house in October. Thus it was that in the summer of 1908 I came to be born in a bedroom in the Central Hotel on the twenty-first day of August — *just*. I say 'just' because Mother says I arrived in a terrific hurry and complaining at the top of my voice, at eleven minutes to midnight. She also says it was a Thursday, and though I have never checked this, I feel it must be true because the old rhyme that starts: 'Monday's child is fair of face', goes on to say that 'Thursday's child has far to go', and that, I am happy to say, has certainly come true for me, for it has been my great good fortune to travel all over the world.

I have gone from one end of India to the other, stayed on a coral island in the Bay of Bengal and another off the coast of East Africa, lived in Peking and Hong Kong and walked on the Great Wall of China. I have sailed through the Inland Sea to Japan and visited 'Nikko the beautiful', where the Shoguns sleep; lived in Egypt and Cyprus, Malta, Persia, Germany and Austria, America, Italy, France and Spain; travelled to Denmark, Norway and Finland and ... Well, you name it and I've probably been there. There must have been more than one good fairy at my christening in Christ Church, Simla, for I was given two invaluable gifts: an excellent memory, and what I can only describe as a personal video set somewhere in my head that I can switch on whenever I wish, and that has recorded, in sound, scent and colour, almost everything that my eyes have seen.

Sadly, my memory is at last beginning to fail me; which fills me with dismay. It seems curious that I should have visualized losing so much, and known and accepted the fact that Time would inevitably afflict me with undignified complaints such as rheumatism, arthritis and indigestion (and if I last long enough, rob me of eyesight and hearing and probably hair and teeth as well!) but never thought that I could possibly forget the past. How foolish can one get? I find it strange too that it was only fairly recently that I discovered that a tenacious memory and a private video in the brain (and, for that matter, an ability to water-divine!) were not things that everyone possessed. Obviously, if you yourself have always had something of that kind, it does not occur to you that there is anything unusual about it, or cross your mind that everyone else may not have it too. It took me a long time to discover how very fortunate I was to have been born with these built-in assets, and I am deeply grateful for them.

My memory, which works almost entirely by sight, goes back to the day I saw mother breast-feeding my sister Betty — christened Dorothy Elizabeth but always known as 'Bets'. I cannot have been more than two-and-a-bit at the time — say two years and two months at the most. Yet I remember it with a photographic clarity that can probably be explained by the fact that it struck me as such a peculiar way of feeding this fascinating new addition to our family (Bill and I got our meals out of cups and plates!). As I write I can still see Mother sitting in a big, white-painted, wicker chair on the screened side-verandah that led off her bedroom at Chillingham in which Bets had been born. She is wearing a lacy, flowing, lilac-coloured robe that in those days was called a 'tea-gown', and her lovely hair is all loose about her shoulders. The year is 1910 and the month is October. Edward VII had died barely five months earlier, but although the Edwardian era had ended, echoes of it were to last well into the reign of his successor. The thin silk tea-gown has a silvery belt that fastens with a Chinese buckle enamelled with a pattern of irises — half of which survived into the early Thirties, even though it was useless without the half that had been lost. I suppose Mother kept it because it was so pretty, despite the fact that by then it had become bent and the enamel was chipped. She probably threw it away when we left India to go and live in North China, and if so, since things outlast people, it will still be around somewhere; as will its other half. India seldom wastes anything!

Another early memory, equally clear, is of being trundled along the Mall in a push-chair by my ayah, and looking down the steep flight of steps that forms a 'cut' (there are many such in Simla), leading from the Mall to the Lower Bazaar. This one was opposite the Green Room door of the little Gaiety Theatre, and strung high above those steep, descending steps, roofing them in, were innumerable strings of brightly tinted paper flags. From where I sat in my push-cart it was like looking down a long tunnel of fluttering colours, and when I asked Ayah what they were for, she said that it was for the Durbar. The word was a new one to me, and I applied it for some years afterwards to any coloured decorations — they were all 'Durbars'! It was not until long afterwards that I woke up to the fact that those flags had been strung up in anticipation of the Great Durbar that was to be held in Delhi in the following month for the new King and Queen: George V and Queen Mary — the same 'Princess May' who had once danced with Tacklow when he was a cadet at Sandhurst. The year was 1911 and I was then aged three-and-a-quarter.

We had moved into Chillingham the previous autumn, and we spent the next two years there. And Simla being Simla, even the children of the Raj led a very social life. Party after party after party.... Unlike Mother, but painfully like my father, I was no party-goer. I hated them: these large gatherings of noisy kids, some of whom — the ones with rich parents or fathers who held important posts in the Civil Service — were accompanied by British nannies while the rest (the offspring of less exalted parents who could not afford British nannies) were in the charge of ayahs. We, the ayah brigade, were fully conscious of our luck and would not have changed places with the nanny-lot for anything in the world: it was snobbery in reverse. Ayahs, with few exceptions, doted upon their little charges; they sympathized with their sorrows and rejoiced in their happiness; aided, abetted and petted them, and invariably spoke to them in the vernacular so that they too learnt to speak it with considerably greater fluency than their mother tongue. Best of all, ayahs could be twisted round their charges' little fingers!

We fortunate ones were not dragooned into good behaviour by martinets in buttoned boots and crisp white uniforms, who spoke in

William and Jane Kaye, my
paternal grandparents.

Below left: Tacklow, aged three.
This daguerreotype is the earliest
extant portrait of my father.

Below right: Tacklow comes of
age — 'He's got the key of the
door, never been twenty-one
before.'

The Dadski: my grandfather, Thomas Bryson, setting out in his covered cart from his house in Wuchang, wearing Chinese dress. He was the first European to live in that great city, which lies on the far side of the river from Hankow.

Left: Tacklow in the uniform of the 21st Punjabis.

Below: Foxy, Tacklow's beloved mongrel.

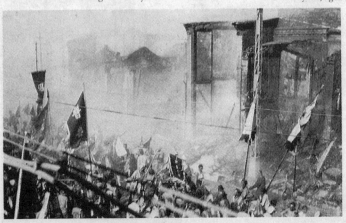

Above: My grandmother, Isabella Bryson ('Isa Carr').
Pastel portrait by her granddaughter, my sister Bets,
from a daguerreotype.

Top right: The last Empress of China. This snapshot was
taken in Tientsin and sent to my mother by a school friend,
Nona Ransome.

Below: Snapshot taken during the Boxer Rising: presumably
of an attack on the Foreign Embassy enclave in Tientsin.

Mother.
Margaret Sarah (Daisy)
Bryson, aged fifteen.

Above: This is the railway station where Tacklow first saw Mother. The fact that the paper-seller in the foreground is wearing his hair in a pigtail shows that when this picture was taken the Dragon Throne was still occupied by a Manchu.

Above: Their wedding in Tientsin. Mother is wearing the 'mingy little veil' that almost ruined her day.

Right: Almost thirty years later her daughter Bets makes it up to her by wearing yards and yards of tulle!

Mother and Tacklow at Pei-tai-ho.

Mother, with Bill in his pram,
in front of the Dâk-bungalow in Jhelum.

Mother: back again, with Bill, at Pei-tai-ho;
but without Tacklow, who had been posted to Simla.

The Central Hotel, Simla. I was born in the right-hand end room on the top storey of the main central block, and learned to crawl on that verandah.

Right: Her Excellency the Vicereine, Lady Curzon. This photograph, in a fabulous silver frame, was presented by Daisy Curzon to the grandparents of my future husband.

Below: Studio portrait of Tacklow and me.

Teeta-ayah, self, Bill and Moko at Chillingham.

Above: The staff; all male except for Teeta-ayah, and minus Mali-ji, who must have taken the day off.

Right: Mother, with Bill and me aboard the rickshaw, in the drive at Stoke Place.

'Rajahs and Ranis' fancy-dress party. Bill (*left*) and self (*right*) — a reluctant Rani.

Below left: Bill and me on the covered water-tank at Fairlawn. This is the one in which a *chowkidar*'s erring wife, missing for many days, was said to have been found drowned.

Right: First visit to 'home'. Tableau from *A Midsummer Night's Dream* at Forres, in Scotland. Bill, complete with ass's head, as Bottom; Cousin Grace as Titania; Cousin Dick as Puck and the sisters Kaye as a couple of fairies. (Bets is plainly bored with the whole show.)

platitudes ('Now you eat that up at once, Miss Enid! Just think how many poor little boys and girls would be only too grateful to have that lovely rice pudding!' 'Don't speak with your mouth full, Master Eddie! It's rude.' 'Smiles before eleven, tears before seven!' — and so on). The nanny-children envied our greater freedom and our ability to chatter to any Indian we met in the Bazaar or the Mall, in our own or other people's houses, or anywhere else. Their nannies would read them stories at bedtime; *Peter Rabbit* or *Little Red Riding Hood*. But our ayahs, together with our many acquaintances in the town, would tell us enthralling tales about the doings of gods and heroes. We learned early why Ganesh has the body of a man and the head of an elephant, how the languars — the grey, long-tailed and white-whiskered monkeys that were Kipling's *bander-log* — acquired their black faces, and how Rama rescued Sita from the demon King of Lanka (which in my day was known as Ceylon) with the help of the monkey god, Hanuman. Our ayahs would sing us to sleep with the age-old nursery songs of Hindustan, and let us run wild in a way that no British nanny would have permitted. We felt truly sorry for the nanny-children.

I loved Simla. I loved passing the time of day with the proprietors of the Indian-owned shops along the Mall and stopping, fascinated, to watch the men who made designs of birds and flowers and butterflies on lengths of cloth, using a curious, white, gooey stuff that looked like very soft putty.* The craftsman kept a lump of this stuff on the ball of the left hand, from where it was transferred with a slim wooden spatula to the cloth, pressed down with one finger and, when the leaf, stem or whatever was complete, brushed with metallic powder in a dozen tints as well as gold, silver and bronze. I have no idea if this particular form of folk-art is still practised, but I hope it is, for watching one of these craftsmen at work was a high spot of any walk along the Mall in my early days in Simla.

Talking of the Mall, I would like to say that of all the lavish helpings of canned twaddle, dished out by those writers who make a mint of money out of denigrating the Raj and all its works on the basis of second-, third- or fourth-hand information, one of the silliest is that before the First World War the British did not allow Indians to walk

* Presumably wax, as the finished product is known a 'wax-work'.

87

in the Mall. Even such well-known writers and reporters as Larry Collins and Dominique Lapierre repeated this anti-British fairy-tale in their bestseller, *Freedom at Midnight*. Do these busy little authors *never* look at old photographs, or talk to any left-overs from the Raj? Or are they so anxious to blacken its name that they invent these tales deliberately? — as E. M. Forster invented some of the preposterous statements he made in that virulent attack on his own race, *A Passage to India*; a book that seems to be regarded as Holy Writ by the trendy who have swallowed every word of it and for some reason like to think the very worst about the British in India. Forster has been equally slanderous and nasty about Indians. Nastier, in fact — though none of his admirers has chosen to notice that. Or perhaps they think that Indians are not quick enough on the uptake to know when they are being insulted?

The 'no Indian could walk in the Mall' story, and others like it, was probably invented on the spur of the moment by some youthful anti-British supporter of the Congress Party or the Muslim League in the 'Quit India' days and, like many similar ones, could be disproved by a few minutes spent on research. Or even a few seconds' thought! How, for instance, would it have been possible for so many of the shops that line the Mall to be owned by Indians if no Indian was allowed to walk there? How did he or his assistants *reach* the shop? Or leave it? Hasn't anyone, hurrying to jump on the *Passage to India* bandwagon ('We are all guilty!'), read *Kim*? That book was written when Queen Victoria was still Empress of India and the British Raj seemed as strong as the Rock of Gibraltar. But anyone who cares to dip into it will learn that Kim goes up from the Lower Bazaar to 'the broad road under Simla Town Hall' — which is the Mall — where he meets a Hindu child who takes him to Lurgan's shop* (which was also on the Mall; and still is — or was when I was last in Simla in the 1960s). The book includes a list of some of Lurgan-Sahib's 'many and curious visitors', most of whom were Indians!

Fancy-dress parties were a popular form of entertaining children as well as amusing grown-ups, and I can remember being dressed up,

* Lurgan was drawn from life. The real 'Healer of Pearls', Mr Jacobs was a famous character who had a book based on him, written by a twentieth-century novelist, Gilbert Frankau, and called *Woman of the Horizon*. Tacklow bought two small carpets that were part of Jacobs' stock. I still have them.

reluctantly, as a Rani to match Bill's Rajah. The jewel on my forehead scratched, and despite the aid of Mother's hairpins I couldn't prevent the sari from slipping off my head. I preferred the Japanese party — which shows plainly in photographs. But though in time I came to enjoy 'dressing-up', I never overcame my hatred of children's parties. Out of scores that I must have attended I can remember enjoying only one — and I must have been a good deal older by then; at least seven or eight.

I have never sorted out the reason for our moves from one house to another during the first four years of my life. It never occurred to me to ask either of my parents why, having rented Chillingham, we didn't stay there instead of moving for a season into another and much larger house called Stoke Place, and then back again to Chillingham; and from there to our old rooms in the Central Hotel once more. I remember Stoke Place very clearly in a series of pictures. A high, two-storied house with a verandah on both floors; myself proudly wearing a pair of Bill's cast-off knickerbockers instead of the hated frilly skirts; a firework display on the tennis court in celebration of the Hindu festival of Diwali — the Feast of Light — with Tacklow touching off rockets and catherine wheels for a deeply appreciative audience consisting of ourselves and the compound children and their equally enthralled parents. Mother in a very long pale-blue dress and a matching hat being photographed in the lower verandah, surrounded by beribboned baskets and bouquets of flowers — the trophies of a last night of, I think, *The Quaker Girl*; it being the custom of the Gaiety Theatre to present floral tributes to every lady in the cast on the final night of any show.

The plays or musical comedies usually ran for about a week, with a total of half-a-dozen evening performances and two matinées; and it was also customary for husbands, fathers, admirers and friends to send up flowers and boxes of chocolates on the last night. This charming habit made the tiny stage look like a florist's shop, but led to a good deal of heart-burning, since the tributes were by no means bestowed in recognition of merit, and it was not unusual for the leading lady to end up with two bouquets — one from the management and one from her husband — while some pretty snippet in the chorus, who happened to be the belle of the season, garnered at least ten or twenty. Popularity could defeat acting talent every time.

Chillingham also stays in my memory as a series of disconnected pictures, as does the Central Hotel. A powder-blue ground-glass globe, scattered with engraved stars of clear glass, belongs to the hotel, where it hung in the main hall, enclosing a strong electric light bulb. I thought it was the most beautiful thing I had ever seen, and that starry globe still stands in my memory as a symbol of loveliness; even though I am well aware that if I saw it again it would probably strike me as hideous. But to a three-year-old it was a beautiful and desirable object, and I used to stop and gaze up at it in admiration every time I passed through the hall. I looked hopefully for it many years later — long after the curtain had fallen on the Raj and the house lights had gone out — when Bets and I were on a sentimental journey to our birthplace and had persuaded an elderly *chowkidar* to take us over the closed and shuttered hotel. But the star-powdered pale-blue globe had gone, and the caretaker could not remember ever having seen it. I hope, for old times' sake, that it is still unbroken and has found a new home with someone whose children are as enchanted by it as I once was.

Chillingham still means Mother's voice singing, to her own accompaniment on the piano in the drawing-room, the sweet, sentimental songs of that day or, on occasions, the rousing hymns that were popular in missionary circles; such as 'Pull for the Shore, Sailor' and 'Beulah Land, Sweet Beulah Land'. People had to provide their own amusements in those days, and since anyone with any pretensions to a singing voice was expected to take some sheet-music with them to a dinner-party, I used to lie in my cot and listen to the duets and solos being sung in the drawing-room. Music heard at night has an enchantment all its own, and perhaps because of those long-ago musical evenings it never fails to catch at my heart. Chillingham also meant the white flowers of the potato-creeper which grew like a weed in Simla and smothered, in a foam of white-on-green, the high fence of criss-cross wooden slats that screened the servants' quarters from the house and the drive.

Since there were no cars in those halcyon times, rickshaws were the taxis of Simla and could be hired in the same way. But all who could do so owned their own rickshaw and kept their own *jhampanis* — the four men who propelled the rickshaw, two pulling from the front and two pushing from behind. Hired rickshaws and those who manned them were, in general, scruffy-looking and unimpressive. But privately owned ones were spick-and-span affairs, gleaming with fresh paint and polished brass lamps, while their *jhampanis*, who wore smart uniforms, looked down their noses at their less fortunate brethren and considered themselves vastly superior beings. Like all the many household servants who were employed by the Sahib-log, they were the firm friends and allies of their employer's children, and rides in the rickshaw when Teeta-ayah* was in charge were always a delight. We could chatter non-stop with the *jhampanis* and hear all their news, and there was little we didn't know about their family affairs or anything of interest that happened in the world in which they lived; that mysterious, exciting, colourful world of close-packed houses and bazaars that clung to the steep hillside below the Mall.

Kipling says in *Something of Myself*, his disappointingly brief and sketchy autobiography, that he and his sister Trix spoke Hindustani far more fluently than they spoke their mother tongue, and that when they saw their parents, the servants would warn them to 'remember to speak English to Mama and Papa'! That was true of all of us: or if not all, of the majority of the India-born children of the Raj. For in our day it was considered a disgrace to be unable to speak to the real owners of the land in their own tongue. It was only later, after the end of the First World War — known then as 'the Great War' — that standards declined and the rot set in as it became fashionable among the Johnny-come-latelys and their wives and children to affect not to be able to speak or understand the language of those whom they professed to rule. Too many confined themselves to a few useful words of command and a smattering of 'kitchen-Hindustani' and considered that this was quite sufficient. But oh, what a lot they missed! For the world behind the bungalow was full of interest. And of dear friends and allies.

Our servants and their families lived in quarters behind their employer's house and since children are indifferent to colour, creed, class or rank (until or unless they are taught otherwise by some grown-up) every inmate of those quarters was a personal friend. There was far more caste discrimination between the occupants of the servants' quarters than there was between them and us, and one learned the

---

* A *teeta* is a partridge. I don't know whether this was her given name or a nickname. Either way, it was pleasantly descriptive!

rules by ear and without knowing it; I suppose one could almost say that we absorbed them through the pores of the skin. Bets and I learned without being told that this or that food or action was taboo to Sundra because of her caste, but all right for Kullu and his nine-year-old daughter Umi because of theirs. That Ahmad Shah could do things that little Hira Singh couldn't, because one was a Pathan and the other a Sikh — and so on. This is the best way to learn anything: particularly languages.

But all these things were merely immutable rules that one's Indian friends obeyed and that we accepted as such: just as they accepted the fact that we had a paler skin (and not all that paler, either!) and lots of habits that they regarded as disgusting: toothbrushes, for instance — *ugh*! It did not prevent our being friends. Or getting into fights for that matter. And it is interesting to remember that the children of my parents' Indian friends, with whom we played, seemed equally oblivious of class distinctions and played and quarrelled, as we did, on an equal footing with *their* servants' children.

Kipling, who knew a lot about India, mentions this fact at the very beginning of *Kim*, in which three children, Kim, 'the poorest of the poor whites', Abdullah the sweetmeat-seller's son, and 'little Chota Lal in his gilt-embroidered cap', are playing 'I'm the King of the Castle' on the great green bronze gun, Zam-Zammah, that stands to this day on a plinth opposite the Municipal Museum in Lahore. Kipling says of Chota Lal that 'his father was worth perhaps half a million sterling, but India is the only democratic country in the world'. By present standards that half-million would be worth more than twenty times as much. But the comment about democracy was still valid in my day: at least, among children. The divisions of caste and class only showed up in later years. But when one was young one found playfellows everywhere, and every man, woman or child in the compound was a friend and an ally. Nor do I think that my parents were in any way exceptional in encouraging this, and it is certain that we gained a great deal from it and never came to any harm.

There were always a great many servants, and the ignorant who criticize the life-style of the 'colonial' British have never failed to use this as a stick (one of many!) to belabour those of their fellow countrymen who spent their working lives in the service of India: condemning it as typical of that ostentation and self-aggrandisement that made such suburban nonentities feel superior — etc., etc. It was nothing of the sort. Anyone who knows the first thing about India must know that in those days (and, whatever is said to the contrary, in these too!) caste dictated everything that an Indian could or could not do.

Looked at in another way, caste was also a splendid device for ensuring full employment; and we who live in an age and a country in which trade-union rules insist that a painter stops work in order to send for a carpenter to bang in a single nail or unscrew a single screw, because the nails and screws are not his business but a carpenter's, or waits for an electrician to come and remove a wall plug before he can finish painting a skirting-board, should have every sympathy for the servants of the Sahib-log who devised this ploy hundreds of years before the unions woke up to its advantages. In my day India had never heard of such a thing as a cook-general, and would have objected strongly to the creation of this useful hybrid. The result was that the lowliest British subaltern or secretary was compelled to employ a whole range of servants to run even the humblest of ménages, and as his pay and position improved, so, inevitably, did the number of his employees increase. . . .

There was the lordly *abdar* (butler), who ruled the Sahib's servants with an iron hand in an iron glove, and the Sahib's *bearer* who looked after his clothes and kept track of the bills. There was the Memsahib's *ayah* who did the same for her — but who would not sew so much as a button on her Sahib's pyjamas! There was the *hamal* who dusted the rooms by the simple process of flapping a cloth which shifted the dust from A to B and back again; the *kansamah* (cook) who produced delicious meals at any hour of the day or night — and for any number of unexpected guests as well — without a murmur. The *khidmatgar* waited at table, laid it, and looked after the knives and forks, crockery and glasses that the *masalchi* (who had a *chokra* to assist him) washed up but would not handle when dry. There was the children's *ayah* as distinct from the Memsahib's, and another and more junior *bearer* for the son of the house; a *bheesti* who fetched and carried water and filled the tin bath-tubs, and a sweeper and/or his wife the *metharani*, who dealt with the disposal of what is euphemistically known as 'night soil' (why only night?). Then there was the *dirzi* who sat cross-legged on the verandah all day behind his whirring sewing-machine, making and mending clothes for the household. Like the cook, he was a genius; he could copy almost anything if one showed him a picture, and all the ladies-of-the-Raj were dressed by him. A *dhobi* and his wife attended to the washing and ironing, and a *mali* and his assistant cared for the garden. There was a *syce* or *syces* for the horse or horses; *jhampanis* to draw the rickshaw and, last but by no means least, a *chowkidar* — a nightwatchman — to discourage robbers and other nefarious persons from breaking in during the hours of darkness. Or at least that was the idea, though in practice these gentlemen did little more than sleep soundly all night in the shelter of the porch, where anyone coming home late from a party must step over a recumbent and sheeted form in order to open the front door: a feat that was always performed without waking the slumberer.

Rumour has it that all *chowkidars* are members of a criminal gang and that their employment is merely a form of insurance — a sort of ancient Asiatic version of the 'protection racket' — and that anyone refusing to hire one would soon discover that it was a lot cheaper to pay the man's modest wage and be free of his gang's attentions! I wouldn't know about that. But as you can see from the preceding list, any family man paying the wages of less than seven or eight servants at the end of each month could consider himself lucky: and probably lived in cramped discomfort in a small flat or half a bungalow! Yet by nineteenth-century standards even a dozen servants was staggeringly modest. That talented and entertaining snob, the Hon. Miss Emily Eden, despiser of Anglo-Indian society, whose acid pen did much towards colouring the views of later writers who, following her example, though unable to match her in the matter of blue blood, wrote off anyone who served in India (Governors-General, peers and all those related to them excepted, of course) as a collection of deadly little provincials married to vulgar dowds from suburbia, would herself have been waited on by considerably more than two hundred servants, since her brother, the deplorable Lord Auckland, happened to be Governor-General. He was also, incidentally, responsible for the calamitous Afghan War of 1839–42 which in the words of my revered kinsman Sir John Kaye, who wrote the contemporary history of that brawl, *'was disastrous because it was unjust. It was in principle and in act, an unrighteous usurpation, and the curse of God was upon it from the start.'*

In Emily's day the household staff was vast and the 'who-does-what' unofficial union rules were a lot stricter. It is interesting to learn that Honoria Marshall, arriving at Calcutta in 1837 to marry Henry Lawrence, a man she had not seen for over nine years, records in her diary that when, amazed by the enormous number of servants in her hostess's house, she inquired how many there were, she was told: 'Not more than sixty. We run a *very* modest household here!' It is also worth noting that in a recent book on the partition and independence of India, there is a group photograph of some four hundred or so of the *five thousand-odd* servants deemed necessary for the running of the then Viceroy's House in New Delhi, in the days of the last Viceroy, Lord Louis Mountbatten. Admittedly the close-packed ranks of liveried men include members of the Viceroy's Bodyguard, but a note below mentions that among the missing thousands who could not be included in the photograph was a man whose sole duty was to pluck chickens, and that no less than fifty boys were employed to scare away birds from the lovely Mogul Gardens. I wonder how many gardeners they had — twenty? thirty? forty? But I still think that the whole scheme was a superlative method of jacking up the employment figures.

Emily Eden and Co. would have been horrified at the smallness of the staff employed by households in my father's day, and he in turn would probably have been surprised by the far smaller size of mine in the 1940s. But everyone in the servants' quarters behind our particular bungalow became a friend and partisan of my two small daughters; as Tacklow's had been to Bets and myself. And my children too spoke English as a second language rather than a first.

Mother thinks we moved from the Central Hotel into Chillingham in the autumn of 1908. I would have been around ten or eleven weeks old by then, so do not recall the occasion. But as Mother's memory for dates is now fairly hazy, I'm inclined to think that we probably stayed put in the hotel until the beginning of the next Simla season, because the smaller roads, such as the steep, winding one that leads down to Chillingham, are deep in snow during the winter months, and only the main ones such as the Mall, the Lakkar bazaar and the Ladies' Mile are kept passable. We had certainly moved by the next spring and summer, for a photograph of Teeta-ayah, Bill and myself, playing in the sun in Chillingham's apology for a garden, is one of those that survived among Aunt Lizzie's collection of Mother's snapshots.

Not many houses in Simla could boast a large garden, because in many places the hillsides on which they were built were too steep to allow for more than a front drive barely wide enough for a rickshaw to turn on; plus, with luck, a small lawn to one side that could just about support a single flowerbed. And that was it. The entrance to Chillingham (nicknamed 'Warmingham' by Mother's many friends!) led straight off the hill road at a right angle, while the drive, having skirted one of those small lawns, turned left onto a level strip of ground bounded on one side by the porch and the front verandah, and on the other by a line of flowerpots and a wooden railing that topped a high stone wall which buttressed the shelf of ground on which the house stood. Below this wall the hillside dropped so steeply that we could look down onto tree-tops and the roof of a neighbour's house, as well as out toward the distant ridges of the foothills that fell away in ever diminishing folds until at last they melted into the yellow heat-haze of the plains.

That gravel frontage was really all the garden that we possessed, and since the hillside rose as steeply behind the house as it fell before it, our servants' quarters were strung out in a line along the curve of the hill, screened from our view by a high, lattice-work fence that was covered in white-flowered potato-creeper and had a green-painted door in it.

My memories of that first stay in Chillingham are so inextricably mixed up with a subsequent one that I cannot really tell how much belongs to the first time. Very little, I suspect. But there are certain things I am sure of; among them, that potato-creeper and the wide drive with its wooden rail giving onto nothingness, which was our playground. I remember, too, being dressed up in a variety of fancy-dresses and being photographed in them by Mother before being taken off by ayah to some children's party. One of these snapshots showed me dressed as a Columbine or a fairy or something of the sort, in a tight white bodice and a very short and very full skirt of white tarlatan. Tacklow presented a print of it to the *mali*, who was a particular friend of mine and was delighted with it. He was gazing at it with deep appreciation when Tacklow, becoming aware that he was holding it upside down, asked him what he thought it was? Whereupon the *mali* scratched his head and after a thoughtful pause said tentatively: '*Shaid fullgobi hoga?*' ('Perchance it is a cauliflower?'). Dear *Mali-ji*!

Then there was my first silk dress. A proper party-dress. Mother had made all our baby clothes herself, many of which still survive in a box in my attic, after having been worn by my own daughters and later by my granddaughter. It was only when we were old enough to walk and run that the *dirzi* was called upon to make us everyday clothes in serviceable materials such as serge and cotton, and party ones in muslin, organdie or *broderie anglaise*. But this was a shop dress — and stunningly beautiful! Made of heavy white Chinese silk with short puffed sleeves and a yoke that was hand-embroidered with sprays of blue harebells, it was a birthday present from an old friend of Tacklow's whom we always called 'the Khan Sahib'. His real name was Khan Bahadur something-or-other, though Khan Bahadur what, I can't remember because we never used it. He was just 'the Khan Sahib' and Bets and I admired him enormously. I have no recollection of any other birthday or Christmas presents until I was at least seven or eight, yet I have never forgotten this one; which makes me wonder why more grown-ups do not give dresses or shoes as presents to little girls, instead of toys.

The Khan Sahib, a big, burly, bearded man with a strong resemblance to the late King-Emperor, Edward VII, owned a house in Simla and another in Delhi. He understood children, and though he spoke excellent English, he realized that Bill and I spoke his language with more fluency than our own and therefore — as he did with Tacklow when they were alone — he always spoke to us in his own tongue; which was a compliment of no mean order. Yet it was from the Khan Sahib that I received one of the first truly traumatic shocks of my life, and the episode has stayed fixed in my mind like a fly in a piece of amber . . .

Teeta-ayah had let me put on the silk dress to show the Khan Sahib how nice I looked in it, but since he and Tacklow were deep in conversation in the study, I settled down cross-legged on the sunny verandah under the study window so that I could waylay him when he came out. From this vantage-point I could hear their voices as clearly as though I were in the room with them, but I was not in the least interested in their conversation and had not been listening to it until suddenly the all-wise Khan Sahib said something so outrageous that it caught my attention. They had apparently been discussing the difference between Indian and English thinking, and the Khan Sahib gave an illustration of this: 'When the British are asked a question,' he said, 'they will instantly reply with the truth, and perhaps consider later if it might not have been wiser to lie. Whereas we of this land will always answer first with a lie, and only afterwards consider if it might not have served us better to speak the truth.'*

I can still remember the shock that a small girl, brought up to believe that lying was a major sin, experienced on hearing such a loved and admired grown-up calmly admitting to telling lies as though it did not matter at all! It stood all my ideas of morality on their heads and left me totally bewildered. But it taught me an early and valuable lesson: that people of different nationalities do not necessarily hold similar views or think in the same way — just as they do not worship the same God or conform to the same laws. If the Khan Sahib felt it was all right for his people to tell lies, then it must be right — for them. But that didn't mean it was all right for me, for I was an *Angrezi* (English) and *Angrezis* obviously thought differently. And why not? After all, my father only had one wife, but I knew that rich old Mahommed Bux had three, because Jinni, one of his daughters, who was a particular friend of mine, had told me that her mother was only the second wife and therefore of less consequence than the senior one; and also that both Number 1 and Number 2 would gang up on the junior one who, being the old man's favourite, had it in her power to put both their noses out of joint — which, according to Jinni, she did on every possible occasion.

I also knew that the luxurious Simla-style chalets that stood in the grounds of a palatial house owned, and occasionally occupied during the season, by a certain Croesus-rich ruler of one of India's many semi-independent states, were *bibi-gurhs*, women's quarters, that housed three Maharanis — His Highness's mother the Dowager Maharani, and his senior and junior wives — together with at least two other lovely ladies of no specified rank, plus the usual quota of female relations, royal children and a swarm of waiting-women. Of these only the children and one of the lovely ladies (who happened to be Polish),

* 'Was it true,' asked the Wazirs, 'that the English suffered from a strange affliction that made them unable to lie?' (I don't know where that quotation comes from but it seems apt!) Somewhere in *Kim*, Mahboob Ali, the horse-trader, says: 'The English do eternally tell the truth, therefore we of this country are eternally made foolish. By Allah, I will tell the truth to an Englishman!' — and I bet Kipling was quoting!

and the humbler waiting-women, were not in *purdah*. The Maharanis could only attend *purdah*-parties, but their children were invited to all the birthday and fancy-dress parties that Bill and I, and later Bets and I, attended, and ayah would often take us to play in their beautifully kept garden.

I learned a good deal about palace life and palace intrigues from these visits, but I didn't enjoy them much because Teeta-ayah's respect for royalty made her insist on dressing me in my best on those occasions, even when it was only an informal morning visit. I was made to put on, over my vest, a white underbodice (to which a pair of white frilly knickers were attached by buttons), a tucked, starched and lace-edged petticoat, and finally a white, full-skirted, puff-sleeved dress of *broderie anglaise* which scratched abominably and was tied at the waist with a blue sash. Black patent-leather strap shoes over white socks completed this outfit, which was topped by a white topi — a pith hat rather like a mushroom — disguised by a frilled *broderie anglaise* cover. This ensemble was not only uncomfortable but very difficult to play games in, and I recall one full-scale row when I persuaded a young royal to let me borrow one of her outfits instead. This consisted of a loose silk shirt over a narrow pair of *churri-dhan* (cotton trousers), which was infinitely preferable to all the starched clobber into which I had been stuffed and buttoned. But the loan was not popular with either attendant; my ayah or hers. Hers, I learned later, had subsequently burned the garments on the grounds that her young mistress could not possibly be expected to wear them again: thereby humiliating mine, who scolded me for allowing her 'face to be blackened' in this manner. I do not, however, believe for a moment that my playmate's ayah really did destroy the polluted garments; I bet she sold them. Because young children do not have any caste. Caste is something that they acquire later on — as do we all in our own fashion; together with prejudice and intolerance ... *'Isn't it sad that our children must grow into people?'*

Yet I remember another major row on similar lines that did not involve either Asians or caste and was then, and remains to this day, inexplicable to me. It happened like this. I had been playing with a small, red-headed girl who lived in the house whose rooftop we looked down upon from our strip of garden, and whose given name I never knew because she was always known as 'Coppertop' — just as her brother was always called 'Sandy'. She and I had been playing in her nursery when, aware of a sudden call of nature, I went into her bathroom and used her china potty for what chamber-pots are for. It seemed an obvious and an innocent enough action, but her Scottish (not Indian!) nanny was furious with me: the reason for her fury being that I, as the child of Protestant parents, had defiled the chamber-pot of a Roman Catholic! She boxed my ears soundly and I was sent home in disgrace and floods of tears. It was the first time anyone had slapped me: which may be the reason why I remember the incident so clearly and with an odd mixture of shame and horror. I had no idea what 'Roman Catholic' meant, or what a 'Protestant' was. And though I knew all about caste, I had until now supposed that all white people were Christians and that like Muslims they did not have to worry about it. The discovery that Christians too apparently had caste rules of this kind was horrifying, as it meant I was not on safe ground even among my own people, and must watch my step with as much care as when I played with Hindu, Muslim, Sikh, Tamil, Gurkha or Tibetan children.

I still do not understand why my very normal action should have aroused such fury and been so drastically punished, and I can only suppose that the 'Scottish' nanny was in fact a Eurasian one who had imbibed some very odd and mixed-up ideas from an Indian mother or grandmother. But whatever the reason, I never played with Coppertop again or went anywhere near her house if I could help it; though until that fatal day she and her brother had been great friends of Bill's and mine, and Teeta-ayah was always being persuaded to take us down to play with them. The only thing I remember about Sandy is that his father, a keen golfer, had a miniature set of clubs made for him and laid out a child's-size golf course in their garden, and that whenever Sandy drove off he always said: '*Damn!*' because he imagined, from watching his father, that the word was obligatory. Of Coppertop, on the other hand, I remember a good deal, and probably because of the alarming manner in which our friendship ended, her face was indelibly stamped on my brain. So much so that many years afterwards, attending a small drinks party in the cabin of the Commander of a cruiser in the China Squadron anchored off Pei-tai-ho, my eye was caught by a silver-framed photograph of a woman and I stared at it and said: '*Coppertop!*' And it was! She was his wife. In later years, after they were divorced, she was to marry a famous Second World War Air Marshal.

Another Simla house that I remember from those early days far more clearly, and with much greater affection, was Fairlawn: that same house in which Mother had been staying when she heard the nightjars crying in the valley below. Fairlawn stood well down the hillside below the road to Mahasu, and if I am right in thinking that the friend it belonged to in those days, who invited us for weekends, was an Indian, then according to a book called *Simla Past and Present*, by Sir Edward Buck, he would have been Nawab Fateh-Ali-Khan, a Qizilbash of Lahore. We children regarded our visits there as great treats, and the thing that fascinated us most about it, and is certainly the reason why I remember it so well from my very earliest years, was that below one end of the lawn, and covered by a wooden platform, lay an enormous rain-water tank, shaded by a weeping willow. Bill and Bets and I loved to lie out on that sun-baked, shadow-mottled surface and hear the echo that our voices and our drumming heels could make in the space over the dark, unseen water below, and to us that covered tank was an exciting and mysterious place.

The caretaker, an aged *chowkidar*, was always careful to see that the trapdoor through which the *malis* and the *bheestis* descended to fill their watering-cans and *mussacks** was opened only for them, and at all other times kept securely padlocked in case an inquisitive child might fall in and be drowned. But he could be coaxed into letting us peer in when the door was open — one brown, sinewy hand firmly gripping us by the belt as we leant in turn to look down at the shadowy water that glimmered like black satin, stretching away into a darkness where lurked a ghostly voice that would faithfully repeat back even our softest whispers. It was a scary place as well as an exciting one, since it often contained, circling slowly round on that dark oily surface, the corpse of a drowned rat or some other small animal that had lost its footing in the dark. And rumour had it that once, in the days when the tank was new, the body of an earlier *chowkidar*'s wife, who was thought to have run off with her lover — a handsome young wood-cutter who had also disappeared at about the same time — had been

---

* The inflated skins of sheep; used for centuries to carry water in, and still in use today.

found bloated and floating in the tank many weeks after she had vanished.

Bill remembers nothing of those days: apart from being woken up and carried out one night by his father to be shown something that did not make any impression on him. He does not even remember Kullu, who was his bearer, or any of the children, Indian or British, with whom we played. While Bets, of course, was far too young to remember those early days at Chillingham.

Chapter 8

Adieu, adieu! my native shore ...

Byron, *Childe Harold*

Tacklow had had no home leave, and very little casual leave either, since that first return visit to England with Foxy in the closing years of the nineteenth century. His parents had never even seen their eldest son's wife; let alone his three children. But now at last he was granted six months' furlough in which to take his wife and family home, and he moved us back into the Central Hotel for the few weeks prior to our departure.

There are only three things that I remember clearly about those weeks. The first and clearest is Tacklow smacking me for being rude to one of the hotel servants. I don't know what I had said or done, only that my crime was connected in some way or other with the black-painted, tin-lined wooden packing-cases that had been taken out onto the open ground below our verandah to be stencilled with our name and, presumably, our address in England and the name of the ship on which we would shortly be sailing. I had probably been reproved by some room-bearer for hindering the painter at work and retaliated with rudery in the vernacular, or — horrors! — physical assault. Whatever the crime it must have been outrageous, for Mother, a true Victorian, considered it serious enough to be reported to Tacklow with the demand that he, as the Head of the Family, should administer justice. Which he did; with the back of a hairbrush. I was duly spanked twice on the appropriate spot, and though I don't think he spanked me very hard, the punishment, like the box on the ears from Coppertop's nanny, left a lasting impression on my mind. That Tacklow, my *own* Tacklow, could do such a thing to me was appalling. I must indeed be a lost soul; wicked beyond redemption and cast into outer darkness! I wept inconsolably for hours.

The punishment was obviously just and I was careful not to invite a repetition of it. But had I got away with it I would almost certainly have traded upon the fact and pushed my luck again — and again! So *phooey!* to all the chat about the horrors of giving young Edwin or Elsie a swift smack on the bottom and thereby denting the poor little darlings' egos. The egos of the vast majority of poor little darlings are a lot tougher than any tender-hearted trendy is prepared to believe. Nor did I forget Tacklow telling me, as he mopped up my tears, that I must always remember that India belonged to the Indians: that it was *their* country, not mine. This was something he was to repeat on other occasions, but I don't think I ever really believed it; not until much later, when I had reached the dignity of double figures and was sent away to school. Because *of course* it was my country! How could it not be, when I had been born there and never known any other?

The second thing that stays clearly in my memory as a picture of that last brief stay in the Central Hotel is of a cold, grey afternoon of lowering skies and a bitter wind, and Mother singing the hymn that starts '*Far, far away, like bells at evening pealing*'. To this day whenever I hear it, which is not very often as it seems to have lost its popularity, I can see the view through the door of the room that was my nursery: I have just woken up from my after-lunch nap and am sitting in my drop-sided cot looking through its railings at the steep drive that leads up from the hotel towards The Chalet and the Mall on the hillside above, waiting for Mother to dress me. From where I sit I can see Bill and Kullu walking hand-in-hand up the drive, dwarfed by the distance; Bill a dot of red and Kullu a streak of khaki in their warm winter coats. Behind them the pine-clad hills of Simla are dark against a stormy grey sky, and the wind blowing in through the open door smells of fir-cones and rain. I feel cosy and safe behind my cot bars with Mother moving round the room singing to me about bells at evening pealing '*O'er earth's green fields and ocean's wave-beat shore*'. It is only a moment or two of time in an eternity of moments; but for some unknown reason it has stayed with me as clearly as though it had happened only an hour ago.

The last memory is again a heady mixture of sound, smell and sight. I am standing on the wide expanse of gravel that fronts the Central Hotel, watching the tin linings of our wooden packing-cases being made. The sheets of tin have already been cut and fitted, and the tinsmith, with the help of his assistant, is soldering them together. He squats beside a little pile of live charcoal that is kept glowing by a pair of makeshift bellows plied by his assistant, into which he has thrust an iron rod with a slightly flattened point. When this is red hot he draws it out and presses it onto a blob of solder in a stone bowl, causing the solder to melt with a fascinating sizzling sound and a strong and unforgettable smell, before using it to weld the sheets of tin together. Once the lining is complete except for the top piece, it will be placed inside the wooden packing-case where it will be filled by blankets or whatever — not forgetting a sprinkling of dry neem or tobacco leaves between each layer to discourage moths. After which the final piece of tin will be soldered into place and the lid of the packing-case closed over it and nailed down. The sight and sound and smell of soldering was something I enjoyed enormously, and I would squat on my heels, Indian-fashion, for hours beside the tinsmith, chatting to him as I watched him at work, or listening to his tales of life as it was lived in the maze of houses and shops that clung to the hillsides below the sprawling city.

Tin-lined packing-cases, their contents redolent of the dried leaves of neem or tobacco, were among the more familiar hallmarks of the Sirkār — the old Raj that vanished shortly after the ending of the Great War of 1914–18. One of them still stands, a forlorn, empty, rusting relic of Empire, in our garage in Sussex. And perhaps one day (if it is not broken up for firewood before then) it will achieve the status of an antique and be exported to Germany or South America!

I don't remember anything at all of the long train journey from Simla to Bombay, or my first voyage on a P.&O. steamer — the famous Peninsular and Oriental passenger-ships that Kipling called 'the Exiles Line' and which were in time to become just that to me; though not in the way he meant it, since for me the exile was from the other hemisphere. Mother told us later that on the second night out from Bombay, while the grown-ups were all at dinner, there was a cry of '*Man overboard!*' and that she and every parent on board leapt to their feet and raced down to their cabins in a panic, terrified that a child might have strayed onto the deck or managed to unfasten a porthole and fallen into the sea. She said that it gave her a terrible insight into the innate selfishness of human beings, to discover that as soon as she found that her own three children were safe (and sound asleep!) her instant reaction was profound relief and an overwhelming feeling of thankfulness that we were all right! She said the relief was so great that she couldn't have cared less about anyone else's child. Though in fact it wasn't a child at all but a man, a passenger, presumed to be drunk, who had climbed onto the rail and jumped from it. The ship had been stopped and turned back to search for him, but though the sea was like a mill-pond there was no trace of him, and after an hour or two they went on their way. I remembered that story when I had small children of my own and was terrified of them climbing deck rails or crawling through a porthole during one of the voyages we took while following the drum.

My Kaye grandparents, now retired, had bought a large, rambling house called Freshfield, not far from Southampton. It was no great distance from the docks and the city, but in those days the area was completely rural and the house stood among green fields, orchards and meadows that looked out across Southampton Water. A young and pretty English nanny had been engaged to look after us, and together with her we were given a set of rooms in one wing of the house, well out of sight and sound of our grandparents and any other grown-ups, including of course our parents; Grandmother, a selfish and tyrannical old woman, being a firm believer in the old adage that children should be seen and not heard. We were also, to Mother's horror, given different food: a plain and stodgy diet that consisted of suet puddings and boiled potatoes with the minimum of meat, and few fresh vegetables — even though the house possessed a large orchard and an equally large kitchen garden. But it seemed that the choicer fruits and vegetables were grown only for grown-ups, while the nursery was restricted to spinach and boiled cabbage and, on rare occasions, a raw apple. Mother tried to persuade her mama-in-law to give us less stodge and more fresh fruit, vegetables and milk (yes, they also kept their own dairy cows) but she only succeeded in putting the old lady's back up; not a difficult thing to do.

Grandfather, equally Victorian and autocratic, had on retiring written to his children to inform them that he was putting the considerable savings of his years in the Indian Civil Service into acquiring this over-large house and extensive estate — plus the staff necessary to run it with clockwork efficiency and keep house and grounds in immaculate order — *solely* from the most selfless of motives: to wit, that his children and grandchildren should always have a home there. This pious announcement turned out to be pure spinach, for we had been there less than ten days when my grandfather told his son and heir that the bother and noise caused by the presence of three small grandchildren, a daughter-in-law and a nanny was too much for his mother's nerves, so would he please remove himself and his family immediately. The selfish old basket must have known only too well that his dear Jane had never had so much as a nodding acquaintance with a nerve in all her life; and also that all the sanctimonious bilgewater about 'spending his all' to provide a home-from-home for his family was merely an excuse for spending every cent on himself and his own comfort, while at the same time furnishing him with a cast-iron alibi for not being able to give any of them any financial help.

Tacklow, who had accepted his father's noble-sounding fairy-tale as the truth and arranged to spend his leave in this umpteen-bedroom home-from-home, wired his sister Molly to ask if she and her husband, Richard Hamblin, now retired and living in Scotland, would take us in as paying guests until he could make other arrangements. When she replied in the affirmative, he packed us up and removed us with all speed to her house in Forres, a small provincial town in the far north of Morayshire.

I was sorry to leave my grandparents' house, though not my grand-parents, whom I can barely remember having set eyes on during our stay — apart from an occasional and terrifying summons to the drawing-room, for which we were washed and brushed, dressed in freshly ironed and spotless clothes and warned to be on our best behaviour. But since even these awe-inspiring audiences seldom lasted for more than twenty minutes before we were thankfully dismissed back to the nursery wing, the old lady's steely nerves really cannot have suffered overmuch wear and tear. The same cannot be said of ours. The more likely reason for our dismissal from her house was that the presence of visitors, any visitors, upset the ordered routine of her comfortably cushioned days. In other words, pure selfishness — combined with a strong miserly streak which she preferred to call 'thrift' and which made her resent paying for the extra food, coal and firewood consumed by her son and his family. Not forgetting his children's nanny.

Oddly enough, considering how short a time I spent there, I can still remember Freshfield quite clearly. Not the interior. Only how it looked from the outside. The long gravel path that ran past the windows of the nursery wing. A cedar tree that shaded the wide lawn to the south of the house and the bank that sloped towards it, down which we loved to roll — doubtless to the accompaniment of delighted squeals that could well have been the 'noise' that so grated upon Jane Beckett Kaye's imaginary nerves.

There is also one other memory that I took away with me from that pleasant but disapproving house, and which is a small fragment of history. The memory of walking across green, flower-spangled meadows, those fresh fields from which the house took its name, holding tightly to our nanny's hand because I was afraid of cows (I still am) and reaching the long, empty shore of Southampton Water to watch an enormous ship steam slowly past. We walked out, I remember, on to a breakwater of huge wooden piles overgrown with mussels and seaweed, below which the tide-driven shingle lay banked along one side; full of a flotsam and jetsam of shells and assorted debris. When we reached the end of it, nanny lifted me up in her arms so that I could see better, and explained that the great ship was the newest, largest and most luxurious liner afloat. And the safest too, because she had been built with so many watertight doors that it would be impossible to sink her. This last observation both startled and alarmed me, since it had never occurred to me until that moment that the liner on which we had travelled from India could possibly sink!

The ship that we watched steaming majestically down Southampton Water on that long ago day was the ill-fated 'Titanic', pride of the White Star Line. And I can only suppose that the reason why the events of that sunny morning are etched so deeply on my memory is because only a very short time later I heard the shocked voices of grown-ups in the servants' hall and the drawing-room discussing the appalling tragedy that had befallen the great liner — and realized that those vaunted watertight doors had proved useless when, on her maiden voyage, she struck an iceberg which sliced through them and sent her to the bottom of the Atlantic with the loss of over a thousand lives. This appalling news cast a gloom over all Britain, and it is not surprising that I remember the sight of her so clearly, for frankly, I was scared stiff. The thought of that vast ship being sliced open with such ease by an unseen ledge of ice, and all those hundreds of people drowning in a calm, black sea, haunted me for many weeks, and I have never quite trusted ships since then.

A few days after that we exchanged the springtime meadows and orchards of southern England for the snow and fog of north-east Scotland.

✂ All that I can remember of Forres, which in those far-off Edwardian days was a comparatively small town (and for all I know still is) is my aunt's house, Ramnee: a name presumably given to it in fond memory of India days, but which will be bracketed for ever in my memory with boiled cod.

Due to the fact that refrigerators and deep freezers had not yet been invented, and that I had hitherto lived several thousand miles from the sea, my diet had seldom if ever included fresh fish. I do not even remember being offered any on board ship or during our brief stay at Freshfield. But early on during our stay in Ramnee, the starched and elderly martinet who ruled the nursery (Aunt Molly's youngest child, Dick, was roughly the same age as Bill) insisted that I ate up every scrap of a large helping of boiled cod with white sauce which was the cook's idea, and hers, of a suitable lunch for children. The cod, from which neither the skin nor the bones had been removed, tasted unattractively fishy, the white sauce tasted of nothing at all — unless it was wallpaper paste? — and the vegetables (over-boiled cabbage and potatoes) were watery and saltless. I thought it was disgusting, and after one or two cautious spoonfuls, refused to eat any more; though eventually, and reluctantly, I did finish the vegetables. But not the cod.

This, in the view of Dick's nanny, was Mutiny. And she immediately set about putting it down. I was to get nothing else to eat, she announced, until I had finished every scrap of cod — even if it took me the rest of the day! Bill, who for two pins would have followed my example, decided that discretion was the better part of valour and forced himself to swallow the nauseous stuff. So did Bets, who was too young to know better, while Dick, accustomed to this type of nursery-fodder, ate everything on his plate as a matter of course. After which all three were given pudding (probably sago or suet, so I don't suppose I missed much), and lunch being over, Bets was put to bed for her afternoon nap and Bill and Dick sent off to play while I, forbidden to leave the table, sat staring stubbornly at the helping of cod that was by now congealing on my plate.

Tea-time came round with brown-bread-and-butter, bannocks and honey and mugs of milk for the others, and the cold cod and lumpy wallpaper paste for me. Mother, appealed to for help, proved a broken reed, for she was plainly just as scared of the uniformed tyrant as the tyrant was scornful of mere mothers who dared to try and interfere in any way with her running of Nursery Affairs. Supper (biscuits and milk) was duly eaten by Bill, Bets and Dick, while I was again presented with the rejected cod; the nanny remarking menacingly that if I didn't eat it that day I would have to eat it for breakfast tomorrow; or for lunch, if I remained obdurate. I remember taking the plate away and sitting with it on my lap on the nursery stairs, watering it liberally with tears as I wondered if I could possibly force myself to eat it and thereby put an end to the whole ghastly business — which by this time felt as if it had been going on for days rather than hours. The chances are that had I been left alone to struggle with the problem a bit longer, I would have capitulated. But the martinet's patience had given out and she made the mistake of trying to feed it to me forcibly.

Scooping me up off the stairs, plate and all, she plumped down on a chair, and holding me on her lap in an iron grip with my head hard back against her starched shoulder, she forced a spoonful of cold cod into my mouth and ordered me to swallow it. I got it down all right. All of it, as far as I remember. But my stomach evidently felt quite as affronted by the stuff as my taste-buds had been, and refusing to accept the offering, returned it — with interest — all over the woman's glossy white uniform. I was appallingly sick, and Mother, coming up to say good-night, found me pallid and weeping, retching helplessly as the infuriated nanny boxed my ears. There followed an invigorating row, won this time by Mother, and I have never touched cod, or any other fish if I can help it, from that day to this. Nor do I recall having any further trouble from that nurse, so I imagine she must have given in her notice and flounced out.

Apart from the Cod War, my recollections of the months we spent in Forres are hazy. Ramnee has left an impression of a big, ugly, Victorian house with one of those large gardens full of tidy flowerbeds in which the flowers all seem to be red, blue or orange — geraniums, lobelias and border marigolds planted in tidy rows. I remember that when we first arrived it was under snow, and that I wore a thick white coat adorned with a circular shoulder cape, and a bonnet made of white sheepskin that tied under my chin with ribbons; both made by Mother. I remember rehearsals for a series of tableaux, including one from *A Midsummer Night's Dream* which, according to a programme that miraculously still survives among our collection of what Tacklow always termed 'Kag', was followed by one of those single-act farces that were much in vogue in Victorian and Edwardian amateur-acting circles. This one was in two acts and called *Browne with an E*; and as far as I remember the whole performance took place either in some village hall or on a makeshift stage in a private house — a much larger house than Aunt Molly's.

The first tableau was very much a family affair, with Dick's younger sister, Grace, appearing as Titania, Dick as Puck, Bill as Bottom, and Bets and myself as a pair of blue fairies. There were also a pair of pink ones and an Oberon played by a Miss C. Mackenzie; but I don't remember them at all. Or the fact that on the evidence of the programme I seem to have appeared in another tableau entitled 'Ceres and the Four Seasons', in the part of 'Spring'. All that remains is the memory of the sheer boredom of having to remain perfectly still and not fidget or scratch between the times that the curtains parted on the tableau and the moment when they closed again; tempered by the satisfaction of being able to dress up as a fairy, complete with wings and wand. A painfully Edwardian fairy, I'm afraid, and not at all the sort that Shakespeare had in mind when he wrote about that moonlit wood near Athens.

I remember too being shown a drowned swan that lay like a fly in amber just below the glass-clear surface of a frozen lake; and — though this must have been months later — being taken to a magical place called Findhorn where there was a long, curving beach on which the open sea broke in lines of white foam. Behind the level shore and the sea lay a maze of sand dunes, down which one could toboggan, and patches of fat scarlet toadstools with white spots on them, exactly like the ones that elves sit on or under in illustrated children's books.

I have no idea how long we stayed at Ramnee with the Hamblins. Probably well into the summer, if those expeditions to Findhorn are anything to go by. But I don't think we can have been there for more than three to four months, because I know we spent August and the best part of the autumn with a friend or a relative who had a farm at Streatfield, and that it was during this visit that I celebrated my fourth birthday with a family picnic in nearby woods and a home-made birthday cake smothered in white icing and decorated with pink sugar roses whose leaves were cut from angelica. It was the first time I had ever come across angelica, which I thought delicious, and because it was my birthday my hostess (who had made the cake) gave me the whole stick of it to nibble. Even now, angelica reminds me of the farm at Streatfield. Just as cod will always mean Forres.

I loved that farm. We all did. We were allowed to help with the haymaking and the cows and the baby pigs, and with feeding the ducks and chickens and collecting hens' eggs. The house was large, low-ceilinged, old-fashioned and comfortable, and there was only one thing about it that I did not like: a dark, arched passageway through which the farm carts could be driven from the front of the house to the big, stone-flagged yard at the back. I hated having to go through that passage and would go to almost any lengths to avoid doing so; for there was a stuffed fox in it, and though I knew it was not alive I was terrified of it. The taxidermist who had set it up had plainly been a master craftsman, for he had drawn its lips back in a snarl and made it crouch a little as though it were creeping with flattened ears towards some helpless rabbit or hypnotized pheasant. The staring glass eyes would catch the light and glitter as though they were alive, and I was never quite sure that it wasn't pretending to be dead and would not spring at my throat as I passed. Yet because I was more afraid of being laughed at than I was of the fox, I never told anyone that I was frightened of it, and there were always occasions on which I could not avoid being sent through that haunted passageway, shivering with terror and with my heart in my mouth. I would edge past it, my back to the wall, and once past I would run like the wind in case it might leap off its pedestal. I suppose that was my first real experience of fear.

Nothing else of any interest can have happened to me on my first visit to the land that I had been taught to call 'home' but always thought of as *Belait*,* because I have no recollection of anything else. We apparently spent the winter with Aunt Lizzie and her husband in

* Britain. Hence 'Blighty' — Army slang for 'home'. See also musical songs of the era, e.g. 'Hi-tiddley-ighty, take me back to Blighty!', etc., etc.

Bedford, but apart from a shadowy impression of fog pressing against the window-panes, and a man who rang a bell and cried 'Muffins! Hot Muffins!' in the icy, misty street outside, nothing remains. Nothing but Bill in a white sailor-suit looking lost and bewildered and struggling not to cry because Aunt Molly, who had somehow reappeared upon the scene, had just told him sharply that boys never cried: only girls cried — girls and babies! That must have happened in January or February, and during a spell of unusually fine weather, because I associate it with sunshine and green leaves rustling in a sharp, blustery wind; laurels, perhaps? I suppose it could have taken place in a London park, for Mother says we spent a night in a hotel in London on our way to Tilbury and the docks from where the P.&O. liners set sail for India and the Far East.

Tacklow had already left for India some months previously, and now Mother and Bets and I were to return there to join him. But Bill was now six years old, which according to the thinking of that day was considered far too old for a boy to be allowed to stay out in India. Popular opinion held that a boy should be 'sent home' no later than five or six, in order to avoid being spoilt by Indian servants and becoming overbearing and backward as a result of missing the early training, education and discipline provided by British preparatory schools. Fortunately (like crying!) the same standards did not seem to apply to girls, who could apparently grow up to be spoilt, self-willed and dictatorial without anyone giving a damn. Something for which I, personally, have always been deeply grateful, since but for that I too might well have been left behind in England like poor little Bill. Or like my future husband, Goff, who was dumped on a clutch of maiden aunts in Ireland at the tender age of four.

It had been decided in family council that Bill would remain in the care of Aunt Molly and Uncle Richard Hamblin for the next eighteen months or so; after which Mother planned to return with Bets and myself and make arrangements to leave all three of us with one or other of their relatives — a normal but heart-breaking business that for over a century had faced all colonial service parents. Aunt Molly must have come down from Scotland to collect Bill and see us off. But although I had it on her authority that girls were allowed to cry, I was sure that mothers could not possibly count as girls; yet here was mine crying her eyes out after saying goodbye to Bill.

She would probably have cried even harder had she realized, as she stood sobbing and waving to him from the deck of the liner drawing slowly away from the crowded dockside, that she would never again see her darling Willie as a little boy in a sailor-suit. For it was not to be eighteen months before she returned to England, but more than six years. She was to miss the whole of the rest of his childhood; and when they met again they would not even recognize each other!

Chapter 9

~※∂∀∂※~

Mine is the sunlight, mine is the morning!

Eleanor Farjeon, *Songs of Praise*

That voyage was made memorable to me by the fact that like legions of young women before and after me — though in general they were a good deal older than I was! — I fell in love and enjoyed my first shipboard romance. His name was Guy Slater and I am happy to say that his sister Marjorie — 'Bargie' — became my best friend. And still is; even though close on three-quarters of a century has passed since we met on that voyage.

※ Guy must at the time have been at least eight years old: possibly even nine; though to me he seemed a lot older than that since he was a good bit taller and broader than I was. A stocky, sturdily-built child, with sandy hair, a snub nose and freckles, he was a born charmer and I can have been only the first of a long line of young women who were destined to lose their hearts to him. He took me under his wing from the start and I imagine that Mother must have been deeply grateful for the services of this unpaid and totally reliable child-minder. She knew that I was safe with Guy, whom I obeyed as I had never obeyed any nurse or ayah, and who would not let me climb the railings or fall down companionways.

Hand-in-hand we went for daily walks round the deck, explored the ship and leaned over the side to watch the dolphins and the flying fish. And when one day, temporarily on my own, I strayed unknowingly into that male holy-of-holies, the smoking-room, and was angrily rebuked and ordered out by a choleric grey-beard, Guy rushed to the rescue like some avenging knight of the Round Table. Grabbing me by the slack of my pinafore he pulled me behind him, and facing the enemy with clenched fists and blazing eyes said furiously: 'Don't you talk to her like that! She didn't know she wasn't allowed in here — she is only a baby!' And turning away he marched me out leaving the grey-beard open-mouthed and struck dumb with surprise. Can you wonder that I adored him from that moment on? One of the grown-ups, intrigued by his interest in me, asked him one day what he saw in me and why he bothered about a small girl of four-and-a-half? I still remember his reply: 'I like the feel of her hand. It's so small, and it holds on so tight.' The macho male and the feminine clinging vine in embryo, I suppose. Surprising to find evidence of it so early.

I have only the vaguest recollection of Guy's family at that time; and that only because his mother and mine became great friends during the voyage and used to sit side-by-side in their deck chairs and gossip a lot — when not surrounded by a circle of shipboard admirers, for both of them were young, pretty and lively grass-widows. Muriel Slater was a red-headed charmer who was known in Simla as 'the Goldfish'; presumably in compliment to that shining red-gold hair. But her daughter Marjorie and her second son, Tony, were both black-haired, blue-eyed and strikingly beautiful, as was a third son, Dick, born a year or two later in Simla. Only in Guy had that red-gold hair been transmuted to a sandy ginger, and he alone had no trace of the family's outstanding good looks. He did not need them, for he had more than his fair share of the quality that the present generation calls 'charisma', and mine would have called 'charm'. Even at that early age he could, as the Irish say, 'charm a bird out of a tree'. And I well remember howling my eyes out on the down platform of Simla railway station when Guy was eventually sent back to England to become a boarder at some English preparatory school. In fact Anjuli, the small girl who hero-worshipped the boy Ashton/Ashok in my novel *The Far Pavilions,* and the child Victoria, who adored the youthful Eden De Brett in my whodunit, *Death in Kenya,* and who 'wept bitterly and uncontrollably, greatly to Eden's disgust and her own mortification' when she said goodbye to him on the platform at Nairobi, both carry strong echoes of myself when young and my tearful parting with my hero and first love, Guy Slater. It is lowering to remember that when I next saw him, a good ten or eleven years later and, as it happened, on the platform of another railway station, this time in London, he hadn't the remotest idea who I was and couldn't even remember me!

The Slaters and the Kayes, having disembarked at Bombay, travelled up to Simla together, where Tacklow had again rented Chillingham for the season. He had hoped very much to buy it, and had he been able to do so it would have saved us a great deal of money in the years to come and probably made a lot of difference to our lives. But he had no capital, and since he must live on his pay, supporting a wife and two children in India and paying expensive school-fees as well as bills for 'keep', clothes, shoes and endless extras for a son in England, there was no hope of his being able to buy Chillingham unless he could borrow the money, at interest, from his parents. The price, in those days, was a mere £100 for the freehold of the little house and its minuscule garden, and Grandfather paid far more than that for one of his carriage horses, while his wife had a very comfortable income of her own, derived from the Beckett interests in India and safely stashed away in the Funds. It would have been no hardship to lend Tacklow that modest sum, on which he would have paid full interest. But no! Cecil must bear in mind that they had 'saddled themselves' with a large house and extensive grounds solely for the benefit of their children and grandchildren (oh yes?) and therefore ... etc., etc. Tacklow swallowed his disappointment and thereafter, for almost a quarter of a century, paid ever rising rents for houses in or near Simla.

I learned of this episode many years later from Mother, who somewhat naturally resented it bitterly, and the chances are that I too would have held it against that selfish and close-fisted old couple but for the fact that Mother's disclosure, added to the way in which poor Tacklow had been requested to remove his family from the large and comfortable house which (he was expected to believe) had been acquired solely for his and his brothers' and sister's and their children's benefit, relieved me of a secret load of guilt. You see I had imagined, as I suppose the majority of us do, that it was more or less obligatory to love and honour one's grandparents — all my Indian friends did! — and the fact that I found it impossible even to *like* my paternal ones had weighed heavily on my conscience. But having heard how Tacklow's request for a modest loan with which to buy Chillingham had been flatly refused, that load was removed from me permanently, and from then on William senior and his Jane became, as far as I was concerned, non-persons; or as we say in India, '*kutch-nays*' (nothings). It was a great relief.

I also learned something that my grandmother's generation do not seem to have taken in: love between parents and their children is not something that flowers automatically from the act of birth, and since no child asks to be born it is up to the parents to do their best for it when it is, and that 'gratitude' should not come into it. In fact, the popular nineteenth-century cry, 'After *all* I've done for you children!', which still crops up with great frequency in a large part of the world, is pure nonsense. Love, any kind of love, has to be earned. And by that I do not mean 'bought' though I suspect that is often tried. I suppose Tacklow must once have loved his parents, because Victorian children were told that it was their duty to love dear Papa and Mama, and Victorians were great ones for doing their duty. He certainly never said a word against them; or even hinted one. Yet I have my doubts. His black-sheep brother, Alec, who absconded to Canada, obviously had no use for them at all. I would have liked to hear his opinion of them.

Chillingham was not the same without Bill. But I did not miss him too much because the Slaters lived quite near us, so I continued to see a lot of Guy; and I still had a resident playmate in Bets, who was growing up, as were a good many old friends in the big houses, the servants' quarters, the shops and the bazaars of Simla. Growing up much too fast, in my opinion. Umi, for instance, now rising nine, was actually married — and inclined to look down her nose at me and give herself airs on that account, even though she would not be going to her boy husband's home for some years to come, so that her situation did not appear to have altered overmuch. I pretended that I was going to marry Guy, but I'm afraid she didn't believe me. Everyone, retorted Umi loftily, knew that *Angrezi* girls didn't get married until they were old and wrinkled!

A number of the *Angrezi* children with whom I used to play had gone home to England; several Muslim ones had gone into *purdah* and could no longer attend mixed parties, and one of the Maharajah's covey of daughters and/or nieces had been formally betrothed to the youthful heir to some princely state and become as toffee-nosed about it as Umi. But thankfully, my grown-up friends — people like Buckie and Sir Charles, the Khan Sahib and the gentle, soft-voiced Diwan*

---

* Pronounced *dee-wān* — Prime Minister. He either was, or had been, the chief minister of one of the Independent Native States.

Sahib — looked just the same and did not appear to have grown a day older. Which I found very reassuring, as I felt that I had been away for years and years.

There were just as many children's parties as ever and I still hated them. Except, in a small way, for the fancy-dress ones; and that was only because I enjoyed the dressing-up, not the party itself. My heart used to sink into my strapped shoes whenever Mother showed us yet another large, gilt-edged card and told us that we had been asked to little Angelica or Archie or Ashok's birthday party, and wasn't it exciting? I wonder how many children actually enjoy children's parties? Not too many, I suspect. The only time I made a serious effort to get out of attending one of these juvenile gatherings, my anti-social attitude astounded and upset Mother. Herself a great party-girl, she could not understand my objection. Why, parties were fun! They were great treats and I was a very lucky little girl to be asked to so many. In the end I began to think there must be something wrong with me, because *all* children, according to Mother, liked parties, and of *course* I would enjoy myself . . . I would have a lovely time, 'Just wait and see!' When I persisted, I was told not to talk nonsense and that I needed a course of iron tonic (filthy stuff that left a nasty taste in one's mouth) or a dose of Gregory's Powder. I suspect I was given both. But if so it did me no good, for I continued to dislike children's parties.

Worried by this, since it augured ill for the future (how was I ever going to be a success on reaching marriageable age if I refused to go to parties and make the 'right contacts' while I was young?), she urged Tacklow to acquire a pony for me so that I could at least learn to ride. Riding carried a certain social cachet, and few girls got anywhere by keeping their noses permanently stuck in a book (this last in reference to the fact that having taught myself to read because I could not find enough people to read to me, my nose was almost always stuck in a book). But Mother was right about riding. Nearly all my little British contemporaries, certainly the children of the Heaven-Born, could be met with any day of the week, correctly dressed in hard hats and smartly cut jodhpurs and jackets, riding their ponies along the Mall or around Jakko with an attendant syce trotting behind them.

Tacklow obliged, and a pony, plus a second and younger syce, was added to the Kaye ménage. But the addition proved a total loss because I disliked the pony quite as much as I disliked parties. To be frank, I was terrified of it, and even now, when my elder daughter breeds the creatures and my young granddaughter has, since the age of two, treated them with the fond familiarity with which even the most timid of humans handles a baby rabbit, I still subscribe to the minority view that all horses are offensive weapons and not to be trusted a yard. At nearly six years old I was scared stiff of them, and of falling off them, and I remember those daily rides on a lead-rein as purgatory. Particularly the slope leading down to and past the Cecil Hotel, where the pony always broke into a brisk canter and would, had the syce permitted, have galloped; in which case I would instantly have fallen off.

⁂ Mother, Bets and I did not, as planned, return to England in the autumn of 1914, the following year. For on the fourth day of the last month of summer, one day after Bill's eighth birthday and seventeen days before my sixth, the 'Great War' — now known as the First World War — broke out, putting an end to countless plans and uncounted lives.

My adored Guy was one of the first of many British children to be hastily shipped off home for fear that they might be trapped in India without proper schooling (which it never seems to have occurred to anyone to provide) should the optimists who insisted that the war would be 'over by Christmas' turn out to be wrong.

To me, at that age, war was something that I had heard about from ayahs and the story-tellers in the bazaars who told tales from the Ramayana — the great Hindu epic that tells the story of Rama and Sita — and of the campaigns of the Moguls and the sack of great cities; Delhi, Kabul and Chitor, and the bloodstained field of Panipat where the fate of India had thrice been decided in battle. But all these heroic events were just stories which had happened in the distant past and which belonged either to history or to legends and fairy-tales. They could not possibly happen *now*! Not in this day and age. Not in my own lifetime!

I can't remember when I first learned that there was actually a war — a world war! — being fought *now*. But I do remember the shock that the discovery gave me; and also, as though it were yesterday, saying to Tacklow: 'But are people really fighting each other *now*? A real war? You mean they are *killing* each other?' And being aghast when he said

'Yes' and explained how it had come about. Even then it took a long time to sink in. And even longer before I could really believe that it was true and get used to the idea; for it seemed to be an incredibly silly way of settling an argument and I thought that 'grown-ups' ought to know better.

After the initial shock, the fact that there was a war on began to make itself felt in many different ways; the worst of these being that Mother was frequently in tears as a result of some problem involving my father. I could not help being uneasily aware of this, but I only learned the reason for it long after the war was over. It seems that my darling Tacklow, in all other ways an intelligent, peaceable and level-headed man — Tacklow, who would have liked to have been an actor, and failing that a member of the Indian Civil Service or better still a barrister if he hadn't been pushed into the Army sorely against his will! — had written a long letter to his black-sheep brother Alec in Canada, asking if he would give Mother, Bets and myself a home for the duration of hostilities while he, Tacklow, went off to the war. Having posted it and received an affirmative reply, he had gone to the head of his Department and requested permission to leave immediately for England in order to join up in the ranks if he could not obtain a commission in the 'Contemptibles' (the Kaiser had recently referred to the British Expeditionary Force as 'a contemptible little army'). He was after all, he said, a soldier, so he should by rights be fighting in Flanders instead of sitting safe and snug behind a desk in Simla while other and better men died in the fields of France and Flanders.

Permission had been flatly refused. Not only once, but again and again; for Tacklow kept on trying. It seemed to him indecent that while the flower of a generation, thousands of young civilians from every walk of life who had rushed to join the colours, were being blown to bits in the blood and mud of the trenches, professional soldiers such as himself should remain on the side-lines. Alec had written that he and his wife would do their best, and Tacklow went ahead with plans for taking us to Canada and either joining a Canadian regiment bound for France or, if that proved impracticable, taking ship for England and joining up there; a prospect that terrified Mother, who went about the house with a white face and a wet handkerchief clenched in one hand.

She need not have worried. The Brass-hats at Army Headquarters remained adamant. As a soldier Tacklow was no great shakes; but as a cipher expert his value was above rubies. He was irreplaceable. There was no one who could take over from him, for cipher experts are born and not made, and his services could not be spared. The Commander-in-Chief himself sent for him and told him in no uncertain terms that there was not the faintest chance of his being cannon-fodder in Flanders, so he might as well save his breath and get on with the job in hand! To soften the blow he would be promoted to Deputy Chief Censor with a rise in pay, and the fact that he had not seen active service would not count against him in his Army career, for when the war ended he would be treated as though he too had fought in it — with a subsequent rise in rank; possibly to Brigadier General. He would be able to console himself with the thought that he had earned it.

The prospect was not one that held much appeal for Tacklow; and in the event that last promise proved a hollow one, being conveniently forgotten the moment the Armistice was signed. But at least Mother was happy again. She had been petrified at the thought of being hurried off by way of the Pacific to Canada, to be dumped with her two small daughters on an errant and eccentric brother-in-law and his wife whom she had never met, while her husband marched off to embroil himself in the appalling carnage in Europe and left her struggling to make ends meet and living in hourly dread of receiving a telegram from the War Office to say that he was dead or, worse, 'missing believed killed' — that most harrowing of tragic uncertainties.

Army Headquarters' flat refusal to let Major Kaye go came, for Mother, as an answer to prayer, and her spirits immediately soared as high as Tacklow's plummeted. It was not that he had any desire to fight or kill anyone. But he loved his country, and now that she was fighting for her life he felt that the very least that anyone could do was to come to her aid and, if necessary, die that she might live. Since that privilege (he was sufficiently patriotic and old-fashioned enough to regard it as such) was denied him, he turned back to the task that his seniors considered that he was best qualified to do, and drove himself unsparingly; working late into the nights as well as through the weekends, and only very rarely allowing himself to take any leave.

Since I have always been incapable of solving the simplest crossword puzzle, I cannot begin to understand the workings of a mind that can break codes and solve complicated ciphers, and apart from the basic principle I never had the faintest idea how the trick was done. My impression even now is that it involved the use of some form of mental water-divining, and that something in Tacklow's brain sensed the meaning lurking under the surface muddle, just as a dowser's forked stick twitches and turns downward in answer to the pull of something unseen. I realized that mathematics played a significant part in it, though maths had always been a closed book to me — and still is! But it seemed to me that there must be something more than that: a sixth sense that enabled certain people to break ciphers. I still think so, and here are two stories that support my belief —

On several occasions ciphers that had baffled the experts in England were sent on to India in the hope that Kaye might be able to break them. And Kaye did. One such, having landed on his desk after being given up by any number of top cipher-experts in Britain, was broken in double quick time because Tacklow, having looked at it thoughtfully for about five minutes, said to his team: 'I've got a strong feeling that this one works on a key phrase. Quite a short one; not more than two or three words. Let's try it out: we'll start with something obvious like "*Gott Straffe England!*"' So they did. And it was! That of course was a glorious fluke. But it supports my contention that the early cipher-experts must have had a lot in common with dowsers.

Tacklow also broke the Russian cipher, though Russian was not one of the many languages he spoke. Russia was at the time one of the Allies. But being Russia, she had her own private codes to which her allies did not have the key (or would not have had, had it not been for Tacklow's peculiar type of brain). Also, being Russia, the Allies were never quite sure whose side she was likely to end up on — if anyone's, since throughout her history Russia has never been on any side but her own. It was therefore considered vitally necessary to know what the Muscovites were really up to, and Tacklow was asked to give the matter his attention. He duly cracked their code — though how he did it I have no idea, considering that without the help of a Russian–English dictionary he could not have translated their messages even if they had been sent in clear!

But he did even better than that. The Russians changed their code once a month, and always on the same date: let's say on the 24th. And within a day or two, never more than three, Tacklow had cracked the new one. He gained tremendous kudos from this spectacular feat, and only some considerable time after the war had ended, when he was asked to give a talk on ciphers and deciphering to the undergraduates of Oxford and Cambridge, in the hope of interesting the young in this vital branch of warfare and security, did he blow the gaff. . . .

The secret of his impressive performance lay in the fact that the Russians are a methodical people. Their new code came into operation on the 24th of each month, so on the 23rd, to ensure that those who used it should have no trouble understanding it, they sent out the new code in the old one. It was as simple as that! The apparent delay of a couple of days or so (in which Tacklow was supposed to be beavering away at solving it) was merely eyewash designed to distract attention from this glaring breach in the Russian defences. Surprisingly enough, they never tumbled to it. And since Tacklow never let anyone into the secret for fear that someone might think it too good a story and tell it in confidence to one of Simla's many gossips, he gained a reputation for brilliance that was undeserved. Though he had, of course, cracked the original one, in a language he did not speak.

He told me a lot of cipher stories. But here is one I learned from Mother. . . . A Top Secret message from a British General commanding a brigade in action somewhere in the Middle East was delivered by hand at our house late one night, together with a note to say that since it was a very long one the duty officer thought that it might be too urgent to be left until morning, so would Major Kaye please . . .? Hauled out of bed in the small hours, Major Kaye fetched the code book from the safe in his study, and waking his sleeping wife asked her to help him out by reading out the relevant numbers from the 'crib'. Yawning and heavy-eyed (she told me she had only just fallen asleep after returning late from a dance), she put on a dressing-gown and dutifully complied by the light of a bedside lamp. The message was a particularly long one, and as the 'very model of a modern Major-General' who had despatched it was in a potentially dangerous situation she, like Tacklow and the duty officer, was prepared for news of vital importance. The message came out slowly, letter by letter, which as Tacklow wrote them down formed themselves into words: PASSED . . . THROUGH . . . FIELDS . . . OF . . . WAVING . . . CORN . . . At which point Tacklow said something that Mother would not even repeat to me, and telling her to go back to sleep, turned out the lamp and went to sleep himself. But the incident passed into family legend and for many years afterwards anything totally irrelevant and time-wasting was described as 'only a bit of waving corn'.

The war years that wrought such terrible havoc in Europe and the Middle East, killing or maiming appalling numbers of people and breaking the hearts and wrecking the lives of twice as many more, were, for me, the happiest in my-life. A Golden Age that I look back on as Eve must have looked back at lost Eden. I knew there was a war being fought, 'a Great War', because Tacklow had told me so. But then he had also read me Kingsley's *Heroes,* and told me about the Trojan Wars and Thermopylae and of Arthur's last fight, and about Saladin and the Crusaders too. They were just stories in a book. Or in the case of Arthur a poem —

> *So all day long the noise of battle roll'd*
> *Among the mountains by the winter sea;*
> *Until King Arthur's table, man by man,*
> *Had fallen in Lyonesse about their Lord . . .*

I knew that this war was different, that it was real and was happening now. I had also been aware of Mother's fear and unhappiness during the weeks of waiting for Uncle Alec's reply from Canada, and for the outcome of Tacklow's efforts to persuade Army Headquarters to release him for active service on the Western Front. Also of her enormous relief when he was ordered to shut up and get on with it, which was as though a light had been switched on. Her spirits had shot up like the fountains in the gardens of the Taj and she had flung herself with renewed and grateful enthusiasm into war-work: which in those days consisted largely of rolling bandages, filling huge parcels for the Red Cross (which I presume must have contained something other than bandages), and knitting endless skeins of khaki-coloured wool into socks, balaclava helmets and fingerless mittens, which came under the heading of 'Comforts for the Troops'. Or she would help to entertain wounded soldiers who were sent to convalescent homes in Simla and other hill stations, run stalls or raffles at endless charity bazaars in aid of this, that or the other war effort, and act in amateur theatrical or cabaret shows for the same causes.

We children were co-opted to help in all these activities and to us it was either fun or a boring chore. The children's plays were fun but rolling bandages a terrible chore because they had to be done exactly right; if one was rolled too loosely or untidily it had to be undone and done again. I remember with affection an intensely patriotic play called *Where the Rainbow Ends* in which my lost love Guy's lovely sister Marjorie — hereinafter known as Bargie, that being the name by which all Simla's children knew her — played the part of Will-o'-the-Wisp in a tunic of blue-grey chiffon and a sparkly silver head-dress that I thought beautiful beyond words; almost as entrancing as that star-spangled globe in the hall of the Central Hotel. A girl called Betty Caruana played one of the two midshipmen heroes, Jim Blunders. I fell madly in love with 'Jim Blunders'. How, I wonder, do little girls escape getting into a terrible tangle over the sexes? 'Jim Blunders' was a boy: yet he was played by a girl. How could I be in love with the boy and not with the girl? Very strange and unsettling.

I wasn't one of the children who was chosen to act in this play, but I understudied one of them and when she (or was it he?) was smitten by some juvenile disease I went on in his (or her) place. Here, I hate to say, my memory must have gone badly astray, for I could have sworn on oath that I played the part of a white rabbit, and that all I had to do was hop across the dark-green side of the stage. (The dark-green half belonged to the Dragon King, and any human venturing on it could be captured, while the light-green half belonged to England's patron saint, St George.) If it were not for the fact that I possess one of the original programmes, and a photostat copy, donated by a Simla contemporary, of the assembled cast — neither of which include rabbits — I would have continued to swear to it. And I can still see myself hopping across that stage in a white, fluffy suit with long ears and a cottonwool tail, and hear 'Jim Blunders' real-life as well as stage sister, 'Betty' (Kitty Caruana), piping: 'Oh do look at those darling wabbits!'

But whether I was sent on to replace a non-talking rabbit or a tip-toeing fairy, I did go on as someone's understudy for several performances, and the chances are that one of them was watched from the stage box by a small boy called Goff Hamilton who would one day marry me. Sadly, he remembers hardly anything about the play except that he saw it and that somebody was tied to a tree so that the wolves would eat them. He says that he 'remembers all the wolves'. But as a matter of fact, they were supposed to be hyenas, not wolves, and there were only three of them. However, it's nice to know that they made an impression on him. (They scared most of the small fry into howls at the children's matinées.)

Perhaps it was during this same year that Mother took part in a song-and-dance show in aid of the Red Cross that was being held at Viceregal Lodge for a strictly limited number of performances. The amateur actors wore pierrot costumes, half black and half white, while the actresses wore white wigs with pierrette dresses that were half white and half black-and-white checks. There is a snapshot of Mother wearing her pierrette outfit, taken at Chillingham; and I presume there must have been a matinée performance of this show for the benefit of those who were too young to stay up for an evening one, because I remember seeing it. I remember too that there was a huge gold picture-frame in the background of the set in which two of the performers, dressed in seventeenth-century costumes, sang a duet: 'Madam will you walk? Madam will you talk ...' Bets and I thought this song was terrific and for years afterwards we used to sing it, accompanied by a minuet, as a party-piece when called upon to show off for the benefit of indulgent aunts and other elderly relatives who considered it 'sweetly pretty'!

It was only much, much later, long after the Great War had been re-named the First World War because there had been a second one, and after that one too was over, that happening to leaf through an old photograph-album belonging to my mother-in-law, I discovered that she too had been a member of that same concert party and had actually sung that song! Neither she nor my mother had remembered that the other had been in the show, and I regret now that I didn't ask her to identify any of the other performers from the group photograph. She may have done so, of course; but if she did, I hadn't the sense to write down the names.

The only two I can identify are Lady Grant and a Mrs Brocas-Howell who (though one would never have believed it on the evidence of this photograph) had the reputation of being a notable charmer in the Mrs Hawksbee tradition and having a train of lovers. And the only reason why I remember her is because we children learned to detest her when, a year or so later, she played the part of Britannia in a patriotic extravaganza known as 'The Pageant' — a show which, like

127

many others during the war years, was produced and directed by our dancing-teacher, pretty Mrs Strettle, later Lady Strettle, whom we all adored, and who ran a weekly children's dancing-class in Simla during the summer months and in Old Delhi during the cold weather. However, 'The Pageant' and Mrs Brocas-Howell came later ...

❊ 3 ❊

Morning's at Seven

Chapter 10

~ᴷᴰᴼᴳᴶᴷ~

Teach us to bear the yoke in youth ...
Kipling, 'The Children's Song'

I don't remember how or why we came to be living in a long, rambling house called Harvington that stood (and still does) on an outlying spur of the hills a mile or two outside Simla, facing the ridge along which the mountain road to Mashobra, Kufri, Fargu and the Kulu Valley winds and twists on its way to the high passes and the snows of Tibet. Puran Baghat's road —

Harvington belonged to a cosy old lady called Miss Cullen who ran it as a boarding-house: for which reason it was always known as 'Miss Cullen's' and never as Harvington. The girl who played the midshipman in *Where the Rainbow Ends*, and on whom I had a juvenile crush, lived with her parents at Miss Cullen's, and although a good deal older than most of the other children there, was kindness itself to all of us. I still remember the floods of tears when she was sent home to England a month or so after acting in that play, her parents having decided that the dangers of the submarine warfare that Germany had declared on all British and Allied shipping was, on balance, of less importance than having their darling daughter spoiled rotten and growing up half-educated.

Bets and I loved Harvington and Miss Cullen. The wooded hillside that fell away so steeply at the far edge of the lawn was our favourite playground: an enchanted world which in springtime was white with drifts of the wild Himalayan lily-of-the-valley, and later with the sweet, evocative scent of the yellow, climbing wild-roses which spangle our hillsides in the months before the monsoon breaks. After that came the rhododendrons; so many of them that for miles around the hillsides seemed on fire. With the autumn a pink, fruitless blossom tree flowered throughout the hills as though it were a second springtime; and always, maidenhair fern dripped from every rock.

No one who has not been a child in the Himalayas can know how beautiful they are, and how full of colour and scent and wonder. We built an entire fairy world among the tree-roots and moss and wildflowers some fifty yards or so down the hillside below the lawn, and when we put out biscuit and cake crumbs for the gnomes, elves and other 'People of the Hills' and found them gone the next morning, we were certain that they were being served up at some fairy banquet, and would have angrily rejected any suggestion that birds, animals or insects were responsible — though the woods were always full of those, and of other forest creatures.

Two of my earliest recollections of the war years are linked with Miss Cullen's, for Bets and I spent at least two cold weathers there in the charge of a new ayah and an English nanny called Lizzie; our parents having moved down to Delhi when the Viceroy, the Government of India, the Commander-in-Chief and Army Headquarters departed *en masse* for the plains in an annual winter migration. This began as soon as the Simla season finished at the end of October, and would take place in reverse when the approach of the next hot weather drove them back to the cool of the hills once more.

The first of those two early memories of Miss Cullen's is a vivid recollection of being awakened out of sleep late one night by Ayah, who snatched me out of bed, bundled me up in an eiderdown and ran out, carrying me in her arms into the cold black darkness of the garden. Lizzie was already there with Bets in her arms and so were a number of servants and, I suppose, the rest of Miss Cullen's guests; though the darkness prevented me from seeing them. I realized with alarm that Ayah was frightened, but when I asked her what we were running away from she would only say through chattering teeth: '*Zalzala*! ... *Zalzala*! ...' The word being unfamiliar to me, my respect for the wisdom of grown-ups took its first knock, since whatever this monster was, it seemed to me the height of stupidity to run out into the night where it could pounce on us in the dark from behind a clump of bushes or a tree-trunk. Surely we would be far safer if we hid from it under one of the beds or locked ourselves into a cupboard? The grown-ups must have taken leave of their senses! In fact, it was an earthquake; and a fairly severe one at that. But as I had been sound asleep when

Ayah snatched me from my bed, and had, throughout, been clutched in the arms of someone who was shivering with fright, I had not been aware that the ground was shaking, or that inside the house the ceiling lamps were swaying to and fro and pictures and ornaments were tumbling off walls and table-tops as though a hurricane were rampaging through the house. I was to experience a fair number of *zalzalas* in the future; but that was the first.

The second and equally vivid memory is of being taken for our daily walk by Ayah or Nurse Lizzie, or both; I on foot and Bets in a push-cart, week after week along a narrow, slippery path between high walls of hard-packed, discoloured snow that had frozen solid. These icy walls were far taller than I was, and even Nurse Lizzie could not see over them; for as in *Kim*, 'Jakko Road was four feet deep in snow that year.' And when a path is cleared through roads that lie under four feet of snow, the surplus shovelled onto the initial depths raises it by another four feet to create icy canyons through which one walks without ever seeing anything but the sky or the black, dripping deodar branches directly overhead.

With the spring our parents returned from Delhi and we all moved back into Chillingham, and while we were here one of Mother's Indian friends presented her with a magnificent fan made from peacock feathers. It was a dazzling affair almost the size of a complete peacock's tail, and Mother was delighted with it. Fans being rather the 'in' thing in the way of room decoration (see any contemporary photographs), she set it up as a fire-screen in the drawing-room, against the advice of several of her girl-friends who assured her that peacock feathers in a house brought bad luck. '*Pooh!*' said Mother. 'As if anything so beautiful could be unlucky!' But that same afternoon she tripped over the stand of her cheval-glass, which toppled over and smashed into smithereens. And as all superstitious people know, to break a looking-glass is supposed to herald seven years' bad luck. Mother, as a missionary's daughter, had no time for such superstitions, but she was shaken by the accident. And even more shaken when less than half an hour afterwards Bets, who was supposed to be in bed enjoying her afternoon nap, appeared in the doorway complaining that her head ached and her throat 'felt funny'.

Mother carried her back to bed, took her temperature, and finding it alarmingly high, sent for a doctor (of whom there were three in

Simla at that time; rejoicing in the names of Slaughter, Blood and De'ath; can you believe it?) The doctor examined Bets and announced that she had diphtheria, and though in these days she would have gone straight into hospital, in those, people were whenever possible nursed at home. A night-nurse arrived within the hour and after a frantic SOS to that great friend of the family, Sir Charles Cleveland, who lived a luxurious bachelor life in a large house at the other end of Simla and had no fear of infection — or anything else! — I was despatched with Ayah, a suitcase and that tiresome pony and its syce, to stay with him until Bets should be out of danger. The danger was very great, for in those days diphtheria was a killer and ranked among the most dreaded of children's diseases. The moment I had gone Mother rushed into the drawing-room and taking that wonderful peacock-tail fan out into the garden, poured kerosene oil over it and set a match to it. And from that day to this she has been incurably superstitious about peacock feathers, and will not have one in the house.

Bets, I am happy to say, recovered. But I can't say that I enjoyed my stay under Sir Charles's roof, for though I was truly fond of him, and devoted to his silky black retriever, Kate, I was terrified of the stuffed leopard who peered out realistically from a clump of dried grass in a large glass case that adorned his hall, and I detested the riding lessons he insisted on giving me every morning. My antipathy to horses was to prove a grave handicap when I grew up and was old enough to be asked out to parties and dances during various horse-show weeks up and down India; for the Cavalry Regiments ranked next to the Heaven-Born in the social scale, and cavalry officers preferred their girl-friends to be horsey and 'debby'; and I was neither. But since that wretched pony had been sent along with me, together with its syce, Sir Charles considered it was his duty to ensure that by the time I was returned to my family I should be so proficient a rider that I would win all the prizes at the Children's Gymkhanas that were held at intervals on Annandale — the Simla racecourse that lies in a cup among the hills over a mile below the Mall.

With this end in view he would spend half an hour every morning between *chota-hazri* and breakfast, sitting on his verandah steps and calling out instructions, strictures and encouragements while I rode up and down or round and round the lawn in front of him; scared to death that the pony would get bored and bolt with me, and struggling to do all the things I was being ordered to ('Keep a straight back', 'Relax!', 'Grip with your knees', 'Keep your hands low', 'Trot!', 'Canter', 'No, no, *no*! don't bump in your saddle — rise in your stirrups!', and so on and so on).

Oh God, how I hated it! I never once felt in control of my mount, who did more or less as it liked while I, willy-nilly, went along with it. And though I was sincerely sorry when some months later it came to a sticky end,* it was a tremendous though unacknowledged relief to discover that shortage of money (those day- and night-nurses had cost poor Tacklow a packet) prevented my dear parents from buying a replacement. As great a relief as it had been when, Bets being convalescent and all danger of infection past, I was allowed home again and knew that I had no longer to face those dreaded daily riding lessons. I regretted disappointing dear Sir Charles who had had my best interests at heart, since he knew the importance of the Raj's social snob-charter even if my unworldly father and feather-headed mother did not.

Tacklow and Mother had honestly believed that I would enjoy having a pony to ride; other parents' children seemed to do so! — but only, I noticed, the British ones; when it came to girls, the fortunate daughters of our parents' Indian friends were not expected to ride, and I used to envy Chote and Moni, Pushpa and Hamida and other friends of my own age-group who were spared the shame of having to display a deplorably bad seat and hands in public and live in terror of being ignominiously thrown or bolted with.

That year when the Simla season ended, our parents packed up the house and returned to the plains once more; leaving us, after tearful farewells, at Miss Cullen's in the un-tender care of Nurse Lizzie. This harridan had come to us with the highest possible recommendation from personal friends of my parents. These friends, describing her as a 'treasure', must have been as fooled by her as my mother was, and did not realize that children do not tell tales about those into whose charge they have been placed. When in the course of time the truth leaks out, the parents of children who have suffered at the hands of

* It fell down the *kud* (hillside) and broke its neck.

sadistic nannies, governesses or tutors ask: 'But why didn't you *tell* us?'

There is no satisfactory answer. Or there was not in those far-off times. Nowadays, when children are being turned into little monsters by parents who refuse to discipline them in any way (when not battering them to death or imbecility) that question cannot arise very often. But in my young days discipline was given a high priority in bringing up children to become responsible citizens, and the young accepted this. We accepted anything that grown-ups did (however foolish, inexplicable or downright fatuous it may have seemed to us) as right and proper, for the simple reason that it was a responsible grown-up, 'She-Who-Must-Be-Obeyed' (or he, as the case might be), who did it. We never questioned their right to order us about or to punish us when we misbehaved. And just because we regarded our elders as our betters, it would never have occurred to us to tell tales or carry complaints about them to other grown-ups; least of all to the parents who had selected them to take charge of us.

I always think of Lizzie as being 'old'. About fifty or sixty. But looking back, I realize that she cannot have been much more than thirty, if that. Memory paints her as a thinner and bonier version of the Red Queen in *Alice Through the Looking Glass*; the one who was always yelling 'Off with her head!'. I don't know how accurate this is, but as no snapshot of her survives I cannot check. In character she was every bit as ferocious as the Red Queen and we were soundly beaten for every peccadillo, however trivial. She would put us across her knee, pull down our frilly drawers, yank up our vests and belabour our small bare bottoms with the back of her hairbrush until they were sore and scarlet and exceedingly painful to sit down on. Hardly a day passed without one or other of us being beaten, and I am convinced that she enjoyed it, because I honestly cannot remember either of us being a particularly naughty child. On the contrary, I think we were very ordinary and peaceably disposed children who never got up to any spectacular mischief and were, in consequence, probably thoroughly boring.

Unfortunately for me, I not only grew to hate Nurse Lizzie with a bitter hatred I remember to this day, but I was sufficiently stubborn to resolve that never, under any circumstances, would I let her make me cry. I used to set my teeth and concentrate on hating her when she beat me, but I wouldn't scream and I wouldn't weep, and I can remember only one occasion when I broke this vow. That was when, realizing that she could not reduce me to the weeping, screaming pleas and apologies that she could draw so easily from poor little Bets, she decided to punish me instead by burning my most cherished possession: a white, silver-spangled scarf that someone, I think Sir Charles, had given me for my 'dressing-up box'. (They still make these scarves in India to this day: the material is coarse net and the glitter is applied by innumerable narrow strips of silvery metal threaded through the net and pressed flat so that the shimmering stuff feels as heavy and cold and slippery as a snake.) I would not plead with her not to burn it, so she threw it on the fire. And having watched, appalled and disbelieving as it shrivelled and turned black and melted into nothingness, I crawled into bed and pulled the blankets over my head so that the hateful woman could not see that I was crying.

I had nothing else that I valued enough for her to burn, except Roller-bear, my adored white teddy-bear who accompanied me everywhere, and without whom I would not (could not!) go to sleep. I imagine that she would have burned him too if she had dared. But the bitch-woman must have realized that everyone, even a small girl, has a breaking-point, and that I would fight for Roller-bear with teeth and claws — or a knife or a pair of scissors if I could get my hands on them! She would also have known that my parents would be bound to ask what had become of him when they returned and discovered him to be missing, and that if asked a direct question I would reply with the truth. So she never touched Roller-bear, but she devised another form of punishment, the effects of which have lasted the rest of my life and can still cause problems.

She knew that I hated having to take castor-oil. I loathed the taste, detested the oiliness and suffered cramping tummy pains shortly before the beastly stuff took effect. In those days a dose of castor-oil was prescribed for any child suffering from low spirits or lethargy or anything else that could be ascribed to constipation, which was considered the root cause of any childish ailment, from loss of appetite to acne. (I believe an earlier generation looked upon Gregory's Powder as a similar cure-all.) How that dreadful woman discovered my loathing for castor-oil I don't know. But discover it she did, and it served to provide her with a splendid new way of punishing me; in addition to a splendid new reason for doing so in the first place.

Lizzie was being courted by a certain Sergeant Smith who used to meet her by the bandstand on the Ridge; and for this reason our daily walk was always the same one. Every afternoon, come rain or shine, we would set off for the Ridge: Punj-ayah,* Lizzie, myself and the push-cart boy pushing Bets whose short, fat little legs could not keep up with my thin, bony ones; let alone with Lizzie's or Ayah's. Our route took us past the unalluring Victorian pile of Auckland House — built in the heyday of the East India Company for the Governor-General of that name — and on up a steep hill to the Lakkar Bazaar, where it joined the level road that circles Jakko — the wooded hill that is crowned by a monkey temple. Turning right in the bazaar, our road passed Davico's Ballroom' and came out on the Ridge here Christ Church stands, and the bandstand and the Library. From where, on one side, you can see down over the rooftops to Simla bazaar descending the mountainside below in a ramshackle avalanche of houses, and from the other onto fold after fold after fold of hills, to where the snow peaks lie in a glittering rampart along the far horizon.

Here Lizzie would meet her Sergeant and Punj-ayah would be ordered to take charge of Bets and her pram-pusher and me, and keep us out of the way for the next half-hour; which she did by taking us down to the Mall to watch one of our favourite sights — the men who applied those paste decorations to shawls and wall-hangings that I have already described, and who could be guaranteed to keep us riveted in admiration for their skill as the patterns flowed and glowed under their swiftly moving fingers. Punj-ayah would allow us to squat on the shop front watching the workers and chatting to them for twenty minutes or so, before herding us back to the Ridge to rejoin Nurse Lizzie for the return to Miss Cullen's. And it was at this point that my purgatory would begin ...

The walk from Miss Cullen's to the Ridge was not a short one for a child, and though there was a ladies cloakroom at the Library, Lizzie

---

* So called because of her inability to pronounce the word 'sponge'. We once unkindly locked her in the bathroom and threatened not to let her out until she said it properly. But it was no good. The best she could ever manage was 'Ish-punj'. Hence Punj-ayah. She was a dear.

would never allow me to visit it. With the result that half-way back to Miss Cullen's the effect of a dose of castor-oil would invariably catch up with me, and the most that Lizzie would allow was to let me run on ahead in the vain hope of reaching the house in time. I never made it. I would run ahead, sobbing and breathless, racked with pains that signalled the imminent approach of disaster, to arrive befouled, smelly and desperate, weeping with despair and embarrassment as I rushed, too late, into the bathroom and sank down on to the seat of the 'thunder box' — the only type of lavatory that Simla homes boasted in those days. Lizzie would arrive as I was frantically trying to clean up the mess with wads of Bromo paper, and after a furious tirade would decree the usual punishment: *another* whacking dose of castor-oil which would be repeated if, as so often, I failed to keep down the first one; and which led, inevitably, to the same crime followed by the same punishment, day after day.

It is strange to think that in the years that led up to the Second World War, Mussolini and his Blackshirts inflicted the same punishment on those rash enough to disagree with them out loud. The shaming embarrassment suffered by the victim was part of the fun; as Lizzie discovered a long time before the Italian Fascists woke up to it. I wonder if she ever married her Sergeant and had any children of her own? Heaven help them if she did, for not unnaturally my insides have never worked properly since then. (Well, just try dosing a child almost daily with massive dollops of castor-oil and see what happens to its interior plumbing!) It could even be that I shall live for fewer years than I would otherwise have done had I not met that sadistic 'treasure of a nanny'.

Mother no longer remembers how she found out about Lizzie. It was certainly not because either Bets or myself had uttered a cheep of complaint, for it had not occurred to us to do so; frightened little twits that we were. But she learned of it somehow. Some other woman, Miss Cullen perhaps, had noticed that I was getting thinner and peakier and having to be bullied to eat any food, and instituted inquiries. I myself am inclined to think that Punj-ayah, my only refuge in those dark days, talked to the Harvington servants, and that either Miss Cullen's ayah, or her old bearer who was a particular friend of ours and a great power in the house, told on the Nurse-Missahib, and that Miss Cullen — or someone — wrote to Mother. Whatever happened, it was enough to bring her hurrying up to Simla a month early and without any warning.

She had, I know, been worried about us, for she used to come up to Simla for short visits whenever she could afford to, just to see that we were all right, and I suppose she had found me looking pale and listless and generally out-of-sorts — and probably shockingly constipated. For Lizzie-the-treasure naturally suspended all punishments while Mother was there, and without their normal 'fix' of castor-oil my insides no longer worked at all, having become hooked on the beastly stuff — with withdrawal symptoms that were most uncomfortable. There is also the possibility that poor Bets's tearful shrieks while being spanked with a hairbrush had been overheard by a sympathetic fellow guest, who blew the gaff on Nurse Lizzie.

The upshot was that Bets and myself were sent out for a walk with Punj-ayah and the pram-boy — for once in the opposite direction to our usual route — and when we returned it was to find Lizzie had gone, bag and baggage.

Mother scolded me, between tears and hugs, for not having told her about Lizzie's reign of terror. Why had I never mentioned it in those carefully printed letters that had arrived once a week in Delhi? Well, that was a silly question if ever there was one! I hadn't because Lizzie vetted every letter as well as stamping them and personally placing them on the tray in the hall, from where all letters from Harvington were collected by a *chuprassi** and taken to the nearest pillar-box. Then why hadn't I told Miss Cullen? Because kind as she was, she was another grown-up and so would presumably agree with Lizzie that I needed punishing. And also because I was far too embarrassed to explain what it was that Lizzie punished me for, even though it was the direct cause of the subsequent crime.

I don't know what happened to Nurse Lizzie or where she went. She must have left Simla, for we never saw or heard of her again and she would have known that her chances of being employed there as a child's nurse were nil. I hope she married her Sergeant and became a model wife and mother, because no one can know what drives another person to behave like that. How is one to know? I am sorry I ever met her, but I hope things came right for her in the end.

* Peon.

The Great War — the 'war to end war' — never became quite real to me. I knew that it was happening, but it was happening on the other side of the world. I also knew that it was horrible and terrifying, for Tacklow had once explained trench warfare to me and told me that to him almost the worst thing about it was the thought of the mud. He said he used to dream about it; of having to plod through it, stand ankle-deep in it, sit in it, lie down to sleep in it ... Mile upon mile of wet, sticky, shell-splattered mud, pocked with craters and spiked with the shattered remains of what had once been trees. A grey wilderness on which the rain fell steadily and unceasingly and bullets pattered down like nuts in autumn. That was a horrible part of war. So were the books of propaganda cartoons in the Public Library on Simla Ridge.

Children were not supposed to look at these particular books and we knew it. They were appalling; and as with Tacklow and the mud, they gave me bad dreams. I don't know who drew them or published them, and I know that Tacklow strongly disapproved of them; as he disapproved of all forms of propaganda aimed at arousing hatred and rage and disgust. According to him, almost all this type of stuff was lies, and when there *was* a grain of truth in it, even that was barely a grain of a half-truth that had been twisted and exaggerated to make it into a full-blown horror story.

The black-and-white cartoons did not need any captions. And as far as I can remember, did not have any. They depicted vicious-looking, pig-featured German soldiers spitting small naked babies on their bayonets; terrible skeletons in ragged uniforms, their grinning skulls topped with German helmets, mowing down screaming, terrified women and children with Father Time scythes, or spraying the helpless bodies of wounded British soldiers with clouds of poison gas. There were pictures of tattered corpses hanging from barbed wire or lolling in rain-filled shell holes, and of hysterical women in nightgowns and traditional caps of Liberty, sporting sashes labelled 'Serbia', 'Belgium' or 'France' and clutching weeping infants as they fled across a shell-torn landscape, pursued by a gloating Kaiser and his grinning elder son, 'Little Willie' — both armed with dripping swords. Gerald Scarfe at his most savage could have taken lessons from them.

Those books of cartoons were obscene. There is no other word for it. But the climate of the 1914-18 war allowed them to be available in the reading rooms of a public library where even young children could take a look at them when the adults were not watching. I still have the illusion that they gave off a frightening smell. An evil smell: the stench of corruption — which is a familiar one in any Eastern country where dead animals and sometimes dead people are left to the mercy of those indefatigable undertakers, the vulture and the carrion crow, the pariah-dog and the jackal. The pictured horrors frightened me stiff, for until I laid eyes on them the world had seemed a safe place, full of kindly people; friends and playmates and wise, all-powerful grown-ups. Yet somewhere in the world these appalling things were happening; and it was grown-ups who were doing them. It was as though the earth under my feet was no longer solid, and I was never again to feel confident that grown-ups knew best: a view that had already received a body-blow from Nurse Lizzie.

Following Lizzie's departure Mother engaged another English nanny for us; this time a young and pretty one whom we loved dearly. But we did not keep her long, for she like Lizzie was being courted by a Sergeant (hers was named Grey) and since this one proposed and was accepted, when the Government moved up to Simla the next spring and my parents returned, she left us to get married. And that year we did not go back to Chillingham but left it to move into another rented house called Oaklands.

⚹ Oaklands was a small two-storey house built just below the crest of a ridge above the little hill village of Mahasu that lies by the side of the Mashobra road some five miles outside Simla. A mule-track, along which the Tibetan traders brought their wares to Simla's markets, ran along the ridge just behind and above the back of the house, and in the village below there was a wooden finger-post (it is an enamelled tin one now) which announced with classic simplicity, 'TO TIBET'. Even at the age of seven that struck me as intensely romantic, and I fell in love with Oaklands on sight. It was the loneliness that appealed to me so much; that and the enormous views from the verandahs. There were no other houses within sight except, far away on the crest of another fold in the hills, the scattered dots — pale grey or pink by day and twinkling yellow by night — which were all we could see of Simla.

From the verandahs, open on the ground floor but glassed in on the top storey, we could look down on the tree-tops of the forested mountainside that dropped steeply away to a valley so far below us that when the forest stopped and gave place to open slopes sculptured into endless layers of tiny fields, the fields looked no bigger than one's little fingernail and it was difficult to believe that each one was probably as large as or larger than our orchard. On the far side of the valley the mountains swept up again, fold on fold and layer behind layer, to merge into the long, glittering, wonderful panorama of the high snows … '*Himalaya heaven-ward heading*'. To our left lay a small lawn, the chicken-runs, potting-sheds and the servants' quarters, and to the right an orchard, which the bears used to raid when the fruit was ripe, and a wired-in tennis court. Behind the house ran that narrow, stony mule-track, and the stupendous untrodden ranges that stretched away and away to Tibet …

The snow peaks that spanned the horizon were a never-ending delight: a Transformation Scene from a Drury Lane pantomime, performed thrice daily for us to watch free of charge from our private box — the windows of the upper verandah. We could see the cold lilac silhouettes of the high snows catch fire and glow rose pink in the dawn, blaze white at midday and turn every colour of the rainbow at sunset, while below them, spread out like a hundred miles of wrinkled blue velvet, lay the vast, unexplored forests of pine and deodar and rhododendron, into which man has only penetrated a tiny distance around the edges; perhaps no more than a fraction of an inch on a map. A pin-prick only.

I had already made a first determined effort at drawing while we were at Chillingham. The outline of the hills that faced us there made a pattern that intrigued me, and the urge to put it down on paper made me ask for pencils and a drawing-block. Having acquired these, I discovered that drawing from life was a good deal more difficult than I had supposed. The block of cartridge paper was a large one, but I ran off the edge of it long before I had drawn a third of the range, and I remember rubbing it out and starting again and again; and again! — struggling to scale it down so that all that I could see could be fitted onto the paper. I never did manage it, but at least I had begun to draw and to appreciate line and shape and colour: and to store it all away in my head where it still remains, together with all the other fascinating places and things and people that I have seen. The view from Oaklands was far more spectacular than the one from Chillingham, and I tried to draw that too. But mostly it was enough just to stand and stare. And I never grew tired of that.

Oaklands is still enchanted ground to me. The hillsides, the grassy ridges and the forests were our playgrounds, and I cannot ever remember being afraid. Or bored! I do not think that either Bets or myself were bored there for so much as a minute; or would even have known what the word meant. Every day was crammed to the brim with interest and adventure: with play and the endless ploys that children invent for themselves. We helped our parents build a thatched summer-house on the upper lawn and assisted *Mali-ji* and his son to pick fruit in the orchard. And every morning after breakfast we herded the ducks down the long, winding drive to the pond that lay near the entrance gate, taking turns to carry our favourite duck, Quacky-Jack, who, poor fellow, was considered far too special to waddle down with the vulgar herd and must put up instead with the honour of being carried. Which I fear he did not appreciate.

Mother had thought it an excellent idea to keep ducks, hens, pigeons and rabbits for the pot; and for chicken and duck eggs of course. But she might have known what would happen. Every bird and rabbit was instantly given a name and became a member of the family, and I well remember the alarm and dismay when one of the hens was found to be missing. We were afraid that a fox had got it, for we had heard one barking on the previous night. But two days later there was roast chicken for lunch, and half-way through the meal Bets suddenly put down her knife and fork, and staring at Mother with round, horrified eyes, said imploring: 'Mummy, this isn't Emily, is it?'

Mother denied it firmly, but Bets remained unconvinced and thereafter lost her appetite for roast chicken. I suspect it was Emily. But after that any chicken we ate had to be bought by the *khansamah* in Mahasu bazaar. And the same went for ducks, pigeons and rabbits. Poor Mother! So much for her efforts to economize. She did no better with the apricots. There was a wild apricot tree growing out of the hillside behind the house, and for two years running it produced such an enormous crop that its boughs were bent down to the grass by the weight of the fruit, and Mother made pounds and pounds of apricot jam; so many that we were all put off apricot jam for years afterwards.

Then there was the mushroom year. The hillside behind Oaklands,

144

and below the mule-track, being exposed to the full force of the monsoon, was almost treeless, for the monsoon rain flails off all but a thin skin of the surface soil, and though the grass must at times have been green, I always remember it as being gold; hot, dry and rustling, and baked slippery by the sun. Bets and I and our friends used to toboggan on it with tin tea-trays. We had taken a picnic far down the hillside, crossing the lower road to Wildflower Hall to slip and slide down the grassy slopes towards a ridge of ground where the grass gave place to turf that had obviously been cropped by goats or deer. There were wildflowers growing there; and mushrooms! Hundreds and hundreds of mushrooms; to the delight of Tacklow, who was partial to them. We emptied out the picnic basket and filled it to the brim with them, and used our topis and Tacklow's hat as extra containers. Those mushrooms were the best I ever tasted, and there were so many of them that Mother made bottles of mushroom ketchup, and sent us back several days running to pick more. She warned us that we must be sure to leave some unpicked so that there would be more next year. And we did. But there weren't. We never again saw another mushroom on those hillsides, though we searched and searched. Perhaps the deer had taken a fancy to them? Or bears?

I have said that there was nothing to be afraid of in the Simla hills. But I was often afraid at night, for there was one particular sound that scared me: an unmistakable one — the barking of a karka deer, which in our hills is supposed to herald the presence of a leopard.

The Himalayan black bears who used to raid our orchard when the fruit was ripe, and who made a cross, coughing noise, did not worry me at all. I suppose I felt, subconsciously, that all bears were in some way relatives of Roller-bear and Bets's beloved honey-coloured and unimaginatively named 'Teddy', and were therefore friendly; which is, of course, by no means the case. But when I woke to the enormous silence of the hills and heard a karka deer barking, and knew that he was warning the creatures of the forest that a leopard was on the prowl, I would picture the big spotted cat creeping silently along the lower verandah — drawn there perhaps by the scent of Kate, the black retriever who belonged to Sir Charles Cleveland but condescended to board with us during the summer months whenever her lawful owner happened to be away on tour. Leopards are said to regard dogs as a great delicacy; for which reason most dogs whose owners live in the hills wear heavy, iron-spiked collars for protection, because leopards go for the throat. Kate too wore one, but I did not put much faith in it, and since we loved her dearly I never heard a karka deer barking without being convinced that it was calling to warn us that a leopard was coming to get her.

Our two white-painted beds stood side-by-side in the nursery; Bets's bed on the left-hand side and against the wall and mine a few feet away with, bridging the gap between the two, a small wooden chest in which we kept our toys. I had insisted on having the chest put there because it was exactly the same height as our beds, and I made a padded pillow, the same thickness as our mattresses, to cover it and a little eiderdown to lay on top of that, in order that Bets and I could hold hands across it at night in comfort should either of us feel the need to do so. We often did, because the house creaked at night, being an old one (old, that is, by Simla standards; which is new by India's, since it had been built in the last days of the East India Company).

Like the majority of Simla's houses it was a flimsy structure, built of local wood and topped by a roof of corrugated tin painted rosy red. There was no electricity, no main drainage and no running hot water; though the house boasted three cold taps. The *mehta** removed the contents of our wooden commodes several times a day, carrying it away in his malodorous basket and either spreading it upon the land or burying it in the earth where it helped to enrich the soil. Bats, rats, mice, lizards, wild cats and flying-foxes made their homes under the tin roof, and there was a family of swallows who returned year after year to build their nest between the rafters supporting the roof of the lower verandah. All these fellow occupants made curious noises at night: scuffling, scuttering and squeaking, or padding softly to and fro (that would be the wild cat). Then there was always the wind, which would sigh under the eaves and through chinks and crannies in the woodwork, wail sorrowfully on breezy nights or howl on stormy ones. Yet the windy nights were never as disturbing as the still ones, because the shrieking din of the wind-section and the surging, booming orchestral accompaniment of the pine forests, which sounded exactly like a storm at sea, were strangely soothing, while the frequent thunderstorms were exciting enough to make one jump out of bed and run

* Sweeper.

to pull back the window curtains and watch the blinding flashes of lightning illuminate the scenery as vividly as though it were a floodlit theatre set.

I used to begin counting as soon as the lightning flashed, because Bulaki, the old hillman who looked after the livestock and did odd jobs such as mending roofs and fences, had told me that the number of seconds between the flash and the thunder would tell me how many miles away the centre of the storm was, and that when the thunder followed immediately on the flash, the storm was overhead. Once I saw a bolt of lightning strike a tall pine tree and split it in two as neatly as a knife divides an apple; and watched the resulting blaze doused by pouring rain inside ten seconds. Yet although our house stood high on the crest of a ridge, I was never afraid that it would be hit, for it was protected — as were all Simla's houses — by a lightning conductor in which I had such complete faith that I was able to watch these spectacular extravaganzas with awe-struck admiration. The noise was almost as exciting as the lightning. The sound of thunder among mountains is quite different from what it is in the plains, for it echoes round the great peaks and ricochets off a hundred rocky hillsides that act as sounding-boards: '*It is Thor that is striking with his hammer! It is Odin where the sparks fly free*' . . .

A thunderstorm in the plains may be just as noisy, but it does not have the hollow, ringing clang, like a series of gigantic wooden planks being slammed down onto the stone floor of some enormous subterranean cave. And when at last the clouds burst, the rain roars down like Niagara in flood-time in a solid wall of water that is quite strong enough to beat a seven-year-old child to its knees. I would always gladly have exchanged the still nights for the wild ones, for I could sleep through the uproar, feeling extra safe and protected in my own warm bed just because there was so much noise and fury raging outside. But on quiet nights, particularly when the moon was full and there was no breath of wind to set the forest whispering, the silence was something that could be felt. A tangible thing that listened — holding its breath the while.

In these days there cannot be many places in the world where one can lie and listen to the silence and feel it press down on you with the weight of water. Nowadays there is always something making a noise somewhere: a lawn-mower, an electric clock, the hum of a generator, or a car revving up; the maddening, mindless yowling of a transistor radio playing pop, the distant throb of some jumbo-jet striving to equal Puck's record and put a girdle round the world in forty minutes, or the banshee scream of a fighter plane from an RAF training base hurtling overhead. But in those far-off times no mechanical sound disturbed the peace of our hills, and listening to the silence one became acutely aware of the thousands of miles of untouched, unknown country behind and beyond the walls of that little house by the narrow mule-track that wound away through the ranges to Tibet and the high plateaux of Central Asia.

If anything stirred in that white, silent world it was possible to hear it. Every flitter of a bat's wing or hum of a mosquito was loud in the stillness, and the night noises that every house makes after dark became sharply audible. The hoot of an owl or the alarm call of a deer from the world outside could make our nerves leap, and it was on these nights that Bets and I would go to sleep holding hands under the eiderdown across the padded top of the toy-chest.

Chapter 11

~X&X~

From ghoulies and ghosties and long-leggety beasties
And things that go bump in the night,
                              Good Lord deliver us!

                                        Anon. (Cornish)

Tacklow gave up his horse, but although we kept the rickshaw and the four *jhampanis* who pulled it, he seldom made use of it; preferring to walk to Simla and back, a total of ten miles every weekday. Only very occasionally — and then only if he was exceptionally tired or the weather was particularly atrocious — would he ring up and ask for it to be sent to his office in Army Headquarters to fetch him home; and even then he would never let himself be pulled up the steep ascent from Mahasu to the front door of Oaklands, for riding in rickshaws pulled by his fellow men was something that always worried him.

It worried me too, and I remember discussing the whole problem at length with our *jhampanis* in the course of a ride into Simla to attend a dancing-class; and being interested to discover that they held very different views. To them it was both a living and a way of life, and they considered it a good one. What, they demanded, would happen to them if everyone suddenly acquired these foolish views about it being beneath the dignity of one man to pull the rickshaw of another one? *Bah!* work was work, and they, personally, considered themselves fortunate to have achieved the status of the privately employed, which entitled them to wear a smart and distinctive uniform supplied by their employer, plus the right to be referred to as *jhampanis* instead of 'rickshaw-coolies', as was the case with the casually employed.

The gods, being sensible, said Durroo, the head *jhampani*, saw to it that there was work for all kinds and conditions of men; not merely for *bunnias** and those who had brains and book-learning. The rich

* Merchants.

and educated needed people to look after them so that they, in their turn, could look after their own high affairs; which was the making of money — and the spending of it, which created work for others. The rich, according to Durroo, were put into this world for the benefit of the poor and uneducated, without whose labour they would be unable to live or, more important, make the money that paid for that labour.

It was a novel point of view, but an interesting one. And only recently, watching my *Far Pavilions* being filmed in Rajasthan, and taking in the sheer numbers of the multiracial army of fellow humans: actors, extras, stunt-men, directors, producers, cameramen, technicians, costume and set designers, electricians, make-up experts, car-drivers, coolies, *darzis*, jewellers, *mahouts* — the list is staggering even if one does not include the families of all the people who were earning their living by working on that particular film, or the hordes of hotel servants who cooked and fed and looked after the vast number of people who had been flown out by the film company and put up in one or other of the local hotels — I began to realize that Durroo and his fellow *jhampanis* had had a point.

Just because I had kept my nose to the grindstone and worked myself into the ground to write *The Far Pavilions*, I, personally, was for a brief space of time responsible for the employment of all these people: many of whom were making far more money out of that book than I myself had done! Granted, if they had not been working on my story they would have been working on someone else's. But the fact remained that they were all, at that particular time, employed and making a living out of and because of *me* and the work that I had done. It was a slightly awe-inspiring reflection, and I thought of that long-ago rickshaw ride into Simla. 'Full employment', in fact: a slogan that had not been invented then, and would have been regarded as an impossible slice of pie-in-the-sky by two thirds of the citizens of what is now known, with lofty condescension, as 'the Third World'! (*What* 'Third World'? Or, come to that, where's the second one?).

One of the great advantages of being born and brought up in India by liberal-minded parents (or, to be strictly accurate, one liberal-minded one and one fun-loving, bird-brained one who flitted through life with the airy inconsequence of a butterfly on a sunny morning) was that Bets and I were on excellent terms with the local citizens and, being able to chatter to them in the vernacular, acquired a lot of interesting information as to their likes and dislikes, their home life, beliefs, philosophy, superstitions and politics (if any). A great deal of this would, I suspect, have horrified our dear parents had they known about it; for like all Victorians, they valued innocence and would have wished to protect us from the harsher facts of life, in the belief that children would learn about such things soon enough and that a child should be allowed to enjoy childhood to the full.

Well, I'm all for that myself. But I do not remember that the things I learned about real life or real death upset me very much; largely, I suppose, because they were told so matter-of-factly by people I knew and liked, who accepted them philosophically and did not whinge or rail against fate, or take to drink, but just shrugged and got on with the business of living. I loved them because they never treated me as a baby or told me to run away and play, but were always willing to explain and discuss matters in which I was interested or had not properly understood. They were never brusque or impatient with me, as grown-ups of my own race often were, and they were never too busy to answer a question. Time seemed to move far more slowly in Asia, and Asians treat it with a lordly carelessness that takes no account of such abstract things as 'the unforgiving minute' — they wouldn't know what you were talking about! It is an attitude that frequently maddens the West, but it does make life seem a lot longer; and a lot more peaceful than our own swift, frantic scamper from the cradle to the grave.

Perhaps this is why my childhood in India — and my girlhood too — seems to me, in retrospect, to have lasted twice as long as the whole of the rest of my life. And for this 'I thank whatever Gods there be'.

✄ Living at Mashobra did not make much difference to Mother's social life. She would take the rickshaw and go into Simla with Tacklow at least twice a week, and her friends were always coming out to visit us: sometimes only for the day, but often to stay for a night or two. Their children came with them, so Bets and I had a constant stream of young visitors, most of whom I could have done without: the shining exception being Guy's sister, my great friend Bargie Slater, who came whenever she could. It was always a delight to see her and wonderful to have her stay with us, because with her arrival life — which out at Oaklands seemed to flow gently along like a placid, slow-moving river — suddenly woke up and turned into a sparkling torrent that resembled Tennyson's famous babbling brook.

There was never a dull moment when Bargie was around. I would take her to see all my favourite retreats and we would spend hours perched among the branches of one of the orchard trees or lying comfortably in a hot, grassy hollow a hundred yards or so below the mule-track, gazing out at the wooded slopes of the far mountains while we discussed life and our contemporaries, exchanged gossip about the grown-ups and speculated about the future and what we would become when we grew up. We would, of course, get married. That was taken for granted, for we both thought highly of Love and Romance and had every intention of Living-Happily-Ever-After. Yet our interests were by no means confined solely to gallant princes and handsome husbands, for before we got around to marriage we were going to write in partnership a book that would make us rich and famous.

This opus was to be about a haunted house, and the surprise twist at the end was that the twin spectres who haunted it were not the ghosts of people who had lived there, but of their emotions. The hate and selfishness that had motivated the behaviour of two sisters who had been born in the sixteenth century, lived through the reign of Charles II and died unmarried — still at odds with each other because one of the two was a sour and bigoted Puritan, a passionate supporter of Cromwell and his Roundheads, while the other was a frivolous partisan of Charles I and his Cavaliers. These two, having vented their ghostly fury on succeeding generations, were to be finally exposed as nothing more than a couple of nasty, quarrelsome egos, and exorcised — surprise! surprise! — by the true love of the latest occupant and his wife. (He turns out to be a distant cousin; the great-great — or great-great-great? — grandson of a nephew who inherited the house from his unpleasant aunts and came under the influence of the malevolent emanations they had left behind to haunt the place.)

We thought this idea was staggeringly original. And possibly it was, since even if Kipling had written 'The House Surgeon' by then, we were too young to have read or understood that kind of story. I was grown-up by the time I read it, and was fascinated to find that someone of such eminence had had the same idea! Needless to say we never got around to writing this masterpiece; though we got endless pleasure out of discussing it and inventing the various evils that befell the successive owners of the house. And even more out of deciding how we would spend the vast sums of money that would reward our labours! I remember that yachts and diamonds were mentioned. A whacking great diamond tiara for Mother, and a yacht for Tacklow. Tacklow who would, if he had had Aladdin's lamp, have wished for one to take him round the world, hugging the coasts and with no time limit, so that he could stop for as long as he liked — a month or a year or two years, perhaps even longer — in any port that pleased him; moving on at once from those that did not, putting in at the Andaman Islands (from where a long-time and like-minded friend of his who had served several terms as Chief Commissioner had written him lengthy letters extolling their idyllic beauty) and, finally, spending months at a stretch on the Great Barrier Reef. This last, for some unexplained reason, had taken a firm grip on his mind. He had promised himself that he would visit it before he died, and I suspected that if he ever did, his travels would end there; for in those days, and until fairly recently, I believe that anyone landing on one of the great reef's hundreds of tiny uninhabited islands could, if they chose, establish squatter's rights and claim it for their own. Provided, of course, that they lived on it. I didn't put it beyond Tacklow to have this in mind!

When not planning novels and dream-shopping, Bargie and I, accompanied by Bets and her special friend, Bargie's second brother Tony, would climb the hill path to Dukani; a house that stood on the crest of the hill behind Oaklands and which belonged to Sir Edward Buck, known universally as 'Buckie' — 'the finest shot in India'. He was also the author of *Simla Past and Present*, and for more years than anyone could remember had been Reuter's chief representative on the subcontinent. Any number of Simla's children knew and loved Buckie, and Bets and myself, his nearest neighbours except for the Roberts who lived in a house called The Bower on the far side of the hill, were allowed to treat Dukani as a second home.

If Buckie should be out we would take the path at the back of his house that led downward for a few hundred yards to The Bower, and look up Sybil Roberts, another Simla child who has remained a lifelong friend, and whose mother, Lady Roberts, had fascinated me ever since I learned that she was the grand-daughter of 'Afghan' Warburton, whose story had been told to me by the Khan Sahib: a story that, to borrow a favourite phrase of the Kojah's, 'since you have not heard it, I will now proceed to relate' —

%% During the British occupation of Kabul in 1841, a young man in the service of the East India Company, Henry Arthur Warburton of the Bengal Sappers and Miners, while taking a stroll through the streets of the city, had been seen by a beautiful Afghan Princess who had been peering down through the carved wooden lattice that screened the windows of the women's quarters. The Princess was already married to a nephew of Dost Mahommed, the Amir of Afghanistan, whom the British had just deposed. But this did not stop her from falling in love on sight with the young Englishman. She managed to find out who he was and to smuggle a letter to him arranging an assignation, and as soon as he saw her he too fell fathoms deep in love; for she was very beautiful. Eventually the two eloped and her husband divorced her. But though her brother-in-law, Akbar Khan, put a price on her head and gave orders to the Afghan Army that she and her lover were to be hunted down and killed, they managed to escape, and after many adventures were married. Their son was the Warburton I referred to in the last section of *The Far Pavilions*; the one who had been about to leave India when the Second Afghan War began to loom upon the horizon, and who had offered to return to the Frontier. Had he done so, our chances of abandoning that unjust and futile campaign (or, alternatively, of winning instead of losing it) would have been greatly improved, for his mother's kinsmen saw to it that he was kept in touch with Afghan affairs, and the Government of India, had they listened to him, would have avoided stumbling into many fatal quicksands. As it was, they declined his offer and he duly sailed from Bombay — and the repercussions of that war are still with us.

Sybil's mother, Lady Roberts, always known as 'Lady Mickey', was a grand-daughter of 'Afghan' Warburton and his lovely, wayward Princess; and I have been told that another Warburton, this time a great-grandson, arriving to join his unit on the North-West Frontier just after the Second World War had ended, and not long before Partition and Independence, got out of the train in his pyjamas to stretch his legs in the dawn, and found himself faced with a vast crowd of Afghans who packed the little platform from end to end. They were all kinsmen of his great-grandmother, gathered here to welcome and pay their respects to her great-grandchild. And if anyone still wants to know why the British who served in India had such a deep and enduring affection for that country, this episode alone should serve to explain a great deal!

✼ Most of our meals during Bargie and Tony's visits were picnics. Sandwiches, hard-boiled eggs, curry-puffs and cake were packed into rucksacks by Mother and eaten by us on the slopes of the golden, grassy hillsides that looked out across the enormous valleys below us towards the great Himalayan ranges that are the outer bastions of Tibet. Even the nights were exciting when Bargie was a visitor, for we would hold midnight feasts; popular entertainments that were tremendous fun to plan and prepare, though it must be admitted that nine times out of ten by the time midnight struck and our elders and betters were (we hoped) safely asleep, we ourselves were far too drowsy to get much enjoyment out of them. As for the provender that we so carefully collected and hid away in toy-cupboards or under the beds, the best that could be said about it was that it could have been worse. Though not much. This was because the first rule governing such nocturnal bun-fights was that the feast *must* consist of food that had been collected without the knowledge of any grown-up — which restricted it to cold potatoes or soggy lumps of pudding whipped off our plates into a waiting handkerchief during lunch, bits of cake or biscuits filched during tea, and bottles of lemon squash surreptitiously sneaked from the larder when no one was looking. And since the pudding- and/or potato-filled handkerchiefs were then stuffed up our bloomers in order to remove them unseen from the dining-room (children's knickers in those days were invariably bloomers with elastic at the waist and knee) the collected delicacies were not all that appetizing. But then anything eaten by stealth and at an unauthorized hour possessed the charm of forbidden fruit.

These midnight feasts came to be known as 'Chunkychaddles', because Bargie, being of a methodical turn of mind, had on one occasion written down a detailed plan: who was to collect what, the exact time that each one of us left his or her room, etc., etc., in the manner of a military exercise. And having concluded the list, she had thrown her pencil down and said: 'And after that, Chunkychaddle bust!' The newly-minted word appealed strongly to her fellow conspirators and from then on, to any member of our own particular circle of friends, a midnight feast was always known by that name. But the final and most famous of our Chunkychaddles was destined not to take place at either our house or the Slaters', but at Sybil's — or rather her mother Lady Mickey's.

The Bower was one of Simla's oldest houses, having been built in the heyday of the East India Company and later on owned for a time by a certain Lieutenant-Colonel in the Company's 7th Bengal Light Cavalry; one Thomas David Colyear. Thos. David had married twice; both times to Indian ladies. The coffin of the first Mrs Colyear (a Muslim lady who died in 1865 and whom he had buried in an elaborate marble mausoleum in the garden of one of his houses) was eventually dug up and re-interred beside that of her husband in the third of Simla's five cemeteries, after a subsequent purchaser of the house objected to the presence of a corpse in the garden. The Colonel, according to the marriage register in Simla's Christ Church that records his second marriage, claimed to be a son of the Right Honourable the Earl of Portmore. Presumably an illegitimate one, since he is referred to only by his military rank and never as 'Lieut.-Col. the Hon. Thomas Colyear'. His second wife, who appears on the same document as 'Alice, spinster, daughter of Jewtoo, Hindu', hailed from Kangra; which makes me wonder if she could have been the inspiration for Lizpeth, the girl in one of Kipling's *Plain Tales from the Hills* who also appears in *Kim* as the Woman of Shamlegh. Hill women from that region are known to be fair-skinned and very beautiful.

The Colonel married Alice, daughter of Jewtoo, Hindu, only a few months after the death of his Muslim wife. And ten years later when he himself died he left her The Bower (then called 'Alice's Bower') in his will: together with a very comfortable fortune. Buckie says in *Simla Past and Present* that her relations in Kangra Valley immediately descended upon the widow with the intention of getting their hands on the money, and that she 'died soon afterward' — he does not say of what. He adds that 'for a time' her ghost was supposed to haunt

The Bower, and includes a story that was certainly not the one that I was told in the early 1930s by old friends in the bazaars of Mahasu, Mashobra and Simla.

In the years I am writing about The Bower belonged to Buckie, who had rented it to Sybil's father, Sir 'Mickey' Roberts; and it seems that at that time half Simla knew that one room in the house was haunted. But since this particular room was always kept unfurnished and unused, no one bothered much about the ghost of poor Alice, which for its part behaved with the utmost tact and kept itself to itself. That is, until Lady Mickey threw a weekend party for a number of her friends, including Bargie's parents and mine, who were invited to bring their children with them in order to keep Sybil amused — there being nothing more certain to ruin an adult party than a bored seven-year-old tagging around after the grown-ups and generally getting underfoot.

The Bower was a good deal larger than it looked, but with so many guests the only way of fitting them in was to put all the children together in one room, dormitory fashion. And since the adults had been very careful not to breathe a word about the ghost to any of the children (and an order to that effect had long ago been issued to the servants), it was decided that it would be quite safe to put the kids into the haunted room — in the belief that although anyone who knew about the ghost might well start imagining all sorts of peculiar things and seeing and hearing all kinds of imaginary movements and noises (their nerves would see to that!), a bunch of high-spirited and blissfully ignorant children would be entirely unaffected: and in any case, the story was a load of old rubbish! The haunted room was therefore opened and thoroughly spring-cleaned, and five beds were procured and made up in it.

It was an odd-shaped room; in outline rather like one of those old-fashioned square ink-bottles. The neck of the bottle had windows on three sides and a peaked roof overhead which jutted out from the main expanse of corrugated tin (a material that roofed ninety per cent of Simla's houses). Two beds were placed on either side of this neck below the long side windows, and a small dressing-table stood in front of the end one. The rest of the room, the bottle part, was large and square and had been hastily furnished with an almirah, a chest of drawers and a chair or two, in addition to the other three beds. There was a fireplace in the wall facing the windowed neck, and on the two side walls to the left and right of this there were two doors, one opening inwards off a wide landing while the opposite one on the far side of the room opened into a bathroom and loo.

The outer wall of the bathroom was part of the outer wall of the house. And since the house itself stood on a flat piece of ground that had been hacked out of the steep hillside, there was on that side a vertical cut, some fifteen feet deep and roughly eight wide, between the outer wall and the hillside above. This was spanned by a stout wooden bridge onto which the outer bathroom door opened and across which the *bheesti* would carry water for the baths, and the sweeper come with his basket to clean the loo. No one crossing the bridge could do so without advertising their presence, for the planks creaked loudly when trodden on, and every footstep echoed hollowly in the cut below — I remember that because we children preferred to reach the hillside by way of the bathroom and the bridge rather than downstairs and out by the front door.

Sybil, Bets and Tony had the beds in the main part of the room, while Bargie and I, as the two eldest, bagged the beds in the neck of the bottle. And this being a festive occasion, we decided to celebrate it with a super-special Chunkychaddle. So on the Saturday we raided the larder and acquired the usual scraps off the lunch table or during tea — fortunately there was a 'nursery table' in the dining-room where the children ate, so no beady-eyed grown-ups spotted us slipping pudding or whatever off our plates and into the waiting handkerchiefs.

We had a lovely day. I can still remember the scent and the sound of it: the smell of pine needles and flowers, the feel of the hot sun on our backs, the huge iridescent red and green and blue dragonflies that swooped and hovered over the lily-pond in the garden, and, towards dusk, the flying-foxes waking up and sailing down the hillsides from the tops of the tall deodars, dark against a green and gold sky. There was a full moon that night and not a cloud in the sky, and after our respective mothers had heard our prayers and kissed us good-night, Sybil's ayah locked and bolted the outer bathroom door giving onto the bridge, turned out the oil lamps and went away, shutting the door behind her. No sooner had she gone than Bargie and I drew back the curtains she had earlier drawn across the windows, and sat bathed in brilliant moonlight which made the rest of the room seem so dead black by contrast that we could not see Bets, Sybil and Tony, who lay in their beds only a few feet away and talked to each other in whispers for fear that someone in authority would hear them and come in and tell them to shut up and go to sleep.

There was not a breath of wind that warm night, and with no soothing surf-sound of the breeze through pine needles, we could hear the grown-ups talking and laughing below and, later, the sound of a piano and someone singing. As the moon moved up the sky and the shadows of the pine trees shortened, we became sleepier and sleepier and began to wonder if the grown-ups were *ever* going to stop talking and go to bed; but after what seemed an age we heard the drawing-room door open and the sounds of the house-party dispersing to their own rooms. We gave them the best part of another hour in which to fall asleep, and then, when the house was still as a pond in a hard frost, Bargie stopped yawning and announced that the Chunkychaddle would commence. And immediately Tony, Sybil and Bets roused themselves, and having scuffled around under their beds and pillows for the provender that they had collected earlier in the day, brought it over to our beds and settled down there to enjoy the feast.

By now the moon no longer shone directly into our windows, but the five of us sat pyjama-clad in the clear light that was reflected off the roof outside, as we ate (with relish I have no doubt) an assortment of food that almost certainly included cold rice-pudding, squashed blancmange and some very crumbly cake and broken biscuits, washed down with orange juice and water drunk out of tooth-mugs. Our spirits were high and I remember that there was a great deal of giggling and the occasional burst of laughter, hurriedly suppressed.

The Chunkychaddle was going great guns when suddenly we heard someone walking up the hall stairs, and froze where we sat; realizing with horror that we must have been making enough noise to wake up one of the grown-ups. Now we'd catch it! Our only hope lay in making no sound, so that whoever we had awakened would think that we must be asleep and that they had made a mistake. We therefore stayed perfectly still, holding our breath, while the footsteps advanced. But there was something strange about them. They didn't sound right. And when suddenly Bets said in a strained whisper: 'It isn't a person ... it's a *thing*!' we all knew what she meant, for it was as though something — a flying-fox perhaps? — was flumping up the stairs.

Something that was having to jump painfully for every step, landing each time with a muffled thud. Not a human but a creature. Some kind of animal . . .

Bets and Sybil began to whimper and I remember saying as firmly as I could: 'Don't be silly! It won't be able to open the door.' And immediately everyone, myself included, relaxed. The door-handles and catches were all good and solid, handmade by craftsmen who knew their job; and once a door was shut (and we all knew it was shut, for Sybil's ayah, impatient to be off, had closed it behind her with considerable emphasis) no draught however strong could open it: only a firm human hand could do that! The peculiar flumping footsteps came nearer and nearer, and now they were on the landing outside. We stayed very still; listening and for the moment no longer afraid because of that closed door. But the strange-sounding steps came on, and ignoring the door advanced steadily until whatever it was that was making them was in the room with us. It came on as far, I suppose, as the fireplace; where it stopped abruptly as though it had suddenly seen us and had checked, staring at us.

We stared back into that impenetrable blackness for perhaps half a minute . . . which is a very long time if you are scared to death. And then Sybil's nerve broke, and she snatched up my pillow and hurled it into the darkness at the spot where the thing had stopped. There was a sudden, scuttling rush and it had gone. Not back the way it had come, but across the room and into the dark bathroom and out again, without pausing, through the far door and onto the bridge. In the next second we heard the familiar creak and clatter of the planks as it ran over them; and on the heels of that sound something — either the same thing or something else that was startled by it — sprang onto the roof, making a hellish clatter on the corrugated tin, and a black formless shadow flicked swiftly across the moonlight outside the windows.

After that there were no more sounds from the night. Or if there were you couldn't have heard them, because all five of us were screaming at the top of our voices. We sat there shrieking our heads off and I have no idea how long we kept it up; for several minutes at least I expect, since in those days few houses in Simla, and none outside it, had electricity, and kerosene lamps take quite a time to light.

Sybil's mother was the first to get one lit and appear on the scene.

We heard her shouting out to us to stop that noise (we stopped!) as she ran to our rescue; and though scared stiff I wasn't really frightened — not really, *truly* frightened — until I heard her turn the handle of the door and push it open. Until then I was convinced that whatever it was that had flumped up the stairs and into our room was an animal: a flying-fox for choice, or a monkey; an old or injured monkey . . . the door *must* have been ajar and our visitor had simply pushed it open. But no wild creature could have turned that handle and opened a closed door. And hearing her open it, all at once I was frightened rigid, right down to my fingers and toes.

Lady Mickey did not improve matters by informing us roundly that we were a bunch of hysterical little ninnies who must have been telling each other ghost stories and imagined it all, because not only had the landing door and the door into the bathroom been tight shut — she had opened them herself! — but the outside door of the bathroom was both locked and bolted and nothing — but *nothing*! — could have entered the room or got out again! Why, even the fire-screen was still in position in front of the fireplace, so let us have no more of this nonsense!

We had been far too shocked and scared to think of hiding the remains of our ill-fated Chunkychaddle, and as other grown-ups in various forms of night attire arrived panting, clutching oil lamps, candles or torches, the resulting blaze of light illuminated the evidence and drew everyone's attention to the sticky collection of debris on the beds and the floor. Our elders and betters then proceeded to relieve their feelings by tearing an imperial strip off us, and oddly enough, this telling-off returned us to normal as nothing else could have done. Guilty and subdued, we eventually allowed ourselves to be settled down to sleep again, though we refused to close an eye unless a lamp was left burning on the chest of drawers and Sybil's ayah brought her mattress and bedded down on the floor of our room to protect us. She seemed oddly reluctant to do so, but was overruled.

By breakfast time the next morning the adult members of the house-party had had time to discuss the happenings of the night which, I now realize must have shaken them considerably — if only because we could hardly have invented the whole thing, since all five of us had told exactly the same story. Had it been some silly, juvenile practical joke, we would have been bound to contradict each other, even with the most careful rehearsing. And anyway Sybil, Bets and Tony were far too young to have been coached to say half the things they had blurted out between sobs — even if Bargie and I had been sufficiently steeped in sin to put them up to it, *one of them* would surely have cracked under questioning. All that must have been in the minds of the grown-ups when they lectured us next morning, for we were startled to discover that Lady Mickey had changed her mind and her story overnight — presumably as the result of anxious discussion as to how best to deal with the situation.

She can't have known much about psychology. Or about children either, for she now said that the door into our room was in fact open and so was the door into the bathroom, while ayah had merely forgotten to fasten the outer one leading onto the bridge, which must have been blown open by the wind. What we had heard was only a flying-fox or a frightened monkey; probably a langur that had somehow become trapped in the house during the day and been trying to get out. It was all quite simple, and the fright that it had given us was no less than we deserved for being awake at that hour in the first place, and engaged in gorging stolen food!

Well, it was just possible that it might be simple to the three youngest Chunkychaddlers. But not to Bargie and myself! We were not *that* green. There must, we decided, be something very peculiar indeed about The Bower if, in order to cover it up, the grown-ups had actually to descend to the cardinal sin of telling lies. For of course they were lying! We were none of us babies, and if the door had been open we would have seen the light of Lady Mickey's lamp long before she reached it instead of only when she opened the door. And we'd all *heard* her open it — and seen her open the one into the bathroom too, because by that time there was a lamp in the room; *hers*! We'd also heard her try the outer door before she came back and assured us crossly that it was locked and bolted and that nothing could have got out that way. It was no good altering her story now because it only made matters worse; in addition to shocking us deeply. (Surely English people, Sahib-log, shouldn't tell lies? If *they* did, who could one rely on?)

We turned instead to our faithful allies the servants for enlightenment; but they too failed us. They avoided our eyes and would only say shortly that we were too young to understand and would we please run away and play because they were too busy to waste time talking to us. They had, of course, received instructions from our parents not to do so. But their refusal to discuss the matter added the final touch to our terror, and both Bets and I refused flatly and tearfully to spend another night at The Bower. We were so adamant about this that in the end all five of us were sent off to Oaklands for the rest of that long weekend; departing thankfully on foot along the mule-track under the eagle eye of Sybil's ayah and Alum Din, our own (or rather Tacklow's) bearer, to walk the scant mile that separated The Bower from Oaklands where a telephone message had warned our servants of a sudden influx of baba-log, and a delicious picnic lunch was eaten in the summer-house on the upper lawn.

Mother and Tacklow returned to spend the night with us, and on Monday morning Sybil returned to The Bower and Bargie and Tony left with their mother for Simla. We were sorry for Sybil, having to go back to that creepy house. But we consoled ourselves with the thought that now the guests had departed she would be able to move back into her own safe little nursery on the opposite side of it, where her ayah would sleep across the threshold of her door and Lady Mickey would almost certainly let her have a nightlight. For our own part we were deeply grateful that we did not have to stay on in The Bower.

Children's memories are apt to be very short, and life was so full in those days, and such fun, that there were plenty of other things to think about. All the same, none of us ever forgot that night; and only a few years ago, while on a visit to Australia, I — a grandmother — had dinner with Sybil, who had settled near Perth to be near her children and grandchildren (and I'm not sure there wasn't the odd great-grandchild too!). We talked, among other things, of that night at The Bower and discovered that we both remembered every detail of it. Bets and Bargie, also grandmothers, certainly do. As did Tony when I last saw him: though sadly both he and Guy have been dead for many years.

None of us had ever previously heard that The Bower was haunted, and no one would speak to us about it afterwards. Sybil's mother stuck firmly to her flying-fox theory, and the other grown-ups, Indian and British alike, supported it; so recognizing defeat, we gave up asking questions and pushed the whole episode into some dusty attic at the back of our minds. It was only years later, when I returned to

India and to Simla, after having thankfully finished with school, completed a year as an art student and officially 'Come Out', that I asked various old acquaintances about the story behind the haunting of The Bower.

Buckie, who was still very much alive and had recently published a revised and updated version of his *Simla Past and Present*, would only repeat the rather pointless and distinctly silly one that he had put into the old version; which was that for more than forty years after Alice's death some Kangra woman or women of her family had played the part of her ghost. He was rather cross with me when I pointed out that since Hindu Alice had died in or about 1880 and 'Alice's Bower' had become The Bower from then on, surely the phoney ghost must have been a bit long in the tooth by then! And as the house had been occupied by several different sets of tenants since the alleged haunting began, some forty years previously, where did this geriatric hide during the daytime? If she was flesh and blood, she presumably had to eat! As for the ungallant young subalterns who, according to Buckie's account, caught the 'ghost' of Alice and roughed her up so badly that she never haunted the house again, I didn't believe a word of it, for Buckie couldn't recall who had told him that tale or the year in which it was supposed to have happened — which must have been later than 1917 since the house was certainly still on the 'haunted' list at that date. Nor could he even remember the name of a single one of the four subalterns who reportedly caught and ill-treated the by now ancient (and dotty?) old dame who was supposedly impersonating poor Alice. It seemed to me that someone had either been pulling Buckie's leg or else had got hold of another story, tacked it on to The Bower, and repeated it to him at a late hour of night after the port had been circulating too freely.

I applied instead to old Khundun, Buckie's head gardener at Dukani; and also to the proprietor of the grain shop in Mahasu, the *chowkidar* of The Bower, and a number of other local inhabitants whose forebears had lived in those parts for generations and who had known me when I was a child. Their individual stories about 'Alice's Bower' were not only far more entertaining but, bar the odd embellishment here and there, to a great extent actually tallied with each other. So here, for what it is worth, is *their* version ...

When Colonel Colyear died and his will was read, his widow found herself in possession of a house and a fortune; both of which, in the eyes of her Kangra Valley relatives, appeared so dazzlingly large and impressive that they lost no time in descending upon her *en masse* to demand a share of the loot. Alice at first proved tractable, but after a few months of having her house overrun by this horde of locusts, her patience began to wear thin and there were tremendous rows. Fearing that she might wash her hands of them they turned on her in a body; locking her up in her own room and keeping her a prisoner there. And when she attempted to escape, they cut off her feet to prevent her running away.

In another version of this story her relatives decided to make sure of the house and the money by forcing her to marry an ill-favoured and much older cousin, and it was this man who cut off her feet after catching her in the act of eloping with an Englishman who had become her lover. But both versions, and all the stories, included the hacking off of poor Hindu Alice's feet. Also that after she died from the effects of that brutal amputation, her greedy relatives were forced out of her Bower by her ghost, which took to haunting the room in which she had been imprisoned; and that she could often be heard clumping painfully on those bandaged, footless stumps up the stairs that led to it . . .

Well, there it is. My own true ghost story. The only one, I am thankful to say, that I experienced at first hand. There were many others that I heard of during my years in India, and there was also the ghost that haunted the house in Somerset which my paternal grandfather acquired after my grandmother died, and in which he lived for the rest of his life. But thank goodness that, and the others, were tales I heard at second hand: though I have no reason to disbelieve them. Quite the contrary, in fact. Which is why I am a firm believer in ghosts. India is full of them — and of things for which there is no rational explanation. As, for instance Jim Corbett's* true tale of the Demon of Trisul and the Temple Tiger of Dabidhura. And though the very idea of haunted houses scares me just as badly as it scares the vast majority of humans, I also find it comforting; because if there are ghosts, then there *must* be life after death.

* *The Temple Tiger, Man-Eaters of Kumaon, My India*, etc., etc.

�֍ In the months after that terrifying night at The Bower we often went over to play with Sybil. But we never again stayed with her overnight or ventured near that room. Nor did we talk about what had happened there. I think we had all been so scared that we deliberately pushed the whole thing into the back of our minds and refused to think about it. Yet curiously enough, even after all those years, describing the event of that last Chunkychaddle — for it was the last — I felt a distinct cold shiver crawl down my spine, and was back once more in Alice's room on a moonlit night over sixty years ago. *Sixty years!* How quickly the time has gone. How terribly quickly . . .

Chapter 12

~※◇※~

Enter these enchanted woods,
You who dare . . .

Meredith, 'The Woods of Westermain'

Of all the crowding memories that I have of our days at Oaklands,
there are only two other frightening ones; both of which occurred
during the monsoon, a time when the hillsides are so thickly blanketed
with mist that one can barely see more than a yard or two ahead. The
first happened while we were being taken for an afternoon walk by a
temporary governess along the lower road that led to the Viceroy's
weekend cottage, The Retreat.

This road was little more than a footpath through the forest; a
shadowed, moss-carpeted track along the steep slopes of the hillside,
used since time immemorial by the hill folk — wood-cutters, charcoal-
burners, gypsies and *shikaris* — most of whom now preferred to use
the later British-built rickshaw road which took the main traffic,
including the Viceregal cars. From the outer edge of the lower road
the hillside dropped sharply downwards for miles before levelling out
into an unseen valley, while on the opposite side there was a high bank
buttressed by a tangle of tree-roots and draped with maidenhair fern,
wild violets and those pink rock-plants with big fleshy leaves.* Pine,
fir and deodar, rhododendrons and chestnuts towered above it, and
even in fine weather one could seldom catch more than a glimpse of
sky through the dense canopy of leaves, pine needles and tree ferns
overhead.

On this particular day — as on almost every day during the months
of the monsoon — we could barely see more than the dark, dripping
trunks of the nearest trees; and those only faintly, for the mist was

* *Bergenia saxifragaceae* — according to a gardening friend.

curling and creeping between them like smoke from a forest fire. We had heard no sound; not so much as the rustle of a leaf or the snap of a twig. Yet suddenly, barely three or four yards ahead of us, a troop of langurs — the grey, black-faced, white-whiskered descendants of the tribe who alone of all Hanuman's monkey folk refused to help Rama rescue Sita — materialized noiselessly out of the fog like an army of ghosts, and crossing the path, leapt up the high bank to our right, to vanish into the misty forest above. On their heels, acting as a rearguard and walking very slowly on all fours, came the patriarch of the group; the biggest langur I have ever seen, before or since. Until then I had no idea that the species could grow to that size, and the sight of that huge, grey creature frightened me even more than the sound of The Bower ghost had done.

We had checked instinctively on seeing the first of the troop, because langurs are known to have uncertain tempers, and we were standing very still when that King-Emperor of all langurs stalked across the path. He would have dwarfed a Shetland pony, for even on all fours he was nearly the same height as I was, and the temporary governess, a townee if ever there was one, gave a gasp of terror and hastily retreated behind us. The movement made the monster aware of our presence, and he turned his head and favoured us with a long, scornful stare before springing silently up the bank to melt into the mist in the wake of his band.

I remember that after he vanished we stayed where we were, listening, for at least a minute. But though in general langurs on the move can crash through the branches with as much noise as a gang of football fans on the rampage, the misty silence remained unbroken. Apart from the breathing of our panic-stricken governess we could hear no other sound, and abandoning our walk we turned with one accord and hurried back home to Oaklands.

I don't remember anything much about that governess. But neither Bets nor I have ever forgotten our encounter with the King Kong of the forest. And when I hear people doubting the existence of creatures like the Abominable Snowman, and speaking scornfully of travellers' tales and the gullible fools who believe them, I remember the thousands upon thousands of square miles of unexplored rhododendron forest that clothe the lower slopes of the Himalayan ranges, and the sea of wrinkled plush that spreads away in wave upon wave up to the snowline and is in reality made up of billions of trees among which man has barely penetrated. There are, or there were then, few paths and no metalled roads through that trackless wilderness; so who knows how many species hitherto unknown to man are lurking there? After all, no one believed in the giant panda until comparatively recently, and the skins that were brought back from the Far East were pronounced fakes. There could be hundreds of unknown birds, beasts and plants in those vast, untrodden forests, waiting for those who dare to 'enter these enchanted woods' ...

The other frightening incident that I remember from our halcyon days at Oaklands also took place on a misty afternoon during the monsoon. A clutch of baby ducklings whose mother had been carried off by a hill fox had been brought into the house to be hand-reared by us, and that day we had put them into a wooden box, lined with flannel, which we pushed under the window-seat of our dining-room for safety. But sometime during the afternoon a wild cat crept into the room through the door leading into a short covered passageway that ended in the kitchen quarters, where the outer door had been left ajar. There had been no rain that day, but the mist that lay thick on the hillsides stole into the house through every crack and cranny, and by the time we returned from our afternoon walk the day had become so dark that Abdul Karim was already lighting the lamps as Bets and I rushed into the dining-room to peer at the baby ducklings. The box was empty. The little quacking balls of yellow fluff had gone and there were bloodstains on the flannel; and when Abdul, in answer to our howls of woe, came hurrying in with a lamp, we saw that there were drops of blood on the carpet and along the passageway and on the kitchen floor, while on the path outside lay one dead and mangled duckling; presumably dropped by its killer on hearing us arrive back from our walk.

The wild cat, emboldened by the mist, must have been prospecting for scraps outside the kitchen door, and lured by the cheeping of the ducklings, found its way into the dining-room and polished off the entire brood. We didn't recover from the nightmare horror of that for some days. I suppose it was the bloodstains and the fact that it was such a dark and misty day that made us keep on picturing that wild cat creeping into our own familiar house and clawing out those poor, helpless little balls of fluff one by one ... There can only have been just room for it to insert a paw between the top of the box and the underside of the window-seat; yet it had caught all of them. We liked cats. But wild cats, with their pointed ears, their fierce yellow eyes and ferocious faces, were something quite different: creatures of the dark forest and, like leopards, savage and frightening.

There were times when, lying in bed and listening to the karka deer barking, I would think how *safe* children in England must feel at night in a country where there were no wild animals. Not that I would ever have dreamt of changing places with them, for as far as I was concerned every inch of India was enchanted.

I cannot use 'idyllic' to describe my childhood there, because the dictionary defines that word as '*peaceful or romantically blissful scene, incident, etc*'. This is not an accurate picture of India. But then there are different shades of enchantment — just as there are two kinds of magic, black and white. I was always aware of that, and it was part of the charm that a forest that could be unbelievably beautiful on a cloudless day — green, scented, spangled with ferns and flowers and full of bird songs — could change with the mist into a shadowy world in which giant langurs could appear and disappear without sound. Or that the enormous expanse of golden, sun-burnt grass on the mountainside below the mule-track could suddenly turn hostile when something that had looked like a patch of freckled shadow thrown by a thorn bush stirred and stretched, and turned into a leopard that loped unhurriedly away along the hillside to vanish among the nearest outcrop of rock.

There were always two sides and a hundred different facets to India; and I loved and was fascinated by them all. Just as I loved the two completely different aspects of the Simla hills that depended on which way you looked at them, and from where. People who have never been there and think of Simla solely in terms of the youthful Kipling's *Plain Tales from the Hills* or *Under the Deodars* probably imagine it as densely wooded. And they are right. But only half right. For though the slopes that face north and north-east (thereby escaping the worst of the sun because by midday they are in the shade) are thick with trees, the ones facing south and south-west are parched and barren. This is because they take the furnace glare of the sun and the full blast of the hot winds that blow off the sandy wastes of the Thar and the deserts of Rajputana; and lacking shade or any defence against those hot winds, few seeds manage to sprout, and those few, with no thick mat of rotted leaves or the grappling nets of tree-roots to protect the soil and hold it in place, fall victim to erosion as the bare hillsides take the brunt of the downpour when the rain-clouds of the monsoon roll in across the plains to crash down on the Himalayas like storm-driven breakers on a reef.

It was Buckie, standing in the gardens of his beloved Dukani on the hilltop overlooking Oaklands, who first showed me that if one stood on one particular vantage-point on the lawn and looked northwards toward the snows, the enormous ranges appeared as bare as the palm of one's hand except where the shadowed sides of some outlying spur faced north; while if one crossed the lawn to another viewpoint, every hillside as far as the eye could reach was covered with forests. An all gold world or an all dark-green one. Yet both were only the two faces of the same sea of mountains. Two sides of the same coin. India ... How lucky I was to live there!

Looking back at myself as a child and realizing that young children are apt to accept anything, whether good or bad, without question, simply because they have nothing to compare it with or have not yet learnt to make comparisons, I find it strange that I should have been so strongly aware of my own good fortune. It would seem more reasonable if I had taken my surroundings and the manner in which I spent my days for granted. Yet I never did, and the only explanation I can find for this is that my first visit to my native land must have been more uncomfortable and traumatic than I supposed; even though I remember so little of it. But the cumulative effect of the necessary restrictions on board ship, the discipline of an English nursery (and more particularly, a Scottish one), the fact that my Kaye grandparents and my Aunt Molly, together with their respective household staffs, considered that 'children should be seen and not heard', the climate (which was frequently cold and wet) and the general crossness of British grown-ups who seldom if ever had the time and certainly not the inclination to sit on the floor and discuss local affairs and gossip with a child (as any member of an Indian household could be trusted to do at the drop of a hat, and without talking down either!) had been shattering enough to make me draw comparisons between the citizens, scenery and climate of the country I had been born in, and the chilly, unfamiliar and dauntingly unfriendly land that my parents persisted in referring to as 'home' — and in which I must always remember not to speak until I was spoken to!

The trees and flowers in *Belait* had lacked the flamboyance of those in India; as had the plumage of the birds and the colour and size of the butterflies. Then there were no monkeys or pi-dogs or jackals, and (this was a distinct asset) no dangerous wild animals either. But apart from that last, I had seen very little to admire in my native land and had been delighted to see India again. India never let me down; not then or later. And one of the clearest memories I have of my first rapturous homecoming is of standing in the garden of a house on Bombay's Malabar Hill, where we were staying with friends for a few days after disembarking, and seeing the fishing fleet put out to sea in a spectacular sunset — the kind you never see in Western countries. The last low rays of the sinking sun had caught their sails and made them look like a flight of pinkish-gold butterflies drifting out over the darkening water, and overhead the sky was turning green, while on Malabar Hill the trees were full of birds coming home to roost and the air smelt of jasmine and roses, and I could hear all the far-away sounds of the city drifting up from below.

Years later I was to see a duplicate of that lovely sight thousands of miles to the eastward, off the coast of North China; and once again 'it hit me where I lived' — to use an expressive phrase of my father's. Yet it is the earlier sight, that butterfly flight of sails setting out into the Indian Ocean from Bombay, seen from Malabar Hill when I was not yet five years old, that is still the clearer of the two. The other is just an echo of something that had happened before — the memory of a memory.

✗ Right up to the end of the Second World War and the Chinese invasion of Tibet, the mule-track behind Oaklands was in constant use by Tibetan traders bringing their wares to Simla. Enchanting wares, the product of a race of artists and craftsmen who worked in wood and metal and precious stones; men and women who carved, wove cloth, painted fabulous pictures on vellum, made prayer-wheels and devil-masks, sticks of incense and endless other odds and ends for which there was always a ready market in the shops and bazaars of India's summer capital. There is a marvellous description of such artefacts in *Kim,* where they form the bulk of the objects for sale in

Lurgan-Sahib's shop on the Mall. These goods were brought over the passes and along the wandering tracks through the forests and across the bare hillsides in bulging panniers slung over the backs of mules and pack-ponies; and whenever we heard the jingle of the mule-bells, Bets and I would rush out of the house and up to the crest of the ridge, and sitting on top of the dry, grass-grown bank that overlooked the track, watch the mule-train pass and call out greetings to the smiling, slant-eyed Tibetans.

The men wore long, loose robes of hand-woven wool that smelt of wood-smoke and asafoetida, thick-soled felt boots and curious duffle hats with ear-flaps that could be tied down to protect them from the cold. Their women, who walked with them (only very small children rode on the mules, while infants in arms were invariably carried on their mother's backs), were more colourful, for they wore great necklaces of silver set with coral and lumps of raw turquoise, enchanting head-dresses of black felt sewn with flat plaques of turquoise, and a species of hand-woven apron bordered with a multitude of gaily coloured stripes. They were smiling, friendly and gentle people who, being traders, spoke a certain amount of Hindustani, so that we could pass the time of day with them. And sometimes they would throw us small gifts such as a stick of incense, a tiny filigree betelnut box set with uncut garnets, or a little lump of turquoise matrix with a hole in it which one could wear on a string round one's neck, like a charm. In return we would give them whatever fruit happened to be ripe or, when there was no fruit, a flower or two from the garden, which they would sniff delightedly before tucking it behind their ear. Running up the hill to exchange pleasantries and wave to them as they went by was always a favourite pastime of ours. But it was only one of many.

There being no TV and no radio either when I was young, we had to invent our own amusements; and we were, of course, lucky enough to have a fantastically beautiful playground in which to carry out our various ploys. But when we were finally sent back to England and dispatched to a boarding-school, our holidays were spent in any number of different and very ordinary places; among them Aunt Lizzie's house in Bedford, where the garden was no more than a narrow strip of ground separated from its neighbours by a high brick wall, and backed on to a railway siding which ensured that the few horse-chestnut trees, a scattering of gloomy-looking laurel bushes and the even fewer flowers that struggled to survive in that cramped space, were all liberally coated with soot from the steam-driven trains that huffed and puffed past less than a hundred yards away. Yet this far from alluring back garden — together with a derelict house on the abandoned lot next door — provided us with endless ploys, and of all our holiday homes in England, Aunt Lizzie's was our favourite one by far.

Out at Mahasu we had no artificial, ready-made entertainment. We devised our own; which included stalking the bands of brown rhesus monkeys (we never took similar liberties with the langurs), chasing butterflies, constructing and furnishing houses for elves among the roots of pine trees, inventing stories, building tree-houses in which to play Swiss Family Robinson, weaving baskets out of dry grass stems and filling them with moss and flowers, and a hundred other activities. At least twice a week we would climb the hill path (it was little more than a goat-track) to Buckie's house, Dukani, and help — or more likely hinder — his head *mali,* Khundun, a particular friend of ours, in picking up windfalls in the orchard, sweeping the narrow gravel paths or, squatting happily on the warm, sun-baked planks that covered the water-tank, we would listen to tales of his youth and stories of the gods and demons and creatures of the hills.

Khundun's *bibi** would let us play with her latest baby or try our hand at milking the cow, and Khundun would give us handfuls of the brittle-shelled *kargassy* walnuts when they were in season. And if Buckie were in residence and not too busy, he would come out of his office and call down to us over the verandah rail to come up to have a glass of lemonade and a biscuit with him. The lower verandah was wide and shady, and all along the inner wall were narrow wooden shelves on which Khundun ranged pots of cinerarias — those heat-loving hot-house flowers which prefer the shade to direct sunlight — so that one wall of the verandah was always a blaze of colour; blue and cerise, purple and crimson. Bets and I admired them enormously, particularly the blue ones; and to this day cinerarias mean the lower verandah of Dukani to us. Just as maidenhair ferns will always mean the lower road to The Retreat; though it is the smell of maidenhair fern rather than the sight of it that is such a vivid reminder of the

* Wife.

paths through the forests. With the cinerarias, which are scentless, it is the child's-paintbox colours that remind me of the hot, shadowed verandah that looked out across the orchard towards Simla and smelt of pine wood, as did all the Mashobra houses.

Poor Buckie! He attracted children in much the same way as Tacklow attracted cats. We all loved him, and though he could be endlessly patient and good-tempered he never for a moment allowed us to impose upon him or become a nuisance. When he had had enough of us we were firmly dismissed; and we accepted dismissal without argument and with no trace of rancour; 'The King has spoken'! I did not realize at that time how unhappy his private life must have been. His second child, a son, had died in infancy and there is a moving reference to his death in one of Lady Curzon's letters to her mother, Mrs Leiter of Washington and Chicago. Writing in the autumn of 1900, she says:

Tell the girls that Mrs Buck's baby of three months — my godchild — died suddenly on Sunday through neglect of the nurse & I went down to poor Mrs Buck & actually buried the baby. There was no one but another woman & me to put the dead baby in its coffin & Captain Baker-Carr carried it downstairs. We went to the cemetery — the coffin in a rickshaw — & the Mother & Father & I & Mr Kruber a friend behind & it was the saddest, baldest, most miserable funeral.

There had been two other children; another boy, and a girl who had been crippled by polio while still a child. Both, with their mother, had been in England when Buckie first saw Dukani perched on its lonely hilltop some half-dozen miles outside Simla, fell in love with it and bought it from the Maharajah of Alwar. He was sure his wife would be as captivated by it as he was, and because he wanted to surprise her with this charming home he did not tell her about it, but spent months improving and rebuilding it, choosing furniture and curtains, having it painted and wallpapered in the colours she liked best, and setting Khundun and his assistants to work making a superb lawn and garden, planting fruit trees, digging a tank and cutting winding paths through the woods that clothed the northern slope of his hilltop. Everything was in apple-pie order by the time Annie Buck arrived and he brought her up to Simla and took her out along the Mashobra Road to surprise her with the home he had made for her.

She was surprised all right. But unpleasantly so. She hated it on sight. Not because she had any fault to find with the house or the gardens, the wonderful views from every window or the way in which the rooms had been furnished. In all those aspects it was near perfect. But if Buckie thought she was going to live in such an isolated, back-of-beyond spot as Mashobra, miles from the social life and gaiety of Simla, he could think again! Nothing would *induce* her to live stranded out here on the edge of nowhere, so the sooner he sold Dukani and acquired a house in Simla the better. It was a bitter blow to Buckie, but since 'Annie B' (the name she was known by throughout half India) stood firm, there was nothing for it but to rent another house; which he did, though he was never to sell Dukani for he had become too fond of it. He continued to spend as much time as possible there, and the weekend parties he held at Dukani became famous; though they hardly ever included his wife, whom he kept from going there. I don't remember meeting either of his two children during the war years, or even knowing that they existed, so I presume they had both been left behind in England; the boy at a public school and little crippled Lorna in the care of relatives.

Since Annie B was crazy about horses and had no time to bother about anything else, the crippled child was brought up to think that horses were the most important thing in life, and though almost immobile on the ground, once lifted onto a horse's back and settled into a side-saddle, she learnt to ride by balance alone and became an accomplished horsewoman and a 'bruising rider to hounds'. I don't think Buckie saw much of her when she was little, or of his much-loved eldest son either, since his work tied him to India. But when the war broke out his boy, barely old enough to enlist, joined up, and like so many youthful Second-Lieutenants was killed almost at once on the Western Front. Perhaps that was why Buckie was so good with children, though at the time I had no idea that he had lost two sons and had a sorely crippled daughter.

Whenever I think of Mashobra, which is often, I see it basking in bright sunlight. But in fact for at least half of the time, if not more, it was smothered in clouds and hidden under a pall of rain. Delhi, in those pre-fridge and air-conditioning days, became too hot for comfort by the middle of April, so it was then that the Government of India made its stately and cumbersome trek up to Simla. Spring in Simla, with the cuckoos calling and the hillsides awash with wild balsam and lily-of-the-valley, was marvellously cool after the hot winds and dust-storms of the plains, while the pine-scented breezes that blew off the snows seemed like heaven to the parched refugees from the heat. May and June were wonderful months; but towards the end of June all India waited for the arrival of the monsoon, and when at last it swept in from the sea, telegrams would go out to carry the news to every part of the Indian subcontinent, for it was easy to calculate how long it would take to travel northward.

Once it hit Bombay we could be fairly certain when it would reach Simla. And after the first downpour we knew more or less where we were and how long it would last, for there was a pattern to the monsoon; it was not all swirling mist and drenching rain. The initial tidal wave of water would be followed by a long period when the sun would rise every day in a cloudless sky above a thoroughly washed world in which every leaf and twig and blade of grass glittered with raindrops and the far snows looked so near and so clear that it almost seemed as though you could spit a cherry-stone at them and score a hit. On those days Bets and I would walk down Oaklands' long drive as far as the Mahasu bazaar with Tacklow, the rickshaw following behind in case we should wish to ride back (a ridiculous idea, as who, at that age, would not prefer to walk?), and having seen him off on his five-mile hike to his office, we would spend half-an-hour or so chatting to various friends in the bazaar before making our way home in the full blaze of the morning sunlight. And every day without fail we would see, as we walked back up the drive, a little cloud no bigger than a dandelion clock in the waste of blue. It grew with incredible speed until by the time we reached the house it would have covered a third of the sky. Half an hour later the orchard trees would have been swallowed up by the encroaching mist, and within minutes the whole world would be grey and even the tubs of blue agapanthus lilies, that stood a bare eight feet from the verandah's edge, would have vanished. Then the rain would come down again and for the rest of the day we lived with the sound of water drumming steadily on the corrugated tin of the roof.

There were many breaks during the rains. Sometimes for as long as a week and sometimes for only a day or two. The rain-washed air was as clear and as brilliant as a table-cut diamond and the world was full of birds and butterflies, and the scent of flowers and pines and wet grass, and one could see every ridge and wrinkle and glacier among the high snows. Not until the first tree fern died did one know that the monsoon was nearly over. But although there were never enough breaks, and in general the monsoon lasted from the end of June until mid-September, Oaklands and Mashobra stay for ever in my mind in sunlight. Hot, bright, glorious sunlight ...

✳ Mother became worried about our lack of schooling and imported a governess. Two, in fact. One after the other. The first one was young and the second middle-aged. The young one, who was always remembered in the family as 'Miss Violets' because she had a passion for the colour, wore no other shade, drenched herself in cheap violet scent and stunned my poor parents on her first night at Oaklands by sailing down to dinner (which was never more than a light supper) in full evening dress with bunches of artificial violets tucked into the brass-gold waves of her hair. My parents had not expected her to join them, for she had her own sitting-room and was well aware that arrangements had been made for her to take her evening meal there; and they themselves never dressed for supper unless there were guests. Mother explained, for the second time, that although as our governess she would take her breakfast, lunch and tea with us in the dining-room, once the children were in bed there was no need for her to join her employers at dinner, which was a meal that Tacklow, after a hard day at the office, liked to eat *tête-à-tête* with his wife whenever he got the chance. Miss Violets retorted haughtily that she was accustomed to being treated as one of the family and had never before been asked to eat alone in her sitting-room. And telling the *khidmatgar* to lay another place for her, she plumped herself firmly down at the table.

She might have got away with it if she had not insisted on keeping up a non-stop flow of exceedingly genteel chat throughout the meal, which almost succeeded in driving poor Tacklow round the bend. It was more than he could bear, and when she again swept haughtily into the dining-room on the following night (this time in a mass of violet-tinted organdie frills and even more violets in her hair and at her waist) and never drew breath except to do a bit of chewing, he insisted on Mother taking a stand. Mother, deeply embarrassed, took one, and Miss Violets, losing her gentility and her temper, took offence, packed her two trunks, three suitcases and a couple of hatboxes, and flounced out. She made quite a procession of it, according to Mother, who says she had to hire an extra rickshaw and two coolies to convey Miss Violets and her belongings back to Simla only two days after paying for two rickshaws and two coolies to bring her out. I remember that Bets and I hung out of a window in the top verandah and, like the ranks of Tuscany, 'could scarce forbear to cheer'! We hadn't liked what little — very little — we had seen of Miss Violets.

The next governess was a good deal older and lasted a good deal longer, but I can't recall her teaching us anything. In fact if it had not been for Tacklow reading us books at bedtime and giving us such an appetite for stories that we could both read from an early age, I imagine that we would have acquired no education at all. Presumably Governess Number 2 taught us a smattering of arithmetic, geography, history and scripture (though of the two last, I owe my interest in the former to Tacklow and had already received a sound grounding in the latter from Mother). But whatever else she did or did not teach us, she was certainly a disciplinarian and the time-table she drew up for us was strictly adhered to. She kept our noses firmly to the grindstone, which was no doubt very good for us; but her chief drawback in our eyes was that she was continually losing her voice. Not completely, worse luck, since she could always manage to talk to us in a perfectly audible whisper, but enough to prevent her calling out to us to come in from the garden. We were therefore restricted during our leisure hours to playing on the small lawn onto which the nursery window looked, and nowhere else. She could keep an eye on us there, and when play-time was up she would lean out and clap her hands to summon us inside. We were never allowed to move out of earshot of that sound. Or out of eyeshot either!

I don't know how long she stayed with us, but it seemed like years, while to her it must have seemed like centuries, since the poor woman must have been bored rigid. There was no social life for her at all, so far outside Simla. No friends, no one to talk to but a couple of kids who until her arrival had been allowed to run wild and resented their lack of freedom under her rule. The thing I remember most about her reign is the sheer bliss of being able to race about the garden again after she left — down to the pond and the orchard and the tennis court, and up to the mule track and across the hillsides and along the forest paths. We had been barred from all of them for so long that we had almost forgotten what they looked like.

One of the high-spots of that year occurred while Sir Charles Cleveland was spending a long weekend with us. He told us that a very august personage, the Rajah of Bhong, would be calling at Oaklands in order to take tea with him and our parents, and that if we were *very* good we might even be allowed to meet him! But he was a very shy person who disliked crowds and large parties and hated to be stared at by strangers, because he happened to be a dwarf. However, he was very nice and with luck he might agree to see us. We were thrilled to bits, and when we came in from our walk that afternoon we went straight up to our bedroom to change into our best clothes and listen excitedly for the sound of his arrival — we had been warned against being seen peering out of the windows.

Mother hurried upstairs to tell us that Tacklow and Sir Charles had left to meet His Highness on the road and escort him to the house, but that unfortunately he had come by the upper road and missed them, and that as he could not stay long and they were still waiting for him somewhere on the lower road, he would be pleased to see us now. So down we went — and sure enough, there he was! A tiny little man with an enormous head and a long beard, wearing a huge turban and lots of jewellery, and standing on the velvet-draped table in front of the curtained door that led out of the drawing-room into Tacklow's office; which put him more on the level with an ordinary grown-up.

He was the greatest fun! Mother told us to curtsey to him and be on our best behaviour, and he could not have been more friendly and amusing. He cracked jokes that made us double up with laughter, kept on pulling his ear or scratching his head, which nearly made his turban fall off, sang a song for us in a high falsetto voice and actually did a little dance for us, rather like a clog dance except that he was wearing gold-embroidered shoes with long, curled-up toes. He gave us a box of Turkish Delight, and then suddenly said he was feeling tired and would like to take a little nap. We *begged* him not to go before our father and Sir Charles came back, and told him how much we had enjoyed meeting him, and after we had said goodbye and curtsied to him again Mother shoved us out of the room and up to the nursery. Later on we heard Tacklow's and Sir Charles's voices talking to him in the drawing-room and a lot of laughter, and were delighted to know that they had not missed seeing the enchanting little Rajah.

We talked about him for days afterwards, and it was not until we had both reached the dignity of double figures that we learnt — even then with almost total disbelief! — that the Rajah had been Sir Charles using his hands for feet in those golden, curl-toed shoes, while the animated arms and those restless, expressive hands that kept on almost knocking his turban off and rescuing it just in time, belonged to Tacklow who was standing behind him, hidden by the curtain ... To tell you the truth, we would both have preferred not to know, for they had worked the trick so well that we would have been prepared to swear that we had seen a real person who was self-conscious about being a dwarf and did not like people to come too near him or stare too closely — an attitude we had every sympathy with. But that half-hour still remains like a bright scrap of gold tinsel in my mental rag-bag.

Chapter 13

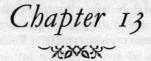

'Hey! diddle-de-dum! An actor's life is fun!'
Collodi, *Pinocchio*

He said: 'I look for butterflies' . . .
Carroll, *Through the Looking Glass*

I can only suppose that the beautiful and indefatigable Mrs Strettle of the children's dancing-classes was responsible for dreaming up and producing the patriotic piece of flag-waving-cum-fund-raising that was known as 'The Pageant'. Because her entire flock seems to have taken part in it.

This oddly named mixture of mime and dance had originally been intended as a Grand Finale to a day-long Garden Fête in aid of the war effort. The Fête was to be held in the grounds of Viceregal Lodge, where there were several lawns (three of them, on different levels, providing an ideal setting for The Pageant), and I believe it was a great success. But shortly before our show was due to begin, the weather went back on us and rain stopped play, forcing us to do our stuff in the State Ballroom instead, with only the inadequate help of a platform on which the Viceroy and his more high-ranking guests were expected to sit in overstuffed chairs and sofas during the intervals between dances at Viceregal balls.

The entire performance must have been incomprehensible to the paying customers, because there should by rights have been two stages; an upper and a lower one (Earth below and a sort of other-worldly Elysium on the upper). But since there had been no time to construct a split-level platform, Earth, the audience and the Viceroy's band were all on the same level, and so inextricably mixed up that I doubt if even those who managed to get seats in the front row caught more than an occasional glimpse of the action — just enough, I imagine, to make them wonder what the heck was going on. However, despite this initial setback (or possibly because of it?) The Pageant was considered good enough to be repeated and was subsequently put on for a proper run, complete with matinées, at Simla's Gaiety Theatre. A double stage was built for the occasion, and *Hi! diddle-de-dee!* — we were off!

The upper stage, which was small and narrow, had a net curtain stretched tightly across it so that the characters inhabiting this cloud-cuckoo-land appeared faintly hazy and unreal. As well they might, considering that they were representing such abstractions as Peace, Plenty, Love, Courage, and so on, played by grown-ups draped like Greek goddesses in yards of white cheesecloth, who, when the curtain rose, were discovered lolling around on grassy banks apparently sound asleep. The lower and much larger stage, minus any net screens, was supposed to represent a portion of the world; and bang in the middle of it, leaning negligently on a plaster pillar that supported a model of a battleship, stood Britannia in the person of Mrs Brocas-Howell, holding a trident in one hand and a large shield painted with a Union Jack in the other.

This sharp-tongued and short-tempered lady was draped in yet another seven yards of cheesecloth topped, if memory serves, by a brassière made of overlapping tin scales and a helmet that looked distressingly like a brass coal-scuttle. Other grown-ups, representing France (another coal-scuttle), Belgium, the Netherlands, Egypt, Greece and Serbia (hands up who remembers Serbia*) and possibly a few more countries, stood dotted about the stage, each with a group of children wearing the appropriate national costume sitting at their feet. Bets and I were little Belgians (not, as one would suppose from the photographs, little Netherlanders). Bargie was a junior Greek, while a kid called Barbara Jacomb-Hood, who was the star pupil of our dancing-class, was little Egypt; solo. The rest of us were in groups of four or more.

The curtain rose on a scene of sweetness and light; Britannia beaming at her battleship and everyone smiling from ear to ear as one after another the little Britons, French, Belgians *et al.*, got up and performed their national dances before exiting L. or R. to great applause —

* It looks as though we may all do so, soon!

183

leaving the mother-countries in possession of the stage. I don't know why we all detested 'Britannia'. I only remember that we did and that she started it. But by the time The Pageant had run its course she must have detested us with equal fervour, for it became a point of honour with us that as each set of child dancers pranced off into the wings, gaily waving to the audience, they would do their best to knock against her shield or upset her column and boat. The trick was to do it so that it looked like an accident; which in the circumstances was not difficult, since we merely pretended that we couldn't wave at the paying customers and watch where we were going at the same time. So poor Britannia had a rough ride, and in retrospect, serve her right! It never pays to be rude to children.

During all this jolly national-dancery the upper stage remained in darkness. But no sooner had the last of the kindergarten element gone waving off into the wings than the lights came slowly up on the Elysian Fields, and, to the strains of the Viceroy's band playing Mendelssohn, the cheesecloth goddesses awoke from their slumbers and began to wander gracefully around with their arms about each other's waists, smiling down approvingly on the lower deck, where Britannia had laid down her trident and shield and was idly tinkering with her ship, while France (or was it Belgium?) operated a spinning-wheel — and so on. Then suddenly, accompanied by a crashing chord from the orchestra, on rushed an enormous uniformed Hun, spiked helmet, grey uniform, jackboots and all, who grasped poor Serbia by her flowing locks (her own hair too, not a wig, so one can safely say that the amateur actress representing that unhappy country really did 'suffer for her Art') and dragged her screaming off the stage. Reappearing in two ticks he weighed in on Belgium and the Netherlands (one in each hand) and, throwing them to the ground, took a slash or two at them with his sabre before turning his attentions to France.

At this point Peace, Plenty, Justice, etc., becoming aware of the fracas, started to run to and fro behind their mosquito net and make gestures indicative of alarm and disapproval. Peace flung herself on her knees before an angel who I think must have been St Michael (a Mr Someone; wings, white butter-muslin and tinfoil armour), who was finally persuaded to unsheath the sword that he wore hanging from a belt, and wave it threateningly at the lower orders, who were instantly blacked out; thus allowing the various countries, prone as well as upright, to scurry off unseen into the wings with their props (battleship, spinning-wheel, and so on) leaving the stage clear for four small girls, Sybil Roberts, Iris Mant, Iris Gillian and one other whose name escapes me, to do the Dance of the Four Winds to the tune of Schubert's 'Moment Musicale'. Even now I never hear that played without getting an instant mental vision of four small, bare-footed figures, wearing minute ragged tunics of pale green, grey and blue chiffon, cross-strapped in the Greek manner with silver ribbon, pretending to play on silver pan-pipes as they skip to and fro in a sort of square dance. I can even remember some of the steps, though I don't remember a single step, or the tune either, of the dance that Bets and I did as 'baby Belgians'. Nor had I, then or now, any idea how the Four Winds got into the act. Could they perhaps have been summoning help from the Empire?

I don't remember how The Pageant ended. The real war was still going strong at the time, so Peace, Plenty and the rest of the cheesecloth brigade, not to mention poor Serbia, could only keep their fingers crossed. I suppose that the real St Michael, who was presumably in the confidence of the Almighty, must have known what was going to happen. But everyone else could only hope and pray; and would go on doing so for at least another year. I do remember that the villain of the piece, the Hun, was still on his feet in the final tableau — tottering, no doubt, but still upright and able to take his bows. This unpopular character had been played with considerable zing by Sir Charles Cleveland's younger brother, after Sir Charles himself had backed out. It had been hoped that he would play the Hun, for not only did he possess the physique of a champion heavyweight boxer in his prime, plus a strong resemblance to a truculent bulldog, but he was judged to be 'the ugliest man in Simla' — or it may have been 'in India'? Unfortunately Sir Charles, who had originally been in favour of playing the part, overheard a fellow member of the United Services Club repeating that last observation, and took umbrage and cried off. A great pity, as he would have played it to perfection and he cannot possibly have had any illusions about his looks. Or his charms either! His mistresses were legion — Britannia being the most notorious, though naturally I did not learn this until years later: together with the story of how that particular and carefully concealed liaison was discovered . . .

It seems that Sir Charles had invited the lady to join a large shooting camp at which her husband would be unable to be present. She accepted and was given a single tent well away from his, and during the daylight hours they sedulously avoided each other's company. But alas, among the guests there was an unkind humorist who one night took the trouble to sneak out and sweep the sand clear between the tents as soon as the last guest had retired to bed. And sure enough, there in the morning as the guests assembled for breakfast, lay a clear line of footprints leading from Sir Charles's tent to Britannia's and back again. Everyone seems to have regarded this as screamingly funny — with the exception of the host and his inamorata and, when he heard of it, the lady's husband, who was furious. But *furious!* The repercussions, I gather, were endless.

From a child's point of view all this patriotic 'in-aid-of' acting and dancing was tremendous fun, since all children, and a great many grown-ups, get a kick out of dressing-up. I certainly did, though I continued to dislike parties, fancy-dress ones included, of which there were a good many. One of these was an Advertisement Party at Viceregal Lodge to which we were all expected to go dressed up as well-known advertisements. Bets went dressed up as the girl on the Erasmic Soap boxes while I went as the one on somebody's tin of talcum powder — I forget whose. Another was a Down-on-the-Farm Party at Peterhof, for which Mother dressed us as dairy-maids in identical dresses and sunbonnets of checked cotton, mine blue and Bets's pink, with white aprons and fichus and armed, if I remember rightly, with a pail apiece.

There was only one children's party that I really enjoyed, and that was a Pink Party given to celebrate the birthday of a girl called Phyllis Moncrieff-Smith whose mother, a truly awe-inspiring woman who looked as though she had been hewn out of a solid block of marocain, obviously had more imagination than one would have given her credit for. All the little guests were asked to wear either pink or white trimmed with pink — a request that aroused considerable hostility among the boys but was fine for the girls — and the rooms in which the party was held were decorated in pink. Everything we ate was either pink or white, and instead of all those excruciating party games (how I loathed them!) or a conjuror or magic-lantern show, we were all issued with large pink aprons and white chefs' caps, given a bag containing a pound of icing sugar, a pastry board and a rolling pin, a bowl and a set of little tin pastrycutters, a bottle of peppermint essence and another of cochineal, and told to make sweets — fondants or peppermint creams, with a prize for the one who produced the best batch. It was enormous fun, like making really glorious mud pies. And we could not only eat the result but take home any that were left over to show off to our parents, neatly packaged in pink paper bags provided by Phyllis's mum. That party kept about thirty children gloriously happy, sticky and occupied for a full two hours or more, and stands out in my memory as the only large birthday party in Simla that I really enjoyed.

On the theatrical side, I have a foggy memory of another 'in-aid-of' song, dance and tableaux show at the Gaiety Theatre in which Bargie and young Tony took part; Tony appearing (under protest) in another of the tableaux, starkers, or very nearly so, as Cupid. Mother and some of her contemporaries sang a song about, '*To Peru we'll hunt the kangaroo, the elephant and the bumble-bee, so pack up your traps and come with me; the newt we'll shoot* — ', etc. It's odd how, if a tune sticks, the words that go with it stick too. A whole raft of First World War songs still stick in my head; no doubt taking up valuable room that should have been used for the storage of more useful items.

Bets and I must have spent a lot of time coming into Simla for rehearsals, performances, or children's parties during our years at Oaklands. And once, in company with Bargie and a few of our friends, we gave a special performance of The Pageant, taking all the parts between us (Peace, Plenty, St Michael-or-whoever, the Hun, Britannia — the lot!) in Buckie's drawing-room at Dukani before an indulgent audience of grown-ups. We enjoyed that even more than the real Pageant I think, as it gave us a marvellous opportunity to show off: though I suspect that the performance must have been a fairly tedious experience for the spectators.

That was a lovely summer! The 'Butterfly Summer' ... I did not know then that it would be our last at Oaklands. Durroo caught a huge black-and-gold one the size of a saucer with my topi. And a small, thin, elderly man called Professor Something-or-other, whom Tacklow said was a world authority on butterflies, came out from Simla to spend a weekend with us during a break in the rains. He was travelling through India in search of new specimens, and Tacklow took him out to Fargu, which lies beyond Dane's Folly on the road to Kulu and Tibet and is famous for its butterflies. But though the hillsides were shimmering with them, the Professor remained unimpressed: they were all ones that he was familiar with — 'common' green-and-gold minauls; yellow or black-and-red swallow-tails; blue-and-black 'window-pane' butterflies; potato butterflies (monarchs), and scores of others. (Those, by the way, are not their proper names but the ones we always called them by.) That was on a Saturday. On the Sunday the Professor went butterfly-hunting in the grounds of Oaklands and was equally unimpressed by the lovely lilting specimens that were taking the air that day. Then suddenly, returning crossly from a foray onto the upper lawn, he spied a very boring-looking butterfly investigating the agapanthus lilies and gave a shrill yell of excitement; an '*I think I've got it! By jove I've got it!*' sort of yell that brought Tacklow up at the double.

Bets and I couldn't think what there was to get so excited about. The butterfly wasn't even a nice colour. It was a sort of dirty white and quite small; a bit smaller than a cabbage white and with rather tattered-looking wings. However, it was evidently something new and special, for even Tacklow was excited, and the Professor's expression as he stalked it, net in hand, was enough to tell even an eight-year-old that this was on a par with finding a real live unicorn nibbling the roses in one's garden. We all held our breath as he advanced, wild-eyed and on tip-toe with his net at the ready. But just as he was about to make his swoop, the butterfly decided against the agapanthus and sailed off — the Professor in hot pursuit.

For the next half-hour it led him an exhausting dance up and down the garden, around the orchard and back again, until eventually, getting bored with the garden, it started off down the drive, lilting carelessly through the freckled shadows and pausing here and there, tantalizingly, to inspect a flower or a blade of grass before sailing on again. When at last it reached the pond it rested for ages on a bough of a tree that overhung the water and was well out of reach of the Professor's net; sunning itself and lazily opening and shutting its wings in a provocative manner.

Bets, Tacklow and I, who by now were losing interest in the chase, subsided onto the sunny bank on the near side of the pond to chew grass-stems and watch Quacky-Jack and the other ducks dabbling about in the water. Eventually Tacklow dispatched the *chokra* who kept an eye on the ducks up to the house with a message for Mother, who presently appeared with the *khidmatgar* and a few helpers bearing a picnic lunch which we ate beside the pond. Not that the Professor ate much. He was too busy keeping both eyes on that butterfly, and when at last it took off and came down to have a closer look at the water, he scrambled to his feet with such haste that he put his foot in the potato salad — or was it a fruit salad? — anyway, something messy in a glass bowl that broke. Bets and I thought this was excruciatingly funny, but Mother was not amused: she had been fond of that bowl. I don't think the Professor even noticed. He was off on the trail like a bloodhound, and that wretched butterfly led him several times round the pond, in and out of the shallow water at the edge and always just out of reach, until finally it drifted out across the water and came to rest on the back of one of the ducks. Its baffled pursuer hesitated on the brink, aware that if he waded in the duck would certainly swim away from him, and he had taken a cautious step into the water, soaking his boots, socks and the bottom of his trousers in pond water and duckweed, when the big drake sailed up and snapped the butterfly off the duck's back as he passed.

The Professor was absolutely furious and it was the first and only time I have ever seen anyone literally dance with rage. He actually took his hat off (it was the regulation topi) and threw it on the ground and jumped up and down on it, shouting the while a good many words that I had never heard before and hastened to add to my vocabulary; though sadly, Tacklow vetoed their use before I had a chance to try them out (he also ticked us off for laughing, and when I pointed out that he had laughed himself, he admitted it and said: 'But not out loud'!). The Professor returned to Simla by rickshaw with his damp boots, socks and slacks in a bundle in the back, and still in such a bad temper that Mother complained that he gave the impression of thinking that the whole affair from start to finish was a put-up job solely designed to upset him, and that she personally had trained that drake to eat rare butterflies off the backs of other ducks — and possibly imported the butterfly in the first place!

Bets and I, who had rolled about laughing and thought the potato/ fruit salad episode even funnier than Charlie Chaplin or the Keystone

Cops, were grateful that it was the big drake and not our beloved Quacky-Jack who had gobbled up the 'unique specimen', and the day of the Great Butterfly Hunt passed into family history.

There were swallows too at Oaklands. Every year several pairs of them built their mud nests high up against the wall of the lower verandah, and it was sometime during the Butterfly Summer that Tacklow and Mother, returning late one night from some official Simla dinner-party in the pelting downpour of the monsoon rains with the thunderstorm raging overhead, saw by the light of the solitary oil lamp that had been left burning for them in the hall that there was a lidless biscuit-tin on the hall table with something alive in it. Six baby swallows! Someone had bedded them down on a bit of flannel on the bottom of the tin, and Mother said they all opened their beaks hopefully when she peered down at them. The nest had fallen a few hours earlier and Alum Din, finding it lying on the wet verandah in the dark, had scooped up the baby birds and carefully deposited them in the flannel-lined tin which he had left on the hall table where it was bound to catch the Sahib's eye when he returned. Well, there was nothing they could do about it at that hour, but Tacklow was up at dawn to nail a hastily constructed wooden box (made by the *mali*) to the spot where the nest had been and pop the babies into it, tin and all.

The parent birds, who throughout these proceedings had been whizzing to and fro twittering hysterically, did not, as we feared, refuse to go near this modern-style jerry-built bungalow, but were back again and busily feeding their young within minutes of the jerry-builders quitting the verandah. What's more, when that lot were fledged, the parents brought up a second brood in the box. And were possibly quite happy to use it again next year. But alas! in the following spring we were no longer there to see our swallows return, for all good times, like all good things, have a sad habit of coming to an end, and inevitably a day came when we had to leave Oaklands and say goodbye to our friends in the bazaar and from Tibet, to all our favourite places, and move back into Simla. This time into a house called The Rookery. Strangers moved into Oaklands, and though we often came out at the weekend to eat Sunday lunch at Dukani, or to spend a day with Sybil at The Bower, we never had occasion to visit Oaklands again. Not until many years later; long after India became independent.

⚘ The Rookery could never improve on Oaklands. But at least it was nearer Bargie and many of our friends and contemporaries, whom we had seen only at odd intervals and could now, if we chose, see almost every day. The house itself was larger than Oaklands and, like a majority of Simla's houses, had been built on a flat piece of ground hacked out of the mountainside and buttressed from below by a high, solid and almost perpendicular wall of stone which prevented the whole thing from sliding downhill on a landslide during some particularly heavy monsoon. It had little or no garden: just a wide, gravelled terrace edged by stout wooden railings that kept one from falling over the wall onto the steep slope of ground below, which in summer and autumn was a wilderness of pink and white cosmos flowers. The tree-covered heights of Jakko which rose steeply up behind it fell even more steeply away below, so that standing on the top verandah you could see, ahead and to left and right, all Simla laid out at your feet. And on clear evenings after rain, during breaks in the monsoon, you could see the golden carpet of the plains.

In the woods behind there were numerous tracks (one could hardly call them paths) zig-zagging up between the tree-trunks and the huge outcrops of fern-draped, moss-covered rocks. Some of these were made by men — woodcutters, charcoal-burners and the like — and others by the forest creatures. Bets and I came to know every track, and one of our favourite ploys was to stalk the bands of *bandar-log* — monkey folk; not the grey, black-faced langurs of Mashobra, but the ordinary brown monkeys who swarm in Simla and are fed by the priests of their temple on Jakko. This was always an exciting sport because we never quite knew when one of the band would take exception to being stalked and turn on us, grunting and chattering and baring its teeth in rage.

I have a soft spot for these thievish, flea-ridden brown layabouts, and a long while later we were to have one of our own. But in those days I was always quite scared of them and I paid only one visit to the Monkey Temple. The sight of so many of them swarming around and on top of the little whitewashed, tin-roofed shrine, bickering and fighting with each other, and the feel of the cold, muscular little hands that snatched the biscuits and grain that I had brought with me, or tugged at my skirts and pulled my hair when I had nothing left to give them, was distinctly unnerving. Besides, quite apart from the risk of hydrophobia, a monkey's bite can be very painful. Their priest rescued me from their attentions; scolding his furry congregation and apologizing for their behaviour. But once was enough, and I never went there again; though it didn't stop me stalking them along the hillsides and among the rocks. Simla without monkeys is unthinkable. They swarmed there, and the din that they made leaping and scampering along our corrugated tin roofs became as familiar as the drumming of the rain during the monsoon. So familiar that one ceased to hear it.

Most of the houses had wire netting over the windows to keep the monkeys out. But sooner or later one of the doors leading out on to the verandahs would be left open, and the next thing you would see would be a monkey springing around a bedroom with its hands and face smothered with Mother's face-powder, or fleeing from the dining-room, liberally coated with castor sugar or guava jelly and clutching a stolen table-napkin that had caught its fancy. Gangs of them raided the orchards or tore off the heads of the roses in the gardens. They snatched the wares from the open-fronted shops in the bazaar — particularly the grain and fruit shops — chased each other, fighting, through the streets of the town, or sat in companionable family groups on railings and rooftops, crooning to their babies or carefully searching each other for fleas, lice or other parasites which, when captured, they would examine with interest and then eat. They did a lot of damage and were a major pest. But Simla would not have been Simla without them, and their presence was an integral part of my childhood.

For a very brief period, only one term, Bets and I were pupils at Auckland House, a coeducational school — which was something of a rarity in those days when the sexes were strictly segregated. The school took its name from the man for whom the house had been built, Lord Auckland, who with his sister Emily had occupied the house during the summers of 1838 and 1839, almost twenty years before the Mutiny. At that time it had been known as Government House, but later on it became a boarding-house, then a hotel, and finally, in 1868, a girls' school which almost half a century later had gone coeducational.

Bets and I detested the idea of going to school. Any school! We had successfully dodged it for a long time, but now we found ourselves caught in the net, and every day we were taken by rickshaw to what we regarded as a prison house. Desks, time-tables, lecturing, hectoring teachers and lessons, lessons, lessons. Our lovely carefree days were over. We bore it because we had to. The verdict had gone out and there was no escape. But it proved easy enough to cajole our *jhampanis* into letting us get out of the rickshaw and walk as soon as we neared the Lakkar bazaar, where we had any number of friends with whom we would pause to pass the time of day, plus acquaintances who would turn a blind eye when, in the manner of the *bandar-log*, we filched a handful of roast *chunna* (gram) from the baskets of the grain-merchants. It was always *chunna* and never anything else; and looking back to those times I imagine that the sweet things — *halwa* and *jellabies* for which I also have a fatal weakness — were too sticky to snatch and conceal. But I have never outgrown my fondness for roast *chunna,* and for some strange reason the *chunna* one paid for never tasted half as good as the *chunna* one snatched on the sly!

True to its name, the Lakkar bazaar (*lakkri** means wood) was where most of the workers-in-wood had their shops: the master crafts-men who could turn a section of oak, pine, sycamore, rosewood or walnut into innumerable charming artefacts. The carvers and joiners; the menders and makers of furniture, toys, ornaments, pipes and walking-sticks. They could all be found there, and the whole bazaar always smelt deliciously of sawdust and pine wood. It was there that the road divided; its left-hand fork plunging steeply down the Lakkar Bazaar Hill while the right went on through the main bazaar towards the Commander-in-Chief's house, Snowdon, and beyond that to San-jowli and Mashobra and, eventually, Tibet. The steep left-hand fork was lined for several hundred yards by shops purveying different merchandise; flimsy buildings, in which were sold grain, fruit, veg-etables and sweetmeats, cloth, medicines, brass and tin-ware, cheap trinkets and fragile glass bangles in glittering, sparkling colours that made the open-fronted shops look like Aladdin's cave. Almost every shop was a treat to the eye, for as anyone who has ever seen an Eastern bazaar will know, the wares, whether grains and spices, vegetables or fruit, are displayed in round shallow baskets that form a patchwork of vivid colours; while the bales of plain or printed materials, piled one on another, wall the cloth-merchants' shops with stripes and

* Pronounced 'Luck-er' and 'luck-ree'.

blocks of every shade and hue — shocking-pink, cerise, scarlet and emerald predominating.

Bets and I never rode in our rickshaw down the Lakkar Bazaar Hill; we ran down it instead. The incline always seemed to us to be nearly perpendicular, so we had to run very fast in order to keep from falling over. We would race the hordes of small children who hang around any bazaar; barking pi-dogs enthusiastically joining in, Punj-ayah scolding fruitlessly far in the rear, and the grinning *jhampanis* holding well back so as not to be run away with by the weight of the rickshaw. At the time it did not occur to me that the kids who raced with us were a cross-section of India; not only as to religion and sect but ranging from ragged little beggar-brats to the sons and daughters of affluent merchants who could have bought out our parents ten times over. For like Kipling's Kim, we too 'consorted on terms of perfect equality' with the small boys of the bazaar: and with the small girls too.

What chiefly shocked poor Punj-ayah about this was that we would race either bare-footed or in our socks, because we learned early that stout strap shoes were all very well for walks on the Mall and at school, but a grave handicap when it came to pelting flat-out down an exceedingly steep hill. If we'd kept our shoes on we would never have won a single race, whereas without them we would occasionally defeat the competition; which was no ordinary triumph, since it was formidable. Even Punj-ayah, for all her disapproval, was pleased when I won and felt that I had done something to uphold the *izzat** of the Away Team.

Our days at Auckland House, together with those races down the Lakkar Bazaar Hill, were brief. The school was strictly for the children of Europeans, which naturally included a very large proportion of what were then called Eurasians, the majority of whom spoke with a lilting sing-song accent that was very like a Welsh one and was known as *chi-chi* (pronounced 'chee-chee', not 'she-she'). It had a catchy lilt that was only too easy to pick up and copy; particularly when almost all our schoolmates spoke it! I can still remember with a mixture of fascination and embarrassment the day on which our teacher made the class rise in turn and recite two lines of Tennyson's 'The Brook' and

* Honour.

194

I suddenly realized that I was the only one who was going to read it in a totally different way from my fellows — unless I deliberately copied their accent, which might give the impression that I was making fun of them ...

I had already had the mickey taken out of me on the playground for speaking in a 'lah-di-dah' voice; and anyway the teacher — who spoke broad Scots — knew perfectly well how I spoke and would think I was being gratuitously rude. However, before I could make up my mind it was my turn to rise, and I did so and stumbled through my two lines in a near inaudible mumble that earned me a sharp rebuke from the teacher and an outbreak of giggling from the rest of the class. But that poem was to save both Bets and myself from any more terms at Auckland House, for when school was over that afternoon and the day-pupils, as opposed to the boarders, left for their several homes, I gave a repeat performance to Bets of my little classmates reciting 'The Brook'. She was as fascinated by it as I had been, and it amused us so much that we took to chanting it, verse and verse about, to each other. We also, somewhat naturally, picked up a good deal of school slang and catchwords which we repeated as we had heard them spoken — in *chi-chi*.

Mother was not amused. She was, in fact, so horrified that I can only suppose that she visualized us speaking with a *chi-chi* accent for the rest of our lives; though she should have known that children can lose an accent just as easily as they can acquire one. She started correcting our pronunciation, and as soon as we realized that she was really worried we saw a way of escaping from any more terms at school by becoming more *chi-chi* than ever.

It worked! It worked like a charm. Once that term ended we did not return to Auckland House. And except in Delhi, where in future we were to spend our winters and go to classes at the house of one of Mother's friends, whose children's English governess agreed to let us join in their lessons, we had no more proper schooling until the war ended and we were taken 'home' and sent to boarding-school. Yet Tennyson's 'Brook' still stays in my memory as I first heard it recited — shrilly and at top speed: '*Chat*-ter, *chat*-ter, *lit*-ell *brook, In* this *ca*-mand *sun*-ee *weath*-er. *Men*-may come and *men*-may go, but *I* go on for *ev*-er.' The cadence is irresistible, and I am deeply grateful to it for saving me hours and weeks and months — perhaps even years — of schoolroom lessons, and for being the means of letting me spend the time instead running wild in the lovely Simla hills.

Only one other memory of Auckland House remains, and that one is connected with the playground where we were released, under strict supervision, to amuse ourselves during the half-hour break at mid-morning. There was a craze at that time for collecting cigarette cards, and the enthusiasts would bring their spare cards out, crying hopefully 'Change-ee? Change-ee?' to advertise the fact they were prepared to exchange their duplicates for ones they had not yet got in their collection. The volume of sound created by some thirty or forty kids all bleating that call at the same time was quite something: rather like nesting-time in one of those bird sanctuaries for black-backed gulls or whatever — plaintive, deafening and unforgettable.

✕ Bets and I and our particular friends continued to be obsessed by amateur theatricals, and when the members of Mrs Strettle's dancing-class were not involved in some official production directed and stage-managed by grown-ups, I would write plays and sketches which our group would perform to audiences of other children and the occasional parent: or, as often as not, merely for our own amusement. Play-acting, however, was by no means our only entertainment, and we continued to find endless sources of amusement. Even without the whole of Mashobra to play in, I still cannot remember ever having been bored — except in class. And then only by some teacher who could not be bothered to explain things clearly, so that one sat there in a fog of misapprehension. Yet even then I could amuse myself by making up stories or inventing future ploys. The Mermaids' Cave, for instance, was invented during an algebra lesson; a subject that has never made sense to me, and I have to confess that I still cannot see why X should equal anything except a kiss, a no-go sign, or simply two crossed sticks.

The Mermaids' Cave was in fact an unused *gussal-khana,* a bathroom, attached to a redundant spare bedroom on the ground floor of The Rookery, which Mother had turned into a box-room. Since the bath-room was never used, I asked if Bets and I could have it as an extra playroom and do what we liked with it. Permission being granted, we began by painting the walls and ceiling greenish-blue, using a bucket of cheap whitewash and a few packets of powdered dye which one could buy in the bazaar for a few *pi* a packet — a *pi* being a small copper coin, now long vanished, worth one twelfth of an anna, of which there were sixteen to every rupee. What an age and what a country to be young in! No wonder we felt rich when our pocket-money was one anna a week; you could buy a lot for one *pi* in the bazaar, and I remember Durroo telling me that a man and his family could live comfortably on two rupees eight annas a month. A *month!* Shades of the Vicar of Wakefield who considered himself to be 'passing rich on twenty pounds a year'.

We already owned a box of crayons, and with these we chalked fishes and underwater scenery, corals and seaweed, on the blue-green walls. Jellyfish and starfish too, and rocks with sea-anemones and crabs on them. We strewed the floor with sand wheeled out of *Mali-ji,* the gardener, collected moss-covered boulders from the hillside behind the house and piled them here and there against the walls, and, having painted more fishes on cardboard, cut them out and strung them up on threads of black cotton, one end of which was stuck to the ceiling with plasticine, so that they swayed to and fro at different levels about our heads and looked as though they were alive. We also cut long, jagged strips of brown paper to look like seaweed and did the same to that; anchoring the top to the ceiling and the bottom to the rocks on the floor. And finally we covered the window-panes with green crêpe paper and painted the single 15-watt electric light bulb with blue paint.

It looked marvellous! Just as though one was standing on the bottom of the sea in a cool, greeny-blue, watery light with weed and fishes swaying to and fro around one in time to the movement of some underwater current. We used to sit there and pretend to be mermaids, 'swimming' whenever we moved about the little room, and making up stories about ancient wrecks and drowned cities.

We went roller-skating at the rink below (or was it above?) the Cinema, with our friends. We built tree-houses and hides in the woods, and played, over a period of months, a long-running and complicated series of games loosely based on 'French and English' (who remembers that one, I wonder?) — though since Tacklow had enthralled us with tales from Indian history, it was 'Maharattas and Rohillas', 'Sikhs and Jats', or 'Moguls and Persians'.

We made our own puppet-theatres, drew, painted and cut out the characters who appeared in them, and spent hours and days constructing a maze of passages and hideaways among the tall, tough stems of the flowering cosmos that formed a dense, feathery jungle on the sloping ground below the buttress wall in front of The Rookery. At a guess, this wilderness of cosmos must have covered a strip of between fifty to sixty yards in width and about half that in depth, ending at the top of another wall and a drop of some ten feet onto the upper road that circled Jakko.

Cosmos grew like a weed on the hillsides, and during its season of bloom the strip of ground between the bottom of one wall and the top of the other was a riot of pink and white. Below this surface roof of colour lay a mysterious grey-green jungle a good deal higher than a child's head, and it was through this that we constructed a labyrinth of tunnels and at least three secret retreats: each one a circular, cleared space in which we could hide from authority, large enough for three to four children to sit in cross-legged to talk and laugh and plan in whispers under a roof of fragile petals.

When the cosmos was in flower all Simla was scented with its sweet, peppery fragrance and the air was thick with pollen dust. That dust, and the scent of the cosmos, is forever connected in my mind with my first experience of one of those strange moments that I presume must come to all of us: a moment when you suddenly see an ordinary and familiar scene with extraordinary clarity — almost as though seeing it through a powerful telescope or in a different dimension — and know with complete certainty that for some indefinable reason it will stay with you for ever; printed on your brain like a snapshot on a strip of film. This happened to me for the first time on a cloudless, windless day in October . . .

Bets and I were leaving Simla with our parents on their annual migration to Delhi — for ever since the débâcle of Nurse Lizzie we had accompanied Mother and Tacklow to the plains instead of being left behind at Miss Cullen's. We were all four standing on the down platform of Simla railway station, waiting for our train, when I turned to look up and back at Simla and saw it through a golden haze of pollen dust: the ridge and the tower of Christ Church, the fringe of ramshackle houses that are the shops on the Mall, with below them the crowded bazaars and behind them the familiar, forest-clad heights of Jakko, daubed now with the yellow and pink splashes of chestnut and late-flowering wild cherry. It was mid-afternoon, but the autumn sun had already dipped below the deodars of Jakko and was streaking the view with long golden spears of light, each one a shimmering, dancing stream of motes from the cosmos pollen. This was the town in which I had been born, and every yard of it was familiar to me. Yet quite suddenly it was strange in a way that I could not have explained, and I knew that I would never forget the way in which I was seeing it now. Well, never is a long, long time. But I have remembered it ever since, and if there is anything in J. W. Dunne's *An Experiment with Time* — and I have every reason to believe that there is — then somewhere back in Time I am still standing there on that station platform, staring up, entranced, through a golden veil of cosmos pollen at the Simla of my childhood.

Yet another official 'in-aid-of' entertainment at the Gaiety Theatre, in which Bets and I took part, must have been very dull, for I can remember nothing at all about it except that we danced a minuet to Paderewski's Minuet in G, and that every time I hear that tune I can see Bets in her costume and remember some of the steps. We also took part in a series of tableaux, plus a very potted version of *A Midsummer Night's Dream,* which was presented at Peterhof — a house that was used as the residence of the Viceroy from 1862 until 1888 when one of them, Lord Minto, moved out of Peterhof and into the newly-built and truly hideous Viceregal Lodge.

I have never understood why the Victorians had such a fondness for tableaux: a static form of entertainment which also seems to have been wildly popular in Elizabeth Tudor's day and on down through Louis XIV and Regency England, into the twentieth-century — if all those early photographs by Cecil Beaton are anything to go by! It certainly survived in Anglo-Indian circles right into my own times, for the last ones I saw were staged at the Gaiety Theatre as late as (I think) 1929, while I distinctly remember some elderly woman — probably all of thirty! — remarking of the Peterhof tableaux that they were 'sweetly pretty'.

Once again Mrs Strettle's dancing-class did their stuff. The first half of the programme consisted of tableaux copied from the books of nursery rhymes illustrated by H. Willebeek Le Mair. I still have my own copies of her books, which continue to enchant me; and for the information of those who are unfortunate enough to have missed seeing them, every illustration, as well as the words and music on the facing page, is set inside an oval wreath of flowers, while the decorative pictures themselves are painted in pale, unshaded water-colours. These were copied exactly on the small stage at one end of the Peterhof ballroom; and while selected members of the dancing-class posed rigidly, doing their best not to twitch an eyelid, some grown-up or other sang the appropriate song: 'Ride-a-Cock-Horse', 'Little Miss Muffet', 'Mary Had a Little Lamb', or whatever. I took the part of Tom in 'Tom, Tom the Piper's Son' and was one of Old King Cole's 'Fiddlers Three', and Bets and her best friend, Tony, were the two small pyjama-clad figures in the shadowy, all-blue bedroom, looking out at 'Twinkle, Twinkle Little Star'!

There were about eight or nine of these tableaux and, after the interval, twenty or thirty minutes of Oberon and Puck, Bottom the Weaver and Titania and her fairies. Bargie, with her lovely black hair loose about her shoulders, made an enchanting Titania, but I don't remember who else played who. I wasn't in it, anyway! In that same year I was in some 'in-aid-of' involving the French Consul which entailed hours of practice in someone's sitting-room at a hotel called Longwood where, among other things, a squad of us had to learn to sing the Marseillaise — in French.

In addition to our personally invented diversions, and all this prancing around on the exciting side of the footlights, there were also the time-honoured festivals of the country, to which our Indian friends could be counted on to invite us. There were the annual celebrations of Holi, which is the great festival of the lowest and by far the largest of Hindu India's four major castes. It is a colourful and joyous Saturnalia that lasts for several days and appeals strongly to the child who never quite dies in even the oldest of geriatrics, since while it lasts people squirt each other with coloured water and pelt each other with fragile tissue-paper packets of vividly tinted powder that explode like miniature smoke-bombs. We enjoyed this exhilarating pastime enormously, but poor Punj-ayah, lumbered with the task of cleaning us up afterwards, strongly disapproved of it. And no wonder! for a topi, a frock, or a pair of shoes that have been doused with alternate jets of scarlet water and green and purple powder is practically a write-off.

Another entrancing Hindu festival was Diwali, the Feast of Lights, which is held in honour of several deities, among them the loveliest goddess in the Hindu pantheon, Lakshmi; and also to commemorate the Lord Krishna's slaying of a demon called Naraka who had captured and imprisoned no less than sixteen thousand maidens! Every Hindu house is decorated with lights at Diwali, and though nowadays those lights are likely to be electric bulbs, in my day they were *chirags* — little doll-sized earthenware bowls filled with oil, in which there floated a wick made out of a twist of cotton. Lined up on window-sills, parapets and walls, and lit after sunset, they set every town and village a-glitter with swaying, shimmering lines of light. It was a magical sight. Diwali is a night for fireworks and feasting, for eating delicious sweets like almond or pistachio *barfi,* and for playing games of chance; since not to gamble at Diwali is inauspicious — even when one can only afford to play with the smallest of copper coins, or sweets! I used regularly to lose my pocket money at Diwali and end up playing for sweets, though on one glorious occasion I won the staggering sum of four annas which, considering the state of my finances, was roughly equivalent to breaking the Bank at Monte Carlo.

Then there was the annual Sipi Fair, where (so Punj-ayah told us with bated breath) there were *brides* for sale! — comely hill-girls, dressed in their best and decked with beads and silver ornaments by parents who were willing to sell them to the highest bidder. And the great Mohammedan festivals of Id-el-Fitr, Shab-i-Barat, and Mohur-ram. The last two cannot really be termed 'festivals', since Shab-i-Barat includes a feast in remembrance of all who have died in the past, while to Shi'as,* Mohurram includes a day of mourning for Hussan and Husain, the martyred sons of Ali, adopted son and eventual son-in-law of the Prophet. On this day flimsy models of the tombs of the martyrs, eight to ten feet high, constructed from bamboo-canes and tissue paper and lavishly decorated with gold and silver tinsel, are carried in procession through the streets, preceded and followed by chanting, shouting crowds of the Faithful. These paper tombs are called *tarzias* — a word that according to Gully, a friend and

---

* Muslims are divided into two basic groups, ninety per cent being Sunnis and ten per cent Shi'as. The reasons are too long to discuss here, but it is another example of religion bringing 'not peace but a sword'.

contemporary of ours (his real name was Ghulam and his father owned one of the shops on the Mall), derived from *ta'ziya,* meaning 'mourning for the dead'. Which is yet another scrap of useless information that remains stuck in my head; though now that I come to think of it, I'm not sure that I ever checked it. But then Gully was a year older than I was, and at that time I thought he knew everything. The chanting processions always ended on the margin of a stretch of water; the sea, a river or a stream, a lake or a village pond, into which the *tarzias* would be thrown or carried and thrust under to be destroyed like the martyrs they commemorated. Next year new ones would be made ...

The first Mohurram procession I ever saw was in Simla, and I suspect that I must have badgered the Khan Sahib to take me to see it. But though I remember being charmed by the glittering, swaying *tarzias,* my clearest memory is of the horror of seeing them followed by squads of vociferous devotees, naked to the waist, who carried short-handled, many-thonged whips, each thong ending in an iron nail, with which they flogged themselves in time to the shouted chant of: '*Yar Hussan! Yar Husain!*' while the blood poured down their backs and stained their white loincloths scarlet. It was a horrid sight and it darkened my day.

❧ 4 ❧

Peacocks and Lilies

Chapter 14

~❧❀❧~

God gives all men all earth to love,
    But, since man's heart is small,
Ordains for each one spot shall prove
    Belovèd over all.

Kipling, 'Sussex'

. . . the most beautiful things in the world are the most useless;
peacocks and lilies for instance.

Ruskin, The Stones of Venice

Simla lies among the foothills of the Himalayas, some seven thousand feet above sea-level; and having been born there, within sight of the high white peaks of the true Himalayas where nothing grows and the snow never melts, you would have thought that my real love would have been for mountains and mountain scenery. And it is true that I love both. But from the moment that we arrived in Delhi to spend our first cold weather there, both Bets and I lost our hearts for ever to the plains.

I cannot explain why this should have been so. It still seems to me completely irrational that anyone who has had the good fortune to be born and spend their formative years among the most beautiful and spectacular mountains in the world should prefer the flat, dusty, often arid and largely featureless plains that stretch away and away towards a limitless horizon. Why does one fall in love — really in love — with a piece of earth? Why should one particular kind of landscape hold such a strong and enduring appeal for me that even after I have seen and lived in some of the most extravagantly romantic places in the world, my real love is still for India's plains? Not even the hill-strewn ones, but the flat lands that lie to the left and right of the Grand Trunk Road: Central India and the Punjab — the 'Land of the Five Rivers' —

and in particular, the once empty plains around Delhi.

I was certainly in the mood to fall in love with Delhi on that first cold-weather move; for which something that occurred at Kalka, where the foothills end and the plains begin, must be held responsible. A small incident which, like that view of Simla seen through the gold-dust shimmer of the sunbeams, has stayed diamond-bright in my memory. This too happened at a railway station; the small station of Kalka where the little toy train from Simla stops and passengers wishing to go further transfer into a broad-gauge one. We had arrived there after dark, and while Punj-ayah and Alum Din and our parents were busy seeing to the removal of our luggage and *bistras** and their subsequent bestowal in a reserved compartment on the Ambala–Delhi train, Bets and I wandered off to explore.

Up in Simla there had been a nip in the air and it had been cold enough after sunset for fires to be lit. But here on the edge of the plains the night was warm and windless, and the full moon that we had watched rise into the dusk like the ghost of some enormous apricot-coloured planet, now blazed bone-white overhead; flooding the world with light that seemed almost as bright as that of the vanished day. We walked across the station yard and back up the main road that led to Simla, the same road that Emily Eden had been carried along in her palanquin, that Kipling and Kitchener and Curzon and our own father, together with thousands of others both English and Indian — among them Kim and Huree Chunder Mukerji! — had driven along in tongas, ridden on horseback or travelled on foot, long before the railway had been laid or the motor-car invented.

Kalka was still little more than a village with a railway station on one edge of it, and the unmetalled road rose in a gentle slope as it led back through a small bazaar and open sandy country towards the hills that lay like wrinkled folds of grey velvet in the moonlight. Once clear of the houses, there seemed to be no one abroad but ourselves that night. The road was empty for as far as we could see, and beside it, on the left, stood a solitary frangipani tree whose shadow, like our own, lay black on the white dust. The tree was in full bloom and its

---

* Long, open-sided canvas holdalls, rolled up and fastened with leather straps, containing one's bedding all ready made up so that when the *bistra* was laid on the berth and unrolled, hey presto! there was a bed. In those days no traveller moved anywhere without one.

pale, waxy blossoms filled the warm night air with their heady fragrance and seemed to gather and reflect the moonlight; almost as though every petal had been carved out of white jade or polished ivory. It was one of the loveliest sights I have ever seen; more beautiful by far than the pale-blue star-frosted globe at the Central Hotel, because it was real; alive and growing and smelling of Heaven.

We stood and stared at it, dumb with admiration; and neither of us has ever forgotten it. To me it became a symbol of the plains, and thereafter any frangipani tree in bloom was special; and still is. I have put that tree into at least two of my books, and it may well have been part of the reason why I, born among the most beautiful mountains in the world, lost the larger portion of my heart to the flat and limitless plains on the very first of our annual moves from Simla to Delhi.

To Bets and myself those journeys were to become one of the highspots of our lives and the most exciting event of the year. As the little train chugged and puffed down the winding gradients of the narrowgauge railway we would hang out of the windows to take a last look at Simla basking all greeny-gold in the afternoon sunlight. Once past Tara Devi and between the gap in the hills, Simla was lost to sight until the next spring, and the next treat was the long Jatogh Tunnel which always enthralled us. Out into the daylight again the track wound back on itself, behind Prospect Hill and then down and down in the waning sunlight until the pine trees and deodars grew fewer and one saw the first sign of the plains in the great clusters of candelabrum cactus on the bare hillsides. One especially popular spot was where the track made a complete loop and we could look out of our carriage window and see both ends of our train at the same time. And as dusk fell the air became warmer and warmer and no longer smelled of pine needles but of the plains — that indefinable, heady mixture of sun-baked earth, dust and spices, kikar flowers and cowdung fires.

On one occasion we made the journey by car. At that date, and well into the Thirties, cars were almost unknown in Simla, and none was allowed further than the road below the Cecil Hotel where there was a row of lock-up garages for the very few who bothered to bring them that far. This particular car, known as the Yellow Peril, was the property of a certain Ronald Graham-Murray, a family friend and Bets's godfather, who had volunteered to drive all four of us down to

Delhi. We were enthralled by the novelty of the journey, but it proved to be a disaster, for I became embarrassingly car-sick and our host, who was driving, had to keep on stopping in order to let me out so that I could be sick over the edge of the road instead of all over his car. Everyone was relieved when the turns and twists and hairpin bends of the hill road were behind us; and deeply grateful, next year, to be going down by train.

The Delhi of my childhood, *my* Delhi, was not the great sprawling city so well known to hosts of tourists who call it New Delhi; for New Delhi had not been built then, and the site that it now occupies was a stony, treeless plain on which the foundations of the new capital were nowhere more than a foot or two high. My Delhi was the old walled city of the Moguls and the British-built Cantonment area that lay beyond it in the shadow of the Ridge — that long spine of rock which juts up from the surrounding plains like the back of a basking whale from a barely ruffled sea. The Ridge is steeped in history, and from its crest you could look down on Shah Jehan's walled city with its battered outer gateways, close-packed houses, bazaars, palaces and great Red Fort. On the marble domes and minarets of the largest of the mosques, the Jumma Masjid that faces the Lahore Gate of the fort across the grassy *maidan*,* and on the winding curves and wide white sandbanks of the Jumna River which in those days skirted the outer walls of the Palace.

Standing on the top of one of our favourite vantage-points, the Flagstaff Tower on the Ridge, and gazing out across the city and the miles of open country that surrounded it, we were looking back over thousands of years of history. For as far as the eye could reach the plain was strewn with the ruins of the Seven Cities of Delhi which, in the course of the long, turbulent centuries, had sprung up successively on these particular miles of India's soil: only to fall victims to war or famine or the ruthless feet of Time. Of these, 'Old Delhi', whose walls were already crumbling, was the seventh. But only a few miles away the foundations of yet another of them, a 'New' Delhi, were being laid above their bones on the stony, sandy, treeless land to the south-east of Shah Jehan's city. And from the Flagstaff Tower, even more than

* An expanse of common land on which horses and dogs can be exercised, children play, and the public stroll and gossip after office hours.

from the hillsides of Mashobra, I had the illusion that on a clear day I could see for ever.

I loved the smell of the plains and the sounds of the plains. The cawing of the grey-headed Delhi crows and the harsh, haunting cry of the peacocks at dawn and at dusk; the screeching of the parrots in flight and their low-toned chatter as they discussed life with each other when they roosted; the soft, interminable cooing of the little grey doves and the shrill chatter of the *galaries* — those small stripe-backed Indian chipmunks that skitter around on walls and creepers and tree-trunks, and are so impudent that if you stay quite still they will come and sit on your knee and eat out of your hand. In the plains when darkness fell you would hear the howl of the jackal packs hunting on the banks of the Jumna, and on white nights the barking of innumerable masterless pi-dogs baying at the moon.

I had grown up with the trees of Simla; pine trees, firs, deodars and the beautiful, blazing rhododendrons. But much as I loved them, I loved the palms and the pampas grass, the kikar trees and bamboos and bougainvillaea more; they were less awe-inspiring. Also — though I know that this cannot be true — I had (and still have) the pleasing illusion that I knew everyone who lived inside the wonderful walled city of Delhi. Now that I come to think about it, I'm not so sure, after all, that that could not have been possible, for according to a census taken no more than seven years before I was born, the entire population of *my* Delhi numbered only two hundred and eight thousand souls: one hundred and fourteen thousand Hindus, eighty-eight thousand Muslims, two thousand Christians and a modest four thousand who were dismissed briefly as 'others'. (What others, I wonder? Buddhists certainly; Confucians too; atheists perhaps? and I suppose those who followed various fancy religions — Madame Blavatski's, for instance. It would be interesting to know.)

But only two hundred and eight thousand people living in Old Delhi! It does not seem believable; I wonder how many millions today live in the sprawling metropolis that is the two Delhis, the Old and the New, now joined together by crowded, ever-growing suburbs? Considering those numbers, I realize how comparatively small the city must have been when I was young. So small that it is even possible that I could have had a nodding acquaintance with a quarter of the citizens who lived between the Kashmir and the Cawnpore Gates;

beyond which, in the days of my childhood, stretched open country all the way out to the Purana Kila (the Old Fort), and on past Humayun's tomb to Okhla, where the Jumna Canal branches off from the main river. Further to the westward lay the beautiful ruins of Haus Khas, which was a famous seat of learning long before Oxford or Cambridge were even thought of; and further still that enormous, lonely minaret, the Khutab Minar, and the curiously Egyptian-style tomb of the Emperor Tuglak — the ruins of whose city, Tuglakabad, look down on his tomb which stands islanded at the end of a long stone causeway in what was once a vast tank that must have provided the water for the city whose crumbling walls gaze blindly across it.

The Old Delhi that I loved so much was fated to become a backwater when New Delhi was finally built. For the senior members of the Government of India and Army Headquarters, together with their staffs, their wives, their families and their servants, moved there; exchanging their old-style bungalows in the green suburbs of Old Delhi for the modern concrete houses nicknamed 'Baker's Ovens' after the architect* who designed them for New Delhi; and as a result of that exodus the focus of official and social life shifted to the new centre of power. Yet when, sixteen years after India became independent, Bets and I went back there again, it was still the familiar place we had known first as children and later as young women, though it had become much quieter and now wore, like a fragile and faintly dusty lace shawl, an air of shabbiness and neglect where once it had been so full of gaiety and life.

Perhaps, having made that sentimental pilgrimage and found all our old familiar places so little changed, we should have left well alone — kissed them goodbye for the last time and never gone back again. And but for the success of *The Far Pavilions,* we would probably have done just that, because we would never have been able to afford to return again. But once the financial side of things became easier, how could we possibly resist? Delhi drew us back again like a magnet with a pair of pins — only to find that most of the things we had loved best had been swept away or crushed under the trampling hooves of that sacred cow, Progress.

The Delhi that still keeps a firm hold on my heart is no more than

* Sir Herbert Baker.

a memory, though even now, returning to it, there have been moments when for a brief space at dusk I have heard a peacock calling from among the shadowy thickets of the Ridge, and found myself back in imagination in the dear city of my childhood and my gay, careless, dancing teens and twenties.

✗ Accommodation in Old Delhi was always in short supply, and a great many people, Buckie and Annie B among them, lived under canvas in the luxurious tented camp originally set up for the use of the VIPs who had come out to attend the great Durbar of 1911. But since there were neither tents nor bungalows available for us, we were allotted two adjoining suites, Numbers 38 and 39, in Curzon House; a large, two-storeyed building that had been put up for the same purpose as the camp, though for an even earlier Durbar — the one held in 1903 to celebrate the Coronation of Edward VII. Later on it had been turned into a cold-weather hostel for Army officers and Civil Service officials and their families; and later still, in the post-war Twenties when New Delhi was springing up out of the empty plain to the south-east of Old Delhi, it became The Swiss Hotel.

The quarters at Curzon House were all alike, each one consisting of a large living-room separated by a tall, curtained archway from an equally large bedroom with a bathroom leading out of it. The only light in the bedrooms came from windows set high up near the ceiling and looking out onto the flat rooftop. These could only be opened and shut by means of long cords that were attached to hooks much lower down the wall. The bathrooms were of the old-fashioned tin-tub and thunder-box variety — India not having got into modern plumbing at that date — and their windows and back doors opened onto long, narrow verandahs; the upper-storey ones being reached by a stout wooden staircase for the use of the *pani-wallahs* who carried up the tins of hot water, and the sweepers who cleaned the thunder-boxes. There were connecting doors between every quarter and the next so that they could, if necessary, be made into larger units, such as ours, which consisted of two quarters. Bachelors and childless couples occupied single ones. The front doors of all these quarters led directly into the living-rooms from long, wide, communal verandahs, paved with squares of red sandstone and carpeted with a long strip of coir matting, and the white, double-storeyed building with its arched frontage and two parallel wings formed a big rectangular U.

There was a formal garden in front and a wilderness of flowers and trees behind, and beyond the left-hand boundary wall stretched the spacious lawns, gardens and tennis courts of a large, single-storey, castellated house, grandly entitled Ludlow Castle. In the days of the East India Company Ludlow Castle had been the residence of the Commissioner of Delhi, but in my young days had become the Delhi Club; later on to be re-titled the Old Delhi Club. Later still, after Independence, it became a college.

Beyond the boundary wall on the right-hand side of Curzon House lay the cemetery in which John Nicholson, 'the Hero of Delhi', who died leading his men into action during the battle for the city in the Mutiny summer of 1857, is buried, together with many of the Mutiny dead. The stone-built wall was not too high for an active child of six or seven to scramble over, and though I don't think our parents ever knew it, the cemetery soon became one of our favourite playgrounds. It was a very peaceful spot: hot and quiet and drowsy, chequered with tree-shadows and freckled and barred with brilliant sunlight. And since Punj-ayah's sari was not adapted to climbing over walls, she couldn't follow us there, but would hunker down in a patch of shade to wait for us on the Curzon House side until such time as we returned; confident that no harm would come to us from her people or ours — either living or dead.

Punj-ayah could never understand our fondness for the cemetery, which she herself regarded as a 'place of the dead' and therefore an ill-omened spot. But it never occurred to either of us to think of those who lay buried there as 'dead'. John Nicholson — *Nikal-Seyn* — and all the men who had died in the battle for Delhi and whose names were carved on the worn, lichen-blotched slabs and headstones, together with the many British men, women and children who had joined them here in the long years since then, were only asleep; drowsing peacefully in the warm silence under the grass and flowers and the lilting butterflies, lulled by the soporific cooing of the little grey ring-doves, and dreaming of home.

There was nothing to be frightened of in this pleasant backwater; and if there were any restless ghosts, they did not walk along the gravel paths that wandered here and there between the worn gravestones, or on the grass that the *malis* kept trimmed but not close-shaved and formal like the lawns of Curzon House and the Club. The grass here was allowed to look like grass, and there was bougainvillaea everywhere and great bushes of roses and jasmine that had run wild and smelled heavenly. The air was always full of scent and birdsong and butterflies — more butterflies than I remember seeing anywhere else — and the whole sun-soaked and tree-shadowed place was strongly suggestive of Frances Hodgson Burnett's *Secret Garden* because, apart from the occasional elderly *mali* pottering around with a rake or a small hand-sickle, no one but ourselves ever seemed to visit it.

Close to the cemetery were the Nicholson Gardens: a public park full of trees and lawns and neat flowerbeds, where there was an ornamental fountain that was supposed to have come from Chats-worth — or was it Blenheim? — and two stately avenues of bottle palms at the junction of which, perched on a high plinth, stood a statue of John Nicholson, sword in hand, facing the battered walls of Delhi and the shell-pocked Kashmir Gate near the spot where he had fallen. Punj-ayah approved of the Nicholson Gardens. It was a nice tidy place in which the *chota-missahibs* were unlikely to get up to any mischief or dirty their hands, shoes or clothes. Besides, there were always plenty of other ayahs as well as European nannies and their charges in the gardens, and she enjoyed a good gossip with her fellow countrywomen.

The Moguls, a nomadic people from the harsh treeless uplands of Central Asia, had a passion for gardens, trees and running water, and there are many of their *baghs** in and around Delhi: among them the Roshanara Bagh which boasts a lake with a tiny island in the middle of it, thickly overgrown with date palms which provide a roosting-place for scores of white ibis. There is also a white marble pavilion, in which Roshanara Begum, the Princess who built it and made the garden, and who died in 1663, lies buried. Her father was the Emperor Shah Jehan who built the Taj Mahal at Agra, and legend has it that she was a marvellous dancer. But our favourite garden by far was the Kudsia Bagh which lay opposite Curzon House; so close that we had only to cross the road to reach its main entrance.

This garden had none of the primness and public-park tidiness of the Nicholson one — except in the 'public facilities' areas devoted to

* Gardens. Pronounced bārgs (singular barch).

tennis and cricket, and a certain treeless space where the grass was worn thin by the feet of Delhi's children who played games, ran races and flew kites there while their elders exchanged gossip or strolled to and fro 'eating the air' of an evening. Apart from that, the rest of the *bagh* was a glorious, planless jumble of creeper-clad ruins, flowering trees and shrubs, bamboo thickets, date palms, eucalyptus, peepul and kikar trees. There were roses everywhere: the old-fashioned cabbage ones as well as the far older Persian variety that Omar Khayyam sings of and from which attar-of-roses is made and all our modern roses are descended. Jasmine too; and canna lilies; poinsettias and orange trumpet-flower creeper; and the white, piercingly sweet-scented *rhat-ki-rani* that flowers only after sundown and whose name means 'Queen of the night'. The entire garden had once been enclosed by a high wall inside which Kudsia Begum, wife of the Emperor Muhammed Shah and mother of his son and successor, Ahmad Shah (whose disastrous reign finally brought about the decay of the Mogul Empire), built herself a palace and a mosque on the banks of the Jumna River.

When I was a child in Old Delhi all that remained of these buildings was a battered but still beautiful gateway, and the shell of an enchanting triple-domed mosque facing the river across a stretch of open ground — part of which must have been the courtyard, for it contained a sunken stone-lined tank in which the Faithful would have bathed before saying their prayers. I have heard that the ground beyond this used to be covered by a stone-paved terrace from which a broad flight of stairs descended to the water's edge; and even in my day the Jumna ran almost directly below the bank. However, no trace of the terrace remained, and the Jumna, which like all India's rivers is perpetually changing course, has moved well away from it since then.

A small shallow stream, barely more than a drain, in which we could catch tiddlers but were forbidden to paddle (since who knew, said Punj-ayah darkly, whence it came or what drained into it?) crossed the gardens to join the river; running *en route* under a little wooden bridge shaded by kikar trees whose scented, mimosa-like blossoms seemed always to be in bloom and provided an endless supply of miniature powder-puffs with which we would powder our noses yellow.

The gateway that had once been the main entrance to Begum Kudsia's palace was a massive affair: a vast, tunnel-like archway capable of allowing entrance to a howdahed elephant. There were guard-rooms built into it on either side, two of which had been allotted to the *chowkidar* of the gate; one for his own use (the only one which still possessed its original iron-studded door that could be barred and padlocked) and the other as a storage place for 'second-day flowers' which, as a sideline, he collected each day from Maiden's Hotel and the Tennis Club, exchanging them for fresh ones. Many of these slightly-used flowers, though not at their best, were far from faded, and he would let us select and take away any we liked. The rest, I suspect, were bunched and resold in the bazaar or to the owners of nearby bungalows. The archway in consequence always smelt deliciously of flowers, and for years afterwards the scent of fading roses, sweetpeas and carnations was an instant short-cut to the ruined gateway in the Kudsia Bagh.

The *chowkidar* became a great friend of ours, and it was he who told us that in the days when the gateway was the entrance to a Queen's palace, there used to be staircases in the thickness of the wall leading out of it and up to the roof and the battlements which surrounded a long-vanished inner courtyard. The stairs on the right had fallen long ago, but though the outer wall of those on the left had also fallen, the steps remained; hidden from view by the tall thicket of bamboos growing against that side of the gateway. He himself had never used them, and it obviously did not occur to him that once we knew of their existence we would not be able to resist climbing them. If it had, I am sure he would never have told us, for the staircase, when he showed it to us, was not only very steep and narrow, but lacking several of its treads, while those that remained were deep in debris and in a shocking state of disrepair.

Bets and I were both afraid of snakes and scorpions, and frankly terrified of spiders. But we could no more resist climbing that staircase than Bluebeard's wives had been able to resist entering the forbidden room. We could at least be certain of one thing — that there was no danger of falling off the stair, because the bamboos pressed so closely against its wall-less outer side that nothing larger than a mongoose could possibly have fallen between those ranks of stout stems.

Punj-ayah (no hawk-eyed duenna!) had fortunately met a friend with whom she was chatting happily in the shade of one of the ficus trees, well out of earshot, when, to the accompaniment of agitated warnings from the *chowkidar,* we pushed back the curtain of weeds and creepers that concealed the base of the stairway and the wall to which it clung, and wriggling through, climbed cautiously up through what looked like a green tunnel of bamboo leaves — testing each step before putting any weight on it — to emerge finally on the flat roof of the great gateway.

At first sight it looked a bit like an empty swimming-pool which the jungle had taken over, for the parapet surrounding it was much taller than we were and the bamboos to the left and right soared high above it, shutting off a good deal of the sky. The centre arch of the gateway was comparatively clear of creepers, but bougainvillaea, orange trumpet-flower and jasmine had climbed the walls and the decorative turrets on either side, to foam down over the castellated parapets in fountains and waterfalls of colour. The roof itself was hidden under a foot-deep carpet of leaf-mould, bird-droppings and assorted feathers — the discarded plumage of innumerable crows, blue jays, doves, pigeons, parakeets, peacocks and other birds which down the long years had perched on the parapets and roosted or built nests among the tangled mass of creeper — and though in and under all that debris there was bound to be a whole world of creeping and crawling creatures, and probably a few rats as well, I do not believe that the thought of them so much as crossed our minds. For we had stumbled on El Dorado!

Not Columbus himself, taking his first sight of America, nor 'stout Cortez' staring out at the Pacific, could have felt more awed and excited than we did as we took in the fact that we had discovered a hidden, private world which nobody else knew about! Nobody but the *chowkidar* (who besides being a friend would not, for his own sake, betray us), and Punj-ayah, who would have to be let into the secret, but would keep quiet for the same reasons. It was a marvellous find and we wasted no time over taking possession. By the time Punj-ayah came in search of us we had cleared a portion of the roof and pushed all the rubbish off the stairway, and during the next few days, with the aid of a broom, a rake and a wicker basket used for carrying food and cut flowers, all kindly lent us by the *chowkidar,* we managed to get rid of all the litter from the roof.

After that the place became a permanent source of enjoyment and a safe retreat from the everyday world. It was ours. Our very own! On it we were hidden away where no one could find us, and we spent hours up there, playing 'house', reading, talking, discussing life and our elders, inventing stories, or being Mrs Jones and Mrs Snooks — a couple of harassed housewives and mothers whose children were a perpetual source of worry. I was Mrs Jones and Bets was Mrs Snooks, and our respective children were my Moko, a life-sized toy monkey which had originally belonged to my brother Bill and been annexed by me when he outgrew such toys, and Bets's large teddy-bear. Moko and Teddy accompanied us everywhere. And would still be doing so had they not been eaten by those tiny but voracious insect pests known as 'woolly bears' that attacked them during six months in the late 1930s, when they were in storage with a good deal of our heavy luggage in a godown in Lucknow. When unpacked, so little remained that it was impossible to re-assemble them; and since their murderers had obviously been breeding like fun, there was nothing for it but to consign them with lamentations to the fire; which we did. Cremating them on a pyre in the back garden of my sister and brother-in-law's house in Lucknow, together with the ruined contents of the packing-case in which they had met their end — plus uncounted thousands of their pestilential destroyers and about a billion woolly-bear eggs. It was a sad moment, because I had looked forward to handing Moko on in turn to be loved, cared for and played with by a child of my own who, with luck, would hand it on to a grandchild.

I don't remember how we managed to beg, blarney or possibly blackmail Punj-ayah into letting us go on using the top of Kudsia Begum's gateway as a secret hideaway and playground. We probably used a mixture of all three. But whatever it was, it worked. She refused flatly to climb up after us (she was scared stiff of all forms of creepy-crawlies and not particularly partial to any form of animal life), but she never gave us away and we continued to use it for two glorious cold weathers. But alas, nothing lasts for ever.

In the third year, when we hurried off to visit all our old haunts, we discovered with horror that some interfering official had decided that the bamboos must be cut down and the gateway repaired. Not a single bamboo shoot remained, and without them Kudsia Begum's lovely gateway looked shamefully undressed; rather like some glamorous lady of the harem who has been forcibly removed from *purdah* and deprived of her gauzy veil. The steps were still there, but they had been repaired and given a high brick and plaster containing-wall on the outer side and also, to make matters worse, two coats of whitewash. There was yet more repair work and whitewash on the top, and everything looked painfully clean and tidy and depressingly un-secret. We never played there again. But nor did we ever forget it, and many years later I used it in two of my India novels. It is the Mori Gate, the north gate of Bhithore, in *The Far Pavilions,* and the entrance to the Lunjore Residency in *Shadow of the Moon,* while its flat rooftop with the high parapet and tall screen of bamboos gave me the idea for the Hirren Minar in the latter novel — the ruin in the jungle which four survivors from the massacre at the Residency use as a hiding-place during the first months of the Mutiny.

But though the gateway was our favourite retreat, it was by no means the only thing that we loved about the Kudsia Bagh. Nor was the *chowkidar* our only friend, for we made many in the gardens. Among them were a number of children who lived in several tall, old and beautiful houses surrounded by lawns and flowerbeds and shaded by neem and banyan and jacaranda trees, beside a quiet, leafy side-road that ran between the Kudsia Bagh and the grounds of Maiden's Hotel. They were a delightful lot, and we fraternized with them by way of a gap in the hedge through which we had to crawl on hands and knees. The houses were owned by one family, the Dayals, and in later years Ashok Dayal, the son of one of those children, was to marry Indu, a daughter of one of my husband's greatest friends, Shiv Bhatia, and his darling wife Metta. Sadly, both Shiv and Metta are now dead; but Bets and I keep in touch with Indu and Ashok, and are certain to be seeing them and their children in the near future.

Another good friend that we made in the gardens was an ancient, ash-smeared Sadhu, a wandering holy man, who had hollowed out a resting-place for himself among a big clump of bamboos that grew on the edge of the gardens, on the far side of the empty stone tank that fronted Kudsia Begum's ruined mosque. It was this old gentleman who first gave us the idea of feeding the birds ...

Every morning, as the sky brightened to the dawn, we would be woken by the voice of a peacock who lived among the kitchen gardens of Ludlow Castle, and whose habit it was to fly up to the flat rooftop of Curzon House where he paraded up and down, calling raucously to his friends and relations in the Kudsia Bagh over the way. Within minutes Punj-ayah would appear with our *chota-hazri,* which always consisted of bananas and cream, and as soon as we were dressed she would take us out for an early-morning walk before breakfast. We always made straight for the gardens, which at that hour were deserted except for the birds and the squirrels. And one morning — it was during our first cold weather in Delhi and I imagine the peacock must have wakened us particularly early that day — walking down the path that passes behind the back of the ruined mosque, we decided to explore it, and rounding the end wall saw that all the ground in front of it, including the tank, was a shimmering carpet of emerald green. A split second later the carpet broke up into fragments that whirled up and away in a screeching cloud of parakeets. They had been feeding on the grain that someone must have scattered there for them, and looking across the now empty tank we saw for the first time the figure of an old Sadhu sitting cross-legged in a niche among the close-growing bamboo stems.

We had passed the time of day with many holy men; met with by the roadside out Mashobra way or in the streets and bazaars of Simla and Old Delhi, so it did not occur to us not to speak to this one. And like the other wandering, ash-smeared ascetics of India whom we had from time to time had speech with, this one too presumably regarded the foreign *baba-log* as being below the age of caste, for he did not shoo us away but became a great friend. We called him Bappu-ji, and whenever we passed that way we would stop and talk to him and bring him presents of fruit and rice, which he accepted courteously, though I don't know if he ever actually ate them. Possibly not, though it seemed to me that he was holy enough to have sanctified anything he cared to eat or touch. He had an endless fund of stories to which we listened round-eyed and enthralled; squatting on our heels Indian-fashion in front of him — an art that many Anglo-Indian children learned when young but which few, if any, can have retained, since without constant practice it is soon forgotten; and once that happens it is lost for good. Bappu-ji told us stories about animals, gods and demons, and it was from him that we learned how the little tree-rats, the Indian chipmunks, got their stripes, and how the peacock acquired the eyes in his tail, and scores of other legends and folk-tales of the land. He had been born and spent much of his youth in Delhi, but after he became a *bairagi* he had roamed all over India and visited so many places of pilgrimage that if the tale of his travels had been written down it would have filled a dozen books.

It was fun hearing about the journeys he had made and shrines he had visited — particularly one somewhere in the high mountains where the path was hard on naked feet and the wind bit to the bone, and where there was the ice image of a god in a cave. (Amarnath, I suppose? He must have told us, but if so the name did not stick, though his description of it did.) But the stories that intrigued me most were the tales he told about Delhi during the 'Black Year' — 1857. The year that the *Shaitan-ki-Hawa,* the Devil's Wind, blew through India, and the *pultons** mutinied ...

He told us how, as a boy of ten or twelve, he and a group of young acolytes from a nearby ashram, who had been bathing in the Jumna River very early in the morning, spied a white smoke-like streak stretching out across the dawn-lit plain on the far side of the river, and realized, since there was no breath of wind that morning, that it could only be a cloud of dust raised by a band of horsemen galloping at great speed. Standing knee-deep in the shallows they watched the riders draw near, and presently heard, clear in the stillness of dawn, the sound of their shouting voices and the thunder of their horses' hooves as they raced, yelling, across the planks of the Bridge of Boats.

What he had seen, and what neither he nor his companions ever forgot, were the troopers of the 3rd Cavalry whose regiment, stationed at Meerut, had mutinied on the previous day† and, after an orgy of murder and destruction, had ridden to Delhi to bring the news (grossly exaggerated, as it happened) that they had killed every *Angrezi* in Meerut, and to urge the aged Mogul, Bahadur Shah, still titular ruler of India, to do likewise and rid his people of every white-skinned aggressor throughout the land. That was how the great Sepoy Rising began ...

---

* Regiments.

† A century later to the day, Longmans Green & Co. published my first historical novel, *Shadow of the Moon,* which was set in India in the days of the Mutiny.

Chapter 15

~XƏVƏX~

'Now tell us all about the war,
And what they fought each other for.'

Southey, 'The Battle of Blenheim'

Bappu-ji was by no means the only one who told us about the Mutiny, for almost every townsman and villager in or around Delhi had a fund of stories about it. And as we explored the Ridge and its ruins, played in the dry moat that encircled Shah Jehan's walled city, or strolled along the battlements above the battered Kashmir Gate, I had only to ask any casual passer-by (and I was always doing that) why there were so many holes in the wall and who made them, and what happened here, to get a reply that nine times out of ten would begin: '*Ah!* now my father told me —' or, surprisingly often, 'I myself, when I was young —'. A story would follow; either a description of something seen and experienced at first hand, or else recounted at second hand from someone who had been there and witnessed it. For as I have said, every foot of Delhi is soaked in history, and at that time the most recent bucketful of it (if one did not count the two great Durbars) was the Mutiny, which had ended less than sixty years previously. And what is sixty years to India? No more than a blink of an eyelid!

There were still a great many people around in their sixties, seventies and eighties, whose memories were excellent, and the tales they told of that time were far more exciting than anything in a children's annual or boy's book of adventure stories. I much preferred them to Fenimore Cooper's tales, or *Treasure Island, The Master of Ballantrae, Tom Sawyer* and similar classics, because for one thing they were *true*. And for another they had happened *here,* on the very ground I was standing on! Old Mr Patel, and Mohinder Singh and Mohammed Bux, and old Seeta Begum too, had actually heard the deafening bang as the

Magazine blew up, and the shrieks and screams of the wounded (Seeta Begum said her mother had hidden her under a bed!). Many others had not only heard the explosion but had seen and could describe the column of smoke and fire that had shot up from the wreckage to spread out into a cloud like the head of a gigantic mushroom on a stalk that was 'taller than the tallest tree' ... a cloud that had hung in the sky above Delhi for hour after hour and was still there when the moon rose! Mohammed Din's father and Nunno's grandmother had actually been there when such-and-such an incident took place; Ram Lal's uncle had been one of the crowd that attacked the Bank House on the Chandi Chowk, once the palace of Begum Sombre, while Jaswant Singh's grandfather had seen the bodies of the English prisoners, who had been put to death in the King's palace in the Lal Kila, thrown into the Jumna to be taken down on the current ...

I heard endless tales of the 'Black Year' from Indians who had heard them at first hand, or themselves witnessed or taken part in the event they described, long before I ever read a line about the Mutiny in an English book. They were my favourite 'cops-and-robbers' stories, replacing the Westerns — those 'cowboys-and-Indians' tales that all children seem to enjoy; probably because they are full of gunfire and villains biting the dust.

Sadly, when the next cold weather came round and we returned to Delhi and hurried off to make the round of the Kudsia Bagh and look up our friends, Bappu-ji the old Sadhu was no longer there. Judging from the new growth, he must have left his home among the bamboos not long after we ourselves had left for the hills, and no one seemed to know where he had gone, or when. Certain charitable folk who had kept his begging-bowl filled reported that one day his place was empty and that he had not returned; that was all — 'perchance he would return one day? Or it might be that he was dead; he was an old man ...'

We refused to believe that he was dead and continued to hope that one day the familiar figure would be back in the shelter of the bamboos. But we never saw him again. It was because of him — because he used to feed the parrots — that we decided to deputize for him and feed the birds in the gardens ourselves; and from then on every day we spent in Delhi, right up to the sorrowful day on which we left it *en route* to exile and school in England, we took our early-morning walks in the Kudsia Bagh laden with all the scraps, crumbs and crusts we had been able to collect during the previous day. The parrots never came down to feast on our offerings as they did on Bappu-ji's (for we had no grain) but most of the other birds in the gardens, and all the *galaries,* the chipmunks, were only too pleased to do so. They took less than a week to catch on to the fact that cake and breadcrumbs and other assorted scraps were being handed out, and after that the birds would wait for us each morning, perched in rows on the telegraph wires that ran down the length of the eucalyptus avenue, and on the railings of the wooden bridge, and in no time at all they became almost as bold and as greedy as the pigeons in London's Trafalgar Square or St Mark's in Venice.

But much as we loved to see the blue jays swoop down in flashing arcs of colour, and the sober, yellow-eyed *sāt-bhaī** come hopping round our feet, it was the little striped squirrels that captured the largest share of our affections. We kept the best toast-crusts to the last for these endearing little creatures, whom we fed in the furthest corner of the gardens: the one that looks across open ground towards Delhi Wall and the Water Bastion, near where one of the old siege batteries had stood in the summer of the 'Black Year' — its site marked by a massive sandstone plinth in which a marble tablet recorded the name of its long-dead commander, together with the number and calibre of its armaments and the particular section of the wall that its guns had been intended to breach. In our day, a line of peepul trees, most of which were old enough to have seen that battle being fought, formed a boundary line between the gardens and the waste ground that stretched between it and the battered walls of Delhi. The peepul, a tall, grey-barked tree with heart-shaped leaves and huge knotted roots, is known as the Boh-tree and held to be sacred because it was while sitting under one that the Buddha received enlightenment. The Buddhist scriptures tell us that during the many days that he sat there, fasting and motionless, though the sun rose and set in a cloudless sky the shadow of the Boh-tree did not move, but continued to shield the Excellent One ...

The peepuls on the edge of the Kudsia Bagh grew between the

---

* 'Seven-brothers'; though the British insisted on calling them 'seven-sisters', because they hop around in groups of seven, chattering non-stop like a clutch of excitable schoolgirls.

great stone slabs that had once formed the foundations of the wall surrounding Kudsia Begum's garden and protecting her palace. And though layer upon layer of earth and leaf-mould had long ago covered them, it was still possible to see traces of them here and there, thrusting up between the coarse grasses. Few people came to this corner of the gardens, so the trees were full of birds and squirrels — hundreds of squirrels who soon learned to know us and as soon as we sat down among the tree roots and took out our toast crusts, would swarm around us as boldly as street urchins, snatching the larger pieces from between our fingers and sitting on the palms of our hands to eat the smaller crumbs. We never missed a day if we could help it, and used to worry about them — needlessly, I may say! — for fear that they might go hungry and miss us when the hot weather came and we had to return to Simla.

Those were our morning walks. Our evening ones were either along the Ridge or down to the river which in those days lay on the other side of the dusty unmetalled road that skirted the far end of the Kudsia Bagh, close to the bamboo thicket where our old Sadhu had lived. All we had to do was walk through the eucalyptus avenue and under the arch of the great gateway, and keeping straight on for roughly two or three hundred yards, descend the short bank where the gardens ended, cross the road that lay below, and there we were on the wide silver sandbanks that fringed the Jumna River. The blue water of the main channel ran some way out in those wastes of sand, flowing wide and deep between the shallows on the Delhi side and the steep banks of the plain, today covered with houses, but then an endless expanse of stony, uncultivated land dotted with kikar trees, clumps of high grass and the ruins of those seven other Delhis built beside the broad, slow-flowing river.

As with all India's rivers, there were a number of shallow side-streams which had been gouged out in the rainy season when the river was in spate, and which continued to thread their way through the silver sandbanks when the monsoon ended and the river fell again. Most of these were just too deep for us to ford. But some were possible to wade across in certain places, and we had our own favourite spots among these pools and shallows. Here we would paddle, chase *chilwa* — the shoals of fingerlings that are India's whitebait — and build elaborate sandcastles to which we could return on the following day, confident that they would still be standing.

Whenever they could, our parents and not Punj-ayah would take us down to the sands, where Mother proved a master architect at building sandcastles and Tacklow enlivened the evenings by telling us stories about an old gentleman known as the Kojah. I've no idea where they came from — some Persian or Arabic book I suppose. If so, I don't know what it was called. There were a lot of Kojah stories and they lasted us through one entire season, for Tacklow would never tell us more than one in an evening, and I have to admit that after all these years I can only remember one of them: the one about the Kojah's neighbour who was always borrowing his cooking-pans ...

One day the Kojah decided for a change to borrow one from his neighbour, and when he returned it he sent a little pan with it. 'Oh Kojah,' said the neighbour; 'what is this?' To which the Kojah replied that during the day or so that the borrowed pan had been in his possession it had had a child. The neighbour was delighted and began to badger the Kojah to borrow his pan again, and once again the Kojah did so, and again returned it with a small one — the big pan had had *another* child. On the third occasion, however, no pan was returned, and after a week or so the owner went to the Kojah and asked for it back, to which the Kojah replied gravely that he was so sorry, but the big pan had died. 'Oh Kojah,' protested the owner, 'how can a pan die? It is not possible!' 'Why not? If it can have a child, it can also die,' said the Kojah.

To this day, when I remember those evenings on the sands by the Jumna River, memory not only shows me Mother and Bets, barefooted and with their skirts tucked up round their waists, making sandcastles while Tacklow intones: 'Oh Kojah!' but the Kojah himself, whom I see in imagination walking at Tacklow's elbow; a thin, elderly, white-bearded Persian (why Persian?) wearing a vast green turban, long robes and curly-toed shoes ...

During the long, hot afternoons when half India indulges in a siesta, Bets and I would go off to the rooms of a middle-aged couple who were particular friends of ours and whom we chose to call, for some forgotten reason, 'General and Mrs Ponson'. They were in fact a Colonel and Mrs Tyndale-Biscoe — the Colonel's brother being that Canon Tyndale-Biscoe who founded the famous school in Kashmir that still bears his name and is attended by Muslim, Sikh and Hindu boys regardless of creed or class. But our name for them stuck, and to everyone in Curzon House (and, I was told, throughout Army Headquarters and half Delhi) they became known as 'The Ponsons'. General Ponson was naturally tied to his office in Metcalfe House, but Mrs Ponson, an indefatigable war-worker, did not waste her afternoons in sleep but spent them — and all her free time! — making *papier-mâché* kidney-bowls for the Red Cross hospitals.

She was a thin, grey-haired, Victorian lady of the old school, and to us she seemed incredibly ancient, the sort of age that a great-grandmother should be. I don't think she had ever had any children of her own, but she ought to have had dozens, for she was fond of them and knew exactly how to treat them, and we loved her dearly. She owned a whole shelf of children's books and for an hour every afternoon she would read us a chapter or two from one or other of them while we, in exchange, tore up and soaked the strips of newspaper from which she made her kidney-bowls, and were sometimes even allowed to try our hand at making a bowl ourselves. It was dear Mrs Ponson who first introduced me to *The Secret Garden* and *The Wind in the Willows*; two children's classics which I have read and re-read scores of times and which continue to enchant me to this day. But the 'Ponson-book' I remember best, though I have no idea who wrote it and have never been able to trace it, was called *The Witch's Kitchen*; about a witch who kidnapped some children and held them captive in her kitchen where she used to cook up some kind of alluring (and dangerous!) yellow goo that I think of as looking, and tasting, like uncooked sponge cake, which is always delicious.

Our mornings were occupied with getting educated, for we attended classes given to a handful of children by someone else's English governess — I don't remember whose, or much about the classes. Then once a week there was a dancing-class held by the same much-admired instructress who took them in Simla, pretty Mrs Strettle who was not yet Lady Strettle. These dancing-classes were held in the ballroom of the oldest Old Delhi Club; a long, low building by the side of the Karnal road beyond Metcalfe House and the Kashmir Bazaar, where the Ridge of Delhi peters out on the plain and a huge standing camp had been built to house the VIPs who came out from England and from all over India for the Great Durbar of 1911. Much of that camp was still standing; and, as I have said, many of our parents' friends and their Indian servants lived there under canvas, in great comfort and state, for the tents were lavish affairs; double-lined against rain and cold or the blazing sun, with durable wooden floors on which carpets were laid, brick fireplaces with proper chimneys, and electric fans and telephones.

There were tents furnished as drawing-rooms where pictures hung on the coloured canvas walls. Dining-room tents with tables, chairs and sideboards, and bedroom tents with adjoining bathrooms — though as far as I remember, no running water. Kitchen tents and numerous servants' tents were ranged behind these and each cluster of tents stood in its own compound, most of which had been planted with shade trees, lawns and flowerbeds, beside wide roads and avenues as in the suburbs of any town. Each compound had gates, name-boards and numbers, and the red gravel paths leading to them were edged with bricks sunk endwise into the ground and their visible triangular tops neatly whitewashed. That camp was still there right up to the end of the Raj — and Buckie and his wife and daughter still lived in it in their tented quarters throughout most, if not all, of the Thirties and Forties.

Punj-ayah used to take us to dancing-classes in a tonga since it was much too far to walk, and I remember being involved in what must have been one of the earliest car-crashes in Delhi — for there were not all that many cars there in those days and nearly all the public transport was still horse-drawn. Our tonga had been turning out of the side-road at a spot known as the 'Khyber Pass' where there was a small bazaar, when a car coming along the main road rattled past in a cloud of dust and tooted its horn at us in warning. The tonga pony, unused to these newfangled monsters of the road, almost leapt out of its skin with fright and took off for the horizon. And since I had been engaged in waving to various friends and acquaintances who kept shops in the bazaar, and not paying sufficient attention to the traffic, I was instantly dislodged and tumbled out into the road; incurring no more than a few minor cuts and bruises, but ruining my dancing-slippers, natty white socks and frilly white *broderie anglaise* dancing-dress as I rolled in the dust. An agitated contingent of stallholders leapt out and scooped me in, making soothing noises, while others raced in pursuit of the tonga, which lurched to a noisy halt when its off-side wheel caught the wheel of a passing bullock cart. Punj-ayah, who had been holding Bets with one arm and clinging like a limpet to the woodwork with the other, seized the opportunity to nip down and, still clutching Bets, gave the tonga-wallah a spirited sketch of his ancestry, with particular reference to the female side; not forgetting the sire and dam of his horse. You could hear her all down the road, and the bazaar applauded every word.

She refused flatly to allow us to get back into the tonga or even call up a new one, so we covered the last quarter of a mile to the Club on foot, where she cleaned me up to the best of her ability and the Club ayah anointed my scratches with what I think must have been iodine: I remember it was dark brown, smelt strongly and stung painfully. (It could have been Jeyes Fluid of course.) Today I would probably have been rushed off to a doctor and given an anti-tetanus jab, but we took things more easily in those days. On the whole I was rather proud of myself for having been thrown out of a tonga. It had been an exciting adventure and I boasted about it to the other children at the dancing-class. Someone (I presume Mrs Strettle) rang up Metcalfe House, where Mother spent most of her mornings rolling bandages and packing parcels for the Red Cross, and told her what had happened, and Mother rang up Buckie who lived nearby but invariably lunched at Maiden's Hotel, which was just up the road from Curzon House, and he fetched us in his car. So we rode home in state — much to the gratification of Punj-ayah who had not ridden in a motor-car before.

Bets and I hadn't ridden in one very often either, and it was not until a year or two later that Mother succeeded in badgering Tacklow into buying a car of our own, which she learned to drive; I don't think we could have afforded a chauffeur. After that we stopped going out in hired *fitton-gharies* (open, four-wheeled carriages drawn by one or sometimes two horses) to such delectable spots as Okhla and the Khutab. Instead we were whirled out by motor-car on Saturdays and Sundays to picnic in places which had previously taken hours to reach, since they lay quite a few miles outside Old Delhi so that the journey, at a slow trot, was a hot, dusty and boring one; unless Tacklow was with us.

Tacklow had an exhaustive knowledge of Indian history and could make every bit of country that we passed through glitter with interest as he told us about the great cities and civilizations that had once flourished there, and of violent events that had taken place centuries ago on this or that very spot. He could make it all come alive again; and so real that one could almost see and hear those long-dead warriors charging into battle and the broken fragments of their cities rising again in splendour. Dark-eyed Queens and Princesses, veiled in gauze and shimmering with jewels, peered down again through the marble tracery of zenana windows to watch their men ride out to fight or hunt, to celebrate some day of festival or greet an emissary from one or other of the endless list of sovereign kingdoms, many of them larger than the whole of Britain, which made India a land of Kings — most of whom were perpetually at war with one or other of their neighbours, and very few of whom died a natural death.

A great school-teacher was lost when Tacklow dutifully followed his father into Indian service, for he could turn history into an enthralling story that knocked spots off *The Perils of Pauline* — not to mention *Dallas* and *Dynasty* and all the other serialized 'soaps' — and drove one to read history books just to learn more and find out what happened next. It was on one of these expeditions that he recited, by way of illustration, a poem of Kipling's that begins: '*Cities and thrones and powers stand in Time's eye, Almost as long as flowers, which daily die . . .*'. I never forgot that poem; or lost my fascination with Kipling's verse either.

The return journeys from these expeditions, taken by evening when the sun was setting and the dust gathering over the plains, or, best of all, when there was a moon to light the last few miles, were always a delight, for Mother would sing us the latest songs to pass the time. Tunes that were the pop songs of the First World War: 'If You Were the Only Girl in the World', 'There's a Long, Long Trail', 'My Little Grey Home in the West', and 'Vilja', the hit song from that long-running success, *The Merry Widow*. And if night fell before we reached home, Tacklow would tell us about the stars and show us how to find the Dog Star and the Pleiades, Andromeda and the Great Bear and a dozen others. These all-day picnics took place at weekends, for that was the only time when Tacklow was able to come with us. Too often some emergency would arise that prevented him from doing so.

Of all our picnic places near Delhi the favourite by far was Okhla, where the Jumna Canal began and the main stream was controlled by floodgates and a long weir that spanned the river from side to side. Above the slope of the weir the water was held in check by stout wooden planks supported by baulks of timber, and only a certain amount of it escaped through gaps between the planks to froth down the stony slope below and join the main stream once more. There was a shallow stone gutter, two to three feet wide and not more than six inches deep, just below the slats. It was always full of water even when the river was at its lowest and the weir was dry, and it was here that we would paddle and fish for *chilwa* with long-handled, home-made shrimping-nets. The silver fingerlings used to swarm here, and with them we sometimes caught baby turtles, miniature creatures no bigger than a four-anna piece but perfect in every detail. The turtles were considered great prizes and we would take them down to the flat sandbanks below the weir and dig pools in which we would release them and watch them flippering their way round and round.

In those happy days few people ever visited Okhla, and Buckie, Sir Charles, Tacklow and their friends would often take their shotguns — and sometimes, if we were lucky, Bets and me too — and drive out there for the evening flighting of the duck, teal and geese who daily, as the sun set, would fly in from across the river in long wavering lines, dark against the dusty green and gold sky; swooping in from the croplands of little lost villages miles away on the far bank. Tacklow, who was a poor shot (except, oddly enough, when after snipe), did not take much interest in these impromptu duck shoots, preferring to sit and watch, and admire the evening sky and dusk falling over the plain. But Buckie was said to be the finest shot in India, and when he made one of the party everyone present, including the drivers and *shikaris* and any Canal employee who happened to be around, was sure of going home that night with a brace or two of mallard or teal and the prospect of delicious roast duck or goose dinners. To watch Buckie shooting was an education in the art, for he never missed; and despite the inadequacy of my own parent and other sportsmen, I gained the impression that all one really had to do to shoot a bird that came over at any angle, high or low, whizzing past at sixty miles an hour, was to point your gun at it and pull the trigger. Simple! And to Buckie, of course, it was.

Sometimes at weekends Sir Charles, Tacklow and Mother and a particular friend of theirs called 'Bunting' (I have an idea that his real name was Hunting) would take Bets and me with them and drive out to Okhla for the weekend where we would sleep in the Canal Bungalow or in tents. Sir Charles kept a little motor-boat at Okhla, in which the five grown-ups (the fifth being Sir Charles's head *shikari,* Kashmera, who always accompanied them when they went out shooting) would go upstream to hunt the *mugger* and *gharial* which, in those far-off days could be found in great numbers in the waters of the Jumna, both below and above the weir and the canal head.

Muggers, the blunt-nosed, armour-plated crocodiles of the Indian rivers, are notorious man-eaters. They prefer flesh — preferably well rotted — to any other food; and in those days they were responsible for thousands of deaths every year among people who lived in towns and villages on the river banks and came down daily to bathe, fill their brass water-pots, wash clothes, water their cattle, or set fish traps while their children paddled and splashed in the shallows. It was easy for a hungry *mugger* to snatch a meal, for their diet also included unwary goats, sheep and cattle, as well as incautious wild animals coming down to drink at a spot where the water was deep enough to hide a lurking killer. And when, in times of plague or famine, the death toll rises so high that the survivors can no longer afford to cremate all their dead and consign them instead to the river, placing a token live coal in the mouth of the deceased, the *muggers* compete with the fish and the turtles and other wildlife along the river to dispose of the dead.

Their cousins, the fish-eating *gharials* who have long, slender snouts with a knob on the end, are by comparison gentle and harmless creatures. Yet they are regarded with dislike by the fisher-folk, who complain that they take an unfair share of the fish and cause considerable damage to nets and fish traps, while almost every village, and certainly every bridge and every ford, has — or used to have — a resident *mugger* who is known to have taken any number of lives, but is nevertheless regarded as semi-sacred; a sort of minor nature-demon who must be placated with garlands of marigolds and other offerings flung into the water, often by a local priest.

There were many *muggers* and *gharials* near Okhla, and wandering along the margins of the river in the evening we would come across the unmistakable marks that they had left in the wet sand: the long smear and deep curved groove where the end of an armour-plated tail had slid into the water, flanked by clawed footprints to left and right. Sometimes we would take careful note of these marks and lie up next day on the river bank among the clumps of pampas grass and casuarina scrub within sight of them, to wait for hours until the ugly water-dragon decided to crawl out again. It was always a deeply exciting moment when it did, and worth every minute of the long waiting —

First the glassy surface of the river would be broken by a barely visible ripple, which would presently resolve itself into two small bumps that could have been bubbles or fragments of debris floating down on the current; except that they remained stationary. They were the *mugger*'s eyes, scanning every inch of the shore to check that the coast was clear. Provided we made no movement, those two specks would presently be joined by two more; the creature's nostrils. Then very slowly all four would begin to draw in to the shore until at last the *mugger* grounded in the shallows, at exactly the angle that a log or a piece of driftwood would do, and waddling forward on his four stumpy feet, dragging that wicked-looking tail behind him, would settle down on the warm sand to take a nap in the sun. He is dark when he comes ashore: the dark grey of wet slate. But as the hot sun dries him the river mud on his horny scales turns pale, until he becomes almost invisible against the silver sandbank on which he lies, and if you did not know about *muggers* and were drifting down an Indian river in a barge or a sailing-boat for the first time, you would never notice him. Or if you did, you would take him for a stranded log that had been in the river for a very long time.

Nowadays both *muggers* and *gharials* have become so scarce that I am told that they will soon be an Endangered Species and are already protected in certain parts of India where rivers run through game reserves. Which is fine as far as *gharials* are concerned. But I have to confess that I have never felt anything but loathing for *muggers* ever since a day when I watched Kashmera and some local assistants slit open the stomach of a newly-skinned one and discover inside it, together with a gruesome collection of bones and bits, five unbroken glass bangles, so small that their previous owner could only have been a child and young enough for her murderer to have gulped down her entire arm without breaking the bangles.

Bets and I saw a good many *muggers* shot, and I remember one of them in particular: a small *mugger* not much larger than myself, that Tacklow shot on a sandbank upstream from Okhla. Mother wanted to take a photograph of us with it and made us sit down behind it;

but just as she clicked the shutter it suddenly came to life and whipping round with a sound that I can only describe as somewhere between a bark and a growl, snapped at Bets and only just missed taking a nice bit out of her arm. The creatures are not at all easy to kill, and at least seven *muggers* out of ten will flip back into the water with one convulsive and purely reflex-action sweep of their powerful tails the instant they are hit. And what's more, they survive. Their armour-plated suits are almost bullet-proof, and the *shikaris* say that there are only two places where a shot from a rifle can kill them: in the neck, or through the spine where it goes through the thickest part of the tail. The one that nearly took a bite out of Bets had merely been stunned, and as Bets fell backwards with a yell of alarm, head over heels, Kashmera leapt forward and dispatched it with a spear-thrust through its head.

After that we were very careful to make quite sure that a *mugger* was really dead before we got too close to it. I still have a handbag, an attaché case and a make-up box made from the skins of young *muggers* that I saw shot at Okhla, and Mother has a dressing-case and a trunk made out of large ones; all of them made up by the tanneries at Cawnpore. They still look nice, but are far too heavy to be of much use — especially the trunk, which weighs a ton even when empty and now sits in the attic taking up valuable space. I suppose one day we shall have to cease feeling nostalgic about them and throw them away, for they are of no further use and not even a museum would want them. Not that they were ever of much use, for the skin of the Indian crocodile is too thick and too heavily plated to make up well. It's the African and American alligators who make up nicely into shoes and bags and other expensive accessories.

Chapter 16

~⋇⋇⋇~

The barrow and the camp abide,
The sunlight and the sward.

Kipling, 'Sussex'

Anglo-India's favourite way of taking a holiday, particularly the Christmas holiday, was to spend it out in camp and shooting for the pot. Luckily for us we were often allowed to accompany our parents and their friends to these camps, where we could choose between following the guns or being left to our own devices. We usually elected to go with the guns, riding either in the back of a bullock-drawn country cart or in a lorry which must have been the first of its kind in the Punjab, with Kashmera and the other *shikaris* who would tell us tales of tiger and duck and partridge shoots that had taken place long before we were born.

Kashmera's favourite tale, and one that we heard often, concerned Sir Charles (whose *shikari* he had been for many years) and a leopard which had broken cover during a partridge shoot. One of the three or four guns who had been walking up partridge of an evening across a stony plain dotted with patches of high grass had, in the excitement of the moment, lost his head and blazed off at the leopard with both barrels of his shotgun at a range of only a few yards, causing the wounded animal to go to ground in one of the dense patches of grass and kikar trees.

Since there happened to be a village close by, the thought of leaving a wounded leopard holed up near it, and likely to attack anyone who passed, was not one that Sir Charles was prepared to contemplate; for leopards are notoriously bad-tempered at the best of times and a wounded one is as dangerous and unpredictable as a stick of dynamite in the hands of a two-year-old. Fortunately Kashmera had been carrying Sir Charles's rifle in addition to his own iron-tipped *lathi*, and the two of them cautiously entered the patch of head-high grass; Kashmera, an expert tracker, leading and Sir Charles, rifle at the ready, guarding his back . . . .

They followed the splashes of blood with infinite caution, and with frequent pauses to listen, for while they moved their ears were filled with the noise of their own progress through the dry, rustling grass. But soon it became difficult to see because night falls swiftly in the East; the sun had almost vanished below the horizon, and in the fast-fading light it was not easy to make out the blood spots. A warning growl from a little distance away made Sir Charles bring his rifle up to his shoulder and both men stood rigid; but it was not repeated, and presently they began to move forward again; one slow step at a time, and very cautiously, towards the place from where the growl had seemed to come — ahead and to their right. But just then, said Kashmera, the last rim of the sun dropped below the world's edge, and the breeze that comes with twilight awoke and blew across the plains. And after that they could hear nothing more because of the 'voices of the grass' all about them —

At this point they would have left that dangerous place and returned to it at first light next morning. But even as they began to retreat, walking backwards with rifle and *lathi* at the ready, the leopard charged and sprang — Not from the direction that the growl had come from, but from behind: for with the cunning of its kind it had taken advantage of the breeze, and under cover of the rustling grass had made a swift, stealthy circuit and attacked from an unexpected direction.

It buried its teeth and the claws of both forepaws in Sir Charles's arm and, clinging there, attempted to rip open his stomach with its hind claws: a feat that it would certainly have accomplished had its victim been a smaller and less powerfully-built man — or a less resolute one! But Sir Charles Cleveland, as has already been pointed out, was a huge man, and most of that hugeness was solid muscle. He kept his feet. And his wits too, for he realized that he must not allow those ripping hind claws to dig into his side and his stomach, and that with about eighty pounds of raging, snarling fury suspended from one arm it would be impossible to bring the heavy rifle to bear on it one-handed. So he dropped the rifle and concentrated grimly on swinging his arm from side to side in order to keep those lethal hind claws clear of his body. Imagine the strength it must have taken to do that! He did not wholly succeed, for the hind claws ripped through his clothes and drew blood, but did not go too deep.

Kashmera always swore that his Sahib kept the leopard swinging for a full five minutes, during which time he himself tried first to attack it with his *lathi* and the skinning-knife he always carried, and then — diving in under that frenzied pendulum to snatch up the rifle — to put a bullet through it. But the light was fading fast and he was terrified of killing the Sahib instead of the leopard who was being jerked to and fro without ceasing. In the end he took a chance, and pushing the muzzle against its body as it swung past, pull :d the trigger; and by good fortune the bullet smashed its spine and killed it. But that was not the end of the story . . .

There followed a nightmare fight to save Sir Charles's life. He had been appallingly mauled and blood was pouring from his wounds. The nearest hospital (which was in fact only a small dispensary run by an elderly Indian pharmacist) was miles away, and the only transport available was a bullock cart. The other members of the shooting-party — who had been given strict orders to stay outside the limits of the grass, but on hearing the uproar had rushed in to help and, like Kashmera, been unable to fire a shot for fear of killing their friend — put a tourniquet on the arm, and having filled the wounds with permanganate crystals (the only disinfectant which everyone in those days carried when out shooting or in camp), made a rough-and-ready hammock out of their coats and carried the wounded man to the village where the cart waited to take them back to their camp.

Here, at the *Talukdar*'s* suggestion, he was transferred to a palanquin with a team of strong villagers to carry it; that being a quicker and more comfortable method of travelling than by bullock cart. But even so, and in spite of changing bearers every twenty minutes, the miles crawled past and it seemed, said Kashmera, impossible that the Sahib could live to reach a doctor. It was almost midnight before they arrived, and the elderly pharmacist, after one horrified look at his injuries, declared that he could do nothing for him apart from washing his wounds and applying clean bandages, and that this was a hospital case. A tonga was procured and Sir Charles taken a further few miles

* Headman.

236

along a rough country-made road to the first town where there was a small hospital and an operating theatre. But it was morning by the time they got there, and the doctor declared that his wound had turned septic and that the only hope of saving his life was to amputate his arm before the poison spread too far and killed him. It would have to be done at once.

Sir Charles had lost a great deal of blood, and besides being in considerable pain and only semi-conscious, was running a high fever. But the doctor's pronouncement jerked him back into full consciousness and he declared in the strongest possible terms that he would see the misbegotten son-of-a-sawbones in Jehannum before he allowed him or anyone else to chop off his arm! In the end, since he would not listen to reason, the doctor shrugged and gave in, and (thankfully, I imagine) stitched him up while arrangements were made to forward him to the nearest British-run hospital — probably the Hindu Rao in Delhi — and sent him off with the parting observation that by the time he reached it, if he were still alive there would be no point in operating, since it would be much too late to amputate; but if he wished to commit suicide, that was entirely his own affair.

Well, he got there alive. And the English medicos told him flatly what their Indian colleagues had already said: that his only hope had been in amputation, but that it was now too late for that and he had better resign himself to death. Sir Charles, however, was even tougher than he looked and he proved them all wrong. The poison and the fever raged in his blood, but as his friends and the hospital staff waited for the inevitable end, he fought back. And inch by inch it retreated; descending slowly through his body until at last it reached his right foot which, so he told me himself, turned dark purple, swelled up like a balloon and hurt like hell — 'as though it were being stuffed through a red-hot mangle' was the way he described it; which gave me some interesting thoughts about Hell. Then quite suddenly it stopped hurting, returned to its proper size, and he was well again.

He had fought and defeated the poison in his blood as decisively as he had defeated the leopard; whose body, incidentally, had been recovered and skinned, and the head and fore-part stuffed and set up in a lifelike manner by the famous taxidermists, Van Ingams. The hind-quarters having been badly peppered by Number 4 shot and disfigured by a hole made by the heavy rifle bullet that had blasted away part of the lower spine, it had only been possible to set up the front half of the creature, and this was done so that it looked just as though it were alive and springing out from the cover of that tall grass. The large glass case that contained it was the one set up in the hall of the house he lived in in Simla, and I always hated having to walk through that hall during the months of the monsoon when the days were dark with rain, for in the shadows the snarling creature looked horribly alive.

That story was only one of many *shikar* stories that Kashmera told us. But we never got tired of hearing it, even though we must have heard it any number of times — and from a variety of different people, including Tacklow and Sir Charles himself who once showed us his scarred arm, as knotted and misshapen as the twisted bough of some ancient oak tree. We could see clearly where the leopard's clenched teeth had torn out a great mouthful of flesh and muscle when it fell back dead, and the deep pits its teeth and talons had driven into his arm. And once, bathing in the Jumna, we saw the long, silvery scars where the leopard's hind claws had raked his chest and belly as it strove to rip him up. All the various versions we heard of this story differed from each other in minor ways. But since the one we heard most often was Kashmera's, we came to know it so well that if he changed so much as a word we would correct him, and I have therefore given his version plus a footnote from Tacklow who told me, years later, that Sir Charles's version of the poison finally reaching his foot was correct, except for one thing: it did not happen in a matter of days or even months. It took years. The poison would seem to be defeated, only to break out again and affect some other part of his body. His left foot was the last part to be affected; and the last bit of that to be truly painful was his big toe! After exiting from that the poison never troubled him again.

Now why should I remember that it was his *left* foot — and his left big toe? — and not be able to remember which arm the leopard got its teeth into, when I actually *saw* the scars on that arm? It was only when I came to write this story down that I realized the years have taken that memory away from me, even though I can still see Kashmera acting out the whole story in dramatic detail to two small, pop-eyed girls in short khaki dresses and pint-sized solar topis, riding home from camp in the back of a plodding bullock cart.

⌘ The Christmas shooting-camps were the greatest fun. On one occasion we made camp in a mango grove near the famous battlefield of Panipat, which lies some twenty miles to the north of Delhi. Three of the bloodiest and most momentous battles in all the long and violent history of India were fought there.

In the first of these an invader from the North, Zahir-ud-Din Mohammed Barber — 'Barber the Tiger' — first of the Great Moguls — defeated the vastly larger army of Sultan Ibriam Lodi, last of the Lodi dynasty whose tombs make New Delhi's Lodi Golf Course among the most charming in the world. Thirty years later, on the same spot, the army of Barber's grandson, Akbar the Great, soundly defeated the forces of a rival claimant, one Hemu. And just over two centuries later a third Battle of Panipat was fought between another invader from the North, the Afghan ruler of Khandahar, Ahmed Shah Durrani, whose victory over the combined Mahratta forces that opposed him signalled the final collapse of the tottering Mogul Empire and the end of the Confederacy of the Mahratta Princes ...

Every inch of the level plain must in its time have been drenched in blood, and I listened enthralled while Tacklow told me the story of those violent days. Walking me over the historic plain, he showed me a brick-built plinth that marked the site of the battlefield and pointed out exactly where the opposing armies had taken up their positions, and how in each one of the three battles, though the defending army had greatly outnumbered their attackers (and in the case of the last Battle of Panipat, possessed far more guns), they had been defeated by superior generalship.

But it was from the people who actually lived there, in particular the owner of the shooting rights and the land on which our camp was pitched, and from various members of his family, that I learned a great many gruesome details about those homeric contests; the tale of which had obviously been handed down from father to son and mother to daughter in the old families of Panipat whose ancestors had seen the conquerors come and go and must have suffered sorely at the hands of both victors and vanquished.

From them I heard the tale of how the wounded and dying Hemu was dragged into the presence of the young Akbar who, at the bidding of his guardian, one Bairam Khan, finished him off with a *tulwar*.*

* The curved sword of the East.

And of how, after the last Battle of Panipat — which ended with the rout of the Mahrattas and the death of most of the Hindu leaders — Shah Durrani's pursuing Afghans gave no quarter to either prisoners or wounded, but decapitated all who fell into their hands; piling up more than two hundred thousand severed heads in great mounds throughout their camps. And *that* was only the Hindu dead! There must have been heavy losses among the Muslims as well. All those dead men ...! Horses too, and probably elephants as well. All that spilt blood ... What on earth must the place have *smelt* like by next day? How did they know who was who, or discover which of the defeated commanders had been killed and which ones had escaped? There were all sorts of things I wanted to know, and some of the answers I received from the landowner and his family were hair-raising.

I don't believe that adults ever realize quite how much their children learn about facts that doting parents imagine they have been successfully shielded from. They do not fully appreciate how easily the nastiest things slide off the backs of the young, who have a disconcerting habit of accepting the seamy and sordid with perfect equanimity and dismissing it as unimportant. Being the fortunate possessor of a retentive and photographic memory, I did not forget the tales I was told of the terrible deeds that had taken place on the plains of Panipat. But I was far more horrified by the sight of a pi-dog who had snatched a still-born lamb that had been left lying out in a nearby field, and ran with it through our camp, pursued by a yapping pack of other pi-dogs who snatched and tore at the gory remains that dragged on the ground. *That* wasn't a story. That was real; and I can see it still. But those piles of severed heads, and worse horrors, were only stories; and though I did not doubt that they were true, they remained on a par with Jack the Giant Killer and '*Fee-fi-fo-fum, I smell the blood of an Englishman; be he alive or be he dead, I'll grind his bones to make my bread!*'.

The Slaters and their children were among the guests at the Panipat camp, and so the presence of Bargie and Tony was enough to make it a memorable one for both Bets and myself — though apart from those tales of the great battles and the incident of the pi-dog, the things I remember best are the sugar-cane and an evening visit to the local temple. The sugar-cane was being harvested, and while the guns were walking up partridge and quail across the uncultivated land, I stopped to pass the time of day with the *Talukdar*'s field-workers, who were cutting and stacking the tall canes and loading them into bullock carts, and was presented with an entire cane which one of the women workers peeled and cut up into manageable lengths for me. No child who has not experienced the pleasures of chewing the juice out of those deliciously sweet pieces of cane, and spitting out the pith with a careless disregard for where it falls, has really lived!

I can't remember who took me into the temple, except that it was an elderly Indian who had some connection with it. Not a priest, because I would have remembered the clothes, and memory holds a clear picture of a burly, grey-haired man wearing a small gold-embroidered cap, and with a thick woollen shawl wrapped about his shoulders — for even in the plains the night can be very chilly in December. I remember a lot of oil lamps and the blaze of a fire that lit up a small, dusty square crowded with stalls selling sweetmeats and hot food and brightly coloured clay figurines. There was a big peepul tree growing out of the centre of a brick platform on which more people sat and talked and smoked *huquas* in the firelight, and the surrounding shops and houses were blotched and chequered with leaping black shadows against a moonless sky in which fireworks made streaks and splashes and showers of varicoloured light.

I remember too that there was some argument over whether or not I should be allowed into the temple, but the man in the shawl, who was obviously a person of authority, said there was no harm, and together we climbed a flight of steps and went in under a stone archway decked with tinsel and paper flowers and innumerable *chirags* that flickered and glowed from every possible niche in the carved stone. *Chirags* are always lit in time of festival and there was one being celebrated that night, though I don't remember what it was. Certainly not one of the major ones. This was only a modest affair and probably in honour of some minor and strictly local deity. I remember the temple, like the square outside, as a patchwork of shadows and shimmering, smoke-filled, golden light that smelt of jasmine and incense and fading marigolds. There was a fire here too that fizzed and crackled as a priest fed it with oil and crumbs of incense and another priest chanted mantras. I remember how cold the stone felt to my feet — I had of course left my shoes outside — and how the oil lamps and the fire made the tinsel decorations glitter. One of the priests put a *tilak*, a scarlet mark, on my forehead, and I remember leaving as an offering a whole silver four-anna piece! — an enormous sum to me in those days, when my pocket-money was one anna a week.

I have been in other temples since then, many of them far larger and older and more impressive. But none of them ever gave me such a feeling of awe and wonder, and holiness, as this small and relatively unimportant one in a village near the old and evil battlefield of Panipat.

That particular Christmas camp was, like most others, a week-long affair, planned to end the day after Boxing Day. But as Tacklow could not be away for more than three days, he and Mother had offered us the choice of spending the entire week there (in which case Tacklow would come out on Christmas Eve and return with us on Boxing Day) or of spending Christmas at Curzon House — in which case he would come to Panipat with us, and bring us back with him on Christmas Eve. Since we had not realized at that time that the Slaters and their children would be asked to join the camp and that Bargie and Tony would be there, Bets and I had elected for the second option. Our reasons being that Panipat lacked the allure of Okhla and the river and sounded pretty dull; whereas back in Curzon House there would be a Christmas tree to decorate and, more important, a proper fireplace. (We were always slightly uneasy about hanging up our stockings in a tent, for even if Father Christmas was able to trace us to our camp — as Mother assured us he would — how would he be able to deliver the goods on schedule if there were no chimney to come down?) Besides, Tacklow would be home every evening, so taking all this into consideration we had plumped for returning to Delhi.

But when the time came to leave, I for one wished very much that we had chosen differently, for I had enjoyed myself so much at Panipat, and having Bargie here had been an unexpected and delightful bonus. I hated leaving her and the camp, and the landowner and his family — and Panipat. But it was too late to change our plans, because knowing that we would be leaving, others had been asked out to take our place and our tents for the extra days. I still remember vividly the deep depression and regret I felt as I waved goodbye to them all, and which stayed with me all the way back to Delhi. A regret that was made deeper by the knowledge that I had made a wrong and irreversible decision, and had no one to blame but myself! I would come to that same bleak conclusion all too often in the future — as I suppose everyone is bound to do — and I can only conclude that the reason I remember it so clearly is because this was the first time it happened to me.

Fortunately, my gloom did not outlast the arrival of the Christmas tree at our rooms in Curzon House that same afternoon. It was a splendid one that only just allowed space for a Christmas star to be fastened to the top after it was firmly planted in a huge copper coal-scuttle. That done we all went gaily off to the Lal Kila to buy tangerines, which were always available at that season from a stall in the Red Fort's own bazaar — two rows of small shops that face each other from either side of the long, covered arcade that leads out of the vast, double-storeyed entrance hall that is the ante-room of the main gate (the Lahore Gate) of Jehangir's fortress-palace. These tangerines were a part of Christmas and to this day the sight, and more particularly the sharp, spicy scent of them, always reminds me of Christmas in India and conjures up a picture of the shadowy, sun-splashed Lal Kila arcade.

The Christmas tree by family tradition (Bryson, I suspect — not Kaye!) was decorated late on Christmas Eve; long after the children had hung up their stockings, said their prayers and were safely asleep. We would go off to bed leaving it an ordinary fir tree stuck in its tub, and wake up next morning to find it glittering with silver bells, glass balls and spun-glass baubles, strings of tinsel, Christmas crackers, cottonwool snow and innumerable brightly coloured little candles. It was a sight that never lost its magic for us. The most exciting moment of the day, though, was when we woke up in the very early morning and, crawling to the end of our beds, groped in the dawn darkness for the stockings we had hung up on the previous night (there was always the fear that this time we might have been forgotten!) and felt them bulging with little parcels and topped by two or three crackers.

Those stockings were a delight, for every single item was wrapped separately in different coloured tissue paper, so that one had the added thrill of opening them one by one. Small, Indian-made toys and trinkets, bought off stalls in the bazaars or at *melas** by Mother during the past year and hoarded for this occasion; none of them costing more than an anna or two and each one an enchanting artefact. Crackers stuck out of the top of each stocking and there was always an orange

* Fairs.

in the toe and an apple in the heel, with nuts and sweets in between, and a packet of those little grey sticks that crackle and fizzle and spit out showers of silver stars when you light the top with a match. And somewhere in my stocking would be, year after year, an adorable biscuit-china cherub or angel with real hair, each one different from the last. These little figurines, in contrast with the rest of the toys, cost a whole rupee, for they were made in Bavaria and sold in Rago Mull's shop in the Chandi Chowk, Delhi's famous Silver Street. By the time I left India to go to school I had managed to collect seven of them; but alas, they all perished, with so much else, in that disastrous fire at the Elephant and Castle.

The larger presents were always given to us when we burst in on our parents to hand them their parcels and share their *chota-hazri*. And after breakfast there were the *dális* — flat, tinsel-bedecked baskets of gilded Indian sweets, fruit and nuts and flowers, presented to us by proprietors of shops where we had an account, head clerks in Tacklow's office, and our servants, to mark the occasion. Sometimes the *dális* contained money tucked away among the flowers or hidden under the fruit, and sometimes there were jewels for Mother or expensive toys or trinkets for Bets and myself. These could never be kept, however alluring, since they constituted a bribe and the taking of bribes was most strictly forbidden. The only gifts one was allowed to accept were perishable ones — fruit and flowers and things to eat.

I have heard of British officials who regarded these expensive gifts as insults and returned them with loud rude words. And, worse, of others who accepted them and said nothing. But Tacklow would always return them with the polite pretence, if it was money, that it must have dropped out of the donor's pocket by mistake, or in the case of jewellery or any valuable present, with warm thanks for having been given the chance of handling and admiring such a charming object ... The point was taken and there were no hard feelings. But oh, I would dearly have liked to have kept some of those expensive toys! Among them, once, there was a French doll with a Paris wardrobe and eyes that opened and shut, which I longed to possess and handled with enormous admiration before regretfully giving it back! Gifts from close Indian friends were of course a different matter. For one thing the givers had no axe to grind, and for another, one reciprocated with gifts of equal value on *their* special festivals; as well as on birthdays and weddings.

After the presentation of the *dális* and all the thank-yous, we would put on our Sunday-best hats, which were white solar topis of the mushroom variety with removable, and washable, covers of white *broderie anglaise*, and leave Curzon House on foot to walk to church, past the Kudsia Bagh, the Tennis Club and the Nicholson Gardens, and on, under the battered arch of the Kashmir Gate, past the Police-*khana* and the old Quarter Guard, to St James's; the Anglican Church built in the early 1820s by Sikunder-Sahib — Colonel James Skinner of Skinner's Horse. It is said that he built it because of a vow he made while lying wounded on a battlefield, that if he should survive he would build a church; and also that he hedged his bets by building a mosque and a temple as well, just to be on the safe side. But his body lies buried in the Skinner vault in St James's.

I was much too young to know anything about architecture, Palladian or otherwise, yet even my untutored eye found a deep satisfaction in the proportions of St James's; in its lines and planes and arches, and the way in which the sound of the service echoed under its central dome. That day the echo threw back the joyful thunder of the organ and the voices of a packed congregation singing 'Hark the Herald Angels Sing' at the top of their lungs. And suddenly it was Christmas! *Really* Christmas. Not just a day for stockings and presents and parties, plum-pudding and snap-dragon, or even the Christmas tree, but an enormous, world-wide birthday party to celebrate the arrival of a baby who had been born in a cattle-shed nearly two thousand years ago: that 'Saviour who is Christ the Lord'. All the rest of it was no more than pleasant trimmings tacked on to the birthday celebration because this was a time of good-will and rejoicing, and everyone felt generous and jolly and full of optimism. I had of course heard the Christmas story; and read it too in a book called *The Life of Jesus of Nazareth*, beautifully illustrated by a William Hole, R.A. I had both listened to and sung carols and knew a good many of them by heart — a favourite being 'Good King Wenceslas'! But until this particular Christmas the true meaning of the 'Mass of Christ' had been swamped by all those exciting trimmings — the presents and the parties, the tinsel and the tangerines. It took '*Hark the Herald Angels Sing, Glory to the Newborn King!*', sung in Sikunder-Sahib's church in

Delhi, to bring home to me for the first time what it was really all about. There are so many first times when one is young; and all of them milestones.

There are other carols, learned much later, that I like better. Christina Rossetti's 'In the Bleak Mid-winter' for one. But ever since then no Christmas Day has been truly Christmas to me until I have heard or sung 'Hark the Herald Angels Sing'. I have heard it sung in churches all over the world. In Peking in north China. In churches in India from Kohat in the north to Calcutta in the south. In Kashmir and in Kenya, in Egypt and the Andaman Islands, in Switzerland, Spain and Austria, and in divided Berlin as well as in Scotland and England, Ulster and Ireland. Yet every time I hear it I am back again in that little Palladian church in Old Delhi, with the sunlight streaming down from the windows below the dome and a long-vanished congregation singing the carol that first revealed Christmas to me.

That afternoon we went to a party in the Moncrieff-Smiths' rooms in Curzon House, where their daughter Phyllis made a dramatic appearance from behind the curtains that (as in our rooms) divided the front rooms from the bedrooms, dressed as a snow-fairy and sitting on a sledge loaded with parcels which she distributed to her guests. We were much impressed by this original departure from a scenario that usually entailed an embarrassed father pretending to be Santa Claus in a deplorably home-made cotton-wool beard and someone's red dressing-gown, plus a repertoire of nervous 'Ho-ho-hos' that would not have deceived the dumbest two-year-old. But then the Moncrieff-Smiths were famous for their children's parties — as witness their spectacularly successful Pink Party in Simla. We used to play with Phyllis, who was a bit older than I was and inclined, we thought, to be a bit snooty. She never became a real friend, though for a few weeks during which our favourite game, for reasons unknown, was playing at preaching sermons, she showed a remarkable aptitude in the role of Vicar for ticking off the congregation (myself, Bets, Sibyl, Joanie, Iris, Tony and anyone else who happened to be around — I don't remember Bargie ever playing). She was excellent in the pulpit, but not so hot as a member of the congregation.

The next two Christmases were both spent at Okhla, the first in the Canal Bungalow and the second in camp alongside Number 3 Groin, below the weir. I had really enjoyed Panipat, but to both Bets and

Above: Self with Sir Charles Cleveland and Kate, on the garden steps of his house in Simla. He used to sit on these steps every morning and watch me ride round and round the lawn, while he shouted instructions and advice. A daily and much-dreaded ordeal.

Left: Bargie (Marjorie Slater).
Taken on board ship, *en route* to India.

Below: The Mall, Simla.

Above: The Black and White Pierrot Show. Mother is the pierrette seated third from left, while my future mother-in-law is second from the right.

Below: Tacklow butterfly-hunting near Kufri in the Simla hills.

Above: Mother leaves Delhi, driving Tacklow, Percival Landon and his bearer in the Hudson.

Below: Bets and self as small Belgians in 'The Pageant'.

Above: Oaklands; our house in
the hills five miles from Simla,
with (left to right) 'Mrs Ponson',
self, Mother, Bets — and Kate.

Above: Village on the road to Kufri. This might
be any one of a thousand hill villages.

Left: Mother, off to a Viceregal ball, complete
with her opal tiara.

Below: Buckie and friends at Dukani.

The Kashmir Gate as it looked when I was a child in Old Delhi, before the dry moat was filled in. The scars of the Mutiny remain on the gate to this day.

Mother in 1916.

Bill. This photograph, sent by Aunt Molly, is the one that reduced Mother to tears because it was so unlike the little boy in a sailor-suit she had said goodbye to.

Above: Christmas camp at Okhla. The one from which a jackal nearly made off with Bets's doll.

Right: Breakfast in camp. Tacklow, Abdul Karim, Bets and self.

Below: (Left to right) Bets, two camp-followers, Kashmera and self, lined up behind the *mugger* whose stomach contained half-a-dozen unbroken glass bracelets. Those rifles, incidentally, were only borrowed for this snapshot after being unloaded.

Above: Picnic at the Khutab. (Left to right) Tony, Bargie, Lady Grant, Bets and self.

Left: The Khutab Minar.

Below: The Taj Mahal. Note that the only human figure in this snapshot is a solitary *mali* (in the centre distance) armed with a basket for collecting dead leaves. It was taken in the days before the Age of Mass Tourism, when the Taj and its gardens were quiet and uncrowded, and beautifully peaceful.

Above: The Slaters. Muriel Slater with three of her children: (left to right) Bargie, Dick and Tony. Their eldest brother, Guy, my first love, had already been sent home to England by the time this photograph was taken.

Right: Mrs Perrin and the *mahseer* that took her all day to land.

Below: Setting out from Narora for the sandcastle island. Mother holding the youngest Perrin, Mrs Perrin behind her, self and Bets on the right: I am clutching Mrs Perrin's fishing-rod.

The Lakkar bazaar, Simla. The hill down which we used to run races falls away sharply just behind the group of citizens on the left.

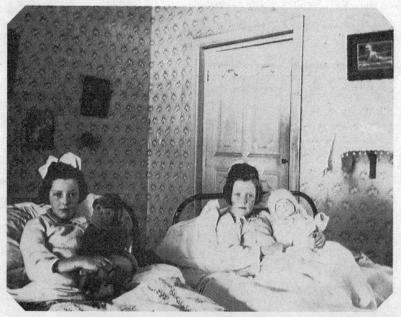

Bets and I both went down with a bad go of the influenza epidemic that swept round the world in the wake of the First World War, killing far more people than the war had done. Here we are, with Moko and Teddy, convalescent but still in bed, at The Rookery.

myself no playground — not even our beloved Kudsia Bagh — could stand comparison with an Indian river.

Oh, those rivers . . .! Why is it that they still keep such a strong hold on my imagination that whenever I hear a really haunting piece of music, like Tchaikovsky's 5th Symphony for instance, or any piece that has real melody, I see to its refrain the quiet, slow-moving, mile-wide rivers of my childhood, flowing through those enormous, sun-baked spaces; and remember the basking rows of turtles lining the sandbanks, the flocks of white egrets pricking through the shallows, wild duck flighting at evening and the parrots coming down to drink in the dawn . . . the smell of it. And the silence: we lost that long ago, but in my day there were endless places where one could hear the wind breathing through the grasses or whispering through pine needles; the whirr of a dragonfly's wings or the fall of a leaf. And even, on certain white nights, the faint '*pop*' that the bud of a moonflower makes as it unfurls.

There were always birds along the rivers. Egrets, gulls, sandpipers, wild duck, herons and storks, sedate flocks of pelicans, stately sarus cranes, and endless other land and water birds. There were always, too, those ranks of sunbathing river turtles which Bets and I used to stalk in imitation of our elders and betters stalking *muggers* — inching forward on our stomachs over the hot white sand and freezing into immobility whenever one of their sentinels turned an alert, snake-like head in our direction. At the last moment, when we had got as near as possible, we would leap to our feet and rush forward in the hope of grabbing a tardy one who had been a bit slow in taking off. We never got one of course, for at the first flicker of movement the somnolent ranks of sunbathers would flip back into the water, and for a good hundred yards up and down stream the sandbanks would be as empty as the back of your hand.

Brooding over our lack of success I came up with the brilliant idea of using Tacklow's butterfly-net. Racing forward after the usual prolonged stalk, one aimed at the water and not the turtles, and generally managed to scoop in an escapee as it swam away. The resulting captives were carried triumphantly back to the camp and incarcerated in our tin bathtub, where we could watch them swimming round and round and scrabbling futilely at the sides. However, Nemesis overtook me, because the butterfly-net did not stand up well

247

to the job of catching turtles and Tacklow became uncharacteristically
testy when he saw the damage they had done to his property (which,
to make matters worse, we had borrowed without his permission). I
got a sharp ticking-off and was in disgrace for at least an hour: after
which he relented and suggested that Kashmera's *muchli-net* would be
more suitable. It wasn't, because it was too heavy for us. But Kashmera
accompanied us on several of our turtle-stalks and caught one or two
for us.

The captives were always returned to the river in the evening, each
one being carried down separately and released on the spot where it
had been caught. But watching Kashmera catch them wasn't half as
much fun as catching them ourselves had been, and we soon gave up
that particular sport and went back to fishing for *chilwa* and releasing
them into pools that we made by digging branch channels off the side-
streams and then constructing dams. Tacklow made up a song about
the turtles which went to the tune of one of his music-hall songs:
'Once there was a little poodle with a coat as white as snow'. It was
never written down and I don't remember it being sung very often.
But it remains firmly in my memory, and here it is —

> *Mollie saw a little turtle in a pool beside the weir,*
> *So she went and tried to catch it, but it would not let her near;*
> *Swam away, she could not follow just for fear of getting wet,*
> *So she called and old Kashmera caught it in his fishing-net.*
>
> *Mollie took that little turtle home and put it in a tub,*
> *Sluiced it down with nice clean water, gave its little back a scrub.*
> *Round and round that turtle scrambled, vainly to escape he tried*
> *But at last he gave it up, because he could not climb the side.*
>
> *Later when the sun was setting Mollie took it in her hand,*
> *Bore it down beside the river, laid it softly on the sand.*
> *Then that turtle winked his eye at Daddy's little daughter*
> *And flipped his funny little tail, and popped into the water!*

This masterpiece by our personal Poet Laureate was, of course,
sung in 'Kaye-language'; which was something else that Tacklow had
invented for our amusement. Various letters and/or combination of
letters were pronounced as z (e.g., 'Then thaz turzel winked its eye at
Dazzy's lizzle dauzer, and flipped its funny lizzle tail, and popped into
the warzer'!). The rules as to which letters were replaced by z were

very strict: but there were exceptions too, of the 'i before e except after c' variety. We all got very good at it and when spoken quickly in ordinary conversation it was quite difficult for non-Kayes to know what we were saying. A nice example of it was when we were driving through a particular bleak and barren stretch of country in which nothing moved but a number of grazing goats, and Tacklow remarked idly: 'A dezolaze country, entirely inhabizez by goze!'

The outfits that we wore in camp were known as our 'scampy brown dresses', and no party frock I ever possessed, however pretty, could touch them for popularity. They represented freedom and fun, and consisted of short, button-through frocks of stout khaki-coloured cotton with white collars and brown leather belts, worn over matching bloomers which, being provided with elastic at top and bottom, made admirable pockets besides enabling us to stuff our skirts into them when paddling. We could have done without the white collars, which showed up too well against the general browny, greeny, sand-coloured surroundings, but when stalking we merely tucked them inside the necks of our dresses. Regulation khaki-coloured topis were worn as a matter of course when the sun was high, since they were supposed to protect us from sunstroke; and always while in camp or at Okhla we were allowed to run bare-foot. It was not long before the soles of our feet became as tough as those of any of the Canal coolies or their children, and we could scamper along the gravel-strewn paths of the Canal Bungalow or the Headworks, or across the open country where the sun-baked ground and the hot dust were littered with flakes of mica, small stones and fallen kikar thorns — those wicked double spikes that can penetrate all but the toughest leather. I still carry the mark of those happy, shoeless days in the form of a small but solid patch of horn (I really can't call it skin!) on the pad of each of my big toes: the last traces of the toughened soles on which I could easily have walked over live coals or broken glass without taking any harm, as Kashmera and his friends did. To know that we could do that too was a source of great pride to us: though we could never summon up the courage to deal with an aggressive scorpion, poised to strike, simply by treading on it as they did.

The first Okhla Christmas, spent in the Canal Bungalow, was made memorable by the fact that Bets actually *saw* Father Christmas. Imagine our excitement!

We had both been asleep, but some small sound had awakened Bets and she had opened one eye and seen that a lamp was still burning in the next room and that a stealthy figure was coming towards the open doorway. The next moment the intruder slipped through and vanished; but as the lamplight caught it (there was no electricity at Okhla in those days) she saw that its cloak was red! *Father Christmas himself!* — it couldn't be anyone else. Then the door closed and she was in the dark again. She didn't dare wake me for fear that he might hear us talking and, realizing that we were awake, magic our presents away. She lay listening for a while in the hope of hearing his reindeer sledge move off, and eventually fell asleep again, so it was not until first light on Christmas morning that I heard about it; and was bitterly disappointed to think that I had slept through it all. Our dear parents were duly impressed when they in turn heard about it, and it must have been sometime during that morning that Mother returned a red dressing-gown she had borrowed from Sir Charles, who was in camp below Number 3 Groin with the remainder of the Christmas-week party.

We had brought a Christmas tree with us which we set up under the punkah in the dining-room, and my 'proper present' that year is the only Christmas present — apart from the little biscuit-china angels that turned up every year in my stocking — that I can still remember. Memory holds no trace of any of the others, but this was something so special that it still surprises me that Mother, who was not over-gifted with imagination, should have been the one who chose it for me. (Tacklow was always too short of free time to do more than choose and buy her present.) She had been buying a pair of ivory-backed brushes as her present for him at a shop called The Ivory Palace in the Chandi Chowk when she saw this and on impulse bought it for me. It was a little ivory dove some five or six inches long and perfect in every detail, sitting on an ebony pedestal that had been carved to look like a broken tree-stump. Except for its colour and the fact that it was only about a third the size of a real one, the ivory dove was the image of the little grey Indian ring-doves which are as plentiful in the plains as sparrows, and whose soft, continuous cooing forms a murmurous and familiar background to each day. I was enchanted by it. It was the first grown-up present I had ever received, and holding it in my hand I felt that I had crossed some invisible threshold and become at least three inches taller. That Christmas was a memorable one for both of us. For Bets because she saw Father Christmas and for me because I was given a work of art: something to keep and to treasure for the whole of one's life — an ivory dove! I kept it and treasured it for years. But alas, the dove too went up in smoke.

The following Christmas we pitched our tents below Number 3 Groin with the rest of the annual shooting-camp. And even though there was no Christmas tree we didn't miss it, because it was a marvellous treat to be back once more on our favourite stretch of river and under canvas again, with the grown-ups shooting for the pot while we fished for *chilwa*. Our catch appeared on the menu as whitebait, preceding the main course provided by the guns which rang the changes between venison (black-buck), jugged hare, wild duck, goose and teal, roast pea-fowl (in place of turkey), partridge, quail and green pigeon, with snipe on toast as a savoury.

In order to differentiate that year's camp from the others, we used to refer to it afterwards as 'the Jackal Camp', because in the course of it a jackal had tried to steal Bets's baby doll. It was one she was especially fond of and had insisted on bringing with her to camp because neither Moko nor Teddy stood up well to river water, thorn scrub or sand. (And anyway Mrs Jones and Mrs Snooks, being townees, did not function outside Delhi.) The doll was made of celluloid and like most infants at that time was dressed in long clothes; the outer robe being of white muslin trimmed with lace, while under that came a top petticoat of white cotton, an under one of flannelette, and then a bodice, a vest and a diaper. It also wore a lace cap tied with ribbons, a caped coat and, on this particular occasion, had been swathed in a knitted shawl and carefully put to sleep on Bets's camp-bed while she accompanied me on some expedition to the river or the weir.

The tents were pitched on hard, sandy ground in the thin shade of some half-dozen kikar trees, and the area in which they stood had been surrounded by a stoutly built zareba of thorn boughs and dead cactus to keep out night-prowling predators. The kitchen tent and the tents in which the servants and *shikaris* slept were outside this zareba and within a similar one of their own, and there were serviceable wooden gates in both which were closed at night but kept open by day. One hot, still afternoon, while the grown-ups and guests were all off shooting somewhere on the far bank, the servants were taking a well-earned siesta and Bets and I were busy with some ploy of our own on the sands, a jackal sneaked unseen into the deserted camp, and entering our tents, saw the baby doll lying on Bets's bed. He presumably thought that it was a live infant, for seizing it in his mouth he was making off with it when Bets and I unexpectedly returned and saw the jackal emerging from our tent with the doll in his jaws, its long dress trailing in the dust.

The doll was less than life-size, but it looked horribly lifelike all the same, and Bets let out a piercing shriek, waking one of the sleeping camp servants who leapt into action, and whizzing out of his tent raced for the gate. The jackal, seeing its retreat cut off, turned and made for the zareba, teeth still firmly clutching its prey, and though one would have said that nothing larger than a tree-rat or a lizard could have found a way through that prickly barricade, it found a weak spot and managed to fight its way out; though fortunately not with the doll, whose robes got so inextricably snagged up on the thorns and cactus spines that its would-be abductor was forced to abandon it — dusty and somewhat tattered, but otherwise undamaged. I never did like jackals anyway, because of Tabaqui in *The Jungle Book*. But after this I really hated them. If that had been a real baby it would have been killed and eaten. A horrid thought.

Apart from that episode, my chief recollection of the Jackal Camp Christmas is of trying my damndest to catch a goggle-fish. I had hoped very much that someone would give me a fishing-rod for Christmas, but despite a lot of heavy hinting, no one had, and I never did catch one of those fish. Nor do I know what a goggle-fish's proper name is. We merely called them that because they went about in small shoals in shallow water with their large, protuberant eyes sticking up above the water, like a brace of doll-sized ping-pong balls. They would come in so close that it seemed as though one ought to be able to catch them with one's hands, let alone a landing-net; or at the very least trap them in one of the small inlets. But they were a good deal smarter than they looked, and those silly goggly eyes were misleading. We laid all sorts of plans to ensnare them, but they invariably outwitted us, and to this day I have no idea what shape or size they are, or what they looked like out of the water. Or even if there is any more to them than just those eyes!

Since a fishing-rod did not figure among my presents I made myself one out of bamboo and boot-button thread, and spent hours trying to entice a goggle-fish to even *look* at my bait (a fragment of *chapati**** donated by the cook and attached to a bent pin). But with no success. In the end I gave it up as a bad job and returned to stalking turtles and building dams, or lying up in the long grass by the river bank to watch a *mugger* or a *gharial* crawl out on to the sand for a bit of sunbathing.

Not all our camps were Christmas-week ones. And nor were they always at Okhla. Another popular site was near Gujrowla on the Ganges, where there is a long iron railway bridge spanning the river. Sir Charles would drive us out in a shooting brake the size of a small bus, and parking it on the near bank, have us all ferried across to the far side in one of the clumsy, flat-bottomed river barges. From these we transferred into tongas or bullock carts that would take us another two or three miles to the spot where Sir Charles's men, who had gone out the day before, would have set up camp near a *jheel* — a stretch of shallow, reed-grown water in the middle of nowhere, where there were always mallard and pintail, widgeon, teal and geese, and plenty of snipe.

Bets and I did not care for the Gujrowla camp nearly as much as Okhla. This was partly because it was well out of reach of the river, and partly because we considered that watching birds being shot was no fun at all (much as we enjoyed the end results, such as duck and green peas with orange sauce, cold roast teal and salad, and similar delicious dishes!). But we loved the getting there and getting back: the early start while it was still dark and the long drive to Gujrowla; first in the pearly, pre-dawn light and later in the sunrise, when the night mists lifted off the croplands and open country and all the shadows lay long and blue and stripy across the white dust on the roadway, and the air was fresh and sharp and full of the clamour of bird voices and the squeals and shrieks of well-wheels.

The sun would always be high and hot by the time we reached Gujrowla. But when we returned again a day or two later, it would be setting and the river would be a blaze of liquid gold as we crossed it once more in one of those slow-moving wooden river-boats that looked as though they had been built by Noah and his sons to a pattern

* The flat, unleavened flour-cakes that are the bread of all India.

that had not changed for centuries. Later, if we were lucky, there would be a full moon; and once again the long, dusty road between the shade trees would be striped with shadows, now black on silver.

Sir Charles would while away the return to Delhi by singing 'Abdul, the Bul-bul Amir' and other familiar songs, and on the outward journey we would all join in singing a song for which Tacklow had written the verses; the first one starting with: *'We're off to Gujrowla today!'*. There was a verse for everyone, but alack, I never wrote them down and all I can remember of them was that one began *'There's Kashmera*, shikari — though no clue remains as to what rhymed with *shikari* — and another: *'There's Kate, the retriever, we never can leave her'* ... Everything else is lost; even my own verse! Yet I have only to hum the tune to remember those long drives out to Gujrowla. Or hear a bar of 'Abdul, the Bul-bul Amir' to hear Sir Charles sing it as we drove back to Delhi by night with herds of black-buck leaping across the road ahead, their eyes glittering in the glare of the headlights. India's plains and forests teemed with wildlife in those days, for there were still vast tracks of country which, except for a thin scattering of small, remote villages, were virtually uninhabited.

Chapter 17
~❋❋~

I called my men from my trenches, my quarries, my wharves and my sheers.
All I had wrought I abandoned to the faith of the faithless years.

Kipling, 'The Palace'

If I have given the impression that our parents always took us with them when they went out camping, let me hasten to say that the only camps we could be certain of being taken to were the Christmas ones. Any others were a bonus. Not all shooting-parties liked children tagging along, and on the many occasions when they went without us, or when Tacklow had to go on tour and Mother went with him, we were left behind in the care of family friends — and Punj-ayah, of course.

On one such occasion, when they both were away for a longer time than usual, Tacklow being on tour — this time, I think, in Burma — and Mother having been invited to join some lengthy celebration in one of the Princely States of Rajputana (a combined birthday-cum-wedding party as far as I remember), Bets and I and Punj-ayah went off to spend two weeks with a middle-aged couple who lived in an isolated, old-fashioned bungalow on the outskirts of Delhi, where the Grand Trunk Road leaves the city behind and drives straight as an arrow across open, scrub-covered country.

None of our friends lived anywhere near here and there was nothing for us to do once we had finished with our morning lessons, to which we were driven in our host's trap accompanied by Punj-ayah. In those car-less days all our old haunts were suddenly as far out of reach as the moon, and the Grand Trunk Road, where every vehicle that passed raised a smothering cloud of dust, was hardly a suitable place for morning or evening walks. We missed the Kudsia Bagh and the sands of the Jumna sorely. But the flat scrub-covered plain was new territory

255

and we set off to explore it and see what it offered in the way of entertainment.

At first it seemed as though there were no landmarks and nothing of interest, and Punj-ayah, satisfied that no danger was likely to befall us in such open and obviously uninhabited country (and unwilling to tear her sari to shreds on the thorn bushes or the dry, knife-edged grass), gave up accompanying us and let us go where we wished. But during the first day or two, extending our explorations to the unknown territory behind the bungalow, we came on an enormous sandpit which, until we were practically on its rim, was completely hidden by the tall grass and the usual sprinkling of kikar trees. It must have been gouged out by water many years before, during a flash-flood in some bygone monsoon when the rain had formed a temporary river that washed away the soft, sandy soil, leaving a deep depression about half an acre in size, whose sides fell steeply away like cliffs below us as we peered cautiously over the edge.

The hooves of black-buck, chinkarra and wandering goats or grazing cattle had worn a track down one side of the enormous sandpit and out at the other; probably in search of water, for there would have been a pool there in the rainy season, though now there was only hard, baked earth and withered grass. But the cliffs below us were pockmarked with holes and the air swirled with the wings of myriads of tiny sand-martins who were nesting in the sides of the sandy cliffs.

The birds took no notice of us and we watched, fascinated, as they swooped and swerved like a swarm of bees; snatching flies on the wing and flashing into their holes in the cliff with a swiftness and accuracy of aim that was almost unbelievable. We watched them for hours, and later, having returned thoughtfully to the bungalow, we set about making ourselves a pair of butterfly-nets; using bamboos for the poles and the ring — a thin, whippy sliver for the latter; you can do all sorts of things with bamboos! That done, we coaxed Punj-ayah into buying us a yard of thin cotton net from the bazaar during the time that she and the driver of the trap had to wait while we sat at our lessons. Our pocket-money, which we were careful to save up for such emergencies, was at that time a lordly one anna a week, so I can only suppose that the price of cotton net was not more than a few *pice* a yard.

Punj-ayah obliged, and we made ourselves two admirably service-able butterfly-nets, much admired by our hosts, who commended us for our enterprise and industry. Little did they know! For the truth is that it had occurred to me that we could easily catch one of those sand-martins. All we had to do was to watch until one went into its hole in the cliffs, and then put a net over the hole and wait, for when it came out it was bound to fly into the net. And I was right. It did. Unfortunately, after we had caught one or two, held them carefully in one hand, stroked their tiny heads with the tip of a finger and let them go again, I had another idea. What about taking one or two of them back to the bungalow and letting them loose inside our mosquito-nets? Then we could sit inside with them and watch them fly around, and perhaps they would become so used to us that when we released them they would come to our hands of their own accord?

I'm afraid our success with the squirrels in the Kudsia Bagh must have gone to my head, for we instantly put this outrageous plan into action. We brought the sand-martins back two at a time and turned them loose inside my mosquito-net, and when we had made several trips and had at least six sand-martins flying around under the net, got in with them ourselves. But here the plan hit a serious snag. Our captives thought nothing of the idea. They were plainly terrified of being boxed in with a couple of human beings and they streaked to and fro in a frenzy of panic, flinging themselves against the netting and clinging to it until their tiny claws became hopelessly entangled as they struggled to free themselves. Our efforts to help them only made matters worse, and by the time we managed to get them all out, the mosquito-net was in tatters and the bed-clothes, pillows and ourselves were liberally spattered with bird-droppings and feathers.

The faithful Punj-ayah would have hushed up the whole affair and mended the mosquito-net had that been possible. But it was so badly torn that it would have taken hours to make good the damage, and it was already tea-time. There was nothing for it but to own up and ask my hostess if I could please have another mosquito-net. She was not pleased, and I don't blame her. She and her husband had never had any children of their own, and though they frequently said how sad this made them and how they doted on children, they did not under-stand them as our beloved Colonel and Mrs Ponson and Buckie did, and were totally incapable of coping with this sort of thing; or understanding it. They were both frankly horrified (more by the mess and destruction, I think, than by the cruelty of trapping birds for fun) and I received a tremendous scolding on that account; and another because I had 'deliberately deceived them in that I had failed to tell them what the butterfly-nets were for'. This was quite true, of course, and I don't remember feeling in the least guilty about that, for if they chose to think the nets were for catching butterflies that was their lookout. In any case, why was it all right to catch butterflies and kill them, and wrong to catch birds and let them go? I simply couldn't follow their reasoning.

In the end I was informed that it would be necessary, as a matter of painful duty, for them to write and tell the whole distressing story to my dear parents; and then sent to bed supperless and in floods of tears. (Bets, it seemed, was too young to know any better and had plainly been led astray by her older sister! Too true.)

Well, at least I had clean bedding and a new mosquito-net. And when I told Tacklow the whole story he laughed and said that it served them right for continually telling Mother how devoted they were to all children, what a pleasure and a privilege it was to have 'young people' about them, and how happy they would be to look after her little darlings if ever she wanted to take a holiday without us. He had, he said, warned them that entertaining a handful of children wearing party frocks and accompanied by nannies, ayahs or parents to tea followed by decorous games was not at all the same thing as having a couple of them as house-guests for close on ten days. They had refused to believe him, and Mother, much touched by their offer, had been rash enough to accept it. (Largely, I suspect, because she herself had very little idea of what we got up to while in the nominal charge of Punj-ayah.)

Mother, to tell the truth, saw even less of us than our hard-worked father did. Her mornings were occupied by Red Cross work, her afternoons taken up by various committees arranging balls, bazaars, cabarets, floor-shows and other entertainments in aid of this or that war effort or charity, and her evenings spent at the Club playing tennis or chatting with friends on the lawn while the Club band played selections from popular musical comedies of the day — *The Merry Widow, The Dollar Princess, Miss Hook of Holland, The Belle of New York, The Quaker Girl* and *The Arcadians* ... Bets and I used to go up to the flat roof of Curzon House to listen to those lovely, lilting melodies drifting through the intervening trees in the dusk, and you've no idea how sweet and gay and romantic they sounded. At half-past seven, just as we were getting to bed, Mother would hurry home to bath and change before going out again to dine and dance. She had a lovely war! The only thorns in her bed of roses were her fears for the safety of her twin brother, Ken, and her two elder brothers, Tom and Arnold, all of whom were with the Expeditionary Force in France and all of whom came safely through the war years; though Tom, her favourite, was destined to be tragically killed in an accident at Singapore while on his way home to North China to join his wife and baby son in Tientsin.

Tacklow still accompanied her to these dinner-parties and, after seeing that her dance programme was full, came home and went to bed. He spoilt her outrageously. Even on his own birthday his presents always included one from himself to himself which invariably turned out to be something for which he found (with surprise) he had no use, and therefore passed on to Mother: such things as silk stockings, scent, some small piece of jewellery or a box of chocolates tied up with a satin ribbon. My chief memory of her during my childhood in India was of her rushing in to say good-night to us before going out to a party, looking perfectly beautiful in a shimmering ball-dress and smelling divinely of a special scent that was Tacklow's favourite and that I never came across on anyone else. It was called *Le Trefel Incarnat* by L. T. Piver of Paris, and everything she possessed smelt of it: her clothes, her furs, her gloves and her evening bags, her luggage, every drawer in her dressing-table and chest of drawers, her cupboards and her bedroom. In later years I had only to close my eyes and sniff a handkerchief or a glove of hers and she was there in person, sparkling and laughing, conjured up like the genie of Aladdin's lamp by the ghost of a scent that L. T. Piver, if they still exist, stopped making a very long time ago.

I used to think how beautiful she was. And how full of laughter. Tacklow, unfamiliar in a dinner-jacket or looking uncomfortable in a stiff shirt, white tie and tails, would escort her to those parties if he came back from the office early enough to do so. And when he didn't, some mutual friend would stand in for him: Buckie or Bunting; Sir Charles or Ronnie Graham-Murray; Harley Alec-Tweedie; Lord Clow or Monty Ashley-Phillips ... Nowadays their names seem to read like a roster of P. G. Wodehouse's famous Club, 'The Drones'! There was never any shortage of escorts and we liked them all — with one exception. The exception was Lord Clow; the 'Lord' being a nickname that someone had bestowed upon him and that had stuck. I don't know how he came by it, for as far as I can remember he was a mere Captain — and not 'Captain the Lord Clow' either! A lordly sort of fellow, perhaps? He was certainly a devastatingly handsome one, and he put himself out to be pleasant to Bets and myself. But neither of us could stand him, and I can only suppose that of all Mother's beaux he may have been the only one she was in danger of taking seriously, and that we sensed this and were jealous — or even afraid? I don't know. I only know that he was far too attractive and good-looking to be true, and that we could not endure him.

We liked all the others though, even the good-looking ones like Bunting and Harley, and some whose names I have forgotten and whom even Mother no longer remembers when I show her snapshots of them. She only frowns and looks on the back to see if there is a name there and then shakes her head and says: 'Yes, I do remember him; he used to make me laugh; but I've no idea who he was . . . Henry someone? Or was it Peter: no, Peter had a moustache — or am I thinking of Alan?' She gives up. Tacklow took all her admirers in his stride, and appears to have had no qualms about leaving her to dance the nights away and be brought home in the small hours by one or other of them. He probably trusted to her mission upbringing to keep her from straying; and in any case he needed his sleep and could not lie in as late as she could of a morning. As, for instance, she did on a certain January night when she stayed dancing into the small hours at the Bachelors' Ball — a yearly fancy-dress affair held by custom at the Old Delhi Club — and, returning to her sleeping husband at around 4.30 a.m., crawled thankfully into bed and thrust her toes down into an ice-cold and sopping wet patch instead of the warm hot-water bottle she had expected. Throwing back her bedclothes with a shriek she leapt out; to find that her hot-water bottle having developed a leak, our faithful Punj-ayah, discovering this, had carefully sewn up the slit in the rubber with a needle and cotton before stowing it away in the bed.

✗ Apart from the weekend picnics and expeditions with our parents, there were always other parents who took their children and their children's friends out for picnics. Buckie, for one, could be counted upon to take a party of us out to Okhla at least once a month. His parties were regarded as great treats because he had three hard-and-fast rules: no parents, no nannies, no ayahs. Just himself and his driver (there were few owner-drivers in those days, Mother being a rare exception) and a selected band of children. He stood no nonsense from any of us, and any child who misbehaved or made a nuisance of itself was never asked again.

At least once a month his enormous car, packed and stacked to the roof with picnic baskets and children, would whisk us off to Okhla where, on arrival, he would line us up like a company on parade near the weir, and announce in a sergeant-major blare that the first one who fell into the water would get their ears boxed — so there! I remember how once, while we were standing in a row near the edge of the river, Joanie Kirkpatrick, who did not know him as well as the rest of us did, took a scared step backwards, and *plop*! there she was in the water. Buckie dealt efficiently with the situation. He fished her out and stripped her, and having rolled her up in a tartan rug, locked her into the back of the car with a bag of toffees to console her, while he took the rest of us off to fish for *chilwa* — bringing us back an hour or two later to enjoy a picnic tea alongside the car so that we could feed poor Joanie through the windows.

Picnics were some of the best things about Delhi. I remember one given by a friend of Mother's, a Lady Grant who later, as Margaret Grant, became a musical comedy actress and whom we last saw when we had tea with her in her dressing-room at — I think — Her Majesty's Theatre in London, where she was starring in a show called *The Good Old Days*. She took us out to the grounds of the Khutab Minar with one or two of her own children, plus Bargie and Tony Slater, Bets, Mother and me. The Khutab is a tremendous minaret that has stood there over a quarter of a century before the death of Genghis Khan, for its foundations were laid and the building of it begun in 1200 A.D. It stands more than two hundred and thirty-eight feet high, faced with red sandstone that is fluted and carved and inlaid with white marble, and is divided into five sections by carved stone balconies that encircle it like fretted bracelets. That picnic stays firmly in my mind because in the course of it Bets and I climbed the Minar three times. (I rather think we all did: except for the Grant children who would have been too young, and the two grown-ups.) We climbed it once on arrival, once after lunch and once after tea.

In those days, and right up to the day on which India became independent, there was no restriction on climbing to the top of the Khutab; anyone was allowed to do it. Nor was there an ugly iron 'lion's cage' plonked on its summit either! There are three hundred and seventy-nine steps, and climbing them is a picnic compared to coming down again. But we seem to have taken it in our stride and thought nothing of it. When I panted up it in 1942, almost a quarter of a century later, there was still no iron cage and I got acute vertigo at the top and had to sit down on the top-step-but-one with my feet firmly below the roof-level — scared to bits of falling! It was then that I stopped seeing anything funny in the story, reported in the *Statesman*, about a villager from Jullunder, who was on the top of the Minar when the last ripple of the terrible earthquake that decimated Bihar reached Delhi and rocked the great tower to and fro. The poor fellow had gasped out to a reporter, who saw him stagger out of the tower some fifteen minutes later, that when it happened he hadn't been able to make up his mind whether to jump off the top or 'risk going down by the stairs'. I thought that was hilariously funny when I first read it, but after that day in 1942 I know just how he felt, for I might easily have had difficulty in deciding myself. (You notice that the gentleman from Jullunder apparently considered that there was no risk — or a lot less anyway — attached to jumping off the top!)

Twenty-one years later still, during one of our nostalgic return visits to the land of our birth, Bets and I decided to climb the Minar for one last time before old age and arthritis got their hooks into us; only to discover that no one was allowed to go further than the first balcony. Beyond that the stair was blocked. This, explained the local *chowkidar*, was because too many people had used the Minar to *kuttum-hogai* themselves (literally 'finish' themselves) by leaping off the higher ones — a messy business that entailed a great deal of bother and trouble scraping the remains off the paving-stones at the bottom. I pointed out that as the lowest balcony was a good forty feet above the pavement, anyone jumping off it would surely *kuttum-hogai* themselves just as efficiently as the ones who went off the top, or one of the higher balconies. But he was not convinced. Unquestionably, a soul-mate if not a near relative of that man from Jullunder. It made me feel even more at home.

Better than the picnics, though not as exciting as the shooting-camps, were the weekends at Agra; for even in those far-off times Agra was only a short distance from Delhi. There was a night train that left a couple of hours after midnight and would get us there in the early morning; which meant that if Tacklow could get Saturday off (most people took Saturdays off as a matter of course!) he could leave Agra by the Sunday-night train that got us back early enough on Monday morning for him to have a bath and breakfast at Curzon House before leaving for his office in Metcalfe House.

Agra was always a magical place to me. It still is. Even though so much has changed and Barber's city is now full of brand-new package-tour hotels, each one crammed to bursting-point with noisy tourists of every shape, size and nationality who bargain loudly for souvenirs when not clicking their forests of cameras or applauding the twice-nightly floor-shows which consist of so-called 'Traditional Indian Folk Dancing', i.e. girls in spangled skirts gyrating to the sound of what in our day were called 'Fu-fu bands'.

But all that still lay in the future; along with the car age and the air age. Back in the teenage years of the twentieth century Agra was still a green and quiet town, living on past memories of the Great Moguls and brooded over by that pearl of pearls, the Taj Mahal. Its great past had gone and its vociferous tomorrow was still to come, and Bets and I were privileged to know it in the sunset of its peaceful days, when the fact that there was a world war raging ensured a total absence of globe-trotting tourists and permitted Agra and its glories to sit back and weave dreams.

For us its spell began to work long before we reached it. First there were suitcases to be packed and a special kind of bottled milk to be bought to take with us, because Mother wouldn't let us drink hotel milk. The bottled stuff had a distinctive taste faintly reminiscent of malt and we considered it delicious. Punj-ayah did not accompany us on these expeditions, but Moko and Teddy went along, and on a Saturday evening, after an early supper, we and they were put to bed in Curzon House with instructions to go to sleep as quickly as possible and not lie awake whispering. It is difficult to do this when one is keyed up and excited, and though we did not dare whisper, I for one would lie awake for a long time, listening to the night noises and especially to the far-away sounds of trains arriving or leaving Delhi. To anyone of my generation there will always be something haunting about the sound of distant trains heard by night: not modern trains that run on diesel or electricity, but the steam-trains of our youth. Which of us will ever forget 'the sigh of midnight trains in empty stations'? To this day the sound of a train in the night speaks to me of Delhi and those magical visits to Agra ... For the space of a few heart-beats I am young again and back in my bed in Curzon House; and wherever I happen to be, no matter in which city or town or country, it is India that lies outside, hidden from me only by the dark.

In the end, of course, we always fell asleep; to be woken at midnight and taken by tonga or *tikka-ghari* to the station which, no matter what the hour, was never empty. There Alum Din would take charge of the luggage and see to the unpacking of *bistras*, and while our parents were busy deciding who should sleep on which berth, Bets and I would escape the eye of authority — easy enough in those swirling, chattering crowds! — and make for our favourite part of the station: the great metal circle that lay out in the moonlight beyond the furthest end of the platform, where the clumsy, coal-burning engines that ended their run at Delhi were turned around on something that looked like a huge turntable, to face the direction they had come from, in readiness for the return journey. It was a sight that never failed to fascinate us, and no arrival or departure from Delhi station was ever complete until we had seen it. It was for us part of a ritual: yet as I look back and remember, I am once again astonished by the amount of freedom we were given. So much, that we could make off alone and dive into the midst of that pandemonium which was, and still is, the normal state of affairs on the platforms of any major railway station in all India, without our parents or ourselves — least of all ourselves! — thinking for one moment that we could come to any harm. We never did. Partly, I suppose, because we always knew we were among friends; but largely because Indians as a whole are a kindly and tolerant people.

Arriving in Agra in the cool, pearly dawn we always drove straight to Laurie's Hotel and a warm welcome from the proprietress, dear Miss Hotz — who was 'young Miss Hotz' then, though to Bets and myself she always seemed old — and as soon as we finished breakfast we were off to the Taj. I don't know how many times I have seen that Wonder of the World, because it never occurred to me to keep count. A hundred, perhaps? though even that may be an understatement. Tacklow, of course, had spent his leaves in Agra, back in the nineteenth century when his father was Commissioner of that town and the district surrounding it, so he had seen the Taj again and again when he was a newly-joined and impressionable young subaltern. I was a good deal younger than he had been then, but to use his own expressive phrase, it 'hit me where I live'. I have never got used to it. Each time has always been as though it was the first time, and it still has the power to make my heart contract.

Many people have tried to describe the Taj, but for me only Kipling has succeeded in putting it into words; and he only saw it in the dawn from the window of a railway carriage taking him down south — and vowed never to see it closer for fear of spoiling that first breathtaking vision. Tacklow quoted me Kipling's description of it, and since I know it by heart and it cannot be bettered, here it is:

It was the Ivory Gate through which all good dreams come; it was the realization of the gleaming halls of dawn that Tennyson sings of; it was veritably the 'aspiration fixed', the 'sigh made stone' of a lesser poet; and over and above concrete comparisons, it seemed the embodiment of all things pure, all things holy, and all things unhappy. That was the mystery of the building ... the thing seemed full of sorrow — the sorrow of the man who built it for the woman he loved, and the sorrow of the workmen who died in the building — used up like cattle. And in the face of this sorrow the Taj flushed in the sunlight and was beautiful, after the beauty of a woman who has done no wrong.

I have to admit that, unlike Kipling, the Taj never struck me as being full of sorrow. Or if it was there, it passed me by. But it was then and is now both the 'sigh made stone' and the 'Ivory Gate through which all good dreams come'. And what made it so perfect was that we could spend the whole day there, wandering up and down, around and all over the buildings and the gardens alike, without anyone ever saying 'You mustn't' or 'You can't'. Very often we would be the only visitors there. It was empty and quiet, and peaceful beyond words. No noises but the birds and the squirrels, the splash of the fountains and the sigh of the wind crooning through the marble tracery and under those serene arches.

There were several reasons for this: the first, strangely enough, being that Indians in general took no interest at all in this marvel of marvels and rarely bothered to visit it. Yet there it was, free for anyone to walk into and explore. No entrance fee to pay, nothing to prevent the humblest, poorest and grubbiest young citizen from wandering in. I know; because I went there again and again and spent hours and days there and played in the gardens with the children of the few (the very few!) Indian families who occasionally dropped in. And had Bets or I ever seen one of the sleepy custodians of the Taj, who spent their days dozing peacefully in the shade of the great entrance gate, turn away an Indian of whatever age or caste, we would have asked to know why. We knew everyone who worked at the Taj, from the head *chowkidar* down to the youngest and lowliest gardener's boy; including the old Mulvi and his assistant who had charge of the underground burial chamber in which Mumtaz Mahal, 'Ornament of the Palace', lies beside the husband who raised this marvellous tomb for her, and by doing so made her name immortal. If any of these people had actively discouraged their own countrymen from visiting the Taj we could not have failed to notice the fact, and be curious about it. And if we had discovered that 'only Sahib-log' were permitted to enter freely, I suspect we would have felt slightly grand and exclusive.

Until a Viceroy, Lord Curzon, began urging India to appreciate and preserve the marvellous monuments of her past, very few Indians seem to have taken any interest in ancient buildings. Temples and mosques being places of worship were OK, since Hindus and Muslims are very devout. A few tombs too, and here and there the odd fort. But that was it, and many a ruling Prince pulled down the glorious palaces that his forefathers had raised and replaced them with some frightful copy of late-Victorian wedding-cakery. Only when mass tourism broke out in the wake of Independence and Partition, and swept round the world like the Black Death, did India begin to take an interest in her historic treasures. Today the crowds that swarm through and around the Taj are three parts Indian to one of Western and Far Eastern sightseers, and hordes of shrill-voiced souvenir-sellers, with their shops and stalls and uproar, insult the approach to their Ivory Gate. Worst of all, the marble itself is being destroyed by the pollution that pours into the air and water from the giant chemical works which, with all India to choose from, some soulless, greedy, money-grubbing politician and/or industrialist thought fit to site a few miles upstream of a building that ranks as one of the Seven Wonders of the World. Anyone, given the money, can build a chemical works. But there is only one Taj Mahal, and when it crumbles the whole world will be the poorer.

However, let me return gratefully to the days of my childhood when so few people visited the Taj that, wandering through the gardens and climbing up the narrow stairway that came out at the foot of the great dome, I could sit on the broad top of the central arch and look back at the entrance gate and the Saheli Burj, one of four monuments erected in memory of the maids of honour in the service of Mumtaz Mahal, or down, down and down the sheer cliff of marble decorated with verses from the Koran, to the wide white terrace below and the long channel of water between a double avenue of cypress trees. When tired of sitting there I could walk round to the opposite side of the dome, from where one could look down on the River Terrace and the water lapping below it, and out across the placid reaches of the Jumna to where, downstream, lay the clustered trees and little half-ruined pavilions that marked the site of one of the gardens that the Emperor Barber, who loved gardens and the sound of running water, had made long, long ago at Agra — long before his grandson Akbar built the great Red Fort, or his great-great-grandson Shah Jehan, the Taj Mahal.

Upstream, a mile or so away and facing the Taj across the white shimmering sandbanks and green patches of cultivated land, the fort rose up like a line of red cliffs along the Jumna. And much nearer at hand, directly opposite the River Terrace and with only the river and the sandbanks between, lay the ruined foundations of the tomb that Shah Jehan had meant to build for himself on the far bank. A second Taj exactly like the first one in every detail — only this one was to have been built from black marble instead of white, with a marble bridge across the river to connect the two. In the event he got no further than the foundations before one of his four sons, Aurenzeb, running true to Mogul family form, deposed and imprisoned him. He was confined to the Jasmine Tower of Agra fort, where he ended his days; and he was lucky not to share the fate of his other three sons, all of whom were murdered by their brother Aurenzeb. I felt sorry for the poor old man; but glad that he had not been able to finish building a black Taj opposite the white one, for it seemed to me that a black copy of the pearl-tinted soap-bubble at my back would have turned out to be a hideous, heavy blot on the landscape. And what would he have done about the bridge? Made it particoloured, or half black and half white?

✕ I have never been able to explain to myself why I find the Taj so satisfying to look at, because there is no doubt that it is, in essence, a biscuit-tin on which someone has plonked half an ostrich egg, and then placed on a chopping-board with a pepper-pot at each corner. Alabaster copies of the thing make hideous souvenirs, and I remember Tacklow being presented with a two-foot-high model of it in solid silver mounted on an ebony plinth, which turned out to be a cruet in disguise. Every bit of it unscrewed and could be used either as a pepper-pot, salt-cellar or sugar-sifter, or a container for vinegar or salad oil — or fruit, if you turned the dome upside down! And you actually *could* keep biscuits in the main body of the tomb. I've never seen anything more horrific, and I considered Tacklow to be straying from the truth when he returned it to sender with the usual polite note saying how *very* kind it was of Rai-Bahadur-Whatever to permit us to examine and admire this superlative example of the silversmith's art — etc., etc. But perhaps it is just because I cannot explain its allure that the original appeals to me so much. One can't pin down the Taj. It changes shape and colour with every hour of the day and every change of the weather; and though its sheer weight in tons must be stupendous, it still manages to look as though it is as perishable and impermanent as a soap bubble, and as easily blown away.

As children we came to know it intimately; every single nook and cranny of it. And because we so often had it to ourselves, we regarded it almost as much a personal possession as our secret hideaway above the arch in the Kudsia Bagh.

There were three other places in Agra which we knew and loved and never failed to visit whenever we went there. A garden, hardly more than a ghost of one (if a garden can have a ghost?) that Barber had laid out. The jewel-box tomb of Itmad-ud-Daula, Persian-born father of Jehangir's Empress, Nur-Jehan, and grandfather of the Lady of the Taj, which is a marvel of intricate, Persian-style inlay-work in coloured marbles and semi-precious stones. And Akbar's great red sandstone fort, crammed with enough palaces, halls of audience, mosques, pleasure gardens, stables, zenana quarters and baths to keep the most earnest and avidly curious of tourists happily occupied for days on end. Nowadays, I'm afraid, the package-tourist is given little time in which to do as we did; wander at leisure through its enchanted and enchanting halls while Tacklow told us stories about the men and women who had once lived and loved, intrigued and plotted and died there: peopling the rooms with lovely ladies who wore silks and gauzes and glittered with jewels and gold-dust, gaily turbaned warriors and statesmen in armour or embroidered *achkans*, scores of priests and pages, servitors, grooms, *mahouts* and men-at-arms; and legions of courtiers and sari-clad waiting-women. All of them at the beck and call of the Mogul himself — Emperor of India and 'Ruler of the World'.

Tacklow also told us about the Mutiny years, and showed us a little mosque which a British military doctor, who had escaped being massacred by the mutineers in Gwalior and managed to reach the safety of Agra fort, had used as a surgery and temporary hospital for the treatment of wounded and dying men, and which ever after had been regarded as defiled and shunned as a place of worship by Muslims; even though many of that faith owed their lives to the treatment they received there!* But I am afraid that of all the fort stories, the one that intrigued us most was the tale of a British sentry who claimed to have found one of the many secret passages which, according to legend and folklore, riddle the walls of Akbar's fort; some of them, it is said, leading to hidden and long-forgotten vaults full of hoarded treasure. The soldier, who should have been on duty, asked a fellow sentry to cover for him while he investigated his find, and the friend agreed to do so. But when the relief sentry arrived to take over, the treasure-seeker had still not returned. Nor was he ever seen again, though a most stringent search was made of the fort, which he could not conceivably have left since it was still under siege by mutineers, and its garrison, fearing another enemy assault, had been at pains to double-lock, bar and place a guard on every possible and impossible exit and entrance.

* It is only recently that I heard the rest of the story from that same doctor's son — who is still very much alive! However, I shall keep it to tell in its proper place, which is well into the 1980s.

269

Since everyone's dream is to find a secret passage ending in a room full of fabulous jewels, Bets and I, conquering our fear of spiders and accompanied by Moko and Teddy, hunted high and low for the one that the sentry had found over half a century ago. But though we found numberless dark and narrow little stairways that dived downward or climbed upward inside the thickness of those formidable walls, they always ended tamely in some open courtyard or deserted ante-room; never in a vault full of golden goblets, bracelets, sword-belts and nose-rings set with emeralds and diamonds. Or even a dungeon containing a skeleton dressed in the uniform of some forgotten East India Company regiment! Oh well, we had a lot of fun and scared ourselves silly trying.

One last 'special place' was Fatehpur Sikri, which is not technically in Agra at all since it lies more than fifteen miles to the south-west, within sight of the borders of Bharatpur. The story goes that a much-revered saint, one Salim Chisti who lived here, foretold the birth of a son to Akbar the Great, who when the prophecy came true built a city on this auspicious spot. But after it had been built and occupied for only a few years, a shortage of water made life impossible, and it was abruptly abandoned; the court returning to Agra and leaving the splendid new city to the foxes and the owls. It was a hot, silent, wind-whispering and bird-haunted place, and in our day few people visited it; for the same reason that few tourists visited Agra — there was a war on.

Here nothing moved except the slow shadows of the red sandstone walls or the swift ones of a pigeon or a parrot flying overhead, and one walked on tip-toe and spoke softly. Which is not as silly as it sounds, for time has dealt so gently with the deserted city that even now you can almost swear that its inhabitants have merely withdrawn for an hour or two to take a siesta, and will emerge again to 'eat the evening air' as soon as the sun moves lower down the sky and the shadows draw out across the stone flags of the courtyards. The stables and the camel and elephant lines, Jodh-Bai's palace, the lovely Panch Mahal, and the great red courtyard marked out like a huge *pachisi* board (*pachisi* is not unlike chess) so that the Mogul and his friends could play that game with beautiful serving-girls as living pieces, all look as new and as unblurred by time as though they had been built well within one's own lifetime instead of that of Elizabeth Tudor, over a decade before that redoubtable Queen granted a charter with rights of exclusive trading to a 'Company of Merchants of London trading into the East Indies'.

Once while Mother was sorting through a bag of miscellaneous kag (the Kaye word for odds and ends: 'kag-bag'), she came across an early photograph of the Taj Mahal taken sometime in the 1860s or early 1870s.* It was a revelation, and I only wish I had had the sense to get my hands on it and stick it in some album for safe keeping. For it showed the Taj as some sort of lost palace, like the palace of the Sleeping Beauty, shut away for a hundred years behind an impenetrable hedge of briar roses. The marble water channels were full of reeds and waterlilies, and the trees and shrubs crowded close to their edges; the higher branches overgrown with trails of creepers dripping down towards the water so that one caught glimpses of the Taj through a veil of leaves and flowers. It could only have looked as beautiful — and as overgrown and neglected! — because of its nearness to the river and the fact that those marble water channels must have silted up and flooded the gardens during the monsoons. But out at Fatehpur Sikri there was little or no water, so weeds and saplings were never able to take it over. Here no creepers veil the walls and grass has not invaded the deserted halls whose stone-paved floors are swept clean by the wind.

Salim Chisti, the saint whose prophecy led to its being built, and who died in 1571, lies buried in an exquisite little tomb whose lattice-work walls, each one carved from a single slab of white marble, look as fragile as lace. The tomb stands in the enormous open courtyard of Fatehpur Sikri's Dargah Mosque, mirrored in a marble-lined pool and looking for all the world like a pearl thrown down on a red carpet, for the courtyard, like the palaces and halls and stables, is paved with red sandstone. Mosque, tomb, pool and courtyard are dwarfed by the towering Gate of Victory which the self-styled 'King of Kings, Shadow of God, Ja-la-din Akbar the Emperor', built to commemorate his conquest of the Kingdom of the South, and upon one wall of which he had inscribed the words: '*Hazrat Isa,*† *on whom be the Peace, said: "The World is a bridge; pass over it, but build no house thereon."*'‡ And,

* For, or by, my Kaye grandmother.

† Jesus Christ.

‡ A sixteenth-century sentiment that is engraved in slightly different words above the door of an Elizabethan manor-house near my home in Sussex: 'Herein we have no abidence'.

'The World endures but an hour, spend it in devotion.'

In the days of the Raj you could climb up to the very top of the Gate of Victory; though the gate-keeper was always careful to warn you to watch out for the nests built by wild bees among the carvings and in the cornices of the galleries, for the fierce wild bees of India can be killers — as anyone who has read Kipling's story 'Red Dog' in *The Second Jungle Book* will know! But provided one took care not to disturb them the view from the top of the Bulund Dawarza was worth the risk, for the huge gate stands at the top of a great flight of stone steps which sweep down to reach the road below, making the height of stairway and gate together a staggering one hundred and seventy-two feet from the road up. Standing on the top, one could look away and away across the roofs of Sikri and Fatehpur and the endless miles of plain, and catch a shimmer of water that showed where the canal and the Bharatpur Gahna lay, with beyond it nothing but the far horizon.

Yet even the Bulund Dawarza was not as popular with us as the Panch Mahal, the 'Five Palaces', which consisted of five graceful red sandstone pavilions perched one on top of the other in the manner of a house made of cards, each one smaller than the one below, and connected to it by flights of sandstone stairways. We liked to picnic in the topmost pavilion, where we could look down on the other buildings of Akbar's red city and, far down the hillside (for the city is built on a ridge), to the Hāthi Minar, 'the Elephant Tower', a circular tower rather like the famous round towers of Ireland, but studded all over with the tusks of elephants. We liked elephants and had mentally put a black mark against Akbar's name for shooting those endearing creatures just to stick their tusks all over his hunting tower. But he went back up near the top of my 'favourite people' list after we found the broken end of a tusk among the grass at the foot of the tower, and realized that it was carved out of stone and not ivory at all!

The very little time we could spare from re-visiting our favourite places in Agra during those weekends was spent in the shops, where our carefully hoarded pocket-money went on mementoes of the visit. If we wanted one (and we always did) it was a hard-and-fast rule that we paid for it ourselves. Each year, on our final visit of the season, we would buy one of those alabaster models of the Taj, and I still remember my envy and anguish when Bets, a more prudent saver than I, bought a far larger one than I could afford and returned proudly to Delhi with a seven-by-five-inch model while I returned sourly with one of the four-by-two jobs — my parents, quite rightly, having refused to make up the difference in price.

I don't know why we should have thought it necessary to acquire yet *another* of these fragile (and, let's face it, not particularly attractive) objects every year; unless it was because we invariably broke them or lost one or more of the detachable minarets. They never lasted long, but that last visit of the season would not have been complete unless we bought a Taj. It was part of the ritual: like visitors to Rome throwing a coin into the fountain of Trevi to ensure that they will return one day. Not that it ever crossed our minds that we would not return to Agra again — many times. To tell the truth, it still does not; and as I write this I feel sure that I shall see it again.

Chapter 18

~%⊃⊂%~

Yes, we'll gather by the river
The beautiful, the beautiful river.

Sankey, *Sacred Songs and Solos*

Agra was not the only place we visited regularly. Once a year during the cold weather we would go to Narora, a small settlement at the head of the Ganges Canal where the head Canal officer and his wife, Mr and Mrs Perrin, lived. The Perrins were friends of my parents and they would put us up in one of the thatched bungalows reserved for visiting inspectors, and feed us in their home, 'Number 1 bungalow', a few hundred yards further along the Canal.

In those days, with very few cars, there was no *pukka* road between the nearest railway station and Narora, so the only way to get there was on a narrow trolley line, riding in an open trolley propelled by a lever pushed to and fro by one of the Canal coolies and an assistant. We would reach the nearest station late at night, and having transferred into the waiting trolley would do that last leg of the journey by moonlight across open and apparently totally unoccupied country. (Since this part of the journey was always done by moonlight I can only suppose that Tacklow selected a date for the Narora visit for a time when the moon was full, because the trip was too hazardous on a dark night.)

How Bets and I loved those trolley trips! They were always the high-spot of the visit: the cool night air blowing through our hair and the vast, dearly-loved plains of India spread out all around us, black on silver, empty and wild and wonderful. *Kala-hirren,** chital and wild boar would start up from among the shadows and race away across the plains, and now and again a roosting peacock would fly out of a

* Black-buck.

kikar tree with an indignant and undignified squawk and a fluster of feathers, or a huge owl would sail past on silent wings. And sometimes if we were lucky we would catch a glimpse of a leopard. The night air smelt of flowers and hot, parched earth, and in some places, very faintly, of wood smoke and dung fires; though we rarely saw a gleam of lamp-light.

The distance was probably not more than five miles and our bunga-low, when we reached it, was always the same one: a big, high-roomed house with a thatched roof, surrounded by a deep verandah and lit by oil lamps. It stood back from the Canal bank in a garden that was little more than a wide lawn of parched and brittle grass, separated from the road by a line of shade trees and a tall hedge of scarlet poinsettias that was always alive with huge black-and-red butterflies. The head-works of the Canal, with its sluice-gates and weir, were very like the one at Okhla, only far larger and longer. For this was not the Jumna River. This was the Ganges, Mother Gunga herself, the enormous, holy river which, rising in the white wastes of Tibet, washes away sin, and yearly carries to the sea the ashes of countless thousands of devout Hindus whose bodies have been cremated on her banks or carried to them to be cast into her waters. Here, unlike Okhla, the river and the weir were over a mile wide, and when the wind sent the silver sand whirling, or a heat haze shimmered in the air, you could not see the far bank and might well have been standing on the shores of some vast inland sea.

The sandbanks changed with every monsoon, and one year a bank that had not been there on any previous visit appeared in the river about two hundred yards out from the shore. Mrs Perrin decided to take us all over for a picnic tea on it, and after that we were rowed across every evening in a big, flat-bottomed wooden boat and in the course of a few days we turned the entire island into a maze of sandcastles; adding new streets and houses, towers, canals, lakes and fortifications every day, until we had built a whole city there. That was a wonderful year! But when we returned the following one, the rains and the currents and the vagaries of the great river had swept the whole island away and the river ran high and unimpeded from bank to bank.

It was during this visit that we rescued a young seagull that had broken its wing. We saw it standing forlornly on the stones below the weir, and having caught it without much difficulty, took it to a local Indian doctor who was a friend of ours and whom we called 'Hakim-Sahib'. He set it most beautifully in tiny home-made splints and narrow bandages, and told us that we must keep the bird from using its wing for at least a week until the bone had set, and to feed it on *chilwa*. So we took it back to the bungalow where we spread sand all over one of the bathrooms, filled two enamel basins with water and kept Gully (I'm afraid our names for our birds and animals were painfully unoriginal) shut up there while we went out fishing for *chilwa*.

For a day or two all went well. Gully caught and ate the *chilwa* that were turned loose in the basins with the greatest enthusiasm. But then, without warning, a spell of unseasonable weather blew in from the south and we awoke one morning to find the world awash with rain and mist and the river totally devoid of fish. Apparently *chilwa* do not fancy cold and rainy weather, and they and every other species of fish in the river seemed to have gone for good. And though Chote and Prem, Mr Dass's children (Ram Dass was a Canal officer), said that they had only gone down to feed on the bottom of the river, we were disinclined to believe them and were in despair, for Gully flatly refused to eat any other form of food.

He turned his beak up at slivers of raw mud-fish procured for him in the local bazaar by the Perrins' *kansamah,* and obviously considered that anything that did not move was not edible. He moped and pined and got hungrier and hungrier while Bets and I grew daily more desperate. At long last, and soaked to the bone by driving rain, we managed to catch a smallish fish in the water below the closed sluice-gates. It was too small to provide a meal for a human and much too big for a young seagull; but at least it was a live fish and we hoped it might cheer Gully up just to see it swimming around in his basin, and give him an appetite for the assortment of scraps that he had hitherto rejected. Well, it cheered him up all right. He gave a loud squawk and the next moment he had pounced on it and was trying to swallow it.

He got it about half-way down his gullet, the fish fighting every inch of the way, before it stuck fast and he could neither get it up nor down. I still don't know why he didn't choke to death. He was in a bad way by the time I got a grip of the fish's slippery tail and managed to pull it out and throw it back in the basin where, believe it or not, it revived. But as soon as he could breathe again Gully lay on his side and played dead while Bets wept and I tore off in the rain to fetch Hakim-Sahib, who dosed him with a few drops of Tacklow's brandy. (Tacklow himself had returned to Delhi as soon as he had seen us settled in.) The brandy worked wonders and got Gully through the night, and the next day the sun was shining and the *chilwa* were back and he stuffed himself with them. A few days later Hakim-Sahib removed the bandages and the splint and said the wing had mended, so we took him down to the weir and put him down very carefully on the spot where we had found him, and presently he fluffed himself up and took off. We had hoped that he might come back to us of his own accord. But he never did. The ungrateful bird joined up with a rowdy crowd of gulls, and left with them when they headed down river.

It was during the first of these yearly visits to Narora that I nearly lost my favourite toy and chiefest treasure. Roller-bear was my first (and last) teddy-bear, and I have no idea who gave him to me or when, or whether he was a Christmas or a birthday present. I only remember that I seemed to have had him for ever, that I loved him dearly and that he owned me and not the other way about. He was quite a small bear, white, and owing to the fact that I refused to move anywhere without him, the bran with which he was stuffed had begun to leak out so that he had lost his stoutness and become endearingly flabby. Naturally he accompanied me on my first visit to Narora, and it was here that one day I pretended that he had run away and climbed a tree to hide from me. I put him carefully up among the branches and walked away, making a show of searching for him and calling out to him that all was forgiven and would he please come back. And then something distracted me and I ran off and forgot him — until bedtime came and I realized with horror that I had abandoned him up that tree!

The scene that followed was heartrending, but Mother was unmoved by my sobs. No, I certainly could not go out searching all the trees along the canal-bank road in the dark! And nor could any of the servants. Roller-bear would be perfectly safe up a tree and hidden by leaves. I must wait until the morning, and that was that. I didn't sleep a wink that night, imagining owls or monkeys discovering poor Roller-bear and tearing him to pieces. Or the child of some Canal worker spotting him and taking him away. I was up at first light, and having woken Bets, we both dressed in a frantic hurry, and letting ourselves out by the back door of the bathroom, ran off to the rescue. The only trouble was that I couldn't remember which tree of the many trees that shaded the road I had hidden him in. They all looked exactly alike and it took us a long time to find him — even with the assistance of a large assortment of sympathetic helpers who had come to look for us as soon as we were missed.

I was in a state of tear-sodden panic by the time Roller-bear was discovered, and I vowed that I would never forget him again. And I never have. But alas, a year or two later, hurried out of the train at Simla by impatient grown-ups, I took my eyes off him and he was left behind. And this time we did not find him again; though my grief was such that a large reward was offered for his return and I prayed every night that whoever had him now would hear of it and bring him back. In the end, having at last resigned myself to the sad fact that I had lost him for good, I changed that prayer, and for years afterwards prayed instead that God would please let whoever had found him love him and take good care of him and see to it that he was tucked up warmly every night. That was the only comfort that I had, and even Moko never displaced dear Roller-bear in my affections.

Some years later, discovering that I had still not forgotten him and still blamed myself bitterly for failing him, Mother at last managed to find another white bear, which she gave me for my birthday — and whom I hated on sight. Poor Mum! She had gone to enormous trouble to find that bear, for though the shops were full of bears of every shade of brown, white bears were as rare as oysters in July. But she should have known that Roller-bear was not replaceable: particularly not by a large, stout, straw-stuffed and vulgarly glossy interloper. Nothing except his colour in any way suggested my dear departed Roller-bear, and I can only suppose that I lost this unwelcome replacement at the first opportunity, since apart from my first shocked sight of it lying smugly in the large cardboard box which I had just unpacked, I don't remember anything more about it, and I certainly never played with the creature.

✄ Our third visit to Narora was made memorable by Mrs Perrin's day-long battle to land a *mahseer*; those great pink and silver fish that are frequently referred to as 'the salmon of the Indian rivers'.

Mrs Perrin, whose favourite pastime was fishing, combined business with pleasure by personally catching the fish-course for her household, and on this particular morning she went down to the river bank before breakfast and was almost immediately into a fish. *Mahseer,* like salmon, are fighting fish, and this one took her line out as though he had been a torpedo, or a marlin! Bets and I watched the battle, fascinated, for a good hour and then, as neither combatant showed any signs of tiring, went back to the bungalow for breakfast.

Returning some time later we discovered Mrs Perrin (supported by an enthralled audience of Canal workers, coolies, villagers, the local *shikari,* a number of fishermen and the odd *jani-wallah,** all vociferously offering advice and encouragement while she hung grimly onto her arching salmon-rod), still reeling in the line or watching it go screaming out across the river. Tacklow, always a dedicated fisherman, was riveted by the contest, and not in any way surprised when his hopeful offer to take over the rod for a bit and give her a rest was tersely refused, since nothing would have induced him to hand over that rod had it been *his* fish on the line! He therefore settled down to watch. But as the morning advanced the mahseer stopped fighting and went down into deep water on the far side of a sunken sandbank in the middle of the river and at the extreme limit of the line, where it sat and sulked. There was no way of shifting it, for the bank obviously ran straight in both directions, while the weir, with the Canal head lying at right angles to it, lay less than a quarter of a mile downstream. It was stalemate.

All that Mrs Perrin could do was to hold on until the fish felt sufficiently rested to come out of its bolt-hole and resume hostilities: which it did at longer and longer intervals as the day wore on. Tacklow suggested that the main current must have worn out a deep overhang on the far side of the underwater bank, providing a shelter in which the mahseer could hold out for hours, and if that were so, the only way of dislodging it would be to go out in a boat and play it from the other side. But Mrs Perrin would have none of it. She was going to stand her ground. Lunch-time came round and a picnic meal was brought down to the riverside for the grown-ups, but Bets and I, who by then had become a bit bored by the whole business, elected to

* Passer-by.

279

return to the bungalow and eat our lunch with the Perrins' small daughters. The meal remains memorable because the servants had hastily laid it out on the sideboard before rushing off with the picnic baskets to join the throng by the river, leaving us to help ourselves; and since I had not encountered mayonnaise before, I thought it must be custard and poured it lavishly all over my stewed fruit.

By tea-time the fish had still not been landed and most of the spectators had lost interest and drifted away to deal with their own affairs: Mother presumably to sketch in some more paintable spot and Tacklow and Mr Perrin to take their customary evening walk. Bets and I arrived back to find that there was no one on the bank but the intrepid Mrs Perrin and one or two idlers, and as the sky began to turn gold and green with the sunset she belatedly threw in her hand. Deciding that Tacklow could have been right, she called up a stalwart young man who had been squatting on his hunkers watching the proceedings for the past hour or so, and asked him to row her out in one of the flat-bottomed river-boats that were moored nearby. Bets and I immediately clamoured to come too, and the four of us set out across the river; the young man rowing and Mrs Perrin standing up amidships, rod in hand and reeling in as she went.

Tacklow *had* been right. Somewhere well below the deceptively smooth surface of the great river the currents had scoured out a deep channel, and the fish had only to sink below its overhanging rim and face upstream and nothing could shift him. But once out in mid-stream and above the hidden channel Mrs Perrin could play him again; and he was exhausted by the day-long struggle. Nevertheless he put up a good fight before admitting defeat, and by the time he did so and allowed himself to be drawn alongside and scooped into the boat, Bets and I were completely on his side. I thought he deserved to get away and hoped that Mrs Perrin would throw him back; but then I am not a fisherman. Instead she knocked him on the head and returned in triumph with the captive of her rod and reel. I believe the grown-ups ate him for lunch on the following day; and if so it was lucky for me that I don't eat fish because I would certainly have jibbed at eating that one!

The poor fellow turned out to be a good deal smaller than he had looked from the flashing glimpses we had had of him as he swirled and leapt at the end of the line. A fairly modest size for one of his species, judging from the snapshot that Mother took of Mrs Perrin holding her trophy on the following morning. But despite the evidence of that snap, in memory he still seems enormous: a huge, almost mythical fish that took a whole day to capture.

✳ Back once more in Delhi we got our first look at what the twentieth century had in store in the way of mass entertainment. The Cinemascope!

Bill had already been taken to see this modern wonder during our brief stay in England — Bets and I had been considered much too young — but the treat had proved a failure, because the film that Mother plainly found riveting, and had wrongly supposed would appeal to her six-year-old son, contained shots of lions, rhinos and charging elephants, with a lengthy sequence involving a python or a black mamba, or some species of large snake. Turning to ask Bill if he was enjoying it, she was horrified to find that he had vanished, and a hasty search revealed that he had been so scared by this reptile that he had gone to ground under his seat and was crouching there with his eyes tight shut. But despite this inauspicious introduction to the joys of canned entertainment, Mother must have agreed with Kipling that small girls have stronger nerves than small boys (he wrote some verses about how Shakespeare got the material for his plays which contain the following lines: '*How at Bankside, a boy drowning kittens Winced at the business; whereupon his sister — Lady Macbeth aged seven — thrust 'em under, Sombrely scornful*'). At all events, she took a chance on it and allowed Punj-ayah to escort us to a brand-new cinema on or near the Chandi Chowk.

I don't think she can have realized that she was in fact committing herself to allowing us to go there once a week for the remainder of the season. But that was how it turned out, for the cinema was showing a serial that featured one of the very earliest stars of what is now referred to as the Silent Screen. Her name was Pearl White and the serial, which ran for weeks and weeks, was called *Lost Island*. Having seen the first episode it was, of course, out of the question that we should miss the next one; and then the one after that; and that, and that ... In the end we saw them all, and the whole thing made such an indelible impression on our minds that we can both remember the tune and most of the words of the title song played at the beginning and end of every performance on one of those wind-up gramophones with a horn like an outsize arum lily: '*O sweet girl of Lost Island I'm longing for you, Won't you come back to my land where hearts beat true? ...*' and so on. I remember it started with the eruption of a volcano — the lost island getting lost perhaps? — and the frantic exodus of hundreds of silently screaming extras fleeing from the special-effects fireworks. The heroic Miss White (played as a tot by some forerunner of Shirley Temple) finished up every episode in dire straits, hanging by a rope over a snake-pit or about to be sacrificed to some ferocious Eastern Idol, and we had to wait until the matinée next Thursday or Tuesday or whatever, to see if she was going to be rescued in the nick of time. She always was, though that did nothing to allay our anxiety on the next occasion when crocodiles were advancing upon her or the man-eating lion was preparing to spring. For how could we be sure that the square-jawed and long-suffering hero wouldn't oversleep this time, or break a leg or something, and arrive on the scene too late? The suspense was terrible!

That cinema, as far as I recall, was a shocking flea-pit constructed out of several rickety shops or warehouses, hastily knocked into one and furnished with rows of seats, a screen, a projection-room and a piano. And that gramophone, of course. The front was quite impressive; well plastered with lurid posters. But there were always a good many non-paying customers in the form of rats who ran to and fro along the rafters overhead and the odd nesting pigeon and its mate whose coos and flapping accompanied the pianist and/or gramophone throughout the performance. However, these were trifles and we enjoyed the show enormously. As did Punj-ayah, regardless of the fact that, since she could not read the subtitles, she had no idea what was going on up there and we had to explain it to her as it went along. I suspect it made her a movie-addict for life.

I suppose we must have seen other films, but the only other one that I remember was one that we saw in Simla in a cinema that had started up above the roller-skating rink. I don't remember its title, but I do remember the name of the star. It was Annette Kellerman. She was a forerunner of the much later talking-and-Technicolor swimming stars such as Esther Williams, and a champion swimmer off as well as on the screen. The film was about a mermaid who fell in love with a human — or vice versa — and I remember it vividly as a sort of dream-cum-nightmare, because I happened to be running a high temperature at the time and was feeling fairly peculiar. I would not admit this for fear that Mother would insist on taking me home and I'd miss seeing the rest of it; even though the story seemed to repeat itself over and over again in a meaningless manner and sometimes the mermaids on the screen were real and swimming towards me and sometimes they grew so hazy that I could barely see them at all.

Eventually, perhaps in the interval, Mother spotted that all was not well, and despite my tears and protests took me home in a rickshaw and put me to bed. I have a dim recollection of her taking my temperature and rushing to the telephone to call a doctor, and after that nothing much else for several days. Which was not surprising: for the year was 1918 and I and several million others had fallen victim to the virulent influenza epidemic that swept the world in the wake of the war; a result, it was widely believed, of the hundreds of thousands of corpses rotting on the battlefields of France and Flanders. It was to claim the lives of far more people than the total casualty figures of the entire 1914–18 war, and India was one of the worst sufferers. Bets caught it a few days later and there is a snapshot of the two of us, convalescent but still confined to our beds at The Rookery, clutching Moko and Teddy and staring wanly at the camera.

There had already been one children's play that year, staged as usual by Mrs Strettle and her dancing-class. It was called *The Lost Colour* and it concerned the smallest colour in the rainbow, Tiny Tint (pink, and if memory serves, played by a girl called Iris Gillan) being kidnapped by some bad character and rescued by the Rainbow King, one Gerry Ross, a pretty creature a few years my senior who possessed a head of lovely copper-coloured curls and wore a gold tunic to match. The curtain rose on the sleeping rainbow composed of members of the dancing-class in order of size, two of each colour (Bets and I were respectively small and large yellow), who to the strains of the Viceregal orchestra's arrangement of Sinding's 'Rustle of Spring', woke up, yawning and stretching, got to their feet and danced in a dreamy manner before rushing all over the stage in alarm as the lights dimmed, sheets of tin were energetically clashed in the wings, and lightning flashed all over the place to indicate that a thunderstorm had blown up. Under cover of all this uproar, the members of the dancing-class nipped into the wings and collected long silk scarves, each in her own colour, and as the storm died out and the lights came up we did a dance with the scarves, waving them in time to the music — the rainbow coming out after the storm. 'How charming!' sighed all the proud mamas in the audience.

I rather think that Tiny Tint must have been shanghaied during the storm, for the next act was a wood on Earth where Bargie, looking as pretty as paint as a wood nymph, did a solo dance followed by a *pas de deux* with the Rainbow King; after which Gerry staged a fight with the villain and rescued Tiny Tint. I imagine there *must* have been a smattering of dialogue, but I don't remember any. Only a lot of dancing and prancing, scarf-waving and mime; and even after all these years I have only to hear the opening bars of 'Rustle of Spring' and I am back again on the dusty little stage of Simla's Gaiety Theatre, dressed in a skimpy yellow silk tunic with a gold girdle (bazaar tinsel, no doubt), bare-footed and with a gold filet in my hair — and fancying myself no end.

A second play, staged in the early autumn, was a peculiar one-act version of *Peter Pan* that coincided with the arrival of the flu epidemic in Simla. This potted playlet was preceded by a lot of dancing — to which Bets and I contributed yet another minuet! This filled the first half of the programme and in the second half, Gerry Ross played Peter and Bargie played Wendy, while Bets and I were a couple of non-speaking, pyjama-clad Lost Boys. Nana had been eliminated from the script, together with Mr Darling, Captain Hook and the entire Never-Never Land, but Mrs Darling was still present and correct, played by the pretty daughter of the Governor of the Punjab, Una O'Dwyer, who sang a charming Irish lullaby, 'Husheen', to send us all to sleep before the arrival of Tinkerbell and Peter. Though what half-a-dozen Lost Boys were doing in the Darlings' nursery is anyone's guess!

No one did any flying and the play ended with Peter, Wendy, Tinkerbell and the Boys going into another dance routine. Curtain. I still remember the words and music of 'Husheen', but that's about all — which is not surprising, considering that the killer epidemic had broken loose in Simla, and was striking down people left and right and playing havoc with the show. One by one the juvenile cast went down with it, and Bets, among the last to be smitten, ended up dancing several other performers' dances in the first half of the show and acting several other people's parts in the play as each one fell ill. The ranks of the non-speaking Lost Boys were reduced daily and Bets took over playing Michael, and then John, and finally Tinkerbell, before collapsing in her turn. I still can't think why the grown-ups didn't cancel the whole thing. It is possible, of course, that the full seriousness of the epidemic had not yet been recognized and even our parents had no idea what had hit them. They may even have thought that it was just as well to keep us all busy and interested — and on our feet. If so, they could have been right; for though some of the British children only just pulled through, I don't think any of them died. But it was quite otherwise with the children in the crowded bazaars and close-packed, insanitary houses below the Mall, and their parents and grand-parents. Yet what we had seen in Simla was only the beginning of the horrors to come . . .

In the late autumn of that year, after we had moved back to Delhi, Tacklow and Mother accompanied Sir Charles and a few of his friends on what was to have been a ten-day trip down the Ganges by boat from either Gurmuktaser or Gujrowla, to the head of the Ganges Canal — our beloved Narora. It was not the first time they had spent a short leave in this fashion, but on this occasion the object of the trip was to shoot *mugger* and *gharial* for their skins, since Sir Charles, anticipating retirement, had been thinking up ways of supplementing his pension while enabling him to keep one foot in India, and had come to an agreement with a tannery in Cawnpore to supply them with skins to be made up into crocodile-leather suitcases, trunks, shoes, women's handbags and so on, to their mutual profit. This scheme was doomed to prove a disastrous flop for a reason that I have already mentioned: the unsuitability of Indian crocodiles' skins for such pur-poses. However, Sir Charles's retirement was still some way off, and this ten-day trip down the Ganges was merely intended to be a trial run.

His party planned to embark on one of the big, open, wooden-built river-boats that are steered by a single oar; the servants and various hired assistants following some way behind in a second and even larger and slower one, bringing the tents, food and luggage, and picking up *en route* any *muggers* that had been shot by those in the first boat — whose occupants would mark them by a yellow flag fixed to a stake that had been driven into the sand near the creature's head. Towards evening Sir Charles and his lot would pick a suitable spot in which to camp for the night and wait there until the second boat hove in sight with the tents and equipment. After which they would go off to shoot duck and partridge for the pot, while the camp was set up and meals prepared, and Kashmera and his henchmen got down to skinning the crocodiles and then pegging out and salting the skins. These would later be rubbed with ashes and dispatched by runner to the nearest railway station to be sent to Cawnpore to be tanned; or that, at any rate, was the plan. But it did not work out like that, and within three days of setting out the entire party arrived back in Delhi again.

It was years before I discovered the reason for this hasty return. And then only because I happened to come across an envelope containing a few snapshots that I had never seen before and which had certainly not appeared in any of the photograph-albums that Mother kept up to date with such care. The snapshots showed a single short stretch of sand on the banks of the Ganges, taken on that abortive trip. It was strewn with rotting corpses.

Hindus cremate their dead, but in times of pestilence or famine, when thousands die, cremation becomes impossible for the poor as wood becomes scarce and its price soars. This year, with people dying like flies in a black frost, the poor could not afford to cremate all of their kin who perished in the great epidemic, so they simply consigned the bodies to the river.

Mother said that no one in the boats had realized, until they actually set off down the river, what it would be like, because the banks near the town were kept clear of corpses and none of the local authorities had warned them. When they got further downstream and saw the numbers of the stranded dead they were horrified, but thought that these must be people who had lived and died in the town and that there would be none further on in the open country away from the towns and villages. But the further they went the worse it became.

At every bend in the river the sandbanks showed more and more bodies in every stage of decay. There were so many of them that even the vultures and carrion crows were satiated and stood around too gorged to fly. Worst of all — worse than the stench and the sight of the legions of dead — were the pariah dogs, those cringing, masterless pi-dogs that haunt every town and village in India and are such cowardly creatures that normally one had only to flap a hand at them to make them turn and run, tail between legs and yelping with alarm.

This year, gorged and made bold by feasting on human flesh, they formed themselves into packs that attacked, snarling and without provocation, and made the dark hours hideous, barking and howling and quarrelling over the dead. No one slept that night, and the next day, since they could not take the heavy boats back up river against the current (the plan had been to abandon the boats at Narora from where teams of coolies would have pulled the empty hulks back up the Ganges in the manner of the Volga boatmen, taking many days to make the journey), they went on foot to the nearest village, where they hired bullock carts to take them across country to the nearest railway station and so back to Delhi.

Tacklow told me that the river had been alive with *muggers*; more of them than any of the party had ever seen before; and that Sir Charles had shot several. But when the skins reached Cawnpore they were found to be green and spongy and could not be tanned; and the same was true of every crocodile shot in any of India's rivers during the time that the flu epidemic raged through the land.

That cold weather we did not visit Okhla even once, and nor would Punj-ayah allow us to play on the sands of the Jumna on the far side of the Kudsia Bagh, because (though I did not know this at the time) Mother was afraid that the Jumna too might be full of corpses. She did her best to prevent us from learning about the appalling tragedy that was taking place in India — and, for that matter, in most of the rest of the world — for fear that it might upset us. In the same way, we, who had known about it from the start through our numerous Indian friends, playmates and acquaintances, had never mentioned it to her because we were afraid it might upset her! But then I don't think she ever realized that the servants and shopkeepers, the children of her Indian friends with whom we played and squabbled and laughed, and every other person whom we met and passed the time of day with in the streets and bazaars of Delhi and Simla, talked freely to us or in our hearing on a score of subjects that no Western adult of that period would have dreamed of mentioning in the presence of young children.

Neither birth nor death, nor poverty, sickness, disaster or crime, held any mystery for me. It was not that I was ever indifferent to it — how could I be? Such things would always have the power to shock me or make me shudder, or reduce me to fury or tears or both. But one learned very young to accept the beauty and wonder of that most beautiful and wonderful of lands, and with it the ugliness and cruelty that was an integral part of it. For is not Shiva the Creator — *'Shiv, who poured the harvest and made the winds to blow'* — also the Destroyer? And is not his consort, lovely Parbati, also Kali the Drinker-of-Blood and Sitala — Mata — the Smallpox?

Chapter 19

~※⊗⊗⊗※~

And we won't go home 'til it's over,
Over there!

George M. Cohan

(popular song of the First World War)

Bets and I must have been among the very first people in India to hear that the Great War, the First World War, was over.

We had been playing in the cosmos jungle below The Rookery one sunny autumn morning while Tacklow, who for once had not set off for the office, sat at work in his study and Mother busied herself packing trunks and suitcases in the upper rooms of the house, in preparation for our annual move to Delhi. It was November, but the weather was as clear and hot and glittering as an English June, and though the tall stems and feathery foliage of the cosmos were already turning dry and brittle, there was still a lavish sprinkling of pink and white blossoms over our heads. The windless air was full of pollen dust, and without the surf-song of the pines, all the familiar noises of Simla drifted up from the town and the bazaars that lay spread out far below us; muted by distance but still clearly audible in the stillness. Above us in The Rookery every door and window stood wide, and the big clock in the hall had just begun to strike eleven when we heard someone run out of the house and down the stone steps into the porch, and out onto the gravel drive. And suddenly the warm, sleepy silence of the morning was shattered by the deafening clangour of the bronze Burmese gong that hung in the hall and was normally sounded, discreetly, to summon us to meals.

It was not being sounded discreetly now. The din was so violent and so unexpected that we were stopped in our tracks (we had been crawling along one of our carefully constructed paths through the cosmos stalks), and regardless of the fact that we might be giving away the whereabouts of our secret tunnels, both jumped to our feet and rushed out headlong to discover what on earth was happening. I think we both expected to find the house on fire or some similar disaster. But it was, astonishingly, Tacklow who was creating this appalling din. He had unhooked the gong and was marching up and down in front of the house, banging on it like some demented drummer-boy.

Mother came tearing out onto the top verandah to lean over the rail and shout down to him, demanding to know if he had gone out of his mind, and everyone else in the place came swarming out from the back of the house, the kitchen, the go-downs and the servants' quarters, convinced that they were being summoned to help put out a fire or, at the very least, attack a gang of robbers. I can still see their startled faces which must have mirrored the shock on my own, when they discovered that the 'Burra-Sahib' had apparently gone mad and was grinning from ear to ear as he woke the echoes of Jakko with the help of the dinner-gong. But as the last, unheard stroke of eleven sounded on the grandfather clock in the hall, we saw a white puff of smoke and a bright flash from Summer Hill on the far side of Simla; so far away that the crash of the gun must have taken a full four seconds to reach us. A minute later the bells of Christ Church began to peal, hooters started to blare and whistles to blow, while the crew of the noonday gun that was fired once a day to tell all Simla that it was exactly twelve o'clock and they could knock off for lunch, broke abruptly with tradition and embarked on a joyous twenty-one-gun salute ... The war was over! At last, after more than four hideous years of slaughter, it was all over. An Armistice had been signed; and I was badly shaken to see, for the first time in my life, that even as he laughed and banged that Burmese gong, there were tears running down my father's face.

Tacklow had known for many hours that an Armistice had been signed and would come into force at eleven o'clock that morning. He had been the first person in India to know, for the news came in cipher. He had decoded it and, late on the previous evening, informed the Viceroy, who presumably informed the Commander-in-Chief and the Governor of the Punjab. But since the order was that the news must not be made public until the following day, and in every part of the Empire at precisely the same time — each part keeping strictly to its own time — Tacklow had not even dropped a hint to Mother. I remember her being extremely annoyed about this and insisting that even if the Viceroy *had* told him not to breathe a word to anyone before the eleven o'clock deadline, he could at least have told his *own wife*! (If she really did think so, she didn't know her husband nearly as well as I knew my father!) 'I bet Lord Chelmsford told *his* wife!' said Mother indignantly.

By afternoon all Simla was *en fête,* decked out with coloured bunting and strings of coloured flags and launched on two days of rejoicing and non-stop *tamashas.** Services of Thanksgiving were held in the churches and there was a Victory Parade of all troops on the Ridge. A *feu de joie* crackled up and down the lines of khaki-clad men, bands played and there were endless side-shows in the form of Kuttack and other regional dances of India, which intrigued me far more than the military parade. Someone gave Bets and me a flag each, and Mother took a snapshot of us waving our Union Jacks. Then it was all over. And after that the grown-ups took to talking interminably of 'going home' and indulging in excited speculation on their chances of getting a passage on a homeward-bound steamer.

I had reached the dignity of double figures earlier that year and was now ten years old. Bets and I had got up early on the morning of my birthday and walked up and down our end of the top verandah, discussing the implications of maturity in whispers so as not to wake our still sleeping parents. Now that I had reached it, ten suddenly seemed to me an awesome number, and I was sobered by the thought that I would never be in single figures again. I remember that we talked of the future and speculated, gloomily, that it would not be long now before either I was sent away to some school in Bombay or Calcutta, or that Punj-ayah was replaced by an English governess. For at that time the Great War still seemed set to go on for ever, and I don't think either of us seriously visualized what would happen to us when it ended. I remember too that our conversation was brought to a close by the familiar crash and clatter of a troop of monkeys chasing each other along the tin roof over our heads, which woke our parents. And also that my presents that year were a wristwatch from Tacklow — which made me feel older than ever — and a morocco-bound copy of

* Entertainment, spectacle; a show, fun.

Daily Light from Mother which I still have (it is disintegrating rapidly but I hope it will see me out).

That had been in August. Then, less than three months after Tacklow had run out of the house banging our Burmese gong, my whole view of the future changed as swiftly and dramatically as the coloured chips of glass in a kaleidoscope change patterns at a single twist of the wrist. One minute everything had been blue and gold and brilliant, and then, suddenly, it was all dark purple, grey and forbidding, and I was full of foreboding ...

'Home'! Yes, I remembered Freshfields. Forres too. And Ramnee. And the farm at Streatley and Aunt Lizzie's house at Bedford. I hadn't thought much of any of them, and it had been wonderful to come back to India again. Why did everyone call England 'home'? *This* was home, and I wanted no other: certainly not that grey, drizzly and definitely chilly place which I had been fortunate enough to escape from once and would not care if I never saw again. Oh yes, of course I knew that we'd all have to go back there one day: I wasn't stupid. But I had quite simply not bothered to think about it. When one is young and completely happy, and all is going well, one doesn't bother to think much about the future unless one is gripped by an ambition to do something special — discover El Dorado or fly an aeroplane, or become a great actor or a great dancer. My ambition was simple. I wanted to spend the rest of my life in India.

Now that the Armistice had been signed, everyone who had had to spend the war years in India, leaving children and relatives back in Britain, could not wait to return. But passages were few and far between, and people had to wait their turn. The wounded and convalescent, all British soldiers who had been in action, senior civilians who could 'pull rank', and so on, had first claim. The rest had to wait; and since our priority was a low one, there was little prospect of our getting passages for some time to come.

Buoyed up by this discovery, and by the fact that the normal amount of goods and chattels were, as always, stowed away in packing-cases and left in a storehouse in Simla to await our return, we left for the plains as light-heartedly as ever; and back once more in Delhi found nothing changed. The Kudsia Bagh was still as beautiful, Okhla as alluring, and the Christmas camp and the annual visit to the Perrins at Narora were as enjoyable as ever. The only blot on our lovely landscape was the absence of Bargie and Tony, whose parents were spending the winter in Calcutta. Bets and I missed them a lot. But we had many other friends, and even if the old Anglo-Indian community began to show gaps as family after family left for Bombay to take ship to England, at least our Indian friends were not leaving; lucky things! Moni and Veena and Lakshmi, Rehana and Karan, Neelum, Vika and Shafi would all be staying. So *that* was all right!

It was during this cold weather that Bets and I had our first sight of the new city the British were adding to the seven cities of Delhi which in the course of the long centuries had risen in turn on this particular stretch of plain.

I knew about this latest Delhi because Tacklow had told me how at the great Durbar of 1911, held for King George V and Queen Mary, the new King-Emperor had announced that plans had been approved for the construction of a modern, eighth Delhi on the open plain a few miles to the north of the present city. And of how their majesties had proceeded with due pomp and ceremony to lay a pair of suitably engraved foundation stones on the proposed site. But either the architects or the Public Works Department had skimped their work, for the chosen spot turned out to be entirely unsuitable. Apparently it was apt to turn into a bog whenever the Jumna overflowed its banks — which it did whenever the monsoon was a particularly heavy one. An alternative site was hastily selected on higher ground, some ten or twelve miles distant on the opposite side of the city and on a barren, rock-strewn plain that was crossed by the Ridge. The foundation stones were hurriedly dug up under cover of darkness, to be transported and re-erected by night on the new site where they would be discovered *in situ* next morning ... A miracle, no less! — the intelligent stones, disliking the prospect of getting their feet wet every time the Jumna burst its banks, had removed themselves to a safer and more auspicious location! Or that (it was hoped) was how it would appear to super-stitious people and the more credulous and simple-minded peasantry. Maybe it did. If so, it shows that they preferred to believe that even a slab of Indian marble (or sandstone or whatever) had more sense than a committee of bureaucratic British planners.

The 1914 war had put a temporary stop to building activities on this newest Delhi. But with the Armistice work had begun again, and that winter Mother drove us all out to the aerodrome — at that time no more than a flat, dusty expanse of earth flanked by an ugly galvanized-iron hangar and a few makeshift sheds — to see the arrival of the very first plane to fly from England to India: a flight that had taken a number of days and endless stops for refuelling, but was regarded at the time as a marvellous feat. The plane, a De Havilland, had been piloted by one of the First World War flying aces, 'Biffy' Bourton; who on arrival promptly fell in love with Bargie's mother and eventually married her. The pilot of the next plane to do this trip, which arrived shortly afterwards, was another ex-Royal Flying Corps officer, one Harley Alec-Tweedie who fell heavily for my mother, but fortunately for all of us ended up as no more than a valued friend of the whole family.

I remember watching Tacklow walk off across that vast, dusty expanse of ground one afternoon to talk to Harley, and the next thing we knew he was clambering up into the cockpit, wearing a borrowed flying-helmet and goggles, and they had taken off. Mother nearly had hysterics, which didn't surprise me, because those early 'flying machines' looked like children's toys. They had open cockpits, out of which I suppose one could easily have fallen if not strapped in, and conveyed the impression of being made out of a few sheets of cardboard and a ball of string. The single propeller had to be swung over by hand to start the engine, and as I never could fathom how they became airborne or managed to stay up once they were, I watched the gyrations of that fragile bit of nonsense containing my courageous but foolhardy Tacklow with my heart almost literally in my mouth, expecting it to disintegrate at any moment. However, it returned him safely and I have a snapshot of him, taken by Mother, looking rather smug and pleased with himself in his borrowed flying outfit.

It was on this same afternoon that Mother decided to take us back by a different route so that we could see how New Delhi was progressing. And as we drove towards it I remember seeing, a mile or so away and against the black rain-clouds of a distant storm moving across the enormous and almost featureless plain, a perfect triple rainbow. I had seen double ones before, but never three of these glorious, ephemeral arches, the palest of which was sharply clear and almost as bright as a normal rainbow. It seemed that we were going to drive right under them; but they retreated before us with the retreating storm, and when we reached the top of the low, stony ridge known as Raisina Hill, on which Sir Edwin Lutyens planned to build a splendid Viceroy's House, the ground all around us was wet and glistening from the rain that had passed across it, and the newly-washed air was so clear that one could see for miles.

Mother stopped the car on the crest of a long slope that would one day be a wide road sweeping down from the open space in front of the Viceroy's House, to pass between an imposing pair of Secretariat Buildings before merging into a long, level avenue that for a brief span of time would be known as King's Way and is now the Rajpath — which means the same thing. And looking about me I saw, sprawled all around me on the wet and glistening earth, the foundations of the present capital of India, New Delhi, which was then no more than a crude map on the ground; all trenches and substructures with here and there the beginnings of a wall.

It was hard to believe, that evening, that this would one day be a great city housing well over a million people. Or that anything more than camel-thorn and cactus bushes could ever flourish on that harsh and stony earth. I thought I had never seen a more desolate spot, and I could not understand how anyone could want to live here instead of among the trees and gardens and orchards of Shahjehanpore — the Old Delhi that the Emperor Shahjehan had rebuilt and beautified on the bank of the Jumna. From this vantage-point, and in that clear, rain-washed air, I could see its close-packed rooftops, red sandstone fort, marble domes and soaring minarets, rising out of a green foam of trees and bordered on the far side by the silver ribbon of the Jumna. And see too the scattered ruins of those other Delhis; the ancient city where the Khutab Minar stands, Siri and Jahānpanāh; Tuglakabad and Indarpat; and Firozabad, which covers both Shahjehanpore and the ruined traces of the city of Shere Shah ...

Tacklow must have known what I was thinking. Or else he must have been thinking the same thing, for he recited some verses that I had never heard before and which so caught my imagination that I looked them up later and learned them by heart. It was a poem about a King who started to build a magnificent palace, and in doing so came across the traces of a former city that someone else had built many centuries earlier, and saw, carved on the ancient stones, '*After me cometh a Builder. Tell him, I too have known!*'. In the end the King is forced to abandon the work he has begun, and the last verse says ...

> *I called my men from my trenches, my quarries, my wharves and my sheers.*
> *All I had wrought I abandoned to the faith of the faithless years.*
> *Only I cut on the timber — only I carved on the stone:*
> *'After me cometh a Builder. Tell him, I too have known!'*

The poem is called 'The Palace' and when I asked Tacklow who had written it he said, 'Kipling.' I ought to have known that. It is a poem I cherish because it can give me back, exact in every detail, one special fragment of time: the brief interval I spent on the crest of Raisina Hill, looking out across the minimal foundations of what would one day be New Delhi, at the ruins of six previous Delhis that lay strewn across the plain — and at the seventh that I knew so well and thought of as 'home', but whose time, like the days of my childhood in India, was very nearly over ...

That last sad fact was still not real to me; though it was soon to become so. A few days later we set off as gaily as in other years to visit Agra, which we found as enchanting as ever. True, Mother discouraged us from acquiring yet another alabaster model of the Taj apiece, on the grounds that when we left for England we were going to have to cut down on luggage and the models took up too much room. But though we settled for pin-boxes instead, we didn't take her warning very seriously, and our optimism received a boost from Miss Hotz who, when we waved goodbye to her and to Laurie's Hotel, called out as usual: 'See you again soon!' So there was nothing to worry about yet.

The blow fell with shocking suddenness. When spring came and the Government of India returned with other migrants to the hills, only one member of our family would be returning with them: Tacklow would be going back to Simla again. But without Mother, Bets or myself, for whom three berths had been allotted on the S.S. 'Ormond', sailing from Bombay to Tilbury Docks in England.

Tacklow had not asked for leave for himself so that he could accompany us, because with everyone clamouring to go, *someone* had to stay behind. And he felt strongly that since he had not been able to fight in the war, the least he could do was to stay at his post and give others, who had, a chance to go to the head of the queue — along with mothers who had been parted for years from their children, and children who had been away from their native land too long and should be going to school there.

I heard the news with horror. It was bad enough to learn that I might never again see Simla or our many friends there, to whom we had so gaily waved goodbye never dreaming that we would not all meet again when the next hot weather came round. Or that for all I knew I could have paid my last visit to Agra and might never travel by moonlight on the rail-trolley to Narora again. But to have to leave Tacklow behind, perhaps for years, was such an appalling prospect that I refused to face it and merely shut my mind against it. It hadn't happened yet and perhaps it would never happen, and I took to repeating one of the copy-book maxims that other children's governesses were so fond of quoting: 'We'll cross that bridge when we come to it, shall we?'

One faint consolation was the news that the Slaters would be returning to England on the same ship, so at least I should have Bargie's company. And in the meantime I was still here. Still living in our own familiar rooms in dear Curzon House. Still awakened every morning by the peacocks in the Kudsia Bagh and the parrots in the big peepul tree that grew in the compound where the servants' quarters were. Still able to hear by twilight, in the lovely, late, dusty evenings, the romantic strains of those nostalgic sugary waltzes drifting through the shadows from the wide lawn of the Old Delhi Club that had once, in the days before the Mutiny, been Ludlow Castle . . .

While Mother saw to the collecting, sorting and packing of the many things we would have to take with us, Bets and I set about making our own collection of necessities, which were in no way similar. From every one of our special places in and around Delhi we took a souvenir; an amulet that we could look at and touch whenever we felt homesick for India. A leaf from the avenue of eucalyptus trees in the Kudsia Bagh. Another from the bamboos that had once hidden the stairway to our hideaway on the roof of the ruined gateway. A flake of sandstone and a scrap of marble from the surrounding parapet. Other leaves from the squirrel trees, the peepul behind Curzon House, the lemon, sweet lime and orange trees in the Roshanara Gardens, and neem leaves and rose petals from the cemetery where Nicholson lies buried. We took a sliver of stone from the Kashmir Gate and a piece of bark from a tree in which we used to sit for hours in the back garden of Curzon House; a fallen feather shed by a parrot, a peacock, a jay, a *sat-bhai* and a dove. A pinch of silver sand from the Jumna, and another, together with the dried and crumpled egg-shell of a river turtle, from Okhla. Red gravel from the Curzon House drive, a pebble from the Ridge, and any number of flowers and grasses, carefully dried — wild ones, picked out on the plains among the ruins of the seven cities. The little dusty yellow balls that are the blossoms of the kikar tree, purple and red bougainvillaea, orange trumpet-flowers, petals from roses, canna lilies, jasmine and Lady of the Night, a stick of incense and a tiny bottle of *'itr*;* a little packet of dust gathered from the Maidan that lies between the Red Fort and the Jumna Masjid, and a twig from the tree that used to grow through the Cloth Shop near the Clock Tower in the Chandi Chowk, together with many other bits and pieces, some of which, such as a fragment of sandalwood and a lucky blue bead, were given to us by friends in the city or in one or other of Delhi's public gardens (it was the old *chowkidar* of Kudsia Begum's gateway who gave us that stick of incense). Kashmera's contribution was a little string of scarlet and black jungle seeds, while another friend, Devika (whose family was once described to me by a member of our dancing-class as being 'rich as creases'), donated a miniature *paan*† box no bigger than a four-anna piece, made of beaten silver and beautifully decorated. It contained small pieces of areca-nut and a pinch of powdered lime, and I have it still, though I lost its contents many years ago.

These and scores of similar souvenirs were carefully stowed away in a glossy cardboard box that had once held a dozen tablets of Erasmic Soap (and was itself a treasured object), and neither Bets nor I would have parted with that assorted collection of dust, sand, pebbles, feathers and dried flowers for all the diamonds in Tiffany's! That Erasmic Soap box and its precious contents left India with us, and during the lean years that followed it became a kind of talisman — a *hawa-dilli*, we call it — a 'heart-lifter'. For whenever we felt homesick or lost or forgotten, we had only to open it and the past was there in our hands. We could touch it and hold it and say: 'Do you remember . . .?' And of course

---

* Essence of roses.

† Areca-nut and lime wrapped in a green *paan* leaf, to be chewed. The red betel juice is spat out all over India!

we remembered. We knew exactly where every single item had come from, and singly or collectively they proved to be strong magic against despair and depression. In time the flowers, leaves and grasses crumbled and the paper disintegrated until, to an incurious eye, the contents would have looked like a boxful of old, dried breadcrumbs. But it still held the scent of India and continued to lift our hearts. I would certainly have had it to this day if it had not been for that warehouse fire; but all that survives of our *hawa-dilli* is 'Vika's little silver box, which I had removed only because the metal was helping to crush the more perishable objects in our cardboard treasure-chest.

One thing I learned during our last few days in Delhi was that Time, which can so often move as slowly as a slug crossing a dusty road, can also move with the swiftness of cloud shadows on a windy day. Until then, a week had seemed a very long time to wait for anything one wanted, while a month ahead was something far out of sight. As for a year — well, one might as well say 'never' and be done with it! But those last days in Delhi rushed past with appalling speed, and on one of them, paying a goodbye visit to Okhla, we witnessed something I have never seen before or since, and which no one was able to explain to me.

It was a dark, overcast day, heavy with thunder, and the air seemed to crackle with electricity. There was no lightning and no rain; though it must have been pouring somewhere further north, for the Jumna had risen dangerously close to flood-level and all the sluices, both on the canal and the river, had been opened. Downstream the water appeared to be boiling with fish. Myriads of *chilwa* were fighting their way up the fish-ladders, leaping like miniature salmon, and beyond the roaring sluices the river was alive with turtles. Hundreds of them. I presume they were catching *chilwa,* but they looked to me as though they were merely coming up for air, turning over so that for a brief moment you saw the pale plates of their bellies show white against the churning mud-coloured water, then diving, and doing it again. Up, over, down. Up, over, down. It was the weirdest sight and it made the wild water look as though it were alive, for there were big fish there too among the turtles. *Mahseer* and catfish, jumping, swirling, turning ...

Raucous clouds of gulls, chalk-white against that black, forbidding sky, were swooping and diving as they competed with the kites and crows for the swarming *chilwa,* and we could not venture onto the weir because the river was already level with the top of the stout wooden barrier that was normally sufficient to hold it in check, and beginning to lap over it. Here and there a plank had given way before the strain and was letting a smooth, head-high spate of water surge through and pour down the stony slope below, and all the sandbanks had vanished, while below the weir the Jumna ran unimpeded from bank to bank with only frothing patches of white water to show where the stone groins lay submerged. Upstream of the canal and the river sluices the tall silk-cotton trees were in flower. The ground below them was littered with their fallen scarlet blossoms, and I took one back with me to add it to the other souvenirs in the treasure-box.

It was a strange afternoon. A rather ominous one, because Okhla suddenly seemed to have turned into a totally unfamiliar place which I did not recognize at all. It was like one of those dreams in which you know that you are in a certain well-known spot even though it bears no resemblance to it, and for some unknown reason, curiously reminiscent of the day I saw the raw beginnings of New Delhi rising out of the 'spent and unconsidered earth', and sensed uneasily the approach of a future that was destined to destroy much that I had loved and thought of as indestructible, and to put an end to an enchanted childhood.

Morning after morning, as the date of our departure drew nearer, we would set out with Punj-ayah on a tour of Delhi to say goodbye to all our friends; returning with tear-stained cheeks and loaded with a weird selection of parting-presents that included a stuffed baby *gharial* that smelt like nothing on earth (and was immediately confiscated and disposed of by Mother), scores of glass bangles and endless paper packages containing a varied selection of *halwa, jellabies,* roast *chunna, paan* and dried fruit, and a whole Noah's Ark of brightly painted toy animals: elephants, camels, tigers, parrots and peacocks, in papier-mâché, carved wood, brass and stone. All of this gubbins (with the exception of the stuffed *gharial*) was, we hoped, to go with us; and it was only when our boxes were unpacked in England that we discovered that Mother had left them behind to be distributed among the children in the servants' compound.

Tacklow and Abdul Karim* would be accompanying us as far as

* Alum Din was away on sick-leave.

Bombay, but we had to say a tearful farewell to Punj-ayah in Delhi, to the entire staff of Curzon House, and a host of other friends who came to the station to see us off. Dear Buckie, Sir Charles, the Diwan-Sahib and the Khan Sahib, Nazir and Ameera, and 'Vika and her family, a number of buddies from the Dancing Class, and many of Mother's friends as well as ours, were on the platform to say goodbye and wish us good luck and a safe return.

A safe return . . .! If only I could have been sure of that! If only I had known for certain that I would be able to come back again one day. But how could I be, when I had recently learned that I was unlikely to leave school until I was seventeen? Seven years! *Seven whole years!* It was a lifetime. Only three years less than the whole of my present life-span, which seemed to me for ever. Besides, Tacklow had already told me that now that the war was over his job was bound to end and very soon he would be retired on a Lieutenant-Colonel's pension — there being little or no chance of promotion for an Army man who had seen no active service during the war years. If that were so, then he himself would be leaving India for good long before my schooldays were over.

I very seldom cried in public, for I knew that it was one of the things that one should not do, whatever the provocation. But I was in floods of tears as the train pulled out of Delhi and I leaned from the carriage window and waved and waved; and for the next few miles or so, as we puffed and chugged and rattled past a score of dear, familiar places on the plains beyond the walled city, I could barely see for crying. I was leaving them all behind: the Janta Mantar, the walls of Shere Shah's Delhi, the Purana Kila — its gateways glowing copper-coloured in the late afternoon sunlight. Humayun's beautiful red-and-white tomb and the heavenly blue of the Persian tiles on the dome of the Nil Burge — the tomb of one Fahim Khan, of whom nothing seems to be known except his name. The Pepper-pot Bridge and the road to Okhla; the *suttee* monuments by the Meerut road and, far away across the plain, the Khutab Minar and the crumbling ruins of the once great citadel of Tuglakabad . . .

I don't remember much about that three-day journey across India to Bombay, except that I spent most of it staring out of one or other of the carriage windows, watching India glide past me and striving to imprint every yard of it on my memory. Chugging across the enormous empty spaces of the Central Provinces and the borders of Rajasthan, I played a game with myself, one that Bets and I always played on long train journeys. The game was to see how many times you could count to sixty before you saw a fellow human (as soon as you saw one you stopped and began to count again). I remember that the average time between one sighting and the next turned out to be over twenty times: more than twenty minutes! This must have worked out at roughly twelve miles — fourteen at most, I imagine — as I am told that the trains of that day would not have travelled at more than thirty to thirty-five miles an hour. Nowadays I suppose the count would be nearer one human every fifteen seconds. But in 1919 there had not yet been a population explosion on the scale of that in later years, and though herds of black-buck and families of wild pig, chital and monkeys were a common sight, there were still enormous tracts of India in which wild animals outnumbered humans by a hundred to one.

As the train rattled southward I saw an occasional wolf, and when the line crossed a river or skirted a *jheel* there were always great flocks of water-birds, while every half-mile seemed to have its pair of sarus cranes; the big, blue, crested cranes which mate for life. Every village and hamlet was surrounded by a circle of cultivated fields and crop-lands; patches of bright green against the parched, lion-coloured plains. And however barren and uninhabited the country, wherever a low line of hills thrust up from the plain you could see that once upon a time, very long ago, there had been a fortress on the heights — or a hunting lodge or a lookout. For the ruins were still there, silhouetted against that enormous sky.

Once, looking out of the carriage window in the very early morning in the middle of nowhere, I saw on the crest of such a ridge a lone pavilion; a little *chatri,* its slender pillars and graceful dome dark against the yellow dawn: the last lonely remnant of some forgotten city. And to me at that moment the sight of the little ruined *chatri* seemed the personification of India and History and all Romance. It still does; for I have never forgotten it. But on that particular morning it was also a reminder of all that I was leaving behind; and watching it grow smaller and smaller as the train raced on, I knew that even if I was fortunate enough to come back again one day, nothing was ever going to be the same. Because I could only come back as a grown-up.

I made another daunting discovery when we reached Bombay. It was there that I learned for the first time that in comparison with the parents of many of our friends and acquaintances, mine were pretty badly off. I had never thought about it before; and if I had I would probably have supposed that Tacklow's pay was roughly the same as theirs, if not more. I knew we had to be careful, and that was about all. But arriving in Bombay my hopelessly unworldly father directed the driver of the *fitton-ghari* we had all piled into to take us to the Taj Mahal Hotel; presumably because it was the only one he had heard of! I remember Mother asking anxiously if he was sure we could afford it, and Tacklow replying that he meant to go in and ask what they charged for their cheapest rooms, and if it was more than we could afford, he would ask them to recommend some cheaper hotel — there were sure to be others. To which Mother replied firmly that she had no intention of allowing the Deputy Chief Censor to be seen dickering over the price of rooms with the hotel clerks, and that if anyone had to do it she would. She made the *ghari*-driver stop in a side-street near the hotel and, leaving us sitting in it, went off alone to cope with the situation; returning triumphantly to say that she had tackled the Manager and beaten him down to a reasonable price for two single rooms on the top floor, into each of which they had agreed to put a second bed for no extra charge. I remember feeling desperately embarrassed that she should have had to do such a thing — it seemed terrible to me then. I knew that we weren't rich, but I had no idea that we had to watch every penny — in this case every anna — and I was shaken by the discovery.

That brief interlude in Bombay, during which Tacklow, Bets and I in our hired phaeton-*ghari,* and Abdul Karim in a luggage-laden tonga, lurked in a side street near the Taj Mahal Hotel while Mother was finding out if we could possibly afford to spend a night there, and bargaining for the cheapest possible rate, taught me something that I never forgot: that far more than three-quarters of the men of my race who spent their lives in Indian service were not overpaid and pampered 'Burra-Sahibs' lording it over 'the natives', but were really people like Tacklow who worked themselves to the bone to serve, to the best of their ability, a country and a people whom they had come to love so much that they were willing to pay the heavy price that was exacted for that service. And just how heavy it was became apparent to me a bare twenty-four hours later, when I said goodbye to my father and saw, with a terrible contraction of the heart, that he, like me, was in tears.

He had not seen his only son for six years, and now he did not know how long it would be before he saw his little daughters again — and children grow up, and grow away, so very quickly. Poor Tacklow! I remember clinging to him like a frenzied octopus as we said our farewells in a cramped cabin on the S.S. 'Ormond', striving to express without words how much I loved him; and when the ship's hooter blew to warn all visitors to go ashore and he had to leave, watching him walk down the gangplank and turn to wave to us from the crowded dockside.

He was not a tall man and it was a family joke that he claimed to be half an inch taller than Mother. But though his heart was enormous his lack of inches, combined with his total refusal, under any circumstances, to shove himself forward, went against him now; for within minutes he was swallowed up in a mass of taller husbands, fathers and friends who stood waving on the dock and I lost sight of him — for two long years: an eternity when one is a child ... The steamer began to draw slowly away, and as the rubbish-strewn harbour water widened between ship and shore the people on the dock seemed to shrink and dwindle until they were barely more than a blur of tiny dots. And presently the 'Ormond' was steaming out of the lovely, island-strewn harbour which some fifteenth-century Portuguese adventurer had named *Bomm-baie* — 'Beautiful Bay' — heading for the open sea.

Mother went down to the cabin to unpack and Bets and I mopped our eyes and blew our noses, and turning from the deck rail made our way to the stern of the ship from where we could watch the towers and domes of Bombay, the green outline of Malabar Hill and the rocky islet of Elephanta, grow smaller and smaller; all gold and gleaming in the low afternoon sunlight. And as the coast of India faded into the haze, we made a solemn vow never, ever, to desert her. Never to let England replace her in our affections. Never, even if we were not able to return, to forget her, but to remember her always with love. We were deadly serious about it, and we repeated it aloud in Hindustani in case any of her many gods and godlings should happen to be listening and could bear witness. Then we shook hands on it, waved goodbye to her as she vanished, and went off, a little comforted, to look for Bargie and Tony and forgather with our friends.

♓ I remember quite a lot about that voyage; starting with lifeboat drill, which was taken as seriously as we had taken our solemn vow. The Great War had not been over all that long, and as ships' companies were very much alive to the danger of floating mines, boat-drill was held with boring frequency. Which was perhaps just as well, since at least one passenger-ship on her way home was sunk by a mine that had drifted far off course. I remember the flying-fishes and the dolphins, and a school of whales basking and spouting on a calm day near the mouth of the Gulf of Aden — and how horrid the 'children's meals' were. Particularly the eggs, which tasted strongly of some form of preservative. The milk too. I was a skinny child and I grew a lot skinnier on the voyage owing to my reluctance to eat the food provided for the young.

There were a good many of our friends and contemporaries on board, and since we had all been well and truly infected with the Amateur Dramatic bug during the war years, we put on a children's song-and-dance show for our long-suffering elders, in which Bets and I sang and danced to 'Madam, will you walk?' and Bargie brought the house down singing 'I'm Gilbert the Filbert, the Kernel of the Nuts', decked out in white tie and tails which she must have borrowed from some schoolboy of her own age among the passengers. She also made a sizable dent in the heart of one of the ship's officers, who fell madly in love with her and was for ever inviting her to his cabin to look at his photograph-albums or drink tea or whatever. (I do hope he was a bachelor.) Admittedly, he was extremely good-looking; but in my opinion far too old to carry on like that. Why, he could easily have been as much as *thirty!*

I could not blame him, for I too thought Bargie must be the most beautiful thing since Helen of Troy. Now rising fourteen, and, by Indian standards a woman grown, she had the violet eyes, the ebony hair and perfect features of a famous film-star as yet unborn, Elizabeth Taylor, when that gorgeous creature was at the height of her beauty. But though Bargie was beautiful she was by no means dumb, and on the rare occasions when her love-sick officer managed to persuade her to accept one of his invitations, she insisted on taking me along with her. Not until much later did I realize how he must have detested the skinny, ten-year-old chaperone who kept a close and beady eye upon him while cheerfully scoffing the lion's share of the chocolates, lemon squash, ice cream and sugared cakes he provided for the purpose of luring the lovely Slater-child into his cabin.

Port Said, which I had last seen the year before the Great War, seemed quite unchanged and astonishingly familiar. The white-painted Victorian-style hotel on the sands. The rows of bathing-huts and deck chairs. The brilliant blue of scores of jellyfish stranded and melting in the hot sun above the high-tide mark. The *gully-gully* men who addressed every white woman as 'Missis Queen Victoria' and who produced adorable, cheeping, day-old chicks from our ears or the crown of our hats or hair ribbons. The round wooden boxes of Turkish Delight which we bought at Simon Artz, and lunch in the big, white dining-room of the hotel that looked out on the sands and the sea ...

To all home-bound Anglo-Indians, the East was only left behind when they entered the Mediterranean. After that there was no longer any need to protect themselves from a savage sun with a solar topi, and for this reason it had become a tradition to throw these emblems of servitude overboard while the ship was still within sight of Port Said. A legend had grown up that if your topi sank you would never return, but if it floated you were sure to go back. So those who had hated their time in India, and had no wish to set foot in it again, would cheat by weighting their topis with a soda-water bottle or a handful of annas wrapped in a sheet of newspaper, or anything else heavy and expendable, and cheer when it sank. The rest would watch with bated breath and feel relieved or depressed according to whether theirs floated or sank. But Bets and I (who by this time knew every lascar on the ship by name and had taken the precaution of asking them for advice) did not fling our topis into the wake, but dropped them very carefully, holding them as though they were bowls of water. And Glory, Glory, Alleluia! they floated! We watched them bobbing away in the glitter of the Mediterranean sunlight, and felt as though a weight had been lifted from our shoulders. We would come back!

Bargie and Tony had also dropped their topis overboard, but though unweighted, both sank almost immediately, so perhaps there was something in that old Anglo-Indian legend after all, for neither of them ever returned to India.

According to Mother, we went ashore at several other places in the course of that voyage; among them Aden, Malta and Marseilles. But if so I don't remember doing so. I only remember Port Said and, towards the end of the voyage, a truly horrendous storm in the Bay of Biscay. It was so violent that the Captain of the 'Ormond' had to turn the ship about so that she went with it instead of fighting it. We were apparently blown many miles off course, and we learned later that the storm had been responsible for an appalling number of wrecks on the coasts of half-a-dozen countries, including England. We had run into the fringes of it shortly after passing through the Straits of Gibraltar, and Mother and most of the adult passengers had made for the privacy of their cabins and collapsed with seasickness. But a handful of children, including Bargie, Tony, Bets and myself, who were not in the least affected by seasickness (a failing that I, for one, have been fatally prone to ever since!), had a whale of a time tobogganing down the drenched and tilting decks on tea-trays that we had filched from a pile outside one of the galleys.

It was a wildly exciting sport, in the course of which we all got soaked to the skin, and I still cannot imagine why none of us were swept overboard. For the 'Ormond' was bucking and pitching and throwing herself to and fro like a frenzied colt in some rough-riding competition, and every wave looked as though it was bound to engulf her. Only once in my life would I see such waves again. They looked more like huge dark cliffs with ragged white bushes growing along the top of them; as though the whole Atlantic had reared up as the Red Sea had done to let the Israelites pass through, and was now about to crash down again as it had crashed onto the pursuing Pharaoh and all the Chariots of Egypt.

The decks were swept again and again with foaming water and the air was full of stinging spray as we whizzed to and fro, shrieking with excitement, until Authority, in the form of a justly infuriated ship's officer, grabbed us, boxed our ears (instant disciplinary action was not discouraged in those days), and, having confiscated our tea-trays, marched us all below and gave us a tongue-lashing that made our faces burn more than our ears had done. He took our names, but nobly refrained from reporting us to our parents, and we decided unanimously that it had been well worth it.

Unwillingly to School

Chapter 20

~%∞%~

My native land — Good Night!

Byron, *Childe Harold*

By the time the S.S. 'Ormond' entered the English Channel the wild weather had passed, and the Thames was as flat as an old unpolished pewter plate as the liner edged slowly up it on a dawn tide in the care of two squat black tugs.

I have never forgotten that traumatic day. Even now I can recall it as clearly as though I have gone back in time and am living it once again; standing on the wet deck to watch the dank grey wharfs and the gaunt cranes and warehouses slide slowly past through a veil of the faint, persistent drizzle that the British call a 'Scotch mist'; a drizzle that was barely visible to the eye and did no more than dampen the winter coat that Mother had taken out of mothballs and made me put on before I went up on deck.

So this was *Belait!* This was 'home'. This wet, flat, dark-grey country with its black, oily river, ugly buildings and drably clad dock-workers. It seemed to belong to another world from the one I had left behind less than three weeks earlier, so different was it from the crowded docks at Bombay in the blinding Indian sunlight, the noise, the heat, the hurrying coolies and the colours — the brilliant clashing colours ...

There had been a breeze blowing in from the sea at Bombay, but today in the docks at Tilbury there was barely a breath of wind to stir that small rain, and only a few passengers were on deck. I heard one of them, an elderly man in an overcoat, ask a ship's officer why the flag was flying at half-mast; and learned that a small child who had been in the sick-bay for some days had died during the night. The child was not one I knew, and nor did I know its mother except by

311

sight. But most of the women on board had known that the child was seriously ill and had done what they could to help and encourage its anxious mother. And now it was dead. I remember looking up at the sodden bit of bunting that drooped at half-mast and feeling the rain on my face, and thinking that it was only fitting that the day should be grey and dreary as though it too, like the flag, was in mourning.

The tugs were easing the great ship along the left bank of the river, the Gravesend side opposite Tilbury, when either the current caught her or the pilot made an error, for we crunched into a pier which must have had some tall structure on it that damaged the 'Ormond's bridge; and suddenly the quiet of the early morning was shattered as shouts, splinters and bad language flew in every direction. A startled passenger hustled me below deck, where I forgathered with Bets and we ate breakfast in a state of deep gloom and made another vow that we would never love this depressing foreign country or regard it as 'home' — so there!* That vow too remained unbroken for the larger part of my life, and was only partially lifted when I came to live in Sussex; for to this day the word 'home' instantly conjures up a picture of India as clear as the one of Bombay that the Thames and Tilbury Docks showed me on that long-ago morning.

In the end the 'Ormond' must have anchored in mid-stream, because I remember Mother taking us up on deck — where there were now many more passengers — to lean over the rail and watch for Bill who would, she had been promised, be brought to Tilbury to meet us. By now it must have been getting on for mid-morning, and though the rain had stopped there was a nasty, cold little wind. Then suddenly Mother cried: 'There he is! That's him! — *Willie!*' She began to wave wildly. There were tears running down her cheeks, and I felt as deeply embarrassed for her as I had for myself when I found that I was crying in public on the station platform at Delhi, and on the deck of the 'Ormond' as I watched Tacklow walk away. For had not that fountain of wisdom, Kashmera, once told me sternly when I wept because I had cut my arm badly on one of the wicked double-pronged thorns of a kikar tree, that I must remember that I was English and that '*Angrezi-log kubi nai rota!*' ('English people never cry!'). I had tried to

* Bargie (now Lady Cunningham) says she remembers me trying to make her take the same oath; with no success!

312

live up to that; and had envied my Indian playmates for whom it was obviously OK to howl their eyes out whenever they happened to feel like it. (Even the boys — some quite big boys — were allowed to yell the roof off, and instead of being scolded, were petted and coaxed and made a fuss of.)

To make matters worse, I knew that Mother had dressed very carefully for this meeting. She was wearing her best suit and her most fetching hat, and looking as pretty as paint in them. Yet here she was, busy spoiling it all by acquiring red eyes and a runny nose and tear-spots all down the front of her jacket. One consolation was that Willie, in that rowboat, was probably much too far away to be able to see such details, so I stopped worrying about Mother and stared down instead at the occupants of the little rowing-boat that was bobbing about on the water some fifty feet below. Two of them were grown-ups; one presumably the owner, since he was rowing it; the other, I recognized with annoyance, was Lord Clow — not my favourite person. The third was a boy between twelve and thirteen years old, who was a complete stranger to me and plainly suffering, as I was myself, from acute embarrassment.

When one is a child, a snapshot or a studio photograph gives a misleading impression of the sitter: particularly when it is in black-and-white — and in those days colour photography had not been invented and most snapshots were taken with a Box Brownie. So it is not surprising that poor Willie had only the vaguest idea of what his mother looked like, or which of the many faces that peered down at him from somewhere near the top of that enormous towering cliff of a ship belonged to her. Even when her wild waving and calling enabled Lord Clow to spot her and point her out to him, he did not recognize her — or his sisters either. All three of us were as much strangers to him as he was to Bets and myself, and even to Mother, who had left behind a little six-year-old son and was now looking at a schoolboy of more than double that age.

Bill told me a long time afterwards that it was the most embarrassing moment of his life, for not only were we all strangers to him, but he had no idea what to do or say to us, and when Mother waved and called out to him he felt as though the eyes of every single one of the massed ranks of passengers looking down from the 'Ormond's decks were focused on him. It was as though, he said, he was standing on a stage in the glare of a spotlight and had forgotten the lines he was supposed to say.

He looked like it too, and I felt for him. They should never have brought him out in that dinghy, but waited until the ship had docked so that he could have met us in our cabin or a corner of the saloon; or even in the crowded Customs shed on shore. As it was, he was compelled to stay put for what seemed like hours to me and days to him; getting colder and colder in the biting wind and beginning to feel seasick from the constant bobble of the little boat and the strain of looking up and waving, keeping a fixed and nervous grin on his face and occasionally shouting some fatuous question or answer which the wind blew away. Until at long last Lord Clow took pity on him and, having yelled up to us that they would see us in the Customs Shed, told the boatmen to row them ashore.

I don't remember what I felt or what any of us did when we finally met. In fact I don't remember anything at all of all that business of disembarkation, except for saying goodbye to Bargie and managing by a superhuman effort not to cry, even though I was by that time bleakly convinced that I would never see her again. I can't even remember if my first love, Guy, was there to meet her and the rest of his family. He probably was, but if so I was too depressed to register the fact. Yet once out of the Customs Shed, I remember very clearly piling into a crowded second-class carriage so full of strangers that I and brother Willie (hereinafter to be known as Bill) had to stand, while Bets sat on Mother's lap.

There were no corridors on trains in those days, and so little standing-room in the narrow second-class carriages that I stood sandwiched between the bony knees of strangers, with my back to the carriage, staring bleakly out of the window at this hideous country that my parents spoke of as 'home'. I had never travelled second-class in India, though I had often thought it would be fun to do so because the passengers, jammed together as they were with their bundles, baskets and babies, always seemed to be enjoying themselves, chattering and laughing together like a flock of parrots in a date palm. Well, now I was doing so. But here no one spoke, let alone laughed. They sat in glum silence, reading their newspapers or staring stodgily ahead of them at nothing. I hated every minute of that journey.

Because of the vast distances that were covered by India's trains, their first-class compartments were always sleepers; each one large enough to accommodate four berths, two to each side, with ample room between for luggage. And since this was before the days of corridor trains, each compartment had its own adjoining lavatory, complete with handbasin and running water. In this train too there were no corridors. But no loos either! I dreaded to think what would happen if I had need of one. Did one have to jump out when the train stopped at a station? (and if so, what if the train left again before one had finished, leaving one stranded in this daunting place?) It was a terrifying prospect!

If the 'Ormond' had docked at Southampton or Dover I might have taken a slightly less unfavourable view of my native land. But to arrive at Tilbury on a cold, wet, overcast day, and have to make the dreary train-journey from there to Central London, through some of the most depressing built-up areas in the country, was a terrible introduction to England. As I gazed, horrified, from the rain-spotted window, it seemed to me as though there were no open spaces here at all. Nothing but mile after mile of squalid, soot-stained walls, warehouses and dingy streets lined with small, grimy terraced houses in which, unbelievably, my native people, *Angrezis* — 'Sahib-log!' — actually lived ...

Tacklow's pay had never run to renting a house of the size and style that the 'Heaven-Born' occupied, and even The Rookery, which was the largest house we had ever lived in in India, had no running water, modern sanitation or refrigerator; and no garden beyond the row of flower-pots on the gravel-covered terrace-cum-drive, and the steep, cosmos-covered slope below the buttressed wall that supported it. Yet in both Simla and Delhi the houses in which the British and the well-to-do Indians lived enjoyed a large degree of privacy, and did not look into each other's windows. Nor was it possible to hear from one's bedroom or verandah what one's next-door neighbours were saying. I can only imagine that it must have been for this reason that the very idea of *Angrezi-log* having to live cheek-by-jowl in those claustrophobic terraces of two-up, two-down houses that faced each other across a rainy street shocked me so much; almost as much as the squalor and dirt!

I had so often heard English people complain of the squalor and dirt of India that I had subconsciously come to believe that England must, by contrast, be a model of cleanliness and order. But nothing I had seen in India — not even the *bustees* and back alleys of her crowded cities, where goats, pi-dogs, monkeys and Brahmini bulls wandered at will among people who flung their rubbish into the streets, defecated in the gutters, chewed *paan* and spat out the resulting streams of scarlet juices broadcast — was more depressingly squalid than this endless wilderness of mean streets. Here everything in sight, including the drizzle and the dingy lines of washing that hung limply in many of the tiny, rubbish-strewn back gardens, seemed to be permeated with soot. And no wonder! For in those days coal was almost the only source of energy. Railways, factories, ships and power-plants burned it, the chimney-pots of every house within sight belched smoke from coal fires and coal-burning stoves, and only lighting and street lamps relied on gas.

My untutored view of my homeland and its natives received yet another rude shock when we finally arrived at our destination, Lord Clow's flat, which occupied the second floor of one of those large, white-painted Victorian mansions in a square near Palace Gate in Kensington. Whoever owns it now probably paid well over a hundred thousand pounds for it and could sell it tomorrow for close on a million; but it failed to meet with my approval. A lift took us and our luggage up to it and there were fires in every room and crumpets for tea. The tall sash windows of the front rooms looked out onto plane trees and down upon a wet street bounded by the high railings of a garden that formed the centre of the square. But our bedrooms, Bets and mine, and I think Bill's and the cook-housekeeper's too, as well as the kitchen and all the 'usual offices', looked out onto an inner shaft: a sort of brick-lined well constructed to allow air and a certain amount of light into the inner rooms of the tall, terraced houses lining the square, all of which, as far as I could make out, had been built back-to-back with the houses in another square behind us. This meant that the view from these inner rooms was restricted to brick walls and windows that avoided looking into each other by being set at different levels. As an added precaution, the windows were provided with a double set of curtains: the outer ones of net or Nottingham lace remaining permanently drawn, while the inner, more solid ones were drawn only when the lights were lit. Though in fact the lights more often than not were on from dawn until bedtime, because England was enjoying a particularly wet spring that year and even when it was not raining the sun never broke through and the days were as dark as an Indian dusk.

Mother arranged various 'indoor outings' for us. She took us to the Natural History Museum, which was a great success, and to lunch with a massive Edwardian dame called Mrs Alec-Tweedie, who turned out to be Harley Alec-Tweedie's mother. Mrs Alec-Tweedie painted highly coloured and very slapdash pictures in water-colours, travelled widely and recorded her travels in books with titles such as *My Adventurous Journey*, *Through Finlandia in Carts*, and so on. She gave us a splendidly grown-up meal in a dining-room crammed with pictures (her own impressionistic efforts competing with large and gloomy family portraits), and afterwards took us to a matinée of *The Lilac Domino*, a musical comedy that we thought was marvellous.

A day or two later Mother took us to a children's matinée of Maskelyne and Devant's Magic Show which we enjoyed; though only mildly, since children who had seen the tricks that Indian conjurors can perform are inclined to be blasé about magic shows. We were far more thrilled, when it was over, to find ourselves emerging from the theatre into a real London fog of the type that used to be called a 'pea-souper'. This was something we had certainly never seen before! The fog was not white or grey, but a curious, dirty yellow that smelt strongly of soot and was so dense that you could barely see your hand in front of your face. Our cabbie took us back to the flat at a snail's pace and Mother fretted the whole way for fear that he would knock someone down and run over them, or drive us all into the river.

Early on during that London visit she took us with her to the bank to deposit the money that Tacklow had given her for travelling and arrival expenses, and I shall never forget the incredulous, pop-eyed amazement of the clerk behind the counter when she handed over a small Gladstone bag which proved to be full of gold sovereigns; coins that he could not have seen for years. But Edward VII had been on the throne and sovereigns and half-sovereigns were normal currency when Tacklow had last been in England.

Then there was our first visit to the Zoo; taken in company with three young cousins and their mother, Aunt Norah Bryson, wife of Mother's eldest brother, Arnold. This 'treat' became a disaster, since the day turned out to be a Bank Holiday and apparently every other paterfamilias in all England had set out with the same intention, accompanied by his wife, children, parents and in-laws and their respective progeny. The crush was beyond anything I had witnessed up to that time. Even the crowds who celebrated Diwali and Id were not greater, and I don't remember being able to see a single animal except the heads and necks of the giraffes and the top half of an elephant who plodded through the mob giving rides to children. The youngest Bryson could not have seen even that much, and my clearest memory of this exhausting day is of his piping voice reiterating tirelessly, like a gramophone whose needle has got stuck in a groove, 'Is this a lift, Mummy? ... Mummy, is this a lift? Is this a lift ...?' It seems — heaven knows why — that since a very early age his infant ambition had been to ride in a lift and Aunt Norah had rashly told him that we would be doing so that day. I believe we did at some point; but it failed to stop that shrill and repetitive question, and I still can't think why some public-spirited Londoner didn't strike the child a hefty clout with a bottle or an umbrella.

An even more disappointing event was a walk in Kensington Gardens — the 'Delectable Gardens' made famous by Sir James Barrie's immortal fairy-tale, *Peter Pan in Kensington Gardens*. They were once the private park of Kensington Palace, where Victoria spent a large part of her childhood and which was her home at the time she was proclaimed Queen. But since they were also the gardens that some fatuous grown-up had assured us were infinitely larger and more beautiful than our beloved Kudsia Bagh, our disillusion that day was quite as traumatic as it had been on the day we docked at Tilbury. So *this* was what the British called a 'garden'! This — this *maidan*! Acres and acres of grass criss-crossed with paths worn by the feet of children and bisected by broad, gravelled roads edged with low railings. Trees of the type one could not climb; neat flowerbeds that bore notices forbidding the public to pick flowers; a plethora of sooty laurel shrubs, a few benches and, dotted about in pairs, innumerable iron chairs on which one could not seat oneself without a watchful park attendant hurrying up to collect a small sum for the privilege of doing so.

How could anyone, even a grown-up, have described this bleak and tidy park as being superior to the flower-scented tangle of Begum Kudsia's garden? We could not understand it, and as we trudged dutifully along the crowded paths and stared silently at the Round Pond and disapprovingly at the statue of Peter Pan (which turned out to be another let-down, being a statue of the wrong Peter — not the baby Peter of Kensington Gardens at all, but the Peter of Captain Hook, the Lost Boys and the Never-Never Land), our aching sense of exile grew greater with every lagging step. It was no surprise when this expedition, like others, ended in rain and a hasty return to the flat in damp coats, hats and spirits.

Many of Mother's efforts at entertaining us were defeated by the weather, for rain and wind kept us flat-bound for the greater part of our visit, and my clearest recollection of that first introduction to London is of the three of us — Bill still a stranger — lying on our stomachs in front of a gas-fire in that dismal back bedroom, with all the lights turned on, and drowning the sound of the wind and the falling rain by playing records on one of those wind-up gramophones with large green-painted horns, our favourite record being a song called 'K-k-k-Katy', ('beautiful Katy, you're the only g-g-g-girl that I adore'). I have never heard it since, yet the refrain and the words still stay obstinately in the jam-packed attics of my mind, and I have only to hum them to see again that dark, rain-beleaguered flat.

There was soon to be a song called 'Roses of Picardy' which will always mean school to me. For the fell matter of school could no longer be avoided. Bill, together with his cousin Dick Hamblin, was already at Lynams, the famous Dragon School in Oxford, since it was to Oxford that Tacklow's parents, having hastily sold Freshfields, had retreated on the outbreak of war — presumably because that city, being too far north of London to be within reach of German zeppelins, was considered a lot safer than Southampton. Their daughter, Aunt Molly Hamblin, now widowed, had moved down from Scotland to keep an eye on them, bringing Bill and her own three children, Maggie, Grace and Dick, with her. It was to her house that we went for a few days after leaving London, so that Mother could meet her in-laws again, see her son back to his preparatory school and discuss the vexed question of a suitable boarding-school for her daughters.

In those days the Dragon School had not become coeducational, so there was no question of Bets and me being sent there. And I can only suppose that my grandparents showed no sign of being willing to take on housing Cecil's daughters in order that they could attend some other local school as day-girls, and that Aunt Molly thought she had done more than enough for her eldest brother by lumbering herself with Bill. For after a few days, Mother took off for Bedford and Aunt Lizzie; possibly with some idea of entering us for her own old school, Bedford High. If so, that too came to nothing, and eventually we travelled down to the Isle of Thanet, to Birchington, to look at a boarding-school where (on the advice of dear 'Mrs Ponson') Mother had finally decided to leave Bets and me.

The summer term was due to start at any moment, but she brought us down to Birchington a couple of days ahead so that we could see the school and its surroundings before being left there. We put up at the Bungalow Hotel (which seemed to be a fairly new addition to the landscape and probably was) and Mother took us for a walk on the beach, which she thought would be a better introduction to the prospect of school than starting with the school itself.

Mercifully it was not raining, and though the day was a grey one it was windless and the sea was calm. But this excellent ploy very nearly foundered when we arrived at the shore to find that the tide was out, and inquired a little blankly why there was no sand. 'What do you mean?' demanded Mother, 'there's masses of it!' 'Where?' returned Bets and myself with one voice, staring around us. 'Don't be silly,' said Mother. 'You're standing on it.' She had forgotten that the only sand we had ever seen, except long ago at Findhorn, was the silver sand of India and Egypt: hot countries where the rocks and reefs and empty shells that make up sand are bleached white by the sun, and where the shores are washed by coral seas and the river banks covered with powdered silver that shows blinding white at midday and by moonlight, and takes on every shade of pearl in between. But this stuff that we were standing on was a yellowish, biscuit-beige colour; and so coarse that you could separate its grains into different minute pebbles on the palm of your hand. We were astounded. And, once again, disapproving. The stuff looked *dirty*! The situation was, however, saved by the chalk cliffs and a wreck —

Owing to the fact that the 'Ormond' had come up the Channel by night, we had missed seeing Beachy Head and the White Cliffs of Dover; which was perhaps just as well, as here the white chalk cliffs were far smaller and much less impressive. On the other hand they were also full of caves and were the first thing in England that really caught my fancy. For one thing, you could scramble up them, and in those days the land that lay above them was all open country: acres and acres of grass and gorse bushes and wildflowers, masses of sea lavender and tufts of sea pinks that bordered the cliff edge along which the feet of strolling villagers and visitors had worn a long, straggling path that ran from The Gap to Minnes Bay. The beach too (apart from that coarse and disappointingly coloured sand) could not, from a child's point of view, have been improved upon; for in addition to those alluring caves there were innumerable rock pools full of anemones, starfish, shrimps and other small sea creatures trapped by the tide. And when we reached the spot where the cliffs dwindled and ended and the bungalows began, the land flattened and curved away in a long, sweeping beach where, stranded some thirty or forty yards out in shallow water and held fast by the rocks, lay the wreck of a Scandinavian freighter driven ashore by the same storm that the 'Ormond' had encountered in the Bay of Biscay.

I had read about wrecks but had never seen one before, and the sight of this one more than made up for the rash of brand-new jerry-built bungalows and the dullness of the landscape behind the bay. We were all fascinated by it, and removing our shoes and socks — in Mother's case, stockings — we paddled out as far as we could in order to see it at even closer range; though as the tide was now coming in fast we didn't make much headway. Still, it added a distinct fillip to the scenery. And what with those lovely rock pools and the charm of those chalk cliffs and smugglers' caves, (for surely such caves *must* have been used by smugglers?) I began to think better of England. Discussing it later that day, we decided that Birchington was really a very pretty place; and we even took a lenient view of the school, Portpool, and the two Misses Barnes who owned and ran it. But not for long.

Mother had taken us there next morning to see the house and meet our future headmistress, Miss Barnes, and her sister Miss Florence who acted as matron. Miss Barnes was thin, bespectacled and grey, and Miss Florence large and bosomy and ditto. Both seemed kind enough and the house, though a school, was not bad as schools go. But Portpool and the Misses Barnes were to do me a great disservice that I would suffer from all my life. The sisters had taken one look at me and, turning shocked eyes on Mother, remarked that anyone could see that I came from India since I was much too thin, skinny and sallow for my age and clearly in need of 'building up'. They had never, they said, had any Anglo-Indian pupils before, but they were aware that the quality of Indian milk — and indeed *all* food in Eastern countries — was lamentable. However, Mrs Kaye was not to worry; they would soon put this to rights and she would see a remarkable change in her little daughter after a few months of good English food, fresh milk, sea-bathing and bracing air.

Mother looked a bit startled, but agreed that I was fairly thin. And to tell the truth, I had two popular parlour tricks which used to amuse my juvenile friends in Simla and which, for what is known in Show Business as a 'limited season', were to prove equally successful with the members of my dormitory at Portpool; I could turn my navel inside out, and hide both my clenched fists under my rib cage — tricks that only the skinny can perform.

The sisters Barnes soon put a stop to that. I was put down for 'extra milk' and given mugs of it at frequent intervals; which I must say I much enjoyed, having discovered with pleased surprise that English milk, unlike its Indian counterpart, tasted delicious. It was like drinking the best single cream and I was all for it. While the rest of the school made do with a scraping of margarine on their bread, I was given butter (another 'extra' on the bill) because I needed 'building up'. And four times a day, for the same reason, I was made to swallow a large, glutinous spoonful of cod-liver oil and malt. Not that I minded that either, since the malt successfully disguised the taste of the cod-liver oil, and the stuff was very sweet — like thick honey.

Stuffed with pints of rich milk, pounds of butter and jars of cod-liver oil and malt, I began to put on weight, and the Misses Barnes and Mother, as well as various women friends and relatives such as Aunt Molly Hamblin, my Kaye grandmother and 'Aunt Bee' Lewis (Mother's friend from the Jhelum days, who had never married and now reappeared on the scene), were delighted with my progress. For it was, unfortunately, an age in which plumpness was considered a healthy condition in children, and the winner of the Best Baby Competition was always some dangerously overweight infant with fat red cheeks and dimples and creases galore. The unsightly excess poundage known as 'puppy-fat' would, one was assured, vanish like the dew of morning as soon as one turned eighteen.

Nowadays doctors have decided that a fat child generally grows up to be a fat adult. How right they are. In my new character of a poor-little-undernourished-shrimp-from-India I was stuffed as systematically as a Strasbourg goose, with the result that I became one of those unfortunate fatties who spend half their life on a diet without ever achieving a slim figure.

Chapter 21

Which is something between
A bathing machine,
And a very small second-class carriage.

Gilbert, *The Gondoliers*

I was not happy at Portpool, and it is a period of my life that I do not enjoy looking back on. That Bets and I made a bad start was not entirely our fault. The two Misses Barnes had told their pupils that two new girls from India would be joining their ranks that term, and for reasons best known to themselves their ignorant little pupils decided that we actually were Indians, and looked forward to meeting a pair of young Maharanis in gold-embroidered saris and diamond nose-studs. The arrival of Mollie and Betty Kaye, who looked no different from themselves, was therefore a sad disappointment which they took out on us.

Their leader, an unpleasant girl whose name I have long forgotten, fancied herself as a singer, and her favourite song, frequently requested by her admiring juniors, was the aforementioned 'Roses of Picardy'. Picardy and Portpool are for ever bracketed together in my mind, courtesy of that school bully ... *'She is watching by the poplars, Colinette with the sea-blue eyes'* ... ugh!

I recall a couple of days during which for some forgotten reason Bets and myself were 'sent to Coventry' by our fellow pupils (which meant that no one would speak so much as a word to us). We retaliated by talking to each other in Hindustani, which both fascinated and dumbfounded them, and when after a couple of days of this they gave up, we continued to use that language because no one else had any idea what we were saying and it maddened them. It also relieved our feelings to be able — smiling sweetly the while — to pass rude and uncomplimentary remarks about them to their faces, which they could neither translate nor resent.

When at last the term ended we spent our first summer holidays, traditionally, at the seaside. And since Tacklow had once spent part of his school holidays at Hunstanton (pronounced, also traditionally, 'Hunstun'), a town on the Wash which he had described to us in lyrical terms and urged Mother to visit, she booked lodgings there for six weeks in August and September. Unfortunately he had neglected to add that there were two Hunstantons — Old Hunstanton and new Hunstanton. His had been the old one. But Mother, writing for information to a newspaper that devoted several pages to advertising holiday accommodation, ended up booking us, for a very reasonable sum, a 'self-service flat only two minutes' walk from the sea front, with exclusive use of a large and fully furnished beach-house, complete with kitchenette'. Or words to that effect. Anyway, it sounded, for the price, too good to be true. And was, of course.

Since our straitened circumstances did not permit Mother to travel to Norfolk in order to inspect this alluringly advertised accommodation, our first sight of it was a horrid shock. The 'flat' was the upper storey of a largish shop in a noisy street in the brash and booming town of New Hunstanton; a mile or two — and a world away! — from the prim, old-fashioned charms of the Old Town. The shop was called 'The London Bazaar', and a bazaar it was: a cheap and gaudy one full of junk goods of every description. Bets and I took to it on sight. Not so poor Mother. The flat, which except for the holiday season was lived in by the owners of the shop, was littered with personal belongings they had neglected to remove. Some of the cupboards and several drawers still held a few ancient coats, hats, boots and peculiar examples of woollen underwear, all smelling as strongly of mothballs as the rooms themselves smelt of bygone meals which (if one's nose was anything to go by) had consisted largely of boiled cabbage.

It was the noisiest flat you can imagine, for the London Bazaar did a roaring trade from dawn until long after dark. The street was a busy one and pubs abounded; so too, inside, did green plush trimmed with bobbles, and red rep curtains edged with fringe. There were also Nottingham lace curtains, several aspidistras in pots, and endless bits of china lettered in gold with 'A Present from Blackpool' or wherever — the towns were all different; any modern interior decorator with a penchant for Victoriana would have gone into ecstasies over it. We thought it was pretty dreadful, and were frankly horrified by the beds, which like too many British beds sagged dismally in the middle. The ones we had been used to in India had thin mattresses laid on tightly stretched interwoven bands of *narwa,* a tough form of webbing which does not sag.

'Never mind,' comforted Mother, 'we won't have to see much of this place. We'll sleep here, and cook our lunch and tea and perhaps supper too at the beach-house, and spend the day there.' We all had high hopes of the beach-house and thought it was very kind of the proprietor of the London Bazaar, from whom we collected the key next morning, when he insisted on sending one of his shop assistants — or maybe a relative — to take us there in case we lost the way. In the event we couldn't have found it without him, for the 'large and fully furnished beach-house' lay over half a mile beyond the outskirts of the town.

The first part of the way took us through a complicated tangle of streets and past the esplanade, and when that was behind us there was a long trudge along a rough and sandy track that meandered between gorse bushes, where the view of the sea on our right was obstructed by a long line of empty and decrepit railway carriages. On our left lay a flat and featureless stretch of singularly unattractive common land that strayed away to the horizon, and needless to say it was another grey and sunless day, though fortunately, windless and rainless: there was that much to be thankful for.

We should have been warned, but I don't believe that even Mother realized what we were in for. Bill, Bets and I certainly did not, and we were left speechless when at long last our guide turned right between the blocks of abandoned railway carriages, stopped and said brightly: "Ere we are then! You 'ave got the key, Madam, 'aven't you? Good-oh! then I'll be getting along now — cheery-bye all.' And departed, whistling: leaving us staring in silent disbelief at the fully furnished beach-house which we had hoped to use as our headquarters for the next six weeks ...

It was in fact the Guard's Van at the end of that particular string of railway carriages, and the 'furniture' consisted of a small and very rusty oil-burning cooker (which presumably constituted 'the kitchenette'), a rickety table and several even ricketier (if there isn't such a word there should be) wooden chairs, a three-legged metal stool (had the Guard once sat on this?) and several exceedingly dilapidated deck chairs. The lock-up cupboards were full of rubbish left behind by the last tenants, and the larder, constructed out of a partitioned section of the van and not much more than a shallow cupboard with a few flimsy shelves, contained a selection of chipped enamel mugs, jugs and plates; none of which matched. A teapot, kettle and a few basic cooking utensils, much battered but still serviceable, hung from or stood on a shelf above the stove. The windows were adorned with faded cotton curtains and the walls with out-of-date calendars and curling postcards fixed to the woodwork with drawing-pins, while the 'all mod cons' consisted of a couple of enamelled buckets that had seen better days, plus a basin and a soap-dish, ditto. And that was it — apart from a strong smell of kerosene oil and decayed seaweed that pervaded the derelict van like a tangible presence.

No one said anything for a long time and I suspect that Mother was on the verge of tears. If so, she swallowed them bravely, and while we three were out taking our first dip of the summer holidays (we had wasted no time over that!) she set about cleaning the place with the aid of a duster and a dustpan and brush she had had the forethought to buy that morning at the London Bazaar, having discovered from the proprietor that nothing of that description was included in the effects of the 'furnished beach-house'.

She was to do wonders with that van; brilliantly demonstrating that one determined woman can bring order out of chaos when she sets her mind to it. Everything she needed was to be found, and at a price she could afford, at that invaluable London Bazaar, and she bought chintz and paint and paint-brushes, a potted geranium, a broom, a scrubbing-brush and a mop, a piece of linoleum, and various other useful items with which she transformed that Guards' Van. The gaily patterned chintz (threepence a yard in those days!) was sewn into new curtains for the windows and loose covers for the chairs and the stool. The doors and walls got a fresh lick of paint and the floor a more easily cleanable covering of linoleum. Even the cooker began to take a pride in itself, and when the overcast skies relented and gave place to a week of sunshine that dried out the damp and got rid of the smell of mildew, kerosene and rotting seaweed (well, *almost* got rid of it), we decided that our now spick-and-span beach-hut deserved a name, and painted a sign for it that said 'Guard's Van Villa'. But we had barely nailed it up when the sun vanished and the clouds rolled up again and down came the rain. And suddenly we were standing under a sieve in place of a roof.

Seven days of hot sunshine had dried it out only too well, and a hundred cracks in its ancient fabric now leaked water onto our heads with so much enthusiasm that we could not have been much wetter if we'd stood outside in the downpour.

After a vain attempt to catch the leaks in cups, bowls, saucepans and buckets, we donned our mackintoshes and took refuge under the table until the worst was over. And as soon as the rain outside eased off a little, we locked up and fled back to the welcome dryness of that dark and stuffy flat, wondering what on earth we were going to do now, since it was clearly impossible to repair the entire roof of the van. Nor could we use the place while it leaked like a sponge, and with the weather showing every sign of being all set for another spell of non-stop rain, it looked as though we would have to resign ourselves to sitting around in the flat. But at this point Mother was visited by inspiration: 'Plasticine!' exclaimed Mother. 'That ought to do it!' And it did. She rushed downstairs to the shop and returned, triumphant, bearing a dozen penny sticks of plain grey plasticine; the kind that one could use for modelling as opposed to the flossier and more expensive coloured varieties that were sold in boxes. Armed with these, we made our way back to the van where we spent the whole of that wet afternoon filling every hole and crack in the roof with plasticine; and from then on, though it was a particularly wet summer, Guard's Van Villa provided us with a safe and comparatively dry retreat.

On the scenic side, our part of the beach could not have been less alluring. There was sand all right; miles of it when the tide was out, because this was the Wash. That huge, square-shaped bite out of the north-east coast of England, with Lincolnshire on one side and Norfolk on the other, both sharing the third, while the North Sea takes care of the fourth or seaward side — but only with a thin layer of water. For this is that same Wash that, back in the year 1216, bad King John, the wicked brother of Richard the Lionheart and chief villain of all those tales about an outlawed folk-hero known as Robin Hood, was attempting to ford when the tide came in with the terrifying swiftness that is still a notable feature of that vast, shallow inlet. It very nearly cost him his life and definitely, according to legend, lost him the Crown Jewels of England which sank with the rest of his baggage. I like to think that the Crown Jewels are still there, somewhere deep down in the sand, and that one day, when the shallow stretch of water finally silts up (or, more likely, when land-hungry men finally succeed in walling it off from the North Sea and turning it into thousands of 'desirable building sites'), someone with a bulldozer will uncover that fabulous, long-lost treasure. Though from all one knows of John, I expect he flogged the jewels and invented the story to account for their disappearance.

The shallowness of the sea off Hunstanton makes its beaches safe for children and non-swimmers, since even at high tide we had to wade out for ever before the water became deep enough to come up to our waists. Which was fine by me, for buoyed up by the knowledge that I only had to put down a toe in order to touch the bottom, I soon learnt to swim. Low tide at that beach uncovered acres of firm, flat sand on which there were no rocks; and therefore no pools — except under the endless yards of an eyesore in the form of an enormous iron pipe that in those days stretched far out toward the retreating sea and was one of the town's main drains. It siphoned a constant stream of sewage into the sea, which was an unpleasant thought for parents, who warned their offspring to keep well away from it. Though why we were urged to avoid it I don't know, since the great iron tube on its cumbersome iron supports did not leak, so the only dangerous part about it was the open end that vomited a thick, khaki-coloured liquid into the Wash. This was only visible for the shortest of short periods every day, and once covered by the tide and safely out of sight and out of mind, was blithely ignored by even the fussiest of parents.

Curiously enough (and not forgetting that apart from a solitary week of sunshine and an occasional fine day here and there, the weather was almost uniformly lousy), the holiday was an immense success. After the initial shock, Bill, Bets and I dismissed the unalluring scenery and trappings and got down to the serious business of enjoying ourselves. The place was crawling with children and it was not long before we had made friends with those whose parents had rented the railway carriages to the left and right of our Guard's Van. In their company we swam, played cops-and-robbers or hide-and-seek among the gorse bushes behind our 'beach-houses', shrimped at low tide or played rounders on the acres of wet sand. That ghastly main drain proved every bit as entertaining as a rock pool, for since it spent half its time under water it was overgrown with seaweed, barnacles and mussels, and its underside dripped with sea anemones. All kinds of small sea creatures would be trapped by each retreating tide in the pools that the water scoured out between its iron supports, and needless to say no child paid the least attention to instructions to keep away from it.

We had become attached to our Guard's Van, but were seldom inside it for we more or less lived in our bathing-suits; and when one is collecting crabs or swimming it doesn't matter in the least whether it is raining or not, so we couldn't have cared less about the weather. Mother took us on a day's expedition by train to see Sandringham, the country-house and estate owned by the royal family and a favourite retreat of the King, George V, who was to die there in 1936. I didn't think much of the house, which is fussy and spiky and very Victoria-and-Albert in design; vaguely reminiscent of Viceregal Lodge in Simla and not at all the sort of house that I had imagined Kings and Queens would live in. I think I had expected a Cinderella-style castle (Buckingham Palace had been equally disappointing). On another day, a non-rainy one for a change, we spent a few hours in Old Hunstanton and realized why Tacklow had cherished such happy memories of the place. But we were having such fun in New Hunstanton that we did not regret the error that had landed us there.

I have only one unpleasant memory of that holiday; in retrospect, embarrassing rather than unpleasant. On our first Sunday, one of those sunny days that caused the leaks, Mother marched us off as usual to church, dressed in our Sunday best. Bill in his school suit and Bets and I in identical white dresses, white socks, black patent-leather strap shoes, and with our hair tied on top of our heads with vast bows of hand-wide black moiré ribbon. On arrival at the church — large, Anglican and on or near the seafront — we were prevented from entering by a black-gowned verger on the grounds that 'the young ladies' (aged eight and ten!) 'were improperly dressed'. Their heads were uncovered. (Hats for the female sex were apparently obligatory.) Mother, unable to believe her ears, began by treating the matter lightly. She said cheerfully that that could be easily remedied, and turning to us, flattened out those huge bows of ribbon until they formed large black pancake hats that more than covered our heads — and looked very smart too! But the verger remained adamant. He knew when a hat was not a hat, and had no intention of allowing any female, however youthful, to enter his church without wearing a proper one.

In the end Mother was driven to insist that he fetch the vicar, and when this reverend gentleman arrived, she was flabbergasted to discover that in the matter of headgear he was in complete agreement with his verger. She explained that as the service was due to start in a few minutes there was no time to return to the flat and collect our school hats, and that no one could say that our heads were not more than adequately covered. When he too remained adamant, she lost her temper and quoted the Scriptures to him in a manner that did credit to the daughter of the Reverend Thomas Bryson and a sister of the Reverend Arnold.

I don't remember much of it, except that she obviously knew her Bible a jolly sight better than the vicar knew his. She demanded to be told exactly where and in what chapter and verse there was any mention of 'hats', and said she had not realized until now that the words Christ had spoken to the Disciples who had tried to drive the children away had not been 'suffer the little children to come unto me and forbid them not', but 'suffer the little children to come unto me and forbid them not — except those girls who are not wearing regulation hats and any boy who may have forgotten to take his off'! I do remember her ending by telling him that he was a disgrace to the Church and that rather than attend any service over which he had the effrontery to preside she would prefer to turn to Rome — or Buddha! With which she swept off, herding her scarlet-faced and deeply embarrassed offspring before her.

Looking back, it still strikes me as extraordinary that such a thing could happen in this century and during my own lifetime, and I am no longer surprised that Christianity seems to have lost its way, and that so many churches are deconsecrated and sold off as private homes or business premises, because they have not attracted sufficient worshippers to keep them going. Men like that vicar and his verger helped to bring about this sorry state of affairs, and one can only hope that their Bishop (to whom Mother wrote to complain, and who took the trouble to write a personal letter of apology on behalf of that unchristian Christian) tore a hefty strip off the culprits and brought them to see the error of their ways. But as Mother angrily reminded that pompous pair of bigots, 'It needs be that offence must come, but woe unto him by whom the offence cometh!'

It needs be that offence must come . . . That 'must' is the operative word, and I find it a daunting one. Yet at the time, and strictly from a child's point of view, the whole shocking episode (and Bill, Bets and I were so deeply shocked and embarrassed by it that none of us has ever forgotten it) had its bright side. For Mother refused to take us to any other church in that town, and instead, on the remaining Sundays, she read us a chapter from the Bible and some of the prayers from the Morning Service, after which we sang a hymn of our choice before being allowed to go off and play on the beach.

We left Hunstanton and the kind and friendly proprietors and staff of the London Bazaar with regret, and as far as I can remember, spent the last two weeks of the holidays at Aunt Lizzie's in Bedford. Bill went back to the Dragon School and Bets and I returned to Portpool. And a fortnight later Mother came down to the Bungalow Hotel in Birchington for a night, to say goodbye to us before sailing for India.

No one who has not experienced them can know just how cruel such partings can be. They were by far the heaviest part of the price that was paid for Empire, and it was the women and children who paid most of it, for their men at least had work to fill their days and occupy their thoughts. I had minded the parting with Tacklow a good deal more than I minded saying goodbye to Mother who, I was well aware, was fonder of Bets, her 'baby', than of me, and fondest of all of her Willie — her first-born and her only son. But it was still a terrible wrench to watch her leave, knowing that I would not see her again for two years at the very least, probably three; and to be afraid that one of the many deadly diseases that were still so prevalent in India might take her away for good. It was a horrible leave-taking and I felt like one of those unfortunate sea anemones that we had so blithely pried loose from their secure foothold on the underside of the town drain in Hunstanton, and attempted to keep alive in a bucket. Bill joined us again when term ended and the three of us travelled to Bedford to spend the Christmas holidays at The Birches with Aunt Lizzie.

✄ For Bets and me, this first-ever Christmas without our parents held none of the excitement and anticipation of those Christmasses in India. Aunt Lizzie supported an indigent spinster sister, Aunt Emily — a thin, bony relic of the Victorian era who never spoke above a whisper and lived in a small back room of The Birches from which she emerged only in order to do a few household chores, eat her meals, and take the same daily walk to the Library and back. We were fond of Aunt Lizzie, but almost fonder of Emily, whose few carefully cleaned and pressed clothes, high-necked leg-of-mutton-sleeved blouses and buttoned boots belonged to an age that had vanished before Mother was born. She could easily have been taken for a ghost out of one of Charles Dickens's novels, for she moved without noise and her curiously dry, whispering voice added to the illusion of other-worldliness. Mother was to tell me later that every Saturday evening, just before Emily returned from her daily walk, Aunt Lizzie would slip into her sister's room and put seven shillings and six pennies under the clock on the mantelpiece: never more and never less. It was the only money Emily possessed, since the work she had done when young (I never learned what it was, but suspect that she may have been a governess) was badly paid and did not carry a pension, so that in her old age she had no savings to fall back on and no recourse but to live on the charity of her widowed sister, with whom she had quarrelled many years ago.

The quarrel must have been a bitter one, and I often wondered if it had been over Aunt Lizzie's handsome husband, Uncle Tom. Had Emily — who must have been pretty when young — expected to marry him, and had he jilted her for Lizzie? That seemed unlikely, since Aunt Lizzie, though a darling, could never have possessed a trace of physical beauty; she looked exactly like the Frog Footman in *Alice in Wonderland,* and cannot have been more than four foot ten or eleven in her shoes. Whatever the cause of the quarrel it had clearly not been forgotten or forgiven, for the two old ladies never spoke a word to each other if they could possibly avoid it.

Perhaps that was why Emily loved to talk to us. And we loved to listen; enthralled by that whispering voice as it described in detail various wonders its owner had seen in the shops that she passed on her daily walk. She was a passionate window-shopper. Poor darling, she could *never* have afforded to buy anything! But to hear her describe something as ordinary as a length of pink satin ribbon entranced us

333

(pink was her favourite colour and she pronounced it *peeeink* giving it two syllables on which she lingered lovingly as though it was something very special). To Emily everything she saw had something wonderful about it, and it was her special gift that she could communicate something of that wonder to others.

That she could also, despite her archaic dress and manner, be surprisingly modern was proved by the way in which she dressed the doll (supplied by Aunt Lizzie) that was put into the top of Bets's Christmas stocking. Aunt Lizzie dressed the other one, which went into the top of mine, and the difference between the two was remarkable. Both dolls were dressed as fairies, and the same materials — white cotton net and silver ribbon — were used for both of them. Mine, dressed by Aunt Lizzie, came straight out of the latter years of the nineteenth century, in a high-necked, long-waisted and long-skirted dress with medium-length leg-of-mutton sleeves. A prim Victorian doll with a neat silver bow plonked straight on top of its head and another at each side of the long waistline. Bets's doll, on the other hand, proved that Emily, while herself still wearing fashions fully thirty years out of date, was by no means ignorant of that fact and had not failed to use her eyes when out window-shopping. *Her* fairy doll wore a short, full-skirted ballet dress with a tiny, tight bodice, silver shoulder straps and a bunch of silver ribbons over one eye — 1920, here I come! I was surprised at Emily; and Aunt Lizzie was plainly shocked. But the stockings in which this very different pair of fairies appeared were destined to prick the delightful, sparkling soap-bubble of Father Christmas, reindeer-sleigh and snow-fairies, and destroy it for Bets and me for ever ...

I had celebrated my eleventh birthday during the summer holidays and in another two years would enter my teens. So I ought to have known better. But Mother had always been so clever over the delivery of our Christmas stockings that neither Bets nor I had ever been able to catch her at it. On the only occasion that Bets had woken up and caught a glimpse of her, the glimpse had merely served to convince Bets that she had actually seen Father Christmas and that the whole story was therefore true — she had proved it with her own eyes! I may at times have nourished doubts, but despite being well into double figures, I too was never a hundred per cent sure, and I always hoped against hope that the lovely story was true — as true as the Christmas story; the Baby in a manger, the star and the shepherds and 'Hark, the Herald Angels Sing'! Why couldn't it be true? My Indian friends and playmates had told me about far stranger things that had happened in India.

Unfortunately Mother had quite forgotten to brief Aunt Lizzie and Emily on how to swap an empty stocking with its pair, previously filled in another room and kept hidden until the recipients were asleep. And since all that the old dears knew about Christmas stockings was that one waited until the children were asleep and then filled the stockings that hung at the end of their beds, Bets and I woke up around half-past ten or eleven on Christmas Eve to find the room bright with electric light and noisy with the rustle of paper as the two old ladies, wearing night-caps and solid woollen dressing-gowns, solemnly wrapped each item in sheets of tissue paper and stowed them one by one in the stocking we had hung up so hopefully before turning out the light.

It was a terrible blow. We had been fooled all along and there was no Father Christmas after all. That cherished, multicoloured soap-bubble burst with an almost audible '*pop!*', leaving nothing but a small wet smudge where something glittering and magical had perished. We shut our eyes tightly and did not stir until the old darlings had finished their work and tip-toed out, clicking off the light as they went and closing the door softly behind them. After a short pause we talked it over in the dark and eventually, having swallowed our disappointment, decided that we had been incredibly lucky in having been able to believe in Father Christmas for so long, and that not for anything would we have missed the anticipation and thrill we had enjoyed on past Christmas Eves as we hopefully hung up our stockings, wondering if Father Christmas would come and fearing that he might not. Nor would we have forgone the wild excitement of waking up in the pre-dawn dark to creep down to the foot of the bed and feel the stocking bulging with delights. Yes, we had indeed been lucky. Enormously lucky! We would never regret having been able to believe in Father Christmas for so long. But oh, how sad we were that it had ended, and that for us that particular magic would never be experienced again.

It was during this same Christmas holiday that we saw our first Christmas pantomime. We had heard a lot about pantomimes and had greatly looked forward to seeing one. Aunt Lizzie had booked seats for *Aladdin* at a Bedford theatre, and since we were of course familiar with the story of Aladdin and his wonderful lamp, we were wildly excited at the prospect of seeing it acted out on a stage. How would they do the Genie? ... the cave of jewels? We could hardly wait! For some forgotten reason, possibly to do with cookery, we arrived at the theatre with only just enough time to find our seats and buy a pro- gramme: and then Aunt Lizzie discovered that she had left the tickets at home. Panic! She remembered the numbers, but the theatre attend- ants were adamant: we could not be admitted without tickets and that was that. It was the vicar and the verger all over again. Bets and I were on the edge of tears as we heard the muffled music of the overture striking up, and even Bill looked shaken. There was nothing for it but for Aunt Lizzie to hurry back to The Birches and fetch the wretched things as quickly as she could. Fortunately, it was not very far; so leaving us in charge of the commissionaire she hurried off, muttering: 'Oh dear oh dear, how very *vexing* to be sure!' — an expression she only made use of when seriously put out (I don't think she knew any stronger ones).

We stood forlornly in the empty foyer, a picture of misery and embarrassment while the minutes ticked by and she did not return. We had so looked forward to this treat and now we were doomed to miss a whole act — perhaps two ... Perhaps half the show! What if she couldn't find the tickets? Supposing she had tripped and broken her ankle, hurrying up the front steps ...? Despairing tears began to trickle down Bets's face and the commissionaire's heart melted. He said that as our seats were in the dress circle we could go in and stand at the back of it until our aunt returned, and he would show us the way and tell her where to find us. Oh joy! We hurried after him and were ushered into the back of the circle and from there had our first sight of a traditional pantomime.

It came as a worse shock than almost anything that had gone before. Worse than Tilbury or Kensington Gardens or the biscuit-coloured stuff that the English called sand. No one — not even Bill, who from the age of six had been taken to see this form of entertainment during his Christmas holidays — had thought to give us any idea of what a British pantomime was like, so we were thrown in at the deep end. There on the stage, in place of ancient China, were three men dancing a species of clog dance while singing a popular song entitled 'Where do flies go in the winter time?'; the middle one got up as a caricature of a cockney charlady complete with apron, hair-curlers and striped stockings, and the ones on either side dressed as British 'bobbies', policemen. Oh lost illusions, where do *you* go in this peculiar country?

It was a very sleazy pantomime put on by a third-rate touring company whose props and scenery were sadly tatty — a defect for which the war years and not the company can be blamed, for it cannot have been easy to get cloth or paint at such a time. But they did their best. And so did Bets and I; dutifully clapping and laughing whenever the audience did, and assuring Aunt Lizzie that we were enjoying it. But it was another sad let-down, as we admitted to each other in whispers after our bedroom lights had been turned out that night. England appeared determined to disappoint us.

We did eventually discover that not all Christmas pantomimes were as tatty and terrible as this one, because a year or two later someone took us to see another; *Cinderella* this time, staged in one of London's largest and most resplendent theatres, Drury Lane. It was wonderful! No tat here, but as much glamour and glitter as even the most critical child's heart could desire. A dashing Prince (we did not realize, poor innocents, that he was a she), a ravishing 'Cinders' and an enchanting Fairy Godmother; a glass coach drawn by *real* ponies and a succession of 'transformation scenes' that left us dumb with admiration.

Yet it was on this occasion that Bets, entering the auditorium, stopped dead in the aisle and, looking indignantly round the huge theatre, announced in ringing tones: 'It isn't *nearly* as big as the Simla theatre!' Alas, the years were passing, and as she herself grew up the memory of that little doll-sized theatre, on whose boards she had last appeared as Tinkerbell, had swelled in retrospect to a size that made Drury Lane seem puny. For the past in which she and I had been so small had stayed still; as it must for all of us. And though we were to see that little theatre again and again, and act in it too, to this day we both still think of its stage as an enormous expanse on which we first danced in The Pageant, when a mere slice of it represented the whole of Great Britain, Europe and the Middle East!

Aunt Lizzie sent us back to Portpool with a large tuck-box crammed with home-made toffee, fudge and chocolates, in addition to several of her superlative cakes; all of which led to a distinct upsurge in our popularity, despite the fact that we continued to speak to each other in Hindustani and were not Indian Princesses, or even Indians — crimes for which we were never really forgiven. But apart from the temporary success of our tuck-box, only three other incidents connected with Portpool remain in my memory. The brightest by far was the day when the entire upper school was taken by bus to see, at a matinée in the Winter Garden Theatre at Margate, that legendary prima ballerina, Anna Pavlova.

In later years some balletomane of the Thirties wrote of her that if you were to ask almost any well-known dancer what had made them take up ballet, the chances were ninety-nine to one in favour of the reply being that either she or he, or their parents, had once seen Pavlova dance. That statement was no exaggeration. I had never seen ballet before, and never imagined that any mere human could create such beauty: could *move* like that. *Dance* like that. It was a revelation. Pavlova danced the Autumn Leaf as though she weighed no more than gossamer being blown here and there in an October wind. She danced as though she was a butterfly; or a mayfly new-hatched, above a trout stream in June. As if she could, if she chose, dance across a field of corn without bending a single stem. And at the last she danced her famous Dying Swan so that there was not a dry eye in the house. Almost every girl from Portpool left that theatre in a daze of ecstasy, firmly resolved to follow in her footsteps and become a prima ballerina: Bets being among the worst hit. I don't know if any of them followed this up, but I am sure that not one of them ever forgot that shimmering afternoon in the Winter Garden at Margate.

The second incident descends abruptly from the realm of the sublime to the painfully silly. One of the girls in my dormitory, an overweight child of about twelve years old, plumped herself down during the night on one of the Victorian china chamber-pots that were provided in case of emergency (pupils were discouraged from traipsing down the passages to the lavatory in the small hours). The pot, proving unequal to the strain, shattered into about fifty pieces, most of which had to be picked out of her wincing posterior one by one. No one could fail to sympathize with her, but at the time, and unkind though it may seem, the incident struck the entire dormitory as hilariously funny and we were laughing ourselves into stitches as we tried to help the shrieking sufferer, while the girl who was sent to fetch help reeled away whooping with mirth, and apparently had some difficulty in making herself understood when delivering her message. Miss Florence refused to see the joke. So did Miss Barnes, who had been awakened by the racket and hurried over to inquire into the cause, and who proceeded to blast us into silence with a brief, blighting speech that would have done credit to a Kommissar in the KGB, and sent us scuttling back to bed as Miss Florence whisked the howling victim off to the sanatorium.

I remember that after our headmistress had turned the lights out and departed, we lay awake for a long time speculating in whispers as to the form of treatment being undergone by our absent room-mate. Prayer or stitches? For by now we were all well aware of something that was officially a secret, but that in the not too distant future was to break up the school: that Miss Florence was a Christian Scientist and that Miss Barnes was undoubtedly aware of it.

As matron, Miss Florence paid lip-service to the parents of non-Christian-Science children by employing a local doctor as the 'school' doctor; but she did not send for him if she could help it, preferring to stick to the lines laid down by her faith. I realize now that this must have been why our dear Mrs Ponson had recommended Portpool — because she herself secretly shared Miss Florence's beliefs; I think it was naughty of her not to tell Mother. The end for the school came when one of its pupils went down with a severe attack of something like pneumonia or typhoid or one of those pre-antibiotic-days killer diseases, and instead of calling in the doctor, Miss Florence relied on prayer and 'inculcating faith' in the delirious child (*'pain is not real ... all sickness is in the mind and can be exorcised by prayer and faith ...'*).

I must have been a poor judge of character, for had anyone asked me, I would have said that Miss Barnes was the dominant sister. But the evidence provided by this affair shows that Miss Florence was the tougher of the two. She stuck to her guns even when the child became far too ill to understand anything that was said to her, let alone exhortations of this nature, and it was only at the eleventh hour that Miss Barnes lost her nerve and sent for the doctor. That gentleman, finding the girl too ill to be moved, hurriedly imported a couple of nurses from the nearest hospital and summoned the child's parents; who arrived by the earliest possible train and naturally raised hell all round. Luckily for everyone concerned the child survived — though it had been a narrow squeak. The school was less fortunate. I gather that the incensed parents wrote to the parents or guardians of every other Portpool girl (in these cash-oriented days they would of course have sued for vast damages), with the result that a good many parents snatched their little darlings away. Of the remainder, some allowed their children to stay with Miss Barnes, while the rest — all of them Christian Scientists — went off with Miss Florence who presumably founded a small school for the Faithful somewhere else.

Bets and I were removed and sent to another 'private enterprise' school on the other side of England; in Clevedon — a small town in Somerset on the shores of the Bristol Channel.

Chapter 22

~~~❊❊❊~~~

... some wet bird-haunted English lawn ...

Arnold, 'Obermann Once More'

Our new school was called The Lawn, and the majority of its fifty or sixty fledgling birds were the children of India-service people. I believe it had begun in a modest way as a home-from-home, plus a certain amount of basic education, for three or four small children whose parents, like Kipling's, were compelled to leave them behind in England for years at a time. But complimentary opinions about it having been circulated by satisfied Anglo-Indian parents, it was not long before the initial home-plus-teaching experiment blossomed into a full-scale boarding-school whose pupils could, if necessary, stay on and be looked after and entertained during the holidays as well as in term-time. It also accepted a small number of day-girls.

At that time there were several well-known schools specially tailored to meet the needs of the children of the Raj, and my parents had originally intended to send us to the largest and best-known of these. But Tacklow had backed out at the last minute because the school in question sent him a copy of the minutes of its latest Board Meeting which, among other things, stated that the chairman, a retired Anglo-Indian, had 'opened the proceedings with a prayer'. Unfortunately the chairman turned out to be a man my parents knew too much about and Tacklow had declared forcefully that no child of his was going to be educated at a school that allowed a hypocritical, two-faced, double-dealing bribe-taker like old Whatsizname, who had never had a Christian thought in his head, to open *any* proceedings 'with a prayer'. It was an affront to the Almighty!

And that was why Bets and I had been abruptly re-routed to Birchington and Portpool — on the strength of a few cosy words from Mrs Ponson and very little else; since apart from the fact that the poet and painter Dante Gabriel Rossetti had died and been buried in the parish church of that quiet little seaside town, they knew nothing at all about Birchington. Or the school either. But now that Portpool had proved unsatisfactory, we were dispatched to The Lawn; a smaller and more modest edition of the original school whose chairman of the Board of Governors had been permitted (despite his own and well-known 'manifold sins and wickedness') to put up prayers in public. I for one was delighted at the move, because among its pupils was my dearest and oldest English friend, Bargie the Beautiful, and the prospect of seeing her again would have made Borstal seem attractive to me!

Since Mother was still in India, all the arrangements had to be made by letter, and we were taken down to Clevedon by that friend of her early days in Jhelum, Miss Beatrice Lewis; hereinafter known to us as Aunt Bee,* to whom Mother had appealed for help and who had agreed to take charge of us during our holiday in return for a 'consideration', plus all expenses.

As at Birchington, we arrived in Clevedon and were installed at The Lawn a day or two in advance of the start of a new term and the arrival of our fellow pupils. Two or three of them spent their holidays there and were therefore special pets of the headmistress, Miss Wiltshire, who could obviously be a totally different and very likeable person during holiday time, though she was an awesome personage during the term — which was the only time the majority of us ever came into contact with her. One of her year-round boarders, Cynthia Hepper, a girl of my own age who became a friend of mine during those first out-of-term days, had been in her care, on and off, since the age of three and was devoted to her. But though Cynthia attached herself to me at once, and I was grateful for her kindness to a newcomer, I was really only interested in meeting Bargie again and could hardly wait for her arrival. Unluckily I had not had the sense to realize that the gap between our respective ages, which had not mattered in the least while we were carefree children in Simla and Delhi, might be an

---

* Victorians and Edwardians had a tiresome habit of making children refer to adult family friends as Aunties and Uncles.

Curzon House, Old Delhi, where we stayed during the cold weather.

The ruined gateway in the Kudsia Bagh, after the bamboo thicket had been cut down.

Above: 'Down-on-the-Farm' fancy-dress party at Peterhof. Bets and I attended as milkmaids; so, according to this photograph, did Bargie. Sunbonnets the order of the day!

Above: In camp. Tacklow chatting to a camp elephant.

Right: Duck shoot on a *jheel* beyond Delhi: Tacklow and Sir Charles being poled out to their 'hides'.

Self off to fish
for *chilwa* at Okhla.

Above: Walled village beyond Tuglakabad,
where there was a friendly pi-dog who used to
lie in wait for us and rush out to race alongside
our car.

Below: The Lal Kila, the Red Fort. The covered
bazaar where we bought our Christmas
tangerines leads inward from the gateway below
the row of white domes.

Right: The Lawn,
Clevedon, Somerset.

Below: Dub-Dub:
Miss Wiltshire, our
headmistress.

Right: Pit Chatham as
MacHeath in Gay's
opera *Polly*, which we
turned into a school
craze.

Below: A few Lawn girls
on a picnic to Walton
Castle, policed by two
mistresses who are
flanked by the Leslie-
Jones twins. Bets is
centre front, with her
best friend, Betty
Norbury, seated extreme
right. I took the picture
with my little Box
Brownie!

Helen Keelan.

Right: Susan, our much-loved 'cook-general', at Kew. All dressed up in her Sunday best in order to go 'walkin' out with my intended'.

Above: Self, thinly disguised as a boy in order to win a bet that I couldn't get out of the school and buy and bring back a handful of ice-cream cornets. I could and did.

Right: Aunt Molly, Grandpapa Kaye and Tacklow at Upton House.

Left: Three Trees, Hillingdon.

Right: Sandy Napier.

Château d'Oex, Switzerland. Bill looking glumly down on the town from a snowless hillside.

Bill, photographed in uniform
before leaving for India
to join his Mountain Battery
on the North-West Frontier.

Right: Aunt Bee-for-Battle-axe Lewis.

Far right: Dear Aunt Lizzie, another honorary aunt, but a much-loved one.

Below: Amateur cabaret on board SS 'City of London'. The chorus line for 'All the Nice Girls love a Sailor'. Captain of the ship in centre. Bets is the third girl from left; self the fourth.

Below: Pyjama Dance and Pillow-fight. I am the second from the left, Bets the fifth.

Home at last!

unbridgeable gulf in the regimented world of a British boarding-school.

Bargie was now in the sixth form; and not only a senior but a prefect, with all the responsibilities, privileges and rights that this entailed, including the right to use the Prefects' Room — a holy-of-holies that no one but another prefect, or a member of the teaching staff, could enter unless summoned. And to the hoi-polloi, a summons only meant that one had erred in some way or another and was therefore about to receive a sharp dressing-down by that august body. I, on the other hand, had suddenly become that lowest and most insignificant of creatures, a 'new girl'; already consigned to the third form and therefore light-years removed from Prefect Marjorie Slater (no one at The Lawn called her 'Bargie' and I had to drop that loving nickname pretty smartly! — though not at her request). The fact was that at least half the junior school and most of the seniors adored her, and had taken instant exception to the use of such a 'hideous' nickname applied to their goddess: and by a new girl, at that — a mere third-former!

In those days, and I suspect in these, it was almost obligatory to select one of the seniors as an object of one's admiration, and I remember my owl-eyed surprise when I was asked: 'Who are you going to Y-A?' — the initials stood for 'Young Adorer', and a prefect's popularity could be gauged by the number of her Y-As: in which respect Bargie (sorry, *Marjorie*), had a slight edge over the head-girl, a statuesque seventeen-year-old called Doreen Hepper, cousin of the friendly Cynthia. When the custom had been explained to me and I replied that I wasn't going to Y-A anyone, I was firmly informed that it was a must; *everyone* Y-Ayed someone until they reached the sixth form and became eligible to be Y-Ayed instead of Y-Aying. 'I suppose' said my informant, 'that you'll be Y-Aying Marjorie Slater, as you used to know her.'

Used! Ah me, what a knell that word sounded in my sore heart! I remember replying tartly that no one could possibly Y-A a friend: it would be too silly. Cynthia urged the claims of her cousin, the lovely Doreen, but I thought the whole idea was too stupid for words, and when the pressure of public opinion became too much for me I selected the senior with the fewest Y-As to her credit, one Beryl Beale, for whom I dutifully fetched and carried, presented with small bunches of flowers and hung about the boot-hole and cloakroom of an evening in order to say good-night when the seniors passed on their way back from supper. I remember becoming quite fond of her in a detached sort of way; rather as though she represented a small firm in which I had bought a few shares. When she left after her final term I did not bother to Y-A anyone else; and I have to admit, regretfully, that as far as I know no one ever Y-Ayed me. But then I never rose to become a prefect or even a sixth-former.

Bets and I lived for letters from India to such an extent that to this day the sight of an Indian stamp on an envelope awakes a faint echo of the thrill it once brought me. Though not all the news those letters contained was good. I remember the shock of learning that people I loved had died: the dear Khan Sahib; our old bearer; and other friends too ... Why is it that children think of the friends of their youth as immortal and are stricken to the heart by the discovery that they are not? I had lost too many of them during that terrible flu epidemic. Raji had been a victim, and Mumtaz and Gully; and my old ally, *Mali-ji*, who had thought that my photograph was a picture of a cauliflower. Their deaths had cast a shadow over our last year in India, but at least we had been there to cry on the shoulders of their grieving relatives and to mourn with their families. But this reading of the passing of some old familiar friend, known to us all our days, made death a very cold and lonely thing; and I became frightened for my parents, particularly Tacklow who was already (horrors!) in his fifties and therefore (if the Bible was to be trusted) had less than twenty years left out of those 'three score years and ten'. It was then that I began to ask God every night to please, *please* allow me to be happily married and with several children of my own before time ran out for Tacklow; so that I should to some extent be insulated against the anguish of losing him.

During the first few years of our exile many of the letters we received from India were from Indian friends, some of whom, the younger and less sophisticated ones, obviously did not realize that although we could chatter to them in their own language we could neither read nor write it. The address on their envelopes had been painstakingly copied out in English, but as the letters inside were in the sender's own beautiful, graceful script, I could never be certain who had written them and had no idea how to get them translated. In the end, though alarmed at the extra cost (stamps on all non-family letters had to be paid for out of our meagre pocket-money), I finally sent them out to Tacklow, asking him to give my love and suitable messages to the writers. This he did; but it was not a popular move. Our young correspondents either did not like the idea of their letters being read by my father, or resented him knowing that they could not write in *Angrezi*; for though I wrote to them I never had a reply. The servants, however, had no such inhibitions. They employed a bazaar letter-writer whose ornate and flowery style has always fascinated me; I enjoyed answering them. But as the months lengthened into years and the years plodded by, the letters came at longer and longer intervals; until at last, as memories began to fade and the past retreated, they stopped altogether. I kept one or two of them for years. But in the end these too perished in that fire.

Contrary to all expectations, I quite enjoyed my years at The Lawn, though I saw little or nothing of Bargie except from a distance, and on the only occasion when I asked if I could walk with her she explained gently that it was unheard of for a senior to pair with a junior when the school went out walking two-by-two in 'crocodile'. She was very nice about it and did her best not to hurt my feelings. But I realized then that the gap between us had grown too great to be bridged and that neither of us could flout the prevailing laws of The Lawn. So I gave up. And anyway I had already blotted my copybook sufficiently badly by insisting on walking with Bets one day a week. Even we did not dare to go further than that, for the opposition that it aroused was fierce and vocal: (a) fourth-formers did not walk with juniors who were only in the second form: it was 'not done'; (b) girls of my age did not pair for walks with mere 'kids' who were two years younger than themselves: it was unsuitable; (c), (d), (e) and (f) sisters *never* walked with each other: even the Leslie-Jones twins did not! It was unheard of . . .

However, since these prohibitions were not officially supported by the headmistress, Miss Wiltshire — known to the entire school, though not to her face (or to her staff either) as Dub-dub* — I defied public

* Shorthand for 'Jungle-drums', which were credited with informing her of everything that went on in the school.

opinion and stuck out for that one day. And since there was nothing that my schoolmates could do to prevent it, Bets and I were able to talk to each other in a limited amount of privacy. For there was a major drawback attached to our transfer from Portpool to The Lawn: a large proportion of Dub-dub's pupils were children of the Raj, so that too many of them knew enough Hindustani to understand anything we said in that language. This meant that even those who, like Bets and myself, had once been able to speak it as their mother tongue, stopped doing so and eventually forgot it — in my own case (due to having a poor ear for music) almost completely.

But although Bets and I could no longer talk to each other in a secret language, we could at least talk of India and our friends there, and we invented a long-running serial story in which we won the Calcutta Sweep and used the money to build an enormous house of glass, on the lines of a bigger and better Crystal Palace, inside which we assembled a life-sized copy of all our favourite places in India. Okhla with its weir and its sandbank and Number 3 Groin. The Kudsia Bagh. The Taj. The squirrel trees. The Purana Kila and the Pepper-pot Bridge. Parts of the Chandi Chowk and all of Curzon House. We could not include Simla or Mashobra, or any part of the hills, because that would have been ridiculous, and the game would have lost half its charm if we went beyond the bounds of the possible. We started with the building, then the heating and lighting, and bit by bit worked out how we would construct a replica of this or that; importing sand and trees, plants and animals, birds and butterflies, and finally paying vast sums to all the people we were particularly fond of to come over to England and live in it, in exact copies of their real homes. I remember that we had a lot of difficulty persuading the jolly proprietor of the Tree Shop in the Clock Tower Square of the Chandi Chowk to bring his family and come to live in our mock-up version of his shop, and that 'Vika's 'rich-as-creases' parents could not be lured into moving!

It was a deeply satisfying game and our make-believe world became so real to us that we almost felt that we really *could* retreat into it, and spend an afternoon stalking river turtles at Okhla when things went badly on the school front or we happened to be suffering from a particularly bad bout of homesickness.

I discovered poetry at The Lawn, and read it avidly because I found that so much of it put into enchanting words thoughts which had hitherto swirled untidily around in my head. There was Housman, for instance: '*That is the land of lost content, I see it shining plain, The happy highways where I went And shall not come again.*' I can remember repeating that to myself on the day that a letter came from India telling us that Tacklow would be retiring in the following year and that he and Mother would be coming back to England for good. '*And shall not come again*' ...! No, that *couldn't* be true. Somehow or other, when I was grown-up, I would manage to walk those happy highways again even if I had to crawl back on my hands and knees as certain pilgrims did to the Cave at Amanath. Or if necessary I'd swim! The prospect of never seeing India again was too bitter to be borne and did not bear thinking about. 'Someday,' said Bets and I to each other; 'one day ...'

Bargie left at the end of the next summer term. She shortened her skirts, shingled her lovely hair and went gaily off into the great world to become a Breaker of Hearts and a fully fledged grown-up. Doreen Hepper had already left; Beryl Beale went shortly afterwards, and I made a new friend: a day-girl called Helen Keelan who was another cousin of Cynthia's. Cynthia was not pleased by our friendship, but Helen turned out to be a real soul-mate. She was a giggler, and people who can giggle have always appealed to me. I don't mean the silly sort of giggling that is really sniggering, and only indulged in by empty-headed schoolgirls of the dimmest variety, but the spontaneous and semi-suppressed variety that rolls you up and makes you shed tears of mirth.

Together we wrote endless plays for our classmates to perform — the whole school, probably due to its Anglo-Indian affiliations, was nuts on amateur dramatics. Every form put on at least one play a year for the benefit and criticism of the other forms, and during my first term at The Lawn my lovely erstwhile chum of Simla days appeared as the heroine of a vaguely medieval drama with music, written and produced by the sixth form, in which the head-girl, Doreen Hepper, playing the hero, serenaded Bargie/Marjorie; the latter teetering dangerously on a step-ladder behind a flimsy canvas tower with her top half sticking out of a window cut in it. The song, a popular dance band tune of that year, was entitled 'Memories', and though I can't remember ever hearing it since, the tune and the words still stick in my mind when much else of far more importance has been forgotten.

Of two other tunes that bring back vivid memories of The Lawn, one — 'My Dear Soul' — used to be played on the seafront by the Town Band in the course of concerts that they gave for the tourists on summer evenings. It is, appropriately, a Somersetshire song, for Clevedon is in Somerset, and the words on the sheet music are written in dialect: 'Zoul' for Soul and 'Zumerzet' for Somerset. Played by a distant brass band on a warm, golden summer evening when the swallows are flying high, it is one of the most charmingly sentimental and evocative melodies one could wish to hear, and I used to hang out of my dormitory window to listen to it.

The other one is MacDowell's 'To a Wild Rose', which I had to play as a piano solo at a school concert. A grisly ordeal, since I have never been in the least good on the piano: or any musical instrument for that matter, unlike Bets, who passed all her public pianoforte exams with flying colours.

But the songs that not only remind me of The Lawn but that I still cherish most are the seventeenth- and eighteenth-century melodies that John Gay adapted for *Polly,* the sequel to his smash-hit success, *The Beggar's Opera.**

Both of these eighteenth-century operas were revived in the 1920s, and Bets and I were taken to see *Polly,* played on tour by a light opera company in the Pavilion Theatre at — I think — Rhyl, during a summer holiday spent in Wales. We had never seen or heard anything like it before and we both, having fallen instantly and madly in love with it, spent every penny of our combined pocket-money on the sheet music and the records, and on our return to The Lawn infected the entire school with our enthusiasm. We made a puppet stage out of a drawer from one of the dormitory chests of drawers, painted a whole set of scenery, drew the entire cast on cardboard (every member of it in at least a dozen different positions), coloured them and cut them out, fixed them on small blocks of wood, and with the aid of records and spoken dialogue, gave endless performances.

Because we saw *Polly* first, we always preferred it to the far more popular *Beggar's Opera.* We still do. One of the records, the best of course (it would be), got broken many years later. But the other two still survive: very scratchy but still greatly appreciated. And Bets still

* No, *not* the one featuring Mac the Knife.

has the original piano score bought with her pocket-money at a music shop in Clevedon.

The last of many songs that remind me of my schooldays is a hymn, the one that we, and probably all British schools in those days, sang at the beginning and at the end of every term: 'Lord, receive us with Thy blessing, once again assembled here' for the first day of term, and 'Lord, dismiss us with Thy blessing' for the last.

There is so much that I remember of those days, but since reminiscences of other people's schooldays come high on the list of 'things we don't in the least want to hear about' I shall pass over the fire that started in the coal-hole in the basement and that the entire school enthusiastically helped to put out; the time that I won a bet by dressing up as a boy and sneaking out of the school and down to the seafront, where I bought half-a-dozen ice cream cones and returned safely with them as proof; and the triumphant success of *The Puddleton Pantomime*, written, produced and acted in by the Misses M. Kaye and H. Keelan (both of whom thought it was *hilariously* funny and laughed a good deal more over writing it than the audience did while watching it).

There are, however, two incidents that should be mentioned; the first because it was a sight that still stands in my memory as one of the most beautiful things I have seen in this beautiful world. I shall always be grateful to Dub-dub for having the imagination to send the entire school down to the seafront, to witness 'The Cutty Sark', that most famous of all the old nineteenth-century tea clippers, moving slowly up the Bristol Channel with the tide and a light breeze. She was under full sail for the last time — or so we were told then — and it was a day of full summer. A hot, blue, almost windless afternoon without a cloud in the sky, but with a soft summer haze lying on the Channel so that one could not see the far shore. Sky and sea were as smooth and as palely coloured as a milk opal, and except for an occasional gull nothing moved; until slowly and softly that stately, white-winged wonder materialized out of the haze like some ghost from a slower and unbelievably lovely past.

The second memorable school experience is not something I saw, but an incident that deserves a mention if only because it illustrates how extraordinarily innocent we were in those far-off days.

I had achieved the dignity of a single bedroom (of which there were only two in the house apart from those occupied by the staff) and

349

Helen, who by then was no longer a day-girl but a boarder, occupied one of the five or six beds in the Explosion Room: a dormitory next door which got its name from the fact that Dub-dub had once accidentally kicked on the switch of the gas-fire one night as she left her sitting-room below, and that holy-of-holies filled with gas which blew up with a horrendous bang when a housemaid with a lighted candle entered it early next morning. The housemaid was blown back across the hall, through the big drawing-room beyond, and accompanied by a great deal of glass, catapulted through the windows and out into the garden; where she was retrieved from a rose bush, unhurt except for a few bruises and a scratch or two. She was the only casualty, apart from the damage to the house. And though the blast was reportedly heard in villages miles outside Clevedon, one member of the dormitory slept right through the whole thing, despite the fact that the blast blew a huge hole through the middle of the floor, leaving her bed poised on the edge of a yawning drop. Hence 'the Explosion Room'. It was before my time.

Helen and I became inseparable. Together we fell madly in love with Pitt Chatham, the actor who played MacHeath in *Polly* and whom Helen had never even seen. We talked a lot about love. Both of us were set on falling in love as soon as we left school, and getting married and living happily ever after: in the meantime we cut out articles about and pictures of the fascinating Mr Chatham as MacHeath, which we stuck in a jointly owned photograph-album. Together we listened, enthralled, to his voice singing those charming songs in the dusty, candle-lit darkness of our secret hideaway — a small, disused cupboard which we named 'Giggleswick', not in honour of the famous public school of that name, but because we laughed so much in it. Closeted in here we nibbled illicitly acquired pickled onions, plotted new plays and composed scurrilous limericks about the teaching staff, or read aloud to each other; a habit that eventually led to our downfall.

Helen would often sneak into my room after lights-out and squash into my single bed where we would either read with the aid of a torch or a purloined candle-end whatever book, poem or piece of homework happened to interest us at the time, or lie and discuss life in general, plot further plays or indulge in fits of giggling in the dark. Very often we would end by falling asleep, and she would whizz silently back to her bed in the Explosion Room in the small hours. Tacklow had given me the inclusive edition, 1885 to 1918, of Rudyard Kipling's verses, and browsing through it one night just on the verge of sleep, we had read 'The Explorer', which begins: *'There's no sense in going further — it's the edge of cultivation ...'.* My bed was of the usual narrow, iron, for-boarding-schools-and-institutions type, and I, as the rightful owner, had the side against the wall while Helen had the outer one. She had a habit of talking in her sleep and an hour or so later I was awakened by her muttering something. Presently she turned over, and lying poised on the extreme edge of the bed said aloud and quite clearly: 'Here's the edge of cultivation ... What's the use of going further?', and fell out onto the floor ...

I exploded into helpless giggles, and she woke in a state of high dudgeon and demanded to know what was so funny about falling out of bed and bruising yourself black and blue? It was some time before my unseemly mirth allowed me to explain, and when it did, she too went off into gales of laughter; in the middle of which the door suddenly opened and in stalked the matron.

Well, I can't say we didn't expect reprisals. Though not to that degree. We simply couldn't understand why she should be so unreasonably furious, and we put it down to the fact that we both kept exploding into giggles during the tirade that followed (we still thought it was funny). Matron didn't, and Helen was practically frog-marched back to her bed while I was locked into my room. First thing next morning, after I had washed and dressed under Matron's stony gaze, I was taken down to Miss Wiltshire's study where Dub-dub herself, every hair of her impressive moustache quivering with outrage, lit into me as though I had been a Victorian scullery-maid caught stealing the spoons.

You never heard such a hullabaloo! It ended with me being banished to Lawnside, the annexe-house next door where most of the form-mistresses and only a handful of senior pupils had rooms, and being put into a three-bed dormitory with Cynthia (who as Dub-dub knew very well had always been jealous of my friendship with her cousin Helen) and an older girl called Netta Something-or-other. Even that was not the end of it, for up to the day that I left school the teachers made every effort to keep Helen and me apart. We were not allowed to stand together, sit together, walk together in crocodile — or out of it — and an embargo was placed on Helen putting so much as a foot in Lawnside. Needless to say these tactics were unsuccessful and we derived enormous entertainment from circumventing them; greatly assisted by the fact that we could still, when pressed, retreat into Giggleswick where no one could reach us, or even think of looking for us, since it was positioned above the stairs leading down to the basement and well above eye-level.

The cupboard itself was merely the enclosed angle between the base of the upper staircase that led up from the hall to the first floor, and I have no idea why that wedge-shaped bit of space should have been closed in to make a cupboard in the first place. Nor do I know why we didn't break our necks getting in and out of it, since the feat had to be accomplished by leaning out across the well of the staircase below, supporting oneself on the far wall with the palm of one hand while walking along a narrow wooden ledge not much more than three inches wide. However, we became so adept at this that we could whip in or out in a matter of seconds, and once inside, lock ourselves in with a bolt bought during holiday-time and firmly screwed onto the inside. This hideaway gave us as much pleasure as Bets and I had got out of our secret place on the top of Begum Kudsia's ruined gateway. In it we stored all manner of possessions including torches, candle-ends and matches, and (the school food being unbelievably dreadful) cheese, jars of pickles and tins of ginger biscuits: commodities that Helen, whose parents were still living in a house in Clevedon to which she returned at weekends, found it easy enough to buy in the town. Once, for a dare, we even spent an entire night in Giggleswick just to prove that we could do it. But that of course was before I was sentenced to banishment at Lawnside ...

Looking back on that sentence in the light of a permissive age in which every child is expected to know everything there is to know about sex from the earliest possible age, I am astounded by the fact that neither Helen nor I had the *remotest* idea why such a fuss should have been made out of what was, to us, a fairly harmless escapade. We could see no reason why so much trouble was taken to keep us apart, or why Dub-dub and her minions should have blown their tops and behaved as if another world war had broken out in their midst. No sense of proportion! — that was the trouble with grown-ups.

Yes, I had heard about Sappho and her Isle of Lesbos. But the word 'lesbian' meant nothing to me beyond that, and I had not given it another thought. Not even when I later got my hands on a copy of a

352

notorious, banned novel, *The Well of Loneliness,* which, since I missed the point completely, bored me stiff. I abandoned it half-way through and was not sufficiently interested to care what all the fuss had been about or why the Lord Chamberlain, or whoever, had bothered to ban it. Why *shouldn't* a woman prefer other women to men, or have a 'pash' on a member of her own sex? All schoolgirls were apparently expected to have 'pashes' for other girls: as witness all that tedious business of Y-Aying! Why, I myself had been pressurized by public opinion into Y-Aying Beryl Beale, and I did not believe for one moment that Dub-dub's jungle-drums would have failed to inform her of the existence of that particular custom in her school. Or that she would have been incapable of putting a stop to it had she disapproved!

It was not until I was well into my twenties and staying with Helen and her parents in Kent that her mother enlightened us. We had been reminiscing about our schooldays, and having touched with some glee on the futility of old Dub-dub's efforts to keep us apart, were writing her off as a monster of injustice, when Helen's mother gave us an odd, sideways look and said: 'Do you mean to tell me that you two *really* don't know why she did her best to separate you? I should have thought you would have worked that out by now! She *had* to do it, after you were found in bed together.' When we still looked blank she explained the mystery a trifle tartly; adding that our headmistress had discussed the matter with her at the time and accepted her word for it that both of us were, in this respect, as pure as the driven snow — or, more accurately I imagine, as dumb as a couple of lead weights. Had Miss Wiltshire not been convinced of this we would both have been expelled. But having been persuaded that there was no vice in us, she agreed to let us stay on 'on probation', though continuing to keep a hawk-like eye on us. 'You see,' said Helen's mother, 'this is something that every headmistress and every headmaster has to watch out for. It is one of the known hazards of boarding-school life.'

Well, you could have knocked us down with that proverbial feather! Dear me, what half-wits we must have been. That was the first time that I realized what a lesbian was — or that they even *existed* outside ancient Greece. And what I longed to ask was: 'What do they actually *do*?' (imagination was boggling like anything). However, I didn't like to and as I have never bothered to find out, I am still in a state of ignorance. Anyway I am all for letting consenting adults get on with it. Provided, of course, that they refrain from frightening the horses.

It was fortunate for me that Helen's mother, whom I had taken to calling 'Aunt Winnie' after the custom of the time, had had the sense to realize, from conversations with her daughter, what a pair of unsophisticated clots we were when it came to sexual matters, and to take up the cudgels on my behalf with the anxious Dub-dub. Otherwise, with the shadow of expulsion hovering over me, my parents thousands of miles away, and only that martinet spinster Aunt Bee (who would have been shocked rigid and probably believed the worst) in my corner, I should have been in dire trouble. As it was, Aunt Winnie, bless her, apparently persuaded Miss Wiltshire to treat the whole affair as a juvenile prank (which in fact it was) and not to worry my parents by writing to them of her fears. So Tacklow and Mother, thank heaven, remained undisturbed.

✳ Mother was plainly having a lovely time in India. She and Tacklow had exchanged their quarters in Curzon House for a bungalow in Old Delhi's Rajpore Road, where Mother grew sweetpeas and roses and experimented with interior decoration. Snapshots of the house and garden, of Tacklow and herself and various old friends and acquaintances, arrived in every letter, filling us with envy and nostalgia. In Simla the new Viceroy and Vicereine, Lord and Lady Reading, gave a Chinese Ball — the 'Feast of Lanterns' — at Viceregal Lodge, for which Mother designed and painted a number of decorations. She sent us sketches and snapshots of painted lanterns, a vast panel on which a dragon sprawled, and others that bore the Chinese characters for good fortune, success and happiness; and later, snapshots of herself and Tacklow in the Chinese costumes they had worn at the ball.

Other letters told us about various festivities laid on for the Prince of Wales, and there was a fascinating account by Tacklow of a Viceregal dinner in honour of King Carol of Romania (or would he have been only Crown Prince Carol then?) in the course of which Mother, on being told the name of the guest of honour, leaned out, laughing, to get a look at him at the precise moment that Carol — bored by the two stout and elderly Very-Important-Ladies sitting on either side of him — glanced down the line of guests and caught her eye. When dinner was over and Lady Reading asked him if there was anyone in particular whom he wished to be introduced to, he replied promptly that yes, there was: the pretty laughing one in the pink-and-gold dress over there. He pointed her out, and an ADC was sent to summon Mother to the dais at one end of the ballroom, where a regal-looking sofa and a number of chairs had been placed for the mighty . . .

Unfortunately one of her shoes had been pinching her and she had eased it off, and had been unable to locate it when the Vicereine gave the signal for the ladies to rise and leave the dining-room. There had been nothing for it but to thank her lucky stars that evening-dresses were still long and that hers included a small train, and to limp out of the room wearing only one shoe. Taken up to meet Carol and seated primly beside him on the sofa, she kept the unshod foot tucked out of sight under her train, and it was only when the band struck up and he asked her to dance that she explained in a whisper why she could not accept. Whereupon Carol went off into shrieks of laughter and said that in that case, would she sit it out with him? They sat together, giggling helplessly, while the rest of the guests waltzed and two-stepped and kept on staring at them, wondering what on earth Daisy Kaye was saying to keep the monarch rolling about with laughter. But Nemesis was about to overtake her, for when the band stopped and the dancers left the floor, the doors at the far end of the room were thrown open and there entered, with as much pomp as the bearer of a boar's head at some medieval banquet, a magnificently uniformed and turbaned Viceregal servant carrying a large silver salver on which reposed a single pink shoe.

Advancing at a slow and stately walk up the length of the ballroom he mounted the dais, bowed and offered it to my flustered and scarlet-cheeked parent, who had no alternative but to accept it. She was forced to withdraw her stockinged foot out of hiding and don the shoe under the pop-eyed gaze of half Simla, and to the accompaniment of uninhibited mirth from the visiting VIP who was later reported to have told the ADCs that he hadn't enjoyed himself so much for years, a sentiment that Tacklow obviously endorsed.

Meanwhile I myself was enjoying a lovely idle time at The Lawn. This was because I could draw, and in those days all but the hopelessly inept members of the art class were expected to take the Royal Drawing Society examinations for which (if you managed to wriggle through) you were awarded either a pass, or a 'highly commended' certificate printed on a piece of flossily decorated card and signed by someone in authority. All school art classes pushed their young hopefuls through these exams, and in our part of the country the school that did best on average was awarded something called the Cuthbert Grundy Shield for Art: a large, ornate and outstandingly hideous silver monstrosity, mounted on a huge wooden shield and surrounded by miniature silver shields engraved with the names of the various schools that had won it. The winning school could only keep this object for a year, after which (with their name now engraved on one of the attendant shields) it was returned to base to be competed for again.

During my last year at The Lawn the art class was fortunate enough to acquire a new instructress; a Miss Hoskins who — though no great shakes as an artist — was that rare thing, an inspired teacher. Under her stimulating influence anyone who could draw or paint at all suddenly began to draw and/or paint better. The art class woke up from its former lethargy and began to enjoy itself and produce good work, and since I was regarded as one of its leading lights, Miss Hoskins decided to enter me for all the RDS exams that I had not already passed. She managed to persuade Miss Wiltshire to let me off a number of classes in other subjects in order to give me time for extra tuition in art, on the grounds that although our school was a small one, if we did well in examination we might, strictly 'on average', bring home the bacon in the form of the Cuthbert Grundy Shield.

Little did the well-meaning Miss Hoskins (or for that matter Dub-dub either) realize that they were letting me out of doing any work at all for the rest of the term. Taking shameless advantage of the situation I absented myself from any lessons that bored me or that I did not like, on the excuse that I had to do 'extra drawing'. I didn't count drawing as work, and Dub-dub's staff must have been a slack lot because no one ever bothered to check up, even when I hadn't understood a problem because of missing a class. Not surprisingly I did terribly badly in the normal end-of-term exams. But I passed all the art ones with honours, and this impressive total, bolstered by sterling work by Bets and Helen and one or two others who also did well in that line, duly won us the Cuthbert Grundy Shield and the privilege of hanging it over the fireplace in the Big Schoolroom for the next year. After which there was no more extra drawing and I had to get back reluctantly to doing some work.

Chapter 23

~%ÐⓋᛞℜ~

For now I am in a holiday humour.

Shakespeare, *As You Like It*

The last chapter was mostly concerned with term-times at school, with only one mention of a holiday. But there were, of course, a good many holidays. Several of these were spent in Bedford in the care of that ancient pair of honorary aunts, Lizzie and Emily, and one in particular, an Easter holiday, was enlivened by the children of a Mrs Richardson, a school-friend of Mother's who had married an Englishman in the service of the Chinese Customs Department. Jessie Richardson, *en route* to Shanghai to join her husband, had parked her three children on the Ransomes, who lived next door to Aunt Lizzie and also had Far East connections — their daughter Nona, another school-friend of Mother's, was at the time acting as tutor-companion to the deliciously pretty little Manchu wife of Pu-yi, the last Emperor of China.

Jessie's son Tommy was about the same age as my brother Bill, and he and his two kid sisters, Beena and Joan, fraternized happily with Bill, Bets and me. The six of us enjoyed a wildly exhilarating holiday that must have put years on poor Lizzie and Emily, not to mention the Ransomes, for Tommy, a born 'boffin', put his fertile brain to work on a variety of schemes calculated to keep the young interested and entertained and to drive their elders into nervous breakdowns.

He began harmlessly enough by constructing an overhead postal-line by which messages could be dispatched from his room in the Ransomes' house to Bill's in Aunt Lizzie's. But on finding that it worked a treat, he advanced to a bigger and better version; one that we could slide down ourselves. I can't think why one of us wasn't killed, but the young are tough, and we survived. His next ploy was a series of tree-houses that we built high up in the soot-caked horse

357

chestnut trees in Aunt Lizzie's narrow, walled-in strip of garden, the far door of which led directly into the shunting yards of Bedford railway station. The tree-houses were brilliantly constructed and very hard to spot from below, and we learned to climb up to them with a swiftness that would have done credit to Tarzan, and to lie low there when we wished to avoid an aunt or a Ransome bent on making us do something we didn't want to.

I still cherish a vivid recollection of Aunt Lizzie's consternation when, following Bets up the steep front-hall staircase, she noticed that the youngest Kaye's knickers were not only black with soot but torn to shreds. She embarked on a horrified tirade, and Tommy, bringing up the rear, remarked nonchalantly: 'Oh, they're *always* like that!'

It was Tommy who scrambled over the wall on the left-hand side of the garden, to explore an empty and dilapidated house that stood there, and who, charmed by the discovery that it had no lock on the back door and was in a shocking state of disrepair inside, immediately decided to take possession of it on the grounds that finders were keepers and that we needed a Clubhouse in which we could play on wet days. The rest of us agreed enthusiastically, and it became a marvellous playground-cum-bolt-hole, far larger than the tree-houses and a whole lot dryer.

Surprisingly, our elders (from whom it had proved impossible to conceal this latest bit of territorial annexation) did not declare the derelict property Out of Bounds, but rather unfairly put us on our honour not to go upstairs to the bedrooms or the attics or down to the basement, for fear that the fabric of the ruined house might collapse on or under us. But as this still left us the main living-rooms, we gave them our word and annexed for our Clubroom what had once been a large Victorian drawing-room whose windows overlooked a weed-grown and rubbish-strewn garden. Here, on wet days, we played badminton, rounders or charades, read and painted, discussed Life and our elders, or just picnicked.

The house had been one of many commandeered by the Army during the years of the 1914–1918 war for the use of troops, either as a hostelry or possibly only as a temporary staging-post for reinforcements bound for the southern ports and those terrible trenches in Flanders. But when the war ended and the last of them marched out, the house was abandoned; together with the furniture, which judging from the state of the garden had obviously been heaved out of the windows or lugged into the open to make a bonfire. Not everything had burned, for the ground was littered with the remains of rusty, fire-scorched bedsteads and bits of chairs and tables, in addition to piles of empty tins and broken bottles, and a few pieces of iron piping, one of which Tommy annexed for future use.

The whole place had been systematically vandalized and we learned a good many new words (ones that even Bill and Tommy had not yet come across) from the graffiti that defaced the flaking plaster walls of that once-elegant Victorian drawing-room. There had also been a great many crude drawings, in both senses of the word. But these Bill and Tommy, who were not unmindful of their responsibilities as elder brothers, had hastily camouflaged with the aid of a box of coloured chalks before their respective sisters were allowed on the premises. When, towards the end of that particular holiday we decided to give a party in the Clubroom, and invite the aunts and the Ransomes to feast on home-made lemonade and a variety of biscuits that we bought with our combined pocket-money (then averaging sixpence a week — the girls got threepence each and the boys a shilling — riches in those days!), we took the precaution of buying a packet of whitewash, and with a bucket and a brush borrowed from Aunt Lizzie, covering up as many of the graffiti as we could reach, before assisting our apprehensive guests over the wall. I hasten to add that they were not required to climb it because we had managed to borrow a couple of step-ladders for the afternoon. But it was a pleasant sight to see those prim, law-abiding relics of the nineteenth century, in their long skirts, befrilled petticoats and buttoned boots, resignedly negotiating the wall to trespass in a derelict house that still, presumably, had a legal owner.

It was, of course, Tommy who thought up a way of using the pieces of iron piping that had been found among the nettles and fireweed growing on the remains of that bonfire. A day or two later he sent me to a chemist's shop to buy two penny-worth of powdered charcoal. I have forgotten what he told me to say if I was asked what I wanted it for, but I feel sure that I was provided with some watertight reason; Tommy never left anything to chance. He and Bill separately, and from two other chemists' shops in Bedford, bought sulphur and saltpetre, and with these three ingredients in our hands, he unveiled his latest invention.

He had heated a short piece of scrap iron, part of a rusty bed-leg, until it was white-hot (little did poor Aunt Lizzie know what went on in her kitchen during the hours devoted to her afternoon nap!) and having hammered it into one end of that length of iron pipe, heated them both and treated them to a bit more hammering to ensure that the metal plug would stay put. After which, to make doubly sure, he did a bit of soldering. A touch-hole was then drilled, and ammunition provided in the form of a long, stout piece of wood, carefully cut and carved so that it would fit snugly into the pipe. Finally a wooden cradle was designed to hold this home-made cannon, with chocks that could lift or lower the angle of the barrel according to the height and distance of the target. When all was ready, Bill and the inventor of this peculiar weapon rode out into the countryside on their bicycles to put it through its field trials in a wood; accompanied by a *vivandière* in the person of myself riding pillion on the carrier of Tommy's bike.

Fixing the gun into its cradle with the muzzle pointing at the trunk of a beech tree some twenty yards away, we mixed together, presumably in the correct proportions, the contents of the three paper packets acquired from different and unsuspecting chemists, and having made the mixture up into small sausage-shaped packets with the aid of Bromo, at that time the world's best-known lavatory paper, dropped one into the mouth of our cannon, rammed it down with the head of a long knitting-needle purloined from Aunt Lizzie, followed it with the 'ammunition' (that length of wood), put a wax vesta into the touch-hole, lit it and stood well back. I have to admit that at this point I put my fingers in my ears because I hate bangs and loud noises. The thing worked splendidly, and though on that first occasion our heavy wooden bullet fell short of the mark, we soon learned by trial and error how much gunpowder to use and how high or low to aim; by the time the holidays drew to a close we could hit almost anything we aimed at, using the same 'bullet' again and again.

That gun brought us endless amusement. But the fact of its existence was kept to the three of us and I wasn't even allowed to tell Bets about it until we were safely back at school; because Tommy wouldn't trust 'the kids' — Beena, Bets and Joan — not to give it away by mistake. He was quite certain (rightly so) that although the grown-ups might stand for aerial railways, tree-houses and a playground in disused premises, if they should hear about this they would put their collective feet down hard. So we kept quiet about it and let them and 'the kids' imagine that our frequent bicycle rides into the country were just that and no more. It was only on the last day of the holidays that things went wrong.

Tommy had decided to use up all the remaining gunpowder in order to see just how far we could fire that home-made wooden bullet. So we took it out through the back door of the garden into ground that belonged to the railway, and having set it up facing acres of empty shunting yards, rain-soaked piles of coke and coal and derelict sheds full of rusty machinery and broken signal-lamps, we packed it with the last of our Bromo-encased gunpowder, jammed in that heavy wooden projectile and touched it off . . .

I can only thank heaven that in anticipation of an even louder bang than usual I had taken the precaution of standing really far back, and that Bill and Tommy had had the sense to move well away on one side as soon as the wax vesta was lit. For this time the T. Richardson Patent Gun literally blew up. There was one blast of flame and a bang that almost split my eardrums despite the fact that my fingers were firmly plugged into my ears, and Tommy and Bill were knocked flat. The back of Bill's suit got smeared with mud, soot and coal-dust, but otherwise he was unharmed. But Tommy, who had been nearer, had his hair, eyebrows and lashes well singed, and suffered a number of superficial cuts from flying chips of stone. Railway officials came running and so did the aunts and the Ransomes, and my recollections of the next half-hour or so are a bit confused. The only thing I can remember clearly is that we all put in a bit of spirited lying. And I mean lying; not 'prevaricating' — though by now I haven't the least idea what our story was. Bill and I merely supported our leader and stuck firmly to whatever he said.

Fortunately there was no proof, the T. Richardson Patent Gun having exploded backwards and buried itself in the process. There wasn't a sign or a sniff of it. Or any trace of that wooden bullet either, though we searched everywhere. For all I know it may have disintegrated. Or even landed up in the next county, chalking up an unofficial amateur record? In any case the holiday that had ended with such a spectacular bang was one of the best and most interesting of my childhood. Never a dull moment, and Tommy temporarily attached to my chariot wheels. We exchanged a chaste goodbye kiss in a dank passageway between the Ransomes' house and Aunt Lizzie's; careful not to be seen doing so for fear of being hooted at by our contemporaries for being 'soppy'.

There were many other holidays. But Mother was only home again for three of them; two summer holidays, one spent in Devon and one in Wales, and a winter one in Oxford. The one in Wales was another Hunstanton fiasco which turned into an unexpected success. Once again Mother had rented lodgings at the seaside, only this time it was a house and not just rooms. The advertisement had described the place in glowing terms: 'Situated in rural surroundings near small, quiet village; garden running down to the seashore, private diving pier' . . . It sounded wonderful! Mother took it, and we arrived to find that the front door opened directly onto the pavement of the main coast road along which buses, cars and lorries thundered at the rate of at least one a minute. (Today it would be six per second, but these were early days.) Also, barely five hundred yards away, there was a quarry where blasting took place once every hour, filling the air with din, dust and flying chips of stone, and causing all traffic to stop — a lot of it just the other side of our front windows — until the quarry's hooter blew the 'All Clear'.

Worst of all was the discovery that although the garden did indeed run down to the sea, a railway line, bristling with notices that forbade us to cross it, ran between us and the high-tide mark, so that in order to reach the shore we had to walk for nearly a mile along the main road to a tunnel that ran under the line. And that private diving pier? Well, *that* turned out to be a huge, disused pier, at least thirty feet high, on which, once upon a time, trolleys containing crushed stone for road-works used to run out on rails to be loaded onto ships that tied up at the pier. Since the quarry had stopped using it long ago, no ships called any more; and anyone mad enough to try diving off it would have had to have been in the Olympic class. (Anyway, there was no way of getting up to it except off the deck of a ship!) However, Mother was back for the holidays; and so, from North China, was Grandfather Bryson, the Grand-Dadski. And that was when we went to see *Polly* at the theatre near Rhyl — or was it Llandudno? — and fell madly in love with the music and MacHeath. So what more could one want?

The holiday in Devon, for which Mother again made the long trip from India, was a roaring success from start to finish, even though she had, as usual, booked our holiday accommodation 'sight unseen'. This time it was a house called Lanka; which is the old name of Ceylon. It had a large garden, and an orchard from where one could either walk down a long, steep path, little more than a goat-track, to reach the seafront, or alternatively, climb up the hillside behind to reach the heavenly heather-clad moors above. It was during this summer that the Dadski, once again with us, told me how he had 'received the call' and become a China missionary. And it must have been towards the end of this year that Tacklow returned to England for the first time since 1913 ...

Tacklow's job had come to an end with the signing of the Peace Treaty, and since none of the promises made to him when he had been refused permission to rejoin his regiment had been kept, he decided on early retirement. Moreover, besides being tired of separation from his family, he disliked and mistrusted the shape of things to come. Now that the war, in which India had supported and fought for the Allies with great gallantry, was over, he and many others like him had confidently believed that plans would immediately be set in train for the Indianization of the Civil Service, the Army, Navy and Police, in preparation for Dominion status, which carried with it the right to secede. A small move in this direction had actually been made. But only a very small one; snail-slow, niggling and guaranteed to exasperate every thinking Indian and turn too many of the unthinking into anti-British revolutionaries and rioters.

To Tacklow, who throughout the war years had been keeping an eye out for talent among the Indian members of his staff, encouraging, training and promoting it in order that there should be men standing ready to step in and take over authority — thereby ensuring that there would be no hitch in the smooth running of his department — the nit-picking and prevarication that was bogging down all progress towards self-government seemed a betrayal of trust. Like his friend Claude Auchinleck, he felt that it could only lead to distrust and the souring of relations between those Indians and British who had hitherto been friends; and since this was something he did not wish to see, he decided to accept retirement. But only a few days before he was due to leave Simla for Bombay and home, he was sent for by the head of the Viceroy's Council, Sir William Vincent, who greeted him by saying: 'If you think I've asked you here to say goodbye and good luck, or anything like that, you're wrong! I've asked you here because I hope to be able to persuade you to change your mind and stay on.'

Tacklow laughed and said 'Not on your life!', or its 1920s equivalent; adding that he was sorry, but he was getting out while the going was good and he still had Indian friends, and that nothing would persuade him to stay on. 'Not even the offer of a totally different kind of job?' asked Sir William.

'Not for anything,' returned my parent. 'I'm going to retire to somewhere quiet like Cornwall where I can grow cabbages and watch my children grow up, and catalogue the Ferrari Collection* in my spare time.'

'Well, at least let me tell you what I have to offer before you turn it down,' urged Sir William. 'There are three jobs for you to choose from.' He listed them in turn, but though the first two were plums, Tacklow rejected both out of hand. The third, however, turned out to be the one appointment in all India that he would have liked to hold but could never aspire to. Because it was strictly reserved for members of the ICS, and so was just another of the many things that he had forfeited so long ago in London when he failed the examination that would have taken him into the ranks of the Heaven-Born. Yet now, unbelievably, Sir William Vincent was inviting him to become Director of Central Intelligence in succession to Sir Charles Cleveland, who after a long and brilliant spell in that post was at last about to retire. Tacklow told me later that he couldn't believe his luck! It sounded too good to be true, for he had always considered Sir Charles's post the most interesting in India: 'I used to envy him so,' confessed Tacklow. He accepted, of course.

We heard the news with mixed feelings. Delight for his sake and pleasure that it would be he and not some stranger who would be stepping into dear Sir Charles's shoes. And also hoping against hope that he would stay in them long enough to allow us to go out to India again once the school years were over (we did not realize that the post was a three-year one, and that Sir Charles had only held it for longer because of the war), but sad because we had been so looking forward

* A famous collection of stamps which had recently been broken up and sold in separate lots at auction.

to having him with us again for good. It was a bitter blow to learn that because of this new appointment our chances of seeing either of our parents, particularly Tacklow, during the next few years were slim. In the event he promised to take short leave in England before starting work as DCI, India.

Mother came back ahead of him towards the end of the winter term at The Lawn, and we were taken down to the Clevedon railway station to meet her. I remember that Bets and I felt curiously shy and embarrassed because we had not seen her for two years and she seemed different from what we remembered; but that wore off very quickly. She stayed for the weekend at a small private hotel at the end of Albert Road, kept by a formidable spinster who ran our school troop of Girl Guides, and next day, a Sunday, took us to morning service in the Anglican church that Dub-dub's pupils always attended. Here she was horrified by the processions, banners and incense — St John's, Clevedon, was very 'High Church' and it happened to be some Saint's Day. To a member of the Kirk of Scotland it smacked of Rome, and Mother complained to Dub-dub, who said coldly that if she preferred a 'Low Church' service for her children it could be arranged for us to attend the small, old and charming church that stood on the slope of a little hill at the far side of a wide shallow bay to the south of the town. Mother marched us off there that same day to attend Evensong. But though service, church and vicar met with her approval, the walk from The Lawn and back again was a long one, and when on the return journey it began to rain and we all got soaked and half frozen, and Bets complained tearfully of a blister on her heel, she abandoned the idea of having us sent there every Sunday. But the incense, and all that genuflecting and banner-toting, continued to rankle.

That year we spent our Christmas holidays in a hideous semi-detached house on the Woodstock Road at Oxford, which Mother had rented so that Tacklow would be able to see something of his parents and his sister Molly as well as his own family. Of all the many rented houses we lived in, this was by far the worst: an ugly little villa with no redeeming features. A foot or two of gravel and a laurel hedge lay between the front windows and the road, and there was a dreary little strip of garden at the back. Inside, the house was furnished with spiky and dangerously unstable chairs, sofas, occasional-tables and a vast hat-stand, all manufactured from the antlers of innumerable stags.

Scores of the creatures must have perished to make that appalling furniture, which was quite the most uncomfortable to sit on, or even to walk past, that anyone could imagine. No wonder the Victorians wore endless petticoats and a crinoline if this was the sort of thing they imagined their Queen went in for at Balmoral! The upholstery throughout was bobble-trimmed plush, and every inch of wall-space was crammed with highly coloured oleographs of religious pictures; bleeding 'Sacred Hearts', 'Our Lady of Sorrows' or saints being martyred wherever one looked. To make matters worse the house was lit and heated entirely by gas (of which, in conjunction with boiled cabbage, it smelt strongly) and the weather was so vile that even beautiful Oxford and its 'dreaming spires' managed to look cold, cross and thoroughly bloody-minded. The only good thing about that nasty little villa were the books ...

There were literally *hundreds* of them of every kind and description. Crammed higgledy-piggledy into varnished pitch-pine bookshelves that lined the landings; stacked up in dusty piles on the floor of the attic, or standing in tidy rows in glass-fronted cupboards and revolving bookcases in almost every room in the house ... I can't think who acquired them; *surely* not the same person who had made or bought that awful antlered furniture. Or the devout and presumably colour-blind one who plastered the walls with holy pictures. The only solution that occurs to me is that whoever owned the house also owned a second-hand bookshop in Oxford, and this was where they kept the spare stock. But whatever their reasons, I fell on those books with the rapture of a treasure-hunter stumbling across a chest full of doubloons, and spent most of my time reading; lying flat on my stomach in front of a wheezing gas-fire in my back bedroom while the rain lashed at the windows and the gas sucked all the oxygen out of the room and gave me a permanent headache.

Since Tacklow had only been able to fit in a very short leave before taking up his new appointment, the best he could manage was to join us here for ten days that included Christmas; after which he and Mother would return to India together early in the New Year. He had particularly asked that we would not meet him at the station; he would prefer to take a cab (he still thought of taxis as cabs) and drive straight to the house. I think he was afraid that he might cry in public when he saw Willie again; the little son whom he could only remember as a six-year-old in a sailor suit, so very long ago.

When the day and the hour of his arrival finally came, all four of us were lined up waiting with our noses pressed to the window-panes of Mother's bedroom upstairs; a vantage-point from which we could see both the road and the gate without being stymied by that laurel hedge. And when at last the taxi stopped in front of the gate and Tacklow got out, Bill, who had not seen his father for the best part of a decade and thought this must be a stranger, said: 'Who's that funny little man?' . . .

Now that is real tragedy. I think both Mother and I, and perhaps, young as she was, even Bets, recognized it as such and were conscious of an appalling sense of shock; because none of us answered. We looked at each other, and then, with guilt and dismay, at the unconscious Bill. It had never occurred to anyone to tell him that his father was a little man; a short, tubby one who in many of the snapshots I have of him could, except for his height, easily have doubled for Winston Churchill (particularly when the latter was photographed in the Middle East wearing a topi). A man who although he was the same height as Mother always looked shorter because of her hair and her high heels. Nor had we realized that the father Bill would remember would be a tall man who towered over him as they walked hand-in-hand along the winding Simla roads. ('What's that house doing, Daddy?' 'Standing up.' '*No,* Daddy! What's it *doing*?' . . .)

Those five short words that were Bill's instant reaction on seeing again the loved and admired parent to whom, as a bewildered and tearful little boy, he had waved goodbye so many long years ago perfectly illustrate something that Rudyard Kipling put into verse in a poem about the P. & O. liners that brought the children of Anglo-Indians home and took their parents back again alone to India:

> *The Tragedy of all our East is laid*
> *On those white decks beneath the awning shade —*
> *Birth, absence, longing, laughter, love and tears,*
> *And death unmaking ere the land is made.*

We never told Tacklow what Bill had said. Their situation was difficult enough without that. And they had so little time in which to resolve it and get to know each other. That they never did succeed in closing the gap left by those lost years is not surprising: it yawned too wide and they had barely ten days in which to build a bridge that would span it. In any case the distance that separates six from fourteen is the widest in one's life, because to the latter a six-year-old is still no more than a little boy who has yet to lose his baby teeth, while the fourteen-year-old has already begun to think of himself as an adult in the making.

Perhaps if they had had a peaceful ten days in which to get to know each other things might have been different. But Tacklow's parents insisted on their full share of his attention and expected him to dance attendance on them; while as for me, I was so delighted to see him again that I could hardly bear to let him out of my sight. So I don't think Bill had much chance. Besides, he was now at public school, which is a giant step up from being a preparatory school boy. And he had gone to Repton and not, as Tacklow had hoped, to Winchester, a disappointment for which the war was responsible. Tacklow had put his name down for Winchester at the correct time and date laid down by the College rules, but a long time later, when it would soon be Bill's turn to clock in as a 'Commoner of this College', he received a telegram to say that by the luck of the draw his son's name had been the last for that particular term, and since owing to some trifling error there was one pupil too many, there would be no vacancy for him after all.

It later transpired that some *nouveau riche* had offered the headmaster a new cricket pavilion if he would wangle a place for his son at the College. So Bill, as the last entry for that year and term, was dropped and as the only public school which could come up with a vacancy at such short notice was Repton, Bill went there. Shortly afterwards the bribe-taking headmaster was quietly moved out and replaced (one hopes) by a more worthy holder of that high office.

It might have helped the bridge-building if Bill had been a Wyke-hamist and he and Tacklow could have discussed the various aspects of life and customs at a school they both knew. But what they needed most was time, and that was something they were never to get. At least we all celebrated Christmas together; though the Christmas dinner, with its traditional and indigestible turkey, plum-pudding, mince-pies, brandy-butter and all the seasonal trimmings that the British owe to a German Prince Consort and an English novelist, Charles Dickens, was eaten at our grandparents' house in company with that ancient and ossified pair and an assortment of their children and grandchildren. We all went to see a pantomime at one of Oxford's theatres, and Mother took us to see a famous Pre-Raphaelite painting that hangs in the chapel of one of the colleges — Holman Hunt's 'The Light of the World'. I admired the intricate detail, because that sort of thing was right up my street; but otherwise I was unimpressed. Then Aunt Bee arrived. And gloom and doom moved in with her.

I never could understand why Mother and Aunt Bee had become friends. Perhaps there had been very few *Angrezi* women in Jhelum when Mother arrived there as a bride? Or perhaps Bee Lewis was one of the few young ones and it was their youth, and possibly loneliness, that drew them together. I imagine boredom played as large a part in it as anything; but the friendship had thrived, and here was Bee Lewis again, preparing to take charge of her friend's children. Well, all one could say was that she was preferable to Aunt Molly!

Poor Bee, having failed to find a husband in India, had returned to England to settle down to the life of an English spinster living on a minute annuity left her by parents, long dead, whose lives had been lived in a time when a yearly income of a hundred pounds had been considered more than adequate for a single woman's needs. No one who lived in those days ever seems to have given a passing thought to the possibility of inflation in the future, and poor Bee eked out her small income by looking after the left-behind children of friends and relatives whose work tied them to India. The trouble was that she didn't know the first thing about children. And did not want to! However, that was something Mother never realized; she merely knew that Bee could be trusted to look after us — which she did with something of the manner of a head-warder at Borstal — and that she needed the money. It was difficult to be fond of Aunt Bee, and we weren't. And now she was about to take charge of us for the last week of that Christmas holiday in Oxford, and see that we got safely back to our respective schools when it was over, because early in January Tacklow and Mother would have to leave for London and Tilbury Docks to board a P. & O. liner bound for Bombay.

They would not let us go to the station to see them off, because there is nothing worse than parting from someone you love very much, and do not know when you will see again, on a crowded platform of a railway station. So we said our goodbyes instead in that dark, ugly little villa among the Balmoral furniture — all those rickety, spiky stags' horns (Mother had taken down the Sacred Hearts and hidden them in a cupboard). Outside it was raining again. And there was a fog too, which made the day even darker, and which was so thick that we could barely see the laurel hedge. We were given our parting presents with instructions not to open them until the taxi had gone, and I remember Mother cried and cried and that Tacklow suddenly looked old: so old that all at once I felt frightened.

How old would I be before I saw him again? And when I did, would I find that I had grown away from him as Bill had done? Would I ever be able to talk to him as freely as I used to? I was already within sight of my teens and had begun to think of myself as almost a grown-up; for had not girls in the days of the Tudors married even earlier than that? Time had begun to move faster. Only a little faster, it is true, but enough to scare me. It was easier to part with Mother. Somehow or other she would go on managing to get back to England every two years, even if it meant giving up all the little luxuries that her friends enjoyed. Tacklow had already given up everything he could possibly give up, and sold everything that could be sold, to pay for her passages: but he would still need every penny he earned to pay for school bills and holidays for us, so I knew he would not come back again for a long time. Perhaps not until I had grown up . . . I remember that day as one of the bleakest in my life; a rehearsal for another and far worse one that still lay far ahead in the future. Because I knew now that my childhood was over for good.

Our parents tore themselves away at last and we rushed to the window and saw them run down the tiny drive and jump into the waiting taxi; heard it start up and watched it vanish into the rain and fog. They were gone —

Chapter 24

~~~❦~~~

Bound to the wheel of Empire, one by one,
The chain-gangs of the East from sire to son,
The Exiles' Line takes out the exiles' line,
And ships them homeward when their work is done.

Kipling, 'The Exiles' Line'

Aunt Bee, with all the tact of a charging rhinoceros, marched briskly into the room and inquired in stentorian tones what we thought we were doing, sitting around moping and snivelling instead of opening our parcels and enjoying ourselves! She then read us a stern lecture to the effect that we were all old enough to know better and to realize that our parents felt just as badly about this parting as we did and were only leaving us for our own good, and that anyway two years, or even three or four, would pass very quickly. And after a rousing exhortation, calculated to drive even the mildest of worms into turning and trying to bite her on the ankle, she wound up by saying that she had a lovely surprise for us. Our dear parents, anticipating a certain degree of gloom following their departure, had bought tickets to a matinée of a musical comedy, *The Dollar Princess*, that very afternoon. There now! Wasn't that exciting?

We agreed wanly: anything to get this brisk Patrol Leader out of the room. And when at last she removed herself we discussed the future with something approaching despair. Were we *really* going to be given into the charge of this bossy, sharp-tongued and acidulated shrew for the next few years? And if so, how were we going to bear it? The answer to the first was yes: we were indeed. To the second, well — we'd have to manage.

I still find it difficult to be just to Aunt Bee. She was the sort of person who is rude to shop assistants, waiters and taxi-drivers, and in the years ahead there were to be endless occasions on which we would try to disown her by edging away and pretending we were attached to somebody else, usually the nearest stranger, while she berated some hapless shop assistant who had had the temerity to tell her either that the store did not stock whatever it was she had asked for, or that its price had gone up a ha'penny since the last Budget. Or when she accused a waiter or a taxi-driver of trying to overcharge her. We never succeeded; for having given someone what she called 'a piece of her mind', she would invariably turn to look for us and cry: 'Bill! Moll! Bets! — come here, children. We'll have to try somewhere else; there must be *some* decent shops in this place!' And having collected us by name (oh, the shame of it!) she would sweep out, herding us ahead of her: to repeat the whole embarrassing process somewhere further along the street. She did not seem able to help it, and we couldn't believe that she had always been like that, for if she had, how could Mother ...? But in those Jhelum days she would have been fifteen years younger. She may even have been pretty and dreaming of romance. And one had to remember that she had been very kind to Mother ...

Poor Aunt Bee! How can one tell what had happened to her to make her so cross and belligerent? There must have been some reason for it; some unspoken tragedy. A love-affair, perhaps, that went wrong? Or one that had gone wrong for her in England before she set foot in India, and led to her being sent out to Jhelum to help her get over it and in the hope that she might meet and marry some Indian-service officer or a rich 'box-wallah' — or even a poor one? (For she was, after all, in her mid-twenties when Mother first knew her, and any unmarried woman of that age was regarded in those days as being at her last prayers.) It was, too, a time when few jobs were open to women of her type except teaching or caring for other people's children. And life had not fitted her for either. She may not have had the qualifications that would have enabled her to teach; and she certainly lacked both the temperament and the patience! So, *faut de mieux*, she settled for the second option; which was bad luck on the children involved and possibly even worse for herself. How she must have hated it!

Years later, when she was old and crippled with arthritis and had been reluctantly re-admitted to a nursing home that she had been thrown out of once (they had only agreed to take her back because none of the long list of nursing homes that she had subsequently tried and ended up being expelled from would have her back, even though by then she was dying), she said bitterly to Mother: 'They say I'm rude to the nurses. *Really* Daisy! How *can* they say such a thing? I've never been rude to anyone in all my *life*!' And this, mark you, reported Mother despairingly, on the heels of being outrageously rude to the unfortunate nurse who had just brought in her tea-tray. What does one do with someone like that who really *believes* that she has never been rude to anyone, ever? 'Oh dear,' sighed Mother, 'poor Bee — poor, dear Bee!'

Poor Bee indeed. But poor us, too. It is not easy to like anyone whose tongue is permanently dipped in acid. Yet she took on all the drudgery of finding and hiring suitable lodgings for our holidays, of fetching us from and taking us to London to catch the trains that would bring us from school or return us there, and of seeing that we went back each term with our school trunks full of the clothes we would need, all carefully listed and marked with name-tapes sewn into every garment. With her we spent three holidays on the Isle of Wight — a winter and a spring one in a house called 'Nesscliff' in Shanklin, and one on the outskirts of that town in a house on the cliffs surrounded by open country, where in the company of several other children whom she was looking after we spent a long summer holiday.

Two of these other children were her nephew and niece, both much younger than we were: Maxine and 'Sprag' Mitchell, whose parents, like ours, were in India. Sprag, nicknamed 'Spraggen' after a character in *Pickwick Papers*, was only a baby and we all spoiled and adored him. But Maxine developed a tiresome passion for us and insisted on following us around like an adoring puppy, carrying a bucket and spade from which she refused to be parted. The handle of the bucket was rusty and it squeaked mercilessly as she panted along the seashore in our wake, driving us to distraction. Aunt Bee was annoyed by our efforts to lose this maddeningly persistent shadow, and on the only occasion that we succeeded in doing so she gave us the mother and father of a dressing-down and sent us to bed without supper. We had told the trusting Maxine that if she lay on a certain patch of lawn under a rug with her eyes shut, and then counted to five hundred, slowly, she would find herself on the other side of the world in Australia. The credulous innocent did so; believing that we, the big children, *must* be right. And as soon as she was safely hidden under the rug we tip-toed away and fled to the beach and our own ploys; free at last. Poor Maxine lay where we left her for what must have seemed like hours, dutifully counting, until at last she ran out of fingers or lost count, removed the rug and found herself alone and not, as promised, among the kangaroos. Whereupon her disappointed howls brought Aunt Bee at the double, breathing fire and slaughter.

Another two Aunt Bee summer holidays were spent on the South Coast. One in the top storey of a tall house on the pebble beach near the top of the steep road that leads up to the seaside town of Folkestone: the same steep road that Mother had walked up when she and Alice went up to Folkestone's Leas to meet the Kentish boys when she was barely fifteen. The other summer was spent in 'rooms with board', in a cottage on the outskirts of the little village of Shaldon on the west bank of the River Dart where it runs into the sea. The owner of Myrtle Cottage was a dear old thing who was very proud of the fact that she had won some local award for 'the prettiest cottage garden' three years running. And she deserved it. The garden was exactly like the English cottage gardens that one sees, or used to see, on the covers of chocolate boxes and birthday cards; tiny and packed with flowers, and smelling of lost Eden.

Two successive Easter holidays with Aunt Bee were spent as paying guests with friends of hers; a pair of elderly sisters who lived in a pleasant house standing in an overgrown garden near Bushey Heath, where we met an equally elderly gentleman who wrote books about birds. His name was Cherry Kearton and Bill was greatly impressed at actually being able to talk to the great man; for at that time, boys by the thousand bought or borrowed his books and attended his lectures. As a result of meeting him we spent every spare moment of those holidays bird-watching in the woods and on the heath. We also, though I don't remember in which year, were taken to tea at a house near Bushey Heath where we met a small, pale and rather pudgy little boy whose name was Peter Scott. I knew all about his father — everyone in the country knew about Scott of the Antarctic; so of course I was interested to meet him. But not nearly as interested as I was at being shown a portfolio of small water-colour sketches of snowfields, icebergs and frozen seas, and being told by my hostess (Peter Scott's mother? grandmother? aunt? — I don't remember who she was) that they were painted by the expedition's doctor who was, I think she said, Peter Scott's godfather and had left them to the child in a Will found in the snowed-in tent in which Scott and his companions had died. I thought that was a most moving story and I often meant to write to Sir Peter and ask if I'd got it right:* *were* those pictures left to him, and where are they now?

Some of the Aunt Bee holidays were fun; in particular those two springtime ones at Bushey Heath, because the old dears whose paying guests we were were just that: old dears. One of them was a talented artist in the Art Nouveau line, and both of them liked and understood children. So did our landlady at Myrtle Cottage who, despite a tendency to get a bit crisp over such matters as seaweed in the bedrooms and damp sandy footmarks in her minute and specklessly clean hall, was a darling. Other holidays included one in a house in Lyndhurst in the New Forest that stays in my memory chiefly because in the course of it King George V's only daughter, Princess Mary, got married with all the fanfare and ballyhoo that attends a royal wedding. Bets and I discussed it endlessly with the cook and the 'daily help' whom Aunt Bee had engaged for the duration of the holiday, and who, like us, thought the whole affair was wildly romantic. This view seemed to be shared by the entire press of Great Britain, for the newspapers and women's magazines were full of articles by dewy-eyed news-hens disclosing 'exclusive' details about the royal love-affair (that nobody but the Princess and her betrothed could possibly have known about) and speculating endlessly on the design of her wedding-dress and where the happy couple would spend their honeymoon. Half the country (or the female half of it, anyway) appeared to be light-headed with romance and orange-blossom. And this notwithstanding the fact that, judging from the newsreels and all those photographs in the daily papers, even the most gushing of sob-sisters could not pretend that the bridegroom was anything remotely like a handsome fairy-tale Prince. Physically, like it or lump it, he was clearly just another frog. She had obviously kissed the wrong one.

I remember being equally disappointed with her wedding-dress, and saying so to some expensive friend of Aunt Bee's who lived in a large and beautiful house near Ringwood and had asked us all over to

---

* P.S. I haven't, and now it's too late.

luncheon. Our hostess had laughed and said that she had been told by a friend who went to the same dressmaker, that according to its designer by the time that Queen Mary had had her say, and the Queen Mother* had had hers, and 'Mary had had her little whimper', there wasn't a trace of originality left in the dress. I had a soft spot for the poor Princess Royal from then on. The only other thing I remember about that holiday is the rain. As usual there was lots of that. The New Forest is a lovely place when the sun shines, but it is not much fun when the rain is pelting down; and too much of that holiday was spent cooped up indoors.

Except when Mother was able to come back to England, which was roughly once every two years, most of our school holidays were spent in the care of Aunt Bee. Though thankfully not all of them: the exceptions were like manna in the wilderness. We spent two whole holidays and part of a third at Croft House in Kidderminster, the home of Tacklow's best friend at Winchester, Cull Brinton. The Brintons were everything that we were not: spoilt, clever, attractive, extrovert, rich and afraid of nothing and nobody. We admired them enormously and a holiday at Croft House was always the greatest fun. They were the sort of family who were, one felt, perfectly capable of suddenly saying: 'There's nothing to do here — why don't we go to Tangier? or Timbuctoo?', and actually *going* there. Heady stuff for children like ourselves who could seldom afford a bus ticket to the nearest High Street.

John, the only son in a family of five, was at Oxford (or possibly at Cambridge). The eldest daughter, Diana — 'Dinnie' — who married an *avant-garde* artist called Rupert Lee, went out to India to stay with my parents and go sightseeing with Mother. Later she became secretary to the society that put on the first Surrealist Exhibition in London, where Dali sprang to fame by giving a lecture wearing a diver's suit and getting stuck inside it because the helmet could not be unscrewed. Noël, the second daughter, was a Bolshevik (the Russian Revolution was less than ten years old) and spent most of her time in Russia; and Anne and Hope were both still at school. The entire family had an endearing habit of deciding at intervals to dress up in togas made from sheets or table-cloths, swathing their brows with wreaths of laurel

* Queen Alexandra; once Princess Alexandra of Denmark.

leaves, and trailing off, bare-footed, to the woods to dedicate an altar to the Unknown God — Cull acting as the High Priest and conducting the proceedings in Greek while the rest of us lit vestal fires and intoned in chorus. A holiday with the Brintons was always stimulating in the extreme, and I was, of course, in love with John who was far too good-looking and didn't even know I was around. Best of all, no one at Croft House ever criticized, lectured or chivvied us — oh, the peace of it!

Then there was one truly magical holiday that we spent at the home of Bets's best friend, Betty Norbury, whose parents owned an old and beautiful Elizabethan house set in acres and acres of some of the loveliest countryside in England: green fields and flower-powdered meadows, woods and spinneys and copses full of primroses and nesting birds. All so unspoiled that one would not have been surprised to hear a horn blow and see the young Elizabeth Tudor and her courtiers come riding out of the woods dressed in green velvet and white satin, as they had done when they rode out a'maying from Hampton Court Palace more than four hundred years ago.

The Norburys' house, Wilmcote Hill, had been built on to a little two-storeyed cottage which, according to legend, had belonged to a Mistress Hathaway whose daughter, Ann, married a young village lad suspected of poaching — one Will Shakespeare. For this was Shakespeare's own county: beautiful, leafy Warwickshire; and the nearest town to Wilmcote Hill was the one in which he had been born, Stratford-upon-Avon.

It did not rain during that holiday. The air always seemed to be alive with the swallows who were building in the barns behind the house, for Mr Norbury farmed his acres; and I never see larch trees in spring without remembering the thousands of daffodils and narcissi that grew under the larches round the lake below the house.

Mrs Norbury used to take us into Stratford when she went shopping, and to matinées at the old theatre — which had not yet been burnt down, and was madly mock-Tudor in contrast to the modern structure that would replace it. Once she took us to a Sunday morning service in the little church where Shakespeare lies buried; and on another occasion to spend a long, sunny afternoon at Warwick Castle. But best of all were the hours and days we spent building ourselves a house in one of the Wilmcote Hill woods; a house that I described long afterwards in a children's book called *The Ordinary Princess* which I both wrote and illustrated.

After I left school Bets continued to spend part of her holidays at Wilmcote Hill, and I was very envious when I heard that she and Betty Norbury had made friends with the Shakespeare Company. Bets did pencil portraits of some of the young actors which they signed for her; among them a future film-actor called Bramwell Fletcher, and the young John Laurie who, in old age, became a star all over again in a TV series called *Dad's Army*.

❋ At last, in November 1925, Tacklow's tour of duty ended. And this time he stuck to his guns in opting for retirement and that little house in the country that he had always dreamed of. Though by now it was far too late for him to watch his children grow up. Bill, whom he had only seen once in the past twelve years, would be leaving Repton in the spring and going to 'The Shop',* for he had opted for the Gunners and, he hoped, the Indian Army. I too had only one more term to go before I left school and became an art student, and Bets alone had still to serve a year or two in the ranks while her brother and sister were demobbed. In mid-December, when the winter term ended, Aunt Bee took charge of us for the last time, and it was under her flinty eye that we three travelled out to Château d'Oex in Switzerland, to meet our parents and spend Christmas with them in the Hotel Rosa, high above the town.

The Channel crossing was a rough one and, to my surprise and indignation, I was appallingly seasick; for remembering the tea-tray episode in the Bay of Biscay I had thought myself immune to wild water. Puberty had obviously altered that as well as other things; though it had not rid me, as promised, of my 'puppy-fat' (for which I blamed Bee, who had insisted, despite all my pleas, on my keeping to the same old 'growing girls need feeding-up' regime, initially foisted upon me at Portpool). Aunt Bee said bracingly that my seasickness was merely due to nerves and imagination and I must 'snap out of it' — Bill and Bets hadn't been sick and nor had she! Well maybe they hadn't. But they all looked pale green and seemed disinclined to eat

* The Royal Military Academy at Woolwich, where future sappers, gunners, miners and signallers are trained.

anything. Unfortunately, Bee's French was good enough to enable her to be dictatorial to the Customs officials and Passport Officers at Calais, and rude to the porters at the railway stations as well as almost everyone we met on the train. It was not a soothing journey and next day we were sadly disappointed to find that very little snow had fallen that year and all the ski-ing resorts were in a panic about it. However, there on the platform to meet us were our parents. Back, this time, for good. We launched ourselves at them with shrieks of joy. Darling, darling Tacklow! It was a marvellous moment and more than made up for our bitter disappointment that as Tacklow had retired, there would be no going back to India for any of us — except Bill if he managed to get into the Indian Army when he passed out of The Shop.

Bee stayed with us as a guest over Christmas before returning to England, and we saw her off with suitable expressions of affection and gratitude. And indeed we really were grateful. Not only for all she had done for us (we had enough sense to realize that we could have been in much worse hands — just look at what happened to poor little Rudyard Kipling, for example), but because we were so thankful that it was all over, and we would never have to be infuriated or embarrassed by her again. We didn't see much of Aunt Bee after that, though we kept in touch; dutifully remembering to send cards and small presents when Christmas or her birthday came round. Sometimes Mother invited her to visit us, or travelled down to Southampton to spend a night or two with her in her top-floor flat in a Southampton suburb; but the last time Bets and I saw her was in the latter half of the Thirties, when she invited us to have lunch with her at a hotel in Southampton —

Bets was married by then and we had both been on a brief visit to her mother-in-law, who lived somewhere around those parts, and were returning to London via Southampton: a circumstance that I suppose Mother must have mentioned in a letter to Bee — hence the invitation. It was a pressing one that left us no option but to accept; though her sister (who was finding Bee more and more difficult to deal with as she grew older) had confessed to Mother that Bee had exchanged high words with so many of Southampton's taxi-drivers that the fraternity had virtually 'blacked' her, and that any call for a taxi in her name was refused; which made it very difficult for her to get around, since she could only walk very short distances with the aid of a stick.

Mother had passed this bit of information on to us and we feared the worst; especially after waiting in the hotel lounge for a good half-hour after the time that Bee had settled on for our meeting. Then at long last we heard a familiar sound floating up to the open windows from the pavement below. A high, authoritative voice was giving a piece of its mind to someone who was returning it with interest. 'That'll be Aunt Bee!' sighed Bets, rising. We ran downstairs and hurried through the foyer; and of course it was. She was shaking that well-known ebony stick at a taxi-driver and telling him just what she thought of him. Apparently he had grossly overcharged her because he took her for a poor, defenceless old woman who could be swindled with impunity, but this time he had met his match for she had taken his number and intended to report him to the police and the City Council and the editor of the local paper ... and so on and so on. Age had certainly not changed the infinite zip with which criticism and invective tripped off that acid tongue. The taxi-driver, no mean adversary, was clearly outclassed, and in the end, having joined the list of the many Southampton taxi-drivers who would no longer answer a call from her address, he drove away, untipped, leaving Aunt Bee the victor on points.

She gave us a blow-by-blow account of the battle over luncheon; complaining bitterly of the insufferable rudeness of public servants in this mannerless age, enumerating many examples, and boasting of the restraint with which she had conducted herself in the face of the shocking and *totally* unprovoked behaviour of the hoi polloi, who 'did not know their place'. She then argued over the bill. It was just like old times! When we kissed her goodbye and saw her leave (by bus) it was with genuine regret; for there is something strangely comforting in discovering, in a rapidly changing world, that even one thing — in this case one person — has remained exactly as you remembered them. We never saw her again. But we have never forgotten her. *Ave atque vale*, Bee; I wouldn't have liked to be in St Peter's shoes when you arrived at Heaven's gate, and I bet you bullied him into letting you go to the head of the queue!

✠ Our stay in Château d'Oex was supposed to help me brush up my French. It failed. Largely, I think, because whenever I groped for a

380

word I wanted in French, it arrived in Hindustani; even though I would have sworn that I had forgotten it and, if asked for it in that language, would have been unable to lay my tongue to it. I only added one new French word to my meagre vocabulary, and that, for some strange reason, has never escaped me. The French for a Jerusalem artichoke.* That one word, and two totally different scenes, stay in my mind to be recalled whenever Switzerland or the name Château d'Oex is spoken. The first scene is in the category of my 'Seven Most Beautiful Things', together with that moonlit fragipani tree beside the Kalka–Simla Road, the Taj Mahal at sunrise and the 'Cutty Sark' under full sail. This is how I happened to see it ...

Our set of rooms at the Hotel Rosa all opened onto a wide private balcony, open to the sky, from which we could look out across the town below us to the snow-covered mountains on the far side of the valley; and sometime between midnight on Christmas Eve and the earliest minutes of Christmas Day, we were awakened by Tacklow and Mother shaking us and urging us to 'Come out and listen to this!' Huddling on our dressing-gowns and slippers and with our eider-downs thrown shawl-wise round our shoulders, we went out onto the balcony and into bright moonlight. There had been a light fall of snow on the previous evening, but now the sky was clear and the windless night was full of stars: stars in the sky and stardust sparkling on the snow where the moonlight struck it — on the mountains on the far side of the valley and the pointed eaves of the hotel, the snow-covered trees and the balcony rails. And silver-sweet in the silence of that still and shining night, an unforgettably beautiful sound: the voices of an unseen choir from the parish church singing carols in the snow among the black tree-shadows below the hotel.

The carols were not ones that I had ever heard before. But even if it had not been Christmas Eve — or Christmas morning — no one could have mistaken them for anything else. This was how the angelic choir must have sounded to the listening shepherds on that hillside above Bethlehem, high, pure, sexless voices singing Hosannas to the Highest ...

The second Château d'Oex memory is also a Christmas one. We arrived at the little English church in plenty of time for the morning

* For those who don't know it, it's *topinambour*. Nice, isn't it?

381

service, only to find that it was already packed solid with visiting Britons. There was no hope of our being able to sit together, but a harassed verger managed to squeeze us in here and there among the congregation, where we were instantly lost to sight. Tacklow had remained standing at the back of the church until he was sure that his womenfolk and his son were seated, and then the kindly occupants of a pew near the door managed to squash up enough to make room for him just as the service began. Only when it was half-way through did it occur to him that, as Keeper of the Privy Purse, he had quite forgotten to dish out money for the collection plate to his family, who would, he felt sure, be gravely embarrassed when it was presented to them and they had nothing to put in it.

Anyone else would have realized that there was nothing one could do about it beyond putting the family's combined collection money in the plate when it came to his turn to contribute, and letting it go at that. Not my Tacklow! He merely waited until the congregation sat down at the conclusion of 'Hark the Herald' or whatever, and then, solemnly climbing on to the pew, stood up and peered over the top of his spectacles at the congregation, like some latter-day Stout Cortez taking a look at the Pacific from that mountain top. Having located us one by one and memorized our several positions, he got down again, sorted out the collection money and trod quietly down the aisle to distribute it — the startled occupants of the pews obediently handing it along the line until it reached the Kaye it was intended for. It never occurred to him to feel embarrassed, or think that we might be. But we were, of course. And all four of us, Mother included, owned up afterwards that we came within an ace of handing the money to our next-hand neighbour.

We had been at the Hotel Rosa for about a week when a flock of letters and telegrams arrived addressed to 'Sir Cecil Kaye'. And that was how we discovered something that Tacklow had known about for some months past: that he was to be knighted. Technically he would not become 'Sir Cecil' until the King touched him on his shoulder with a sword at an Investiture at Buckingham Palace in another month or two. But once such announcements appeared in the New Year's Honours List, everyone chose to ignore that and used the prefix on envelopes and articles. Scores of the letters arriving for 'Sir Cecil' came from India, for he had made a great name for himself during his term as Director of Central Intelligence. He had always believed that the post, which was a top security-and-police job, should by rights be held by a policeman and that it was unfair that it should always be given to a member of the ICS. How, he argued, could anyone expect to persuade the best men to opt for a career in a service in which they knew from the start that however hard they worked, and however good they were at their job, they could never reach the top rung of the ladder because custom reserved that for the Civil Service — a plum for the Heaven-Born.

His own appointment had caused a good deal of resentment because he was an Army man and not a civilian. But it had broken the pattern, and one of the tasks he had set himself was to ensure that the next DCI, and all subsequent ones, would be a policeman. He succeeded in this, and when he retired *The Times of India* wrote a valedictory column that I still cherish and that must have pleased him.*

Buckie told me that it was written by an Indian. I don't know where he got his information from, for the article was not signed. But I expect he was right, for almost forty years later — sixteen years after India became independent and long after both Buckie and my father were dead — a senior Indian police officer, to whom I had to show my passport while revisiting the dear country of my birth, noticed that my maiden name had been Kaye and asked me if by any chance I was related to a Sir Cecil Kaye who had been DCI, India in the years following the end of the First World War? When I said that I was his daughter, he leapt to his feet and embraced me (and for two pins would, I think, have kissed me), babbling excitedly that this was wonderful — *wonderful!* — that when he had been a young man my father had been so good to him. So kind and so helpful. Everyone in the Department had loved and revered him and would be forever grateful for the encouragement he had given them: 'We worshipped your father; he was a truly good man!' That was a great moment for me — and obviously for him too, for I have seldom seen a man so deeply and genuinely moved.

Bill, Bets and I were naturally thrilled to bits by the news of that knighthood, and charmed to learn that our parents would in future be known as 'Sir Cecil and Lady Kaye'. Mother was equally thrilled; but

* This is printed in the Appendix on page 454.

the reactions of the recipient himself were a good deal more muted and could at best be summed up, in Ko-Ko's famous phrase, as 'modified rapture'. Tacklow warned us that it would only mean that from now on everything was going to be a lot more expensive, because the Great British Public believed that anyone with a handle to his name must automatically be rolling rich, and charged him accordingly! The same went for 'abroad': only more so, for there, even a man with a modest 'Sir' before his name was instantly a 'Milor' and, of course, loaded. But the fact remained that we were far from rich, and now that he had retired on a small pension (the job had been a civil one but the pension was an Army one, and his Army rank was Lieutenant-Colonel) we were going to have to count every penny. The salaried days were over.

I don't think I took any of this very seriously. Tacklow, I decided, was only feeling a bit depressed at the prospect of retirement in a country that he had almost forgotten. And probably sad, too, because he foresaw trouble ahead for the one in which he had spent his working life. I knew that this worried my father because he would sometimes talk to me about it. What I did not know at the time, and would never have known but for Mother, since Tacklow himself never mentioned it, was that every letter of the shoals of letters that began to arrive from all over India congratulating him on his knighthood, said the same thing: 'It ought to have been a KCSI or a KBE'* (those being two senior grades of knighthood, while Tacklow's was the most junior grade: 'Kt', or 'Knight Bachelor'). Not until long afterwards did I learn from some old friends of his, Buckie and Claude Auchinleck, who was to become Commander-in-Chief, India — and later a Field-Marshal — and Sir Denys Bray of the ICS, who was, I think, a member of the Viceroy's Council, that Tacklow, together with almost everyone connected with security, had incurred the wrath of the then Prince of Wales (now better known as the Duke of Windsor) when he toured India in the early Twenties. So angry was he, that if he could — and he possibly could — have prevented any of them from getting any award, he would have done so. In the event he had sufficient pull to get the awards held up and pared down. Much later, Tacklow told me what a headache the Prince's visit had been for everyone, and how

* Knight Commander of the Star of India, or Knight of the British Empire.

difficult he had made it for anyone whose misfortune it was to be charged with protecting him from assassination.

I remember asking him what the Prince of Wales was like to meet and talk to; we all knew what he looked like, because the newspapers of the time were always full of his pictures — this handsome, laughing young man who had made himself such a reputation as an adored Prince Charming. Tacklow said he was a 'retarded adolescent'. I had never heard that expression before, and when I asked him what he meant, he replied that the Prince was like a spoilt but very attractive and extremely likeable schoolboy of fifteen or so, who having reached that age had decided, like some older Peter Pan, to stay there for good, atrophied in youth.

I had my own reasons for being interested in the Prince, for I had already heard a lot more about his visit to India than appeared in the newspapers. This was because my room-mate Cynthia Hepper had an elder sister, Joan, who was, at that time, one of the reigning belles of Bombay. She was also a prolific correspondent whose frequent letters were proudly read aloud to us by Cynthia. Netta and I were enthralled by them: understandably, since Joan had actually danced with the Prince of Wales — not once but several times — and was madly in love with one of his equerries! This was life with a capital L. Glittering, glamorous, grown-up life. How we envied her!

Joan, with thrilling casualness, referred to the Prince as 'David', and reported gleefully that he was delightfully unstuffy and had on several occasions stood up some of the 'frumps' he had been booked to partner, some of them the wives and daughters of senior officials and prominent Indians,* while he danced instead with some pretty young thing who had caught his fancy — Joan presumably among them. Such dashing behaviour had obviously impressed her, and I have to admit that we too thought it was pretty impressive, and spared no thought for the humiliation and embarrassment of those poor, publicly slighted ladies.

The press had reported the whole tour as a roaring success. But in fact it must have been a cross between a severe headache and an Imperial nightmare for all those who were responsible for the young man's safety and his public image, for the Prince detested all the

---

* In those days few Indian husbands would permit their wives to dance, so the chosen ladies would have sat out the dances with the Prince.

security arrangements (he called it 'mollycoddling') and proved from the start to be what any nanny would have termed 'a handful'. Landing in Bombay, he celebrated the occasion by sending his anxious parents a telegram in clear that said: 'Wonderful welcome! Forty-six dead, four hundred injured, and a thousand arrested' — or words to that effect — and throughout the remainder of the tour behaved like that little girl in the nursery rhyme who 'When she was good she was very, very good, and when she was bad she was horrid'. One of the latter periods culminated in Peshawar in a ferocious row with his host in that city, Sir John Maffey, over his security measures. He had flown into a royal rage, and Sir John, losing his cool, had exploded in his turn and metaphorically speaking torn a strip off him. Whereupon the Prince, scarlet with fury, stormed off to his rooms: emerging an hour or so later to find Lady Maffey soothing her jangled nerves with a cup of tea on the lawn. She told Mother later that he had come to a stop beside her, and after standing there for a minute or two with his head down and his hands in his pockets, moodily kicking the turf with the toe of one foot and looking for all the world like a guilty schoolboy summoning up the courage to confess to some youthful peccadillo, he blurted out ruefully: 'By jove, Lady Maffey, your husband does talk straight to a fellow!' At which point, she confessed, her heart melted and she would have forgiven him anything. But oh, the sigh of relief that must have gone up from Peshawar to Cape Cormorin when he finally left India, still in one piece . . .

Tacklow admitted that when it was all over he had the first good night's sleep he had had for weeks, and I think that that royal visit must have marked the lowest point in his term of duty as DCI, India. The highest and best (which strangely enough involved another heir to a royal throne), makes a fascinating story that could only have happened in the East, for it concerns the ruler of one of India's Independent States who fell in love with a dancing-girl. She was only a common *nautch*-girl off the streets, already pregnant by some unknown customer when she entered the royal harem; yet despite this, when she gave birth to a son some six months later the ruler became almost as besotted by the boy as he was by its mother. Eventually, since his legal wives had given him no male heir and by now were unlikely to bear him any more children (the *nautch*-girl would have made sure of that!), he petitioned the Government of India to declare her little bastard the legal heir, by adoption, to his throne.

The Government was profoundly shocked and besought His Highness to reconsider; pointing out that he was not yet old enough to give up hope of having a son of his own, and that if at some later date he should acquire one, he would be unable to demote the *nautch*-girl's offspring in favour of his own. The Law was the Law and one could not play games with it; had His Highness fully appreciated that? His Highness insisted that he had, and in time the deed was done. But sadly, the Sirkār had been right. A day came when the *nautch*-girl's charms began to fade and His Highness took another wife, who bore him a son: a fair-skinned child of the blood royal whom he grew to idolize. It was then that, realizing the Sirkār would never go back on its word and declare his own boy the heir, he decided that there was nothing for it but to resort to bribery; and calling upon his ministers he instructed them to draw up a list of every influential man in the entire Government of India, and to write against each one the sum for which that man's support could be purchased. It was done as he ordered. But somehow word of that highly secret list came to the ears of the Government, who instantly became very anxious to get their hands on it, because the sums of money written against each name would serve to pinpoint officials who were in the habit of taking bribes. (A modest figure could be taken as clear evidence that the owner of that name was known to be bribable, for the compilers of the list would make no mistake about *that*.)

To cut a long story short, a copy of the list was obtained and, by his order, placed unread into the hand of the Viceroy, Lord Reading — who for obvious reasons was intended to be the only person allowed to see it. However, having read it he sent for Tacklow (whose department had been responsible for filching it) and said: 'I know that I am not supposed to show this to anyone, even you. But it contains something that I think you should be allowed to see, and I know I can trust you to forget the rest.' With that he handed over a scroll containing a list of names that began with his own, against which (the state in question was a very rich one!) was written a really whopping sum of money. The sums against the other names varied widely; some being suspiciously small. But only one name among all those names had written against it a word instead of a number. The word was 'unbribable' and the name was Tacklow's.

❧ 6 ❧

The Locust Years

Chapter 25

~❋❋❋~

Lord, dismiss us with Thy blessing,
Thanks for mercies past receive;
Pardon all, their faults confessing;
Time that's lost may all retrieve ...

Buckoll, *Hymns Ancient & Modern*

It was while I was at Château d'Oex that I learnt to my amazement that thanks to that eyesore, the Cuthbert Grundy Shield, I would be leaving The Lawn a whole year earlier than I would normally have done.

Apparently my ungrateful headmistress had written to inform my parents that since dear Mollie seemed to be uninterested in anything but art, they would be wasting her time and their money if they kept her at The Lawn any longer, and had much better send her off at the end of the summer term to a good art school: Miss Hoskins strongly recommended her own, the MacMunn Studio in Park Walk, Chelsea ...

Tacklow had replied briefly that in that case he saw no point in my wasting another summer term at her school and would remove me at the end of the Easter term. So that was that.

Considering that I had won that hideous trophy for her practically single-handed, I took a poor view of Dub-dub's letter, which seemed to me distinctly unfair. But apart from that I was delighted at the prospect of an earlier release from school, and I had always hankered to be a painter. Not a painter of pictures that were exhibited at the Academy and bought by city councils for their art galleries, but an illustrator of children's books; fairy-tales for preference. A famous one, of course.

My parents, though a trifle miffed by Dub-dub's letter, were all for my studying at the Slade: and I am proud of the fact that I was actually accepted as a student. However, an interview during which the curriculum was explained to me in detail proved that Miss Hoskins's advice was sound. The Slade produced — or aimed to produce — serious Artists. And since that was not in the least what I was after, I backed down hurriedly and signed on at Miss Hoskins's old studio after all. Which may have been a wise move or a grave mistake; I have never been quite sure about that; because to study at the Slade was, in the Twenties, the height of every aspiring young artist's ambition, and I had been given the chance and thrown it away.

On the whole, I had quite enjoyed my years at The Lawn. Though I was not in the least sorry to leave it and I cannot say that I acquired anything that could be called an Education there. They never succeeded in teaching me to spell or speak French or do the simplest sums. Nor did they attempt to teach me any of the social skills that would have made me popular with the kind of young man whom Mother expected me to marry; skills such as riding, playing golf and tennis, and being an adequate dancing partner on a ballroom floor. I was no earthly good at any of those things. I was, and still am, afraid of horses; I detested card games, was a poor swimmer and an indifferent ballroom dancer, and, worst of all, I was fat!

All that 'feeding-up' had done its worst and doomed me to the fate of all fat girls — perpetual self-consciousness on the score of one's figure and the boredom of diets that never work because as soon as you stop them you instantly put back all the pounds you have so painfully lost (and often a few extra ones by way of a bonus). Nor did the fact that my dear brother had nicknamed me 'Old Piano Legs', when I was at my most sensitive age, do anything for my morale.

The only thing The Lawn had done for me, apart from engaging Miss Hoskins to take over the art class, was to keep me occupied and tolerably happy during the bleak years of separation from my parents and exile from the country I thought of as 'home'; though the stresses and strains of holidays with Aunt Bee undoubtedly served to make the term-times more pleasant than they would otherwise have been. Beyond that, The Lawn had done nothing much, either socially or mentally, to equip me to cope with life in a competitive world, and I can only be profoundly grateful that I was born into a time and a class in which girls were still not expected to go out to work, but only to marry and get on with producing the next generation. Because had there been, as there is now, the pressure to get a job at all costs, I would have found myself at a terrible disadvantage.

Dub-dub was fond of saying smugly: '*All* my girls marry'! But I can remember meeting in middle age one of my school-mates who had not, and who said bitterly that she would never forgive Dub-dub for that fatuous remark, or for failing to provide her with an education that would enable her to get, and hold down, a good job when she left The Lawn. I saw her point, since I have always regarded myself as being self-educated — or rather, Tacklow-educated — and had I on leaving school been told to earn my own living, I could not have held down any job. I would not even have made a good 'daily', since all my end-of-term reports always included the same six-word comment by Matron: 'Mollie is as untidy as ever'; a remark that never failed to irritate my normally placid father ...

'What do I pay these women for?' he would demand. Well actually, for knowing that during our long periods of separation from him and Mother we would be tolerably happy. On the other hand, scholastically the school was dire, and had I not been a voracious reader with a passion for history (for which Tacklow and not my form-mistress was responsible) I would have finished my school years virtually uneducated. Yet the only thing I regret about this was not being taught to speak French. Yes, of course we were *taught* it; but by an Englishwoman who, I suspect, wouldn't have done any too well if she'd suddenly found herself being parachuted into France. She never made the French language come alive, and though I coped within reason with her endless written exercises, I always failed to pass the few oral ones and thankfully forgot the whole thing the minute I left. However, although my weekly position in class was generally somewhere near the bottom, I could sail through the end-of-term exams and come top of the list in subjects like history, English, botany, composition, scripture and, oddly enough, geometry. (Why geometry, when I couldn't do maths, and algebra was always a closed book to me? Could it be that geometry has something to do with drawing?) I was adequate at cookery but ham-handed at sewing and music, and could only *just* scrape past at Latin. The Lawn did not teach physics, chemistry or any modern language except a smattering of that painfully British-French that has recently been immortalized by Miles Kington as 'Franglais'.

Oh well, for better or for worse it was over! The boarding-school era, that had loomed ahead like a threatening shadow during the last bright years of my childhood in India, was past, and life and love lay ahead. Romance, here I come! Yet there was a distinct lump in my throat as I joined in singing the hymn that always ended Prayers in the Big Schoolroom on the last day of term: 'Lord, dismiss us with Thy blessing' . . . I don't think I had ever paid much attention to those words before, but I remember being struck by them that morning. '*Let Thy father-hand be shielding All who here will meet no more . . .*' Strange to think that I myself had at last become one of those who would meet here no more. Suddenly, it was a very sobering thought. Tomorrow I would be a grown-up; and all at once I was not at all sure that that was such an enviable thing to be! '*May their seed-time past be yielding Year by year a richer store; Those returning, Make more faithful than before. Amen,*' sang the assembled school. No more school. No more Clevedon. And with luck, no more Upton House — !

Upton House had been bought by my Kaye grandfather after my grandmother died at Oxford. And there he now lived in peaceful Victorian seclusion with Aunt Molly and her children; keeping bees and waging a non-stop war on the dandelions that persisted in coming up on his lawns. His new home was a large stone-built manor-house with mullioned windows, standing among lawns, flowerbeds and shrubberies, orchards, a tennis court and a large walled garden. The whole was surrounded by a high stone wall and set among sloping meadows full of wildflowers. Beautiful? Well, yes. I hated it! The whole set-up made me feel as though I had stepped backward in time, because Grandpapa Kaye, who was always pleading poverty, insisted on living as though he was the local squire and a young Queen Victoria had only recently ascended the throne.

He kept a large staff, consisting of a cook, a housemaid, a skivvy,* an odd-job man, an ancient gardener and, I rather think, a gardener's boy as well. There was neither electricity nor gas in the house. Oil lamps and candles, and that was it. There *must* have been running water, because I couldn't possibly have forgotten having to take a

* A humble girl who was expected to scrub the floors, peel potatoes, wash the dishes and in general do all the dirty work that no one else wanted to do.

bath in a hip-bath, or using an 'earth closet'. But the mere fact that I can't remember where the bathroom was, or the loo, or even if they were there at all, says a lot about Upton House.

Each day there began with the arrival of a maid with a copper can of hot water, which she would dump in the china basin on the washstand and drape with a towel, to keep it warm while she pulled the curtains. The next thing was family breakfast in a dining-room where the sideboard almost literally groaned with covered silver dishes, each one on its own stand above a tiny flame from a little methylated-spirit lamp that kept the dishes hot. You had a choice of kippers or kedgeree, eggs (scrambled, fried or boiled), grilled kidneys, bacon and sausages, a large cold ham, and always, heading this ridiculously lavish line-up, a huge tureen of porridge; because whatever one chose for 'afters' one was expected to start with porridge. The grown-ups always ate it standing up, out of wooden bowls and with salt, not sugar — a Scottish ritual which, considering that the Kayes originally came from Yorkshire, I regarded as a piece of swank.

The mornings were all right, because one could play in the gardens. And I discovered that I could cope with bees without getting stung; which pleased Grandpapa, who used to take me down with him to the row of beehives in the upper orchard to help him remove old frames or fumigate the hives, and would watch approvingly when (carefully veiled, I may say) I let swarms of the little insects crawl all over my hands. I can only suppose I must have had the sort of smell that bees like.

Lunch, however, was to be dreaded, because Grandpapa liked to drink beer that was drawn fresh from the cask, and it was always one of his grandchildren who had to fetch it for him. 'Let a child do it!' was his invariable command, and we never knew which of us his beady eye would light upon. We all hated fetching the stuff, because the casks were kept in the wine cellar; a damp, pitch-black dungeon of a place with a vaulted roof and pillars draped with cobwebs like something out of a horror film. But it was neither the dark nor the spiders that scared us. It was frogs. Or rather toads, of which there were any number, squatting fecklessly on the wet stone flags and brooding on infinity, regardless of the fact that they were almost impossible to see by the light of a single wavering candle. Have you ever trodden on a frog? Or, worse still, on a toad? I do not recommend it. They explode with a horrid pop, followed by a squish as one slips wildly on the remains of the deceased.

Armed with the beer-jug and a candle I would grope my way down the slimy steps into musty, beer-smelling blackness, praying that I would not tread on a frog or be dropped on by a spider; and having balanced the candlestick on the top of a cask, cautiously turn the spigot and attempt to fill the jug without getting too much froth on top or spilling too much beer. There would always be a certain amount of spillage, of course, and I can only presume that the reason why those wretched toads didn't hop out of the way was because they were permanently sozzled.

I was always terrified that the candle would go out and leave me in that toad-filled darkness, or that I would drop Grandpapa's favourite jug and get skinned by his razor-edged tongue for doing so. The whole business was a terrifying ordeal and probably the reason why I am afraid of the dark to this day. And just to add to everything else, the house was haunted. It had a resident ghost . . .

✕ Given the choice between the ghost and the toads, I would have preferred the ghost every time; in spite of that hair-raising experience at The Bower. For one thing, this ghost was the only truly kind-hearted one I have ever heard of. She had no known history, and even the Oldest Inhabitant in the village could not say when she had started haunting the house; only that it was 'before me time'. One really should not be scared of benevolent ghosts; and if there *had* to be a ghost in the house it was obviously better to have a friendly one. Speaking for myself I would have preferred to have no ghost at all, and the fact that the house harboured one was not conducive to peaceful sleep at night.

The Upton House ghost was that of a young woman; a girl in her late teens or early twenties according to those who had seen her, and judging from her dress she must once have been a housemaid, for even in my day, in the depths of the country young village girls 'in service' still wore print dresses, aprons and mob caps; as they had done for several hundred years. One can only suppose that this one, when she was alive and in service in that house, was treated with great kindness by someone who lived in it, and was so grateful that even after her death her ghost would return to the house whenever those who lived in it were in need of help.

It was not easy, in those post-war years, to find household help even for a modern, labour-saving house, while for one such as Upton House — old and stone-built, with long ice-cold passages leading to large stone-flagged kitchen quarters, not a hint of All Mod. Cons. anywhere, no electricity, no gas, miles from the nearest town where there was a cinema, good shops or, for that matter, a barracks — it was getting almost impossible to obtain staff. The women who once worked in such houses, and had left to work in munitions factories, hospitals and a dozen other spheres during the war years, would never come back; while the young had no desire to take work in out-of-the-way places where there were few if any young men to take them out on their days off.

With no boy-friends, no bright lights, no *fun!* — and that human battle-axe, Aunt Molly, chasing them around to see that they 'kept up to the mark' — it was not surprising that the staff at Upton House were always downing tools and departing at short notice, leaving Aunt Molly and Cousin Maggie, and any other available grandchild who happened to be present, to cope with the housework and cooking while Cousin Grace trundled off in the family car to do the shopping and to plead with the nearest employment agency to find yet another set of replacements willing to take on the drudgery and boredom of Upton House and put up with Aunt Molly's ideas of discipline. On at least two such occasions (there may have been more when she wasn't spotted) the ghostly housemaid rushed to the rescue and did her stuff. That girl really *must* have had a heart of gold.

On the first of those two occasions it was my cousin Tom Polwhele, elder son of Tacklow's beloved sister Nan, who saw her. Tom, a naval Lieutenant, was on leave and due to spend a few days with his grandfather. Since he had written to say that he would be arriving late at night and that no one need bother to stay up for him, a cold supper was left for him in the dining-room and a candlestick in the hall, where all our candlesticks were put out for us every evening; each of us lighting one and carrying it upstairs when we went to bed. We did not hear him arrive and no one had thought to tell him that the staff had walked out *en masse* on the previous day. He came down next morning to find us all at breakfast, and having apologized for being late and dutifully greeted his grandfather, kissed his aunt, and grinned at his assembled cousins, he collected himself a plateful of food from the sideboard and remarked casually that if he hadn't been woken up he would probably not have surfaced until well into the afternoon: 'Who's the new girl who woke me up this morning?' inquired Tom: 'Haven't seen her before. Pretty little thing.'

Everyone stopped eating and there was dead silence in the dining-room as we all stared at him, open-mouthed. Then someone said: 'What did you mean ... she woke you? How?'

'Oh, she just tapped on the door and came in and pulled the curtains, smiled at me and made a nice little bob and went out again. Why? — what else would she do?'

'*The ghost!*' yelped his cousins in chorus: '*He's seen the ghost!*'

Tom, who was a stolid, 'Silent Service' Navy type, not given to practical jokes or playing tricks on people (and besides being unaware that there were no servants in the house, he had never heard that there was a resident ghost), demanded to know what we were all yowling about, and on being told, leapt to the conclusion that one of us had persuaded a friend to dress the part in order to pull his leg. When he realized that this was not so, and that there really were no servants at Upton House, he first became extremely cross and stuffy and said the whole thing was rubbish because no ghost could possibly open and close doors and pull curtains, and then fell back again on insisting that we must have put someone up to doing it and that he didn't think it was in the *least* funny.

The girl was not seen again for the best part of a year. And next time it was Aunt Molly, of all people, who saw her. Once again there had been high words with the staff who, with admirable solidarity, had flounced out in a body. Shortly afterwards, my formidable aunt, feeling cross and distrait, came downstairs to prepare luncheon and, on her way down, passed a housemaid who was on her knees brushing the stair-carpet. The girl drew aside to let her pass, which Aunt Molly did automatically and without thinking, and it was only when she had taken the last step and reached the hall that it flashed into her mind that all the staff had already left. She whirled round and looked back up the staircase; and of course there was no one there.

I gather she tottered into the dining-room and helped herself to a stiff brandy, and spent the next half-hour lying on the sofa in the drawing-room sniffing smelling-salts. She did *not* cook the lunch: I suppose Maggie did.

What with ghosts and toads and Grandpapa and a strong-minded aunt, it is hardly surprising that I disliked staying at Upton House. The room I slept in was known as the 'Battle of the Blues' because its once fashionable William Morris-style wallpaper was a riot of hydrangeas, lilies and larkspur in various shades of blue on a prussian blue background, and there were curtains of navy blue rep on the four-poster bed and at the windows. The furniture was mahogany and massive, and the room so large that the single candle permitted to a child (the older grown-ups had oil lamps) made such a small pool of light in that waste of shadows that on one occasion I spent all my pocket-money on extra candles, because I had come across a book in the library called *Carnaki the Ghost Finder* which so scared me that I did not dare go to sleep in the dark.

The only other thing that I remember clearly about Upton House is that it was here, during a weekend when my parents were also present, that I first realized with an appalling sense of shock that my gay, pretty mother was a complete nit-wit. I can even pinpoint the moment. It happened during a sunny half-term holiday and I was sitting on the grass bank at one end of the tennis court with my cousin Maggie, who was umpiring. Mother was one of the players and I can see her still; the afternoon sun making her hair the colour of horse chestnuts. She is wearing a very becoming white dress and laughing. I haven't the faintest recollection of what it was that she said or did; I only know that whatever it was it made me suddenly aware, as though a blinding light had been switched on and blazed in my face, that she was silly. A charming, butterfly-minded bird-brain ... what Victorians would have called a 'goose-cap'.

It was a horrible moment. Nowadays I don't suppose that anyone under the age of fifty could have any conception what it was like, because with the arrival of the Bright Young Things in the Roaring Twenties, and the appalling prospect of a second world war, standards crumbled, many illusions perished, and it became fashionable to criticize one's parents and anyone of an older generation. But in my day the vast majority of children still regarded their parents as the fount of all wisdom, and the sudden revelation that one's *own* mother was, to put it crudely, plain stupid, was shocking beyond words. It couldn't be true and I must be some kind of horrible freak for even *thinking* such a thing: for didn't the Bible say: 'Honour thy Father and thy Mother that thy days may be long in the land that the Lord thy God giveth thee'? My days couldn't be long at this rate, and for the first time I wished I was a Catholic and could rush off to Confession and be given a penance, and be shriven. Because if I was right about Mother — and I knew very well that I was — then nothing was safe and the very earth under my feet was not solid any more.

It took me a long time to come to terms with that discovery and it was only after I left school, and became used to it, that I mentioned it to Tacklow: and was charmed and comforted by his answer.

'But I never wanted a brainy wife,' said Tacklow. 'I have to use my brain all day in the office, and when I get home I don't want intelligent conversation — I can get that at the Club. I want a beautiful woman who can take my mind off work and worry, and make me laugh; and your mother has always been, and always will be, a source of pride and delight to me.' I felt a lot better after that: and less ashamed of myself. But the incident played its part in casting a shadow over Grandpapa's house. Even though I was beginning to know that cantankerous old curmudgeon rather better because of the hours we spent together messing about among the beehives. I also admired the way he refused to be bossed about by Aunt Battle-axe, and one particularly pleasant memory of him remains with me: his reply to her when she announced at breakfast one morning, after opening her mail, that her dear friends, Eustacia and Hugo Smith-Piggot let us say, had accepted her invitation to spend a couple of nights at Upton House next month and would be arriving in time for luncheon on the fourteenth and leaving after breakfast on the sixteenth — or whatever. She had not asked her father's permission, or expected it; she just stated the fact. Grandpapa merely nodded and said musingly: 'Ah, yes, the Smith-Piggots. The fourteenth to the sixteenth, I think you said? ... Um ... I'm afraid I shall *not* be very well on the fourteenth — or on the next two days either.' And he wasn't. He remained firmly in bed for two and a half days, coming down again only after the guests had departed.

Apart from members of his family, whom he endured rather than enjoyed having to stay, he detested guests, and 'not being well on the twentieth to the twenty-second of next month' (or whenever it was his daughter-cum-housekeeper announced the arrival of visitors), was a well-known gambit of his. But he didn't always win, for I also remember an occasion when Aunt Molly told an extremely over-powering and talkative guest, who had been saying how *very* sorry she was to 'miss seeing your dear father', that Papa was quite well enough to receive a visitor who was such an old friend and who would not expect him to talk too much and tire himself. With which she ushered the 'old friend' into his bedroom and left him to endure an hour of non-stop chat from which there was no escape, since he was clad in pyjamas and tucked up in bed.

Thinking back on the many embarrassments inflicted on us during weekends at Upton House, there is one other incident that deserves mention; Morning Service in the parish church, with whose vicar Grandpapa appeared to be permanently at odds (which did not mean that he would ever consider failing to turn up for the eleven o'clock service every Sunday. Or let any of us skip it, either!). The church was a very old one and the front pews, reserved for centuries by the owners of the few large houses, had high sides and doors that were shut by the verger on the last person to enter. The pew immediately below the pulpit went automatically to the owner of Upton House, and once inside it, with the door closed, only the vicar (or whoever happened to be preaching the sermon) could look into it. Which was just as well, because Grandpapa had a rooted dislike of long sermons. With a view to correcting the vicar's tendency to talk too much he would make a tower of the coins he intended to put into the plate, carefully piling them one on the other before ostentatiously taking out his pocket-watch and placing it beside them where the preacher, looking down into the pew, could not fail to see them. For the first five minutes of the sermon (very occasionally more, provided Grandpapa was interested) the tower remained untouched; but after that with each circuit of the minute hand on his watch one coin was removed until, if the sermon went on too long, the entire lot had been returned to base and the collection plate got nothing at all from old Mr Kaye of Upton House.*

I used to watch this irreverent performance torn between

---

* Years later I read of similar behaviour, in some magazine. The writer must have seen Grandpapa up to his tricks! Or heard about them from someone who had.

embarrassment on behalf of the vicar and a wild desire to burst into giggles as I watched his hypnotized gaze creep back again and again to the shrinking tower of coins, and heard his voice begin to speed up. I still don't know why he didn't ignore the whole business instead of giving in, Sunday after Sunday, to what can only be described as blackmail. At least it worked; and there have been times when, pinned down in a pew and compelled to listen to the droning of some worthy gentleman in Holy Orders who should never ever have been allowed within five hundred yards of a pulpit, I would have dearly liked to follow Grandpapa's example and see if I could make it work too.

In the end, however, much as I may have disliked my school-time visits to Upton House, my memories of the place were sweetened by the fact that on my last visit, a good many months after I had left The Lawn and put my hair up (in those days becoming a grown-up meant putting one's hair up and letting one's skirts down), I fell in love with a friend of my brother Bill's. I haven't the remotest idea what his name was but I can still remember his face as clearly as though I had seen him an hour ago; an attractive puckish face, alight with laughter and made up almost entirely of triangles. He was by no means the first to whom I had lost my heart, for I was always losing it: there was Guy Slater when I was still not five years old, and after him a succession of other idols: young Kurram who wasn't a bit afraid of horses and looked so lordly and handsome as he galloped, nose in air, past my plodding pony on the Mall; Gully, who besides having such beautiful eyes and the whitest of teeth, knew *everything* about everything; Betty Caruana in her character of Jim Blunders in *Where the Rainbow Ends*; as well as endless characters from books, ranging from Robin Hood to Rupert of Hentzau. Then, briefly, there had been Tommy Richardson, who was succeeded by a red-haired and spotty-faced youth who sang in the choir of St John's Church at Clevedon, to whom I never even spoke, and who was soon eclipsed by a long list of actors and film-stars, among them, of course, Pitt Chatham who played the part of MacHeath in *Polly*.

Looking back on my early youth I don't seem to remember any time after the age of four and a half, which was when I met Guy, that I wasn't in love with some member of the opposite sex — not counting Tacklow, with whom I had obviously fallen in love at first sight. I think most of my generation were a sentimental lot who in general thought highly of Love. The whole thing became too raucous later on. It was a lot more romantic when such affairs of the heart were a closely guarded secret.

The 'flicks' — the silent cinema — were really getting into their stride in the Twenties. And since we saw at least one film, and often two, every week during our holidays (in those days the price of a seat in any one of the front six or eight rows was sixpence!) I fell in love with the hero of practically every film that I saw, and lost my heart on an average of one-and-a-half times every seven days; until the day when I met a real live West End actor who switched my attention from the cinema to the stage and was to make an important contribution to my life.

Mother had taken me to an At Home given by Mrs Alec-Tweedie. This outdated function was a relic of Edwardian days at which tea, sandwiches and cakes were served, and friends and acquaintances of the hostess dropped in to exchange gossip and show off their latest hats and dresses. A schoolgirl was definitely *persona non grata* at such gatherings, and Mother had only taken me there because she had been landed with me for half-term, and after a morning spent shopping, didn't know what else to do with me. Attired in my hideous school hat, gym tunic and regulation black cotton stockings, and feeling terribly out of place among all those society women with their high-pitched, pea-hen voices, dauntingly smart dresses and modish hats, I retreated hastily to a dark corner of one of the rooms and tried to make myself as small as possible behind a potted palm. I must have lurked there, hungry and embarrassed, for at least half an hour when I was winkled out by an enchanting elderly man, quite old enough, I thought, to be my father, who brought me a cup of tea and a plate of delicious sandwiches, plumped himself down beside me and kept me fascinated, amused and in gales of giggles for the best part of an hour — and this in spite of our hostess's determined efforts to lure him away! He continued to brush aside all her pleas of '*Dear* Sir Gerald, may I introduce you to Lady Catherine de Burgh who is *dying* to meet you?' with the greatest charm and went on telling me silly stories, and I only learned later that he was a famous actor, Sir Gerald du Maurier, son of the author and illustrator of two of my favourite books, *Trilby* and *Peter Ibbetson*. (And also, incidentally, father of the Daphne du Maurier who would one day become famous as the author of *Jamaica*

Inn, Rebecca, and scores of other best-selling novels, but at that date would still have been in short socks!)

He obviously liked children and knew exactly how to get on with them and put them at their ease, and he was the only person in the room to realize how miserably embarrassed I was feeling — a young and gawky crow among this flock of peacocks and birds of paradise — and to come to my rescue. Meeting him had a long-lasting side-effect, because after Mother returned to India I badgered and badgered Aunt Bee to take me to see him act and eventually wore down her resistance until she actually took us to see a matinée of *The Last of Mrs Cheyney,* in which he played opposite lovely Gladys Cooper in the title role. Had Aunt Bee known what the play was about I am sure she would have considered it unsuitable for children. But fortunately the words 'light comedy' on the playbills outside the theatre misled her, and once we were firmly embedded in our seats in the dress circle she could hardly march us out in the middle of an act. Anyway, she couldn't help enjoying it, even though by the standards of that day it was considered to be very daring; in fact terribly *risqué* — dear me, what an age of innocence that was!

I enjoyed every minute of the play, but there was one brief conversation, I think in Act 2, that was to be of great use to me in the future. Gerald du Maurier as the hero, Lord Something-or-other, says to one of the women guests at a weekend house-party (it was that sort of play) that he wants to ask her a strictly hypothetical question: what would she say if he asked her to marry him? To which she replies promptly: 'I'd be ready in five minutes — no, make it three!'

I don't know why that should have made such a deep impression on me, but it did. Then and there I made up my mind that I would never marry anyone unless I felt exactly like that about him; no doubts whatever; no 'Shall I?', 'Shan't I?' Just *'I'll be ready in five minutes — no, make it three!'* It became my yardstick in the future and saved me again and again from lurching into disaster; for although it didn't stop me from falling in love with regrettable frequency, I always applied that test when it came to a serious proposal of marriage: and the answer that came up was always: 'No — not in three minutes — not even five!' Until one day there was no need even to ask it, since I knew the answer was: 'I'll be ready in three minutes — no, make it *one!*' And for being saved for that day, I shall be grateful for ever to dear Gerald du Maurier, who understood children and recognized the depth of my misery as I cringed in my corner at a fashionable London 'At Home'. I wonder if people still have 'At Homes'? I imagine not. They must have ended with the Second World War. Together with *thé-dansants* and the Charleston ...

Tacklow was knighted at the first Investiture of 1925 by King George V. Sadly, neither Bill nor I, nor Bets, saw that ceremony, for we were all three back at school: Bill and I for the last time. Even Mother did not accompany Tacklow to Buckingham Palace to see him knighted, though she would have loved to do so. But then he did not know that if the recipient of an honour applied to the Palace it was possible to be given permission to take one's nearest and dearest (up to a maximum of three!) to watch it being handed out by the monarch. That was something Mother only discovered later, and she was justifiably annoyed at missing a chance that, since Tacklow had now retired, would never come her way again. I don't know how he managed to talk himself out of that one; but I suspect that this was probably the reason why, shortly afterwards, he took Mother to Menton on the French Riviera for a holiday that he could not really afford, but which they enjoyed enormously.

He had hoped to be able to buy a cottage in the country where he could potter about in the garden and occupy his spare time in compiling a catalogue of Ferrari's famous stamp collection. But the ending of the First World War was followed by inflation and a rocketing rise in the cost of living, and everything went up — except pensions, which remained more or less where they had been in the reign of Edward VII, though there were still school bills to be paid for Bets and art school ones for me, and Bill at Woolwich would need an allowance. So Tacklow went to work again, this time as a civilian. He became the editor of a weekly magazine called *The Near East and India,* and since the head office of that publication was in London, he arranged to rent a tiny furnished house in Kew that belonged to a cousin of his.

The house was about the size of a postage stamp, but after spending a week in it Mother went out shopping and came back with yards of coconut matting and half-a dozen packets of something called Rudell's Salts that claimed to 'comfort tired feet'; because the passage between the front door and the kitchen was paved with red brick and our feet had become so bruised from walking back and forth on it that we could hardly stand up. The coconut matting was a tremendous success, but the Rudell's Salts a disaster; for though they were undoubtedly comforting to soak tired feet in, they merely softened the wretched things and turned them into cissies instead of toughening them up to take more punishment — as Bets and I had done for ours when we ran bare-foot at Okhla. Oh, darling Okhla! — would we ever see you again? It seemed highly unlikely, and there were days when, staring out through a thin curtain of drizzle at the row of small, smug and almost identical suburban houses that faced ours on the other side of the wet grey street, I felt as though I would have sold my soul for the sight of a hot, silver sandbank with a row of mud-turtles basking at the water's edge, or the blaze of crimson and purple bougainvillaeas pouring over a whitewashed wall. '*No more, no more, the folly and the fun: our little day was brave and gay, but now it's done!*' Was it *really* all over and done with? Would I never get back, ever? I couldn't and wouldn't believe it.

Tacklow bought each of us a season ticket to Kew Gardens, and since the main gate was so near we spent a lot of our spare time there; mostly in the enormous glass hot-houses where the tropical plants grew, which provided a lovely bolt-hole on wet or windy days. The gardens were really charming, and armed with those season tickets we almost felt as though they belonged to us. But I was more interested in Kew Palace than the gardens, and liked to imagine Queen Caroline and her children walking along the gravel paths between the formal flowerbeds, or taking the air on the terraces while her husband, the dotty King George III, chased Fanny Burney through the ornamental shrubberies. But my chief recollection of that time is of Susan ...

Susan was our cook-general, a large, fat and comfortable woman with a bright red face and a heart of the purest gold, who came to the house for five or six hours every day except Sundays. She had, she told us, been 'walkin' out', with someone she always referred to as 'my intended', for three years; but though still not officially engaged, she remained blithely optimistic that they would get married 'one of these days'. When dressed in her Sunday best (Sunday was the day on which she 'walked out' with her swain) she was a truly impressive sight. She asked Mother to take a photograph of her 'in me best' and was so pleased with the result that she had an enlargement done for her intended. We learned a lot about him and were enthralled by her stories and her glowing description of this paragon; though we never actually met him and there were times when I wondered if he really existed or if she had made him up. I hope he was real and that he did marry her in the end. She deserved to be happy. And in addition to that heart of gold, he would have won himself a first-class cook!

Not that Susan's knowledge of culinary matters did not have its limits, for I remember Mother staring in surprise at some peculiar off-white substance that lay scattered all over the rubbish heap in a corner of the garden, and on stooping down to take a closer look, realizing with horror that it consisted of a pound of recently purchased and very expensive ground almonds that she had bought to make marzipan for the Christmas cake. 'Oh *no*!' wailed Mother and rushed off to the kitchen to inquire how it got there ...'*That* stuff?' said Susan comfortably, 'oh, you don't 'ave to worry about that, m'lady, it's only a lot of mouldy breadcrumbs wot I found in one of them tins o' yours.' It seems that she had never come across ground almonds before. She also had an endearing habit of advising Mother, whom she insisted on addressing as 'm'lady', on what she should and should not eat, and I well remember the day when my parents entertained a small but distinguished gathering of the Heaven-Born to luncheon, and Susan, dumping down a dish before Mother, said in an encouraging but painfully audible whisper: '*Rhubarb,* m'lady — so good for yer bowels!' And on a similar occasion, warning her that there were spring onions in the salad, adding the loudly whispered admonition: 'You be careful now, m'lady; they do *repeat* so!' Mother did not think it was nearly as funny as we did.

One of the few things that I learned from our stay in that really horrid little house was to be very careful in the matter of interior decoration. There was only one bathroom in the house, and since the bath (an old-fashioned iron affair standing on claw feet) was badly discoloured, we tried scrubbing it with something in a packet that was supposed to make bathrooms and kitchens 'sparkling white in next to no time'. As that didn't work, we bought a tin of white gloss paint and a brush and gave it a couple of coats, one on each of two consecutive days, and were charmed with the result; the dingy old relic looked spanking new. Unfortunately, we hadn't realized that we should have made the coats of paint far thinner, instead of sloshing them on with a fairly lavish hand; for as a result of this error the paint slithered unobtrusively down the sides to settle a good deal more thickly on the bottom. The surface felt perfectly dry when we ran a hand over it before putting on that second coat (which naturally obeyed the laws of gravity and did the same thing), and as we admired our handiwork, we had no idea that though the paint on the sides was paper thin there was a lake of it on the bottom; smooth and shining and, on the surface, as dry as a bone. We gave it two days in which to dry out, just to be on the safe side, and then, since we reckoned that the Master of the House had probably suffered the most from having to strip-wash at a basin, we gave Tacklow the honour of the first bath ...

The water, which came from one of those terrifying gas-powered geyser things, was steaming hot, and Tacklow lowered himself gratefully into it: and stuck fast to the bottom. It took his united family to get him out again, mainly because we were all rolling about with laughter, and to this day I can't think how he managed to escape with a whole skin. We had begun to think that we'd have to send for a doctor and a plumber to pry him loose, when the bath suddenly released its grip on him and he was free. After which we left it severely alone for a few more bathless days, and had no more trouble with it — if you don't count the fact that it bore the clear and unmistakable imprint of Tacklow's posterior, stamped as firmly on it as the hand-print of some film-star on the concrete slabs in front of Grauman's Chinese Theatre in Hollywood. Nothing short of a sand-blaster would have removed it, so we left it alone. And since that bath was the kind that was made to last, it may still be around; though I doubt it, for all the spare iron that England possessed — including the beautiful gates and railings of her public parks and gardens — was melted down to make guns during the early years of the Second World War.

The next Do-It-Yourself interior decorating disaster cannot be blamed on anyone but myself. Given permission to do what I liked with my own bedroom, I looked out at the rain and fog of what was proving, even for England, to be an exceptionally lousy spring, and decided that a bit of sunshine was what was needed to brighten up the general greyness. I therefore painted every inch of wall-space and every scrap of woodwork, including the furniture, a cheerful shade of yellow; made myself matching cotton curtains and bedspread, and wheedled Mother into buying me a set of bright yellow china for the washstand. I can't remember what we did about the carpet, but I bet I insisted on that being yellow too. It certainly brightened up the room and seemed to make it a lot warmer and cosier. But Mother Nature, suddenly deciding to make up for that dreary spring, gave us a really good summer and threw in a heatwave for good measure. My yellow room became a furnace and I swear that the colour sent the temperature up by at least ten degrees; I could feel that glare of yellow even at night when the lights were out and my eyes closed. I learned a lot from that room about the use and misuse of colour, and found that the knowledge came in very handy in future years.

✗ Editing *The Near East and India* kept Tacklow occupied and interested; though I don't imagine it paid very well. However, every little helped, and he must have been grateful for it. But he still hankered for green spaces and quiet, and in spite of our proximity to Kew's famous Gardens, soon grew tired of that poky little semi-detached house with its pocket-handkerchief lawn and single flowerbed; so he advertised for an 'unfurnished house to rent in the country, within easy commuting distance from London, required by retired Indian Army Officer and family of four' — he put in that last because he said it would stop people with two-bedroomed cottages, or those who wanted exorbitant rents, from replying.

His advertisement drew a surprisingly large number of answers and we spent a good many weekends driving around the outskirts of London looking at dozens of houses; none of them quite what we wanted. And then one day a middle-aged couple called on us at the Kew house and explained that they had answered Tacklow's advertisement, and had been greatly taken by the fact that he had bothered to reply. (He had thanked them for their letter and said that, though their house sounded charming, he much regretted that his Indian service pension wouldn't run to paying the rent they were asking.) They had both decided that he was the kind of tenant they wanted, so would he please come and look at the house before deciding that he couldn't afford it? Their car was large enough to take us all, and it would not take long to drive there and back again. Tacklow protested that they would only be wasting their time since he truly could not afford their price, but in the end, because we liked them and they insisted, we went with them: 'but only to look at it'! And that was how we came to live in Three Trees.

We had honestly meant just to look at it and to enjoy the drive. But it turned out to be one of those houses which welcome you with open arms and in which you immediately feel at home and comfortable. The Chinese have a name for that; they call it *Feng Shui,* which means the spirit of a house. Or its soul, if you like. They believe that every house has one and that it is vital for one's happiness and well-being to live in a house whose *Feng Shui* is right for you. No true son or daughter of the Celestial Kingdom would dream of building a house without a priest or an astrologer deciding which way it should face in order to have the right earth currents and the right spirit. And as one who loved China and anything Chinese, Tacklow was a great believer in *Feng Shui,* and Three Trees possessed that intangible asset not only for him but for all of us.

The house stood on the edge of a park in the grounds of what had once been a stately home, Hillingdon Court near Uxbridge, whose owners, like the owners of many of England's great houses, had been so badly hit by the First World War that they could no longer afford to keep it up and were forced to sell. The house itself had been bought for a nunnery, and various people had bought plots of ground on the estate on which they built houses for themselves. A good many of the plots, including the one on the left of the house, were still not built upon, while the park on its right was to remain a park for good — or that was the idea at the time. Three Trees, like most of the other houses on the estate, was a modern one and it had been built with love by the daughter and son-in-law (or perhaps the son and daughter-in-law?) of the middle-aged couple who had driven us over. The son (or son-in-law) had been in the Navy, and he and his wife had planned the house for several years; cutting out from magazines of the *Homes and Gardens* genre anything that appealed to them, and designing their dream house to be just that: a dream. They had found an architect who was as enthusiastic as they themselves were, and who managed to incorporate everything they wanted in the house they meant to bring up their children in and live in for the rest of their lives. And then, when it was finished down to the last lick of paint, and all they had to do was furnish it and move in, something happened ...

After all these years I can't remember what it was. A car crash, perhaps? Anyway, an accident of some kind in which they were fortunate enough to die together. Their house passed to their grieving parents, who could not bear to live in it: and in any case did not want to, since they had their own house. Yet they could not bring themselves to sell it, so they decided to let it unfurnished until they had made up their minds what to do with it. But they wanted a certain kind of person to take it and not just anyone: no one that the two young people who had built it would not have liked. They had already turned down several applicants when they had seen Tacklow's advertisement, and something about the letter he sent them in reply to theirs had made them decide to drive over to Kew and see him, and if they liked him, to urge him just to come and look at the house.

He looked and was lost. He couldn't afford the rent they were asking, but he went up on his maximum figure and they went down on their minimum one, and we furnished Three Trees and settled down to ... what? To live happily ever after? I think that is what Tacklow would have liked to do; for in spite of its sad history, no trace of sadness lingered in any corner of the rooms or the garden of that pleasant, friendly house; and had it not been for us — Mother, Bets and myself — I believe he would have been only too happy to end his days there. Perhaps if he had been able to buy it — ? But he could not possibly afford to do so. And anyway it was not for sale at that time, so there was never any question of our being able to own it. Then there was the added expense of having to furnish it; for apart from pictures and ornaments, a few rugs, and things like china and glass, a certain amount of silver and masses of books, we hadn't a chair or a table to our name, let alone beds and cupboards and all the hundred-and-one things that one needs when moving into an empty house.

Bets went back to school and Bill went off to Woolwich; and Mother and I took on all the cooking and housework, because what with buying furniture and paying more than we had meant to for the rent, we could not afford a 'daily', let along a living-in cook-general. I well remember the horror with which I noticed for the first time that Mother's pretty hands had become red and wrinkled from washing dishes and scrubbing floors. And the day that the first of our neighbours decided to pay a call on Lady Kaye, and Mother, who had been in the kitchen cleaning the silver — or to be strictly accurate, the silver plate — answered the doorbell wearing a duster tied round her head, a vast and rather grubby cooking apron over her dress, and with her hands blackened and her face liberally adorned by the dark smudges that an amateur at the job is apt to acquire when first trying her hand at cleaning either silver or brass.

Confronted by two elderly, grey-haired ladies dressed in their best, hatted and gloved, armed with calling cards and inquiring in impeccable upper-class accents if her mistress was at home, Mother said baldly: 'Yes.' And, having ushered them into the drawing-room, fled upstairs, whipped off duster and apron, washed her hands and face and applied a dab of powder and lipstick, and returned after a few minutes looking as serene as any lady of leisure, apologizing for keeping them waiting. Believe it or not, they never realized that the 'maid' and the 'mistress' were one and the same. Either because they were very short-sighted or, more likely, because they belonged to an earlier generation in which 'the gentry' often did not notice servants.

Mother was no cook. Nor was I much better at that time. But we learned — the hard way. At first the number of dishes that were taken straight from the stove to the dustbin was shaming and Mother was often reduced to tears; not because of the failures, but because of the waste of money. When we spoiled food we either made do with a 'ploughman's lunch' of bread and cheese and pickles, or something out of a tin. But in time we both became pretty good cooks. We also discovered the value of a haybox, which is something I earnestly recommend to anyone who is bothered about electricity bills. We made a double one for ourselves out of one of the wooden boxes in which groceries were delivered in those days, lining it, including the lid, with odd bits of material padded with hay, and then filling it with more hay in which we made two nests, each one big enough to put a covered saucepan in, and finally making another hay-filled cushion to lay on top of them. For those who don't know how to use a haybox, you bring to the boil a saucepan full of stew, porridge, lentils, soup-bones or anything that needs long, slow cooking, cover it and put it into the nest in the hay, place the padded cushion on top, shut the lid and leave it alone overnight. By morning it's cold but perfectly cooked, and all you need do is heat it up. Simple! A saver of time and temper as well as a money-saver if ever there was one, since the stuff in your saucepan can't burn, scorch or boil over, and doesn't need to be watched.

We still had our failures, though. There was the sad case of a

Christmas plum-pudding, made in September because Aunt Lizzie (who gave us her special recipe) told us that the longer you kept it the better; and certainly her own Christmas puddings were the best ever. Unfortunately she was getting very old, and her handwriting had always been early Victorian — very spidery and with a tendency to write her s's as f's — and she had written 'tbs' (tablespoon) instead of 'tsp' (teaspoon). Any experienced cook would have spotted the mistake at once, because it referred to black treacle: '4 tbs black treacle'. Alas, we were only amateur cooks learning by trial and error, and since black treacle is extremely thick and gooey it didn't occur to either of us that four tablespoonfuls of the stuff was far too much. (The mixture seemed stiff enough, goodness knows!) Only when Christmas Day came round and, after boiling it up for the correct number of hours, we attempted to decant it from its bowl and display it in all its glory, did disaster strike. For the treacle having melted, the pudding streamed out in a dark, relentless flood, filling the plate, pouring over the edge onto the kitchen table and from there, within seconds, onto the floor, like lava from an active volcano. Table and floor were awash with the ghastly stuff before we could collect our wits and transfer our sticky Vesuvius to the sink — which in turn filled up. You wouldn't have thought it *possible* that one fair-sized pudding-basin could have contained so much, and I am sorry to report that we received neither help nor sympathy from the non-cooking members of the family who were too busy falling about with laughter.

Mother, frugal to the last, rescued all she could of the liquid pudding and served it up for luncheon for weeks afterwards with flour, breadcrumbs, rice or broken biscuits mixed into the lava to thicken it. It was like that apricot year at Oaklands all over again, and very nearly succeeded in putting us all off Christmas pudding for life.

We were not the only people to have culinary problems, for Mother reported that she and Tacklow, while shopping in Oxford Street, had bumped into Sir Charles Cleveland, now retired and living in a small flat in London. It had been a joyful meeting and they had taken him into the nearest café for lunch and heard all about his struggles with cookery: an art that he too was in the process of mastering on the basis of trial and error. He had instanced the 'Case of the Vanishing Mushrooms', a pound of which he had recently bought off a street barrow. The barrow-boy had told him that a child could cook them —

all that was needed was a frying-pan and some butter, 'and Bob's yer uncle!' — and following these instructions Sir Charles had dumped the entire bag of mushrooms, plus a good dollop of butter, into a frying-pan and had left them to get on with it. On returning he discovered that the mushrooms had absorbed the butter: and they continued to do so in a manner which suggested that they drank the stuff. In the end they shrivelled up into no more than a teaspoonful of small, rubbery flakes of blackness. He found it very disheartening.

This meeting happened on the same day that my parents, returning on the Underground, met another old friend: an ex-Governor of Assam, also retired, who recalled wistfully that on the last occasion that they met he was on an official visit to the Viceroy and had arrived in Calcutta in the Governor's private yacht, to travel up to Simla in a special train complete with platoons of ADCs, assorted hangers-on and acres of red carpet. And now here he was, fighting for a strap on the Underground!

Five days a week, Monday to Friday, except when the Studio was closed for the holidays, I would accompany Tacklow up to London. Leaving together after an early breakfast, we would take a short-cut across the park to the railway station, where we could catch a Metropolitan train to Baker Street: that long, wide street that runs off Oxford Street and is known all over the world because Sherlock Holmes and his friend Dr Watson had rooms in one of the houses that line either side of it. Here our ways parted; Tacklow boarding a bus that would take him to his office and I another that would take me in the opposite direction to Chelsea and the Studio in Park Walk, just off the King's Road. A few hours later we would meet again for a snack lunch at the Kardomah Café in Piccadilly, opposite the Burlington Arcade. And at five o'clock we would make for Baker Street once more to catch a home-bound train and walk back in the dusk across the park to Three Trees.

The Kardomah Café sold and served wonderful coffee, but the thing I liked it for most was the fascinating mural that decorated the walls of the long, narrow, table-filled room. It was painted in the style of Sir Edward Burne-Jones and illustrated the story of Briar Rose, the Princess who pricked her finger on a spindle and fell asleep for a hundred years. I cannot believe that it was by the hand of the great man himself, for if so it would have cost a fortune. But whoever

414

painted it must have been an admirer of the Pre-Raphaelites and a considerable artist in his own right, because its decorative style would have done credit to William Morris, let alone Burne-Jones. I never grew tired of looking at it, and many years later was saddened by the discovery that both the Kardomah and its excellent coffee had vanished from Piccadilly; and with it the enchanted world of the Princess and her courtiers lying asleep among the formalized sprays and tendrils of the encroaching briars. As the Pre-Raphaelites had, at that time, gone so completely out of fashion that you could have bought one of their paintings for peanuts, it is just possible that a masterpiece by one of their lesser lights could have been wrecked in the process of pulling down the Kardomah to make way for another shop. I wonder if anyone else still remembers that mural?

Those daily journeys to London and back became a familiar and pleasant routine which, apart from my Studio holidays, was broken only once; by the General Strike that stunned the whole country in the spring of 1926. Looking back on those days I have the impression that the great majority of the public were taken completely by surprise and could not really believe that such a thing had actually happened. No one seemed to want it, apart from a small group of union militants, and a corresponding number of high-spirited chinless wonders of the P. G. Wodehouse variety who appear to have regarded it as an opportunity for a glorious rough-house on the lines of a Varsity Rag Week. Presumably a lot of people must have seen it coming, but I suspect that most people at that time were, like myself, deeply uninterested in politics. I certainly do not remember seeing anyone in the third-class carriages in which Tacklow and I, and thousands of our fellow commuters, travelled daily to London, reading anything but the sports pages of their newspapers. And that is something that I can swear to, because in the run-up to the strike, when the trains were overcrowded and I was feeling bored by the sea of newspapers that restricted my view, I used to try and read over the shoulders of my nearest neighbours; only to discover, time after time, that they were reading about football or cricket, boxing, racing or tennis. Even Tacklow, who read *The Times,* seemed far more interested in its crossword puzzles — which were new things in those days and tiresomely full of obscure quotations from Horace. But then half Tacklow's editorial job consisted of reading newspapers from all over the world, so I suppose doing *The Times* crossword during the daily journey to London provided a welcome break. I knew that he had been worried about the possibility of a General Strike and took an extremely serious view of a situation for which he blamed the Government, who should, he considered, have been aware of the despair, resentment and anxiety that had been building up among the unemployed, and done something about it instead of adopting a policy of 'Don't look round and perhaps it will go away!'

Had it not been for that new invention the 'crystal set', which made the absence of newspapers no more than a minor irritation, I suspect that the strike would have had far more impact, for with the nation deprived of all news, rumour would have taken over. Which would have made the situation ten times worse, since rumour is always scare-mongering and frequently wildly inaccurate. As it was, the Government controlled the air waves and put out frequent news bulletins; and since anyone who hadn't got a crystal set of their own knew someone who had, people could always cluster round the nearest available one when the bulletins were put out, to learn what was going on and be urged by a hearty voice, speaking through a barrage of squawks, squeaks and crackling, not to panic, to keep calm and ride out the storm — or whatever — and assuring everyone that everything was under control.

Those wirelesses, like the radios in the Second World War, made a great difference to the nation's morale; as did the scores of light-hearted 'strike jokes' that were soon in circulation; most of them concerned with the antics of the Bertie Wooster-type strike-breakers. There was the one about the youthful undergraduate who in his capacity of volunteer engine-driver succeeded in bringing his train into Basingstoke station. To the dismay of the would-be passengers who packed the platform, waiting to board it, the train passed slowly through with its driver leaning from the cab yelling: 'Don't worry! — I'll be back for you as soon as I find out how to stop this damned thing!'

The country refused to panic and there were surprisingly few ugly incidents. Strikers and strike-breakers alike kept their cool and remained firmly and staunchly British and proud of it. The bloodshed and civil war that had been predicted never occurred, largely because the British of that day were still at heart a law-abiding lot who did not approve of violence. Or of civil war either. So when the Liberal leader, Sir John Simon (later Viscount Simon), who was reputed to be the greatest living authority on law, declared the General Strike to be illegal, the nation took a hasty step back from the brink, and the TUC decided to call the whole thing off.

Considering my indifference to politics, it is odd that the two things I remember most clearly about our time at Three Trees should be the General Strike and the introduction of what was known as 'the dole'. And I only remember the dole because of Tacklow's reaction to it. On the day it became law, after listening to the news on the wireless he went out and spent a long time walking slowly up and down the short gravel drive. And during the rest of that day he hardly talked at all; which was not all that unusual, for as I have said, he was a quiet man. But the next morning, after having read the morning papers, he became — even for him — unusually silent and absent-minded. Knowing that he was troubled, I followed him when he went out again to pace to and fro under the three pine trees that gave the house its name, and when I asked him what was the matter he looked at me for what seemed a long time and almost as though he had not heard what I said, and then at last he said: 'This dole business.'

I suppose I must have looked blank, for he explained what it was, and said that it sounded such a marvellous idea. So civilized and humanitarian: something that should have been done long ago, since it was not right that in a country as rich as ours a person should starve and be driven to beg or steal for food, merely because he could not find work or was sick. That was shameful and barbaric, and now it would stop. But all the same, 'I think this may well be the end of us,' said Tacklow. 'Unless they handle it right, this could be the beginning of the end of Britain.' When I asked how (for it seemed to me to be a wonderful scheme), he said that unless the dole was tied to the Labour Exchanges it would end by rotting us. That if a jobless person was offered a job and turned it down, not because he couldn't do it but because he 'didn't fancy it', then he should not be given the dole. If there was no work available, then it was only fair that someone who needed it should be given enough money to keep themselves and their dependants from want. But once dole money was handed out to people who turned down available jobs, we would stop being Great Britain. 'Because,' said Tacklow, 'if people can turn down a job and still get the dole, a day is going to come when everyone who is working will, in effect, be supporting several who are not — for the money will have to come from *somewhere*; and that somewhere will be taxes. Then when India gets her freedom — which she must do very soon — all the Colonies will start demanding theirs; and we shall give it to them because we are beginning to think that having colonies is not such a good idea. But when we lose India, and eventually all the rest of the Empire, we shall no longer be the rich and powerful country that we are now. And since the cost of living is always going up, and never down, it won't be long before a sum that at present a family can manage to live and save on will not be enough to feed a rabbit!'

Tacklow said that when that happened the dole would have to be increased to keep pace with inflation; until in the end it wouldn't be worth anyone's while to do any of the small but necessary jobs unless they were paid more — perhaps a good deal more! — for doing them than they could get on the dole for doing nothing. Since the general public wouldn't be able to afford to pay them that sort of money, they would take the dole instead; and presently hordes of immigrants who couldn't make a living in their own countries would come hurrying over to ours to get a share of the bonanza. Then the next generation would start thinking, and saying, that they were 'owed a living' as a human right; which in Tacklow's opinion was something that no human was 'owed' by its own kind — excepting only its parents who, because they brought them into the world, owe it to their children, and to their country, to bring them up to be responsible citizens who know how to stand on their own feet and not stamp on other people's.

Odd to think that although I should remember so clearly everything that Tacklow said that day as we walked to and fro under those three tall pine trees, I did not realize, until long after he was dead, that though he had in a sense been 'dreaming true' — as he had done twice before when he dreamt the winner of the Derby days before the race was even run — he failed to foresee another and more immediate threat. The then unthinkable one of another world war that would deliver a far worse blow to his country's power and prestige, let alone her riches, than the first had done, and be the means of hastening the disintegration of the Empire on which, like the one that Spain had once possessed, 'the sun never set'.

It has set now. But if historians of the future have the courage to resist the pressures that will be put upon them by the rulers or dictators of their respective countries to re-write history to suit their nationals (you should see some of the stuff that is already being written — how George Orwell would have laughed!), then a time may come when the world will look back on the era of the Pax Britannica as a golden age, and not, as the present tendency seems to be, a dark, disgraceful period of brutal colonial suppression.

Chapter 26

❧⋘⋙❧

Wilt thou be gone? It is not yet near day ...

Shakespeare, *Romeo and Juliet*

When I read any book set in the period between the two world wars, I realize how important a part the General Strike of 1926 played in the history of Britain. Tacklow had given me a strong interest in history, starting me off at a very early age on *Little Novels of English History* and telling me riveting tales of India's past which for action, zip, intrigue, goriness and glamour outdid anything that our forefathers in the United Kingdom ever got up to. Yet despite this I was at the time of the strike (and to a great extent have remained) uninterested in contemporary history. (Unless, of course, it happens to be written up by someone like A. J. P. Taylor, who not only writes as Tacklow spoke, but — if my television set is to be trusted — speaks with his voice, stands as he did, uses his hands in the same way and even *looks* a little like him.)

The reason for this incuriousness must I suppose be because, like so many of us, I find it difficult to think of something that is actually happening here and now as History with a capital H. And also because something that is happening today invariably becomes political. If it's bad, whatever Government happens to be in power gets the blame, while if it's good they grab the credit — even if it's only a matter of a record harvest which is in fact due to the weather! The General Strike therefore meant little to me beyond preventing me from getting to the Studio, which I resented. But then I could always carry on drawing at home; and did. I put in a lot of drawing at Three Trees; and because Bets was still at The Lawn, Bill at The Shop, Tacklow (also housebound by the strike) busy writing articles and editing in his study while Mother coped with cooking, washing, ironing and all

420

the other endless chores that come under the heading of 'housework', I had to use myself as a model, with the aid of the full-length looking-glass on the inner side of my cupboard door or the triple mirror on Mother's dressing-table. Which is why, to this day, the type of face I find easiest to draw is my own.

I enjoyed my time at the Studio, and since the teachers knew their job my work began to improve; though in fact I learnt less from them than from my fellow students. It was both an education and a revelation to see how someone else handled a subject or an object that I myself was looking at and struggling to put onto paper; while the totally different way in which others obviously *saw* exactly the same thing intrigued me enormously. It taught me to look at everything with a new eye, and it was my good fortune to have, for a term or two, three fellow students who were, in partnership, to become famous as theatrical designers under the name of 'Motley': Peggy and Audrey Harris and Elizabeth Montgomerie. The last in particular taught me that if you are bold enough you can put together colours that clash wildly with each other, and make them look marvellous. One of their first successes was the job of designing and making the costumes for *Richard of Bordeaux,* a play starring the young John Gielgud. It was an enormous success, and those three girls produced the costumes for it on a shoestring budget, co-opting members of the studio to stencil medieval patterns in gold, silver and a variety of colours onto the cheapest and heaviest materials available, and making the stuff look like hand-woven brocades and tapestries. The result had to be seen (and touched) to be believed, and it is nice to know that the name of Motley will go down in theatrical history.

Another student, again a girl, with the unusual name of Merlyn Mann, was so good and so individual in style that I confidently expected her to end up among the greats. One of her pen-and-ink drawings was hung in the Royal Academy when she was only sixteen, and when she suddenly took a dislike to an unfinished one and tossed it into the Studio's wastepaper bin, I snatched it out; much to her disgust. 'You *can't* like that,' said Merlyn, 'it's a mess!' But I managed to flatten it out with an iron and had it framed, and I have it to this day — or rather my younger daughter has it now, because she liked it as much as I did. Merlyn's trouble was that she was too good. She needed an old-fashioned 'patron' to buy up all her work and make her fashionable. I could sell bits of rubbish for cheap reproduction, but her work called for an expensive book with really beautiful illustrations: the kind of book that people will pay top prices for. I don't know what became of her. Like Tacklow's young genius who broke the Playfair cipher, she seems to have vanished from the public eye without trace.

The Miss MacMunn who owned and ran the Studio had a brother in the Army (Lieutenant-General Sir George MacMunn, KCB, KCSI, DSO, no less!) whose wife, dear Lady MacMunn, was excessively stout and shaped rather like the Victorian idea of an operatic diva. Back in Simla, her three rickshaw men had been known as Faith, Hope and Charity; the one who pushed at the back being Faith, because Faith, we are told, can move mountains. Lord Reading, a man not noted for a sense of humour, said of her that she was an admirable woman, 'but I do wish,' he said — extending his finger and thumb at arm's length in front of him — 'that she would not wear a carnation out *here*'. He was also rumoured to have made her the subject of his only known joke. Some energetic do-gooder in authority had decided that it would be a good idea to replace the noonday gun, that told the city it could knock off for luncheon, with a siren instead; and on the first occasion that it sounded, his Lordship, caught unawares by its eldritch shriek, leapt in his chair and exclaimed: 'Good heavens, someone must have stuck a pin into Emily!'

Everyone liked Emily MacMunn. But her George was a terrible old bore, and having known him from early on, I was all in favour of avoiding the lecture on Art (with lantern-slides) he was billed to give at the Studio in the afternoon of a half-holiday. The students, who were clearly expected to attend, were invited to bring relatives and friends with them, and typed leaflets announcing this, plus the subject, date and time of the lecture, were distributed to one and all. Tacklow announced firmly that he would, most unfortunately, be *far* too busy on the sixth — er, seventh? — to be able to take the afternoon off (shades of his father!). But Mother, who was fond of Lady MacMunn, insisted on going and taking me with her. We arrived late, and as the lights (with the exception of a single spotlight focused on the speaker) had already been switched off, we groped our way in the gloom to a couple of empty chairs amid a chorus of *shhh*-ing to which the General, already in full flight, paid no attention.

The subject of his lecture had been advertised as 'Art in the Middle East' (which apparently included India and Greece). But in fact it turned out to be largely about himself, and he had arranged for one of the second-year students, a fat, phlegmatic girl in spectacles, to man the magic lantern and change the slides every time he thumped twice on the floor of the model's platform with the stick that he was using as a pointer. Apart from one or two of the slides appearing on the screen upside down (his fault, not hers, since he had loaded the boxes of slides), this arrangement worked well. All the slides were of course in black-and-white, and many of them had been taken by the General himself. But he had managed to appear in all the others, posing in a martial manner in front of famous ruins; Roman, Greek, Persian and Egyptian, as well as the occasional shot of a Hindu temple or a Moslem mosque.

His method of lecturing was simple. Having introduced himself to his audience and told us that he was only a bluff old soldier, but by jove, he knew what he liked when he saw it, and that his career having taken him out into the furthest parts of our far-flung Empire he had been fortunate enough to see many wonderful works of art, he paused and gave the floor two sharp taps with his stick. There followed a whirring noise, a glare of white light, and a photograph of the Sphinx being upstaged by the General appeared on the screen. He then told us how he, not the Sphinx, came to be there and we heard a bit about his war experiences in Mesopotamia, which seemed slightly odd considering that the Sphinx ... oh well, forget it. When he had said everything he could think of about the Sphinx he tapped again and we got the 'rose-red city — half as old as Time', and another view of the General. And so it went on. Drone, drone, drone, blither, blither, blither '... er — um — well I think that's all I can tell you about *that*'; tap, tap, and the slide would vanish and be replaced by another. By endless others ...

Since almost everyone smoked in that age of the cigarette, the atmosphere in the darkened studio became more and more hazy and hotter and stuffier with every crawling minute. The seats of the cheap wooden chairs, hired for the occasion, grew increasingly hard and uncomfortable and the audience became noticeably restless as the Lecturer ploughed on with all the determination of an elephant fording a river in flood. Presently, as yet another slide appeared on the screen, a voice from somewhere ahead of us murmured as though unconsciously speaking a thought aloud: 'Can't *stand* any more of this!' and an enormous, shadowy figure surged up from its seat and made for the door. 'That's Emily!' said Mother, instantly recognizing the shape and size of that familiar outline. And rising in her turn she followed the Lecturer's Lady out into the fresh air.

I would have given much to follow them; and so it seemed, from the number of turned heads and envious profiles, would many others. However, good manners prevailed and we stuck it out through a series of Persian tiles, Coptic frescoes and bits of Babylon, until it petered out — literally. The General, having talked for a good five minutes about a slide showing some battered fragment of statuary dug up by someone or other from the ruins of Troy or Abydos or somewhere, ran out of things to say about it and thumped the signal for the next slide. Nothing happened. He thumped again, louder this time. Still no response. 'Another slide, please!' barked the General in parade-ground tones, repeating his thumps for the third time. 'There aren't any more,' announced the operator flatly. And with that the lecture ended, and I collected Mother and Lady MacMunn from the courtyard, where they had been having a cosy gossip in the dusk while the shops and street lamps of Chelsea lit up around them.

Miss MacMunn had laid on tea and biscuits for the exhausted audience, and afterwards Mother and I caught a bus to Baker Street where we met Tacklow. And all the way back to Three Trees Mother talked of the places and people that she and Emily had been reminiscing about: re-telling scraps of the gossip of Northern India that either Emily or George had told her that afternoon, until I could have wept from homesickness. All through my schooldays I had been sure that once school was over I would be able to go home to India again. And when Tacklow retired and that hope died, I used to tell myself that if I worked hard at art and saved every penny I made, I would one day be able to pay for a passage back to Bombay and see all my friends, and Delhi and Simla and Okhla again. And put up at Laurie's Hotel at Agra and see dear Miss Hotz, and wait once more at twilight in the quiet gardens of the Taj to see the moon rise over the dusty plains of India and transform that wonder in white marble into something as fragile and shimmering as a soap bubble floating above the shadowy mass of the trees.

So many friends; so many lovely places; so many memories. And so much happiness! It wasn't possible that I should not be able to go back again one day. But when I looked at the work of people like Merlyn and Elizabeth and the Harris sisters — to name only four out of at least half-a-dozen outstanding students at one minor studio — and realized how many studios there were in London alone, I became less confident that I could earn the sort of money I would need to get me back to India. And once again England seemed to grow smaller and to close in on me as it had done on the wet, grey day that the 'Ormond' docked at Tilbury.

✳ Tacklow had acquired a cat in the usual way: attracting a stray. A lean, slinking outlaw, probably descended from some barnyard cat who had kept down the rats in the days when Hillingdon was a great house. This shy and unattractive moggy lived in a small, dense wood of lilac trees opposite the garage and the woodshed at Three Trees, keeping body and paws together by preying on the rabbits, birds and rodents that inhabited our garden and the Park. Bets and I had long been aware of a pair of hostile yellow eyes in a whiskered, sandy-coloured face, glaring at us from the undergrowth below the lilacs, and once I had seen the cat trotting across the drive carrying the corpse of a rabbit, almost as large as itself, in exactly the way that a tiger carries its prey. But if we called to it or made any move in its direction, it was off like a flash.

Tacklow never really wanted a cat. It was always the cats who wanted Tacklow, and this one was no exception. It took to watching him as he strolled round the garden of an evening, and when he spoke politely to it, it stood its ground instead of instantly nipping back into cover as it did when anyone else addressed it. Eventually it came out to share his walk, and ended up feathering his ankles and purring when he tickled it under the chin. It never allowed us to do more than stroke it — and that only occasionally — and made no attempt to venture into the house. Nor did Tacklow encourage it to do so; which surprised me a little since he had already dubbed it Chips. But he said that for its own sake it would be kinder to let it remain an outdoor cat. Did he, I wonder, have a premonition that our stay in Three Trees would not be long, and that when we left it could be for somewhere where we could not take a cat with us?

The Hillingdon Chips remained an outdoor cat; catching her own meals and fending for herself even in the worst of weather, until, on a spring morning when the lilac wood was a blaze of mauve and white and purple blossom that smelt as though you had drenched it with bottles and bottles of *Temps de Lilas* — a once popular scent made by Messrs Houbigant of Paris — Tacklow went out to the woodshed to cut some more kindling for the fire and reached automatically into the trug behind the door in which he kept the small hand-axe. Whereupon the trug exploded like a dropped electric-light bulb, slashing him sharply in the process and giving him the fright of his life. In the next second a sandy-coloured strip of fur streaked through the half-open door, yowling indignantly. Chips to the rescue! — 'Here come the United States Marines!'

Our moggy had evidently decided that the woodshed, which had an ill-fitting door that allowed her to get in and out of it even when padlocked, was a better place for her kittens than whatever outdoor spot they had been born in; for they had not been there when we last went into the woodshed for kindling, and they were obviously at least ten days old and probably more, since they had their eyes open — and knew how to spit and use their claws! They had attacked Tacklow's intrusive hand with instant fury and whizzed off in different directions to cower among the piles of logs: three minute balls of terrified multicoloured fluff.

Tacklow tied up his hand with his handkerchief and spent a few minutes apologizing to Chips for upsetting her kittens, and smoothing down her bristling fur, before returning to the house to exchange his handkerchief for a strip of plaster and fetch a saucer of milk. I remember saying that Chips would certainly have removed herself and her family by the time he got back, but he only said 'Nonsense, cats always know on which side their bread is buttered.' And sure enough, when we returned to the woodshed Chips had either carried or herded her family back into the trug and was standing guard over them, looking tigerish and wary. The three small, pansy faces spat at the sight of us, and as Chips made one of those disapproving cat noises that are half-way between a growl and a miaow, Tacklow ordered us all back to the house, saying that if we wanted them to stay around we'd better leave them severely alone until they had had time to settle down.

I remember that he spent most of the rest of that day there, merely sitting on a log by the open doorway of the woodshed, reading a newspaper and smoking one of the cheap Indian cheroots he had acquired a taste for as a young subaltern. Chips graciously accepted the saucer of milk and ended up by going to sleep on his knee in the attitude of one of Landseer's Trafalgar Square lions, and by sunset she allowed him to remove the axe from under her kittens. He would not let us go near them and would not handle them himself until he was quite sure that they had accepted him as a friend, and during the next few days he fed them with morsels of raw meat; only when they were no longer afraid of him did he stroke them with a finger. When at length he could pick them up by the scruff of their necks, as Chips did, and dump them on his shoulder or in his lap, he knew that it would be safe to let us play with them. But though all kittens are appealing bits of fluff when they are the size of a bridge roll, these ones, even when small, looked what they were — wild young toughs. For which reason we named them after three of the then best-known stars of cowboy Westerns: Tom Mix, Harry Carey and Buck Jones. Funny that Bets and I should both remember those names still.

Tom Mix, took after his mother, but goodness knows where she picked up his father, for Buck Jones was mainly black with white markings, while Harry Carey was mostly ginger with a white face, one black ear, and a black patch over the opposite eye which gave him a rakish air and was so distinctive that Bets and I, returning close on ten years later on a sentimental journey to see what had become of Hillingdon and dear Three Trees, seeing a cat who had been lying asleep in the long grass at one end of the garden start up and stare at us over the grass, said with one voice: '*Harry Carey!* – it's Harry Carey.' The cat vanished with the speed of light, but there could be no mistaking that cockeyed white face with its rakish black eye-patch and single black ear. Harry C. had obviously returned to the wild and was doing all right, for he looked very stout and sleek; and the sight of him made our day.

Three Trees had not changed; nor had the Park. But there was now a house on the empty plot next door, built on the spot where in our day there had been a ring of tall Scots pines, and all the once vacant plots had been bought and built on. The whole place was beginning to look crammed with houses, but the house opposite Three Trees looked just the same. Back in the Twenties it had belonged to a Colonel Hutchinson who worked for a publicity firm in London and had written a book that had become a terrific best-seller. It was called *The W Plan,* and I remember him telling us, as though it was a tremendous joke, that its success was entirely due to his knowledge of what he called 'the publicity racket'. He had, he said, had the bright idea of having the title of the book in huge print pasted high up along the side of every London bus, and the expense involved had paid off, since you couldn't move in London without seeing THE W PLAN screaming at you from every angle.

He was an amusing and extrovert man, and an excellent neighbour. We got to know him and his wife and young family well, though I have to admit that I thought nothing of his book. He gave us a signed copy of it which unfortunately perished along with all the rest of Tacklow's books.

I can still see him quite clearly in my mind's eye, but though I may not have appreciated his book — which must have been one of the very first to be hyped into best-sellerdom by expert publicity — I thought that his garden must be the most beautiful in all England. It made me wish I could have seen Hillingdon in its great days, for judging by this one, the gardens must have been spectacular. There were, I was told, four separate gardens, each one in a different colour, and our writer friend had bought a large plot that included the whole of the Blue Garden. It was a dream of a garden! A long strip of velvety grass, flanked by wide flowerbeds, led down an avenue of dark, beautifully cut blue-green yew that broke into arches where other walks bisected it. And in the flowerbeds, in every possible shade of blue, grew delphiniums and larkspur, Himalayan poppies, drifts of forget-me-nots and lobelia, clumps of hydrangea, lilacs and hibiscus, violas, lavender, violets and gentians, campanula and clematis, and all the other blue and bluish-mauve flowers you can think of; plus blue-leaved hostas and lots of things with lacy silver-grey foliage and no flowers.

We were told that our lawn had once been part of the Red Garden. But all that remained of that was an overgrown, nettle-filled avenue of Canadian and Japanese maple trees that lay on the other side of the fence at the far end of our lawn, and belonged to the nuns. The trees turned unbelievable shades of crimson and scarlet in the autumn, but the avenue was so choked with weeds and brambles that you could no longer see even a trace of the herbaceous borders that had once lined it. No one seemed to know where the yellow and white gardens had been, and the only one to survive was that magical blue one.

That's about all I remember about the Hillingdon interval; except a couple of pop tunes, one of which, entitled 'When My Sugar Walks Down the Street', was played dangerously near to the point of justifiable homicide by Bill, who was learning to play the banjo — banjos were the 'in' instruments of the Twenties — and this was the only tune he knew. The other, also played to exhaustion by Bill, but on the gramophone, was a ditty called 'Big Bad Bill is Sweet William Now'. I don't know which was worse.

Surprisingly, since he was an exceptionally good-looking youth, Bill had not started collecting girl-friends, so when the time came round for the first Summer Ball at The Shop, I thought for a brief time that he might — just possibly might — ask me to go with him. Unfortunately, he still thought of me as an unalluring schoolgirl; 'Old Piano Legs', in fact; and I don't think that the idea that he might ask me to the ball so much as crossed his mind. However, being partnerless, he asked Mother instead; which turned out to be one of his better ideas, for much to his surprise she was a wild success with his fellow students who couldn't believe that anyone could have a mother as young and pretty and good company as that. She was at the time just short of her thirty-eighth birthday, and except for her once pretty hands could easily have passed for twenty-five.

I remember that she wore a dress Tacklow had seen in the window of a shop in Bond Street, and had thought so pretty that he did what was, for him, an unprecedented thing: he walked straight in and bought it. 'It looked as though it was made out of opals,' explained Tacklow, 'and I couldn't resist it.' He loved opals above all other stones because, he said, they were the only precious stones that couldn't be faked. All the others could be made out of glass and fool nearly everyone; even pearls could be Mikimoto fakes. But not the opal. So he only bought opals for Mother (he could never have afforded to give her emeralds or diamonds, anyway). The dress was made of smoky-blue chiffon and lace embroidered all over with opal-coloured beads and sequins that shimmered when the wearer moved, and Mother wore her opals with it and went off to the ball looking as glamorous as Cinderella. Bill said he nearly burst with pride when his friends vied with each other to dance with her, and that he only managed to get two dances with her himself; and that with difficulty!

As for Mother, she came back looking like a girl again; or a flower that has been drooping for lack of water and is suddenly revived by a shower of rain. She loved to dance; and for the first time I realized how much life must have changed for her and just how much she must miss the gaiety of India — the dances, the lights and the music — the admiration ... Well, all that was finished and done with. For her the party was over. But for Bets and myself it had not yet begun, and there were times when I used to think gloomily that at this rate it would never begin! For we were not in the 'Débutante Set' with the prospect of a London Season ahead. (Few India service people, outside the Heaven-Born, were.) And anyway Tacklow could not have afforded to 'bring us out'. Nor were our present neighbours — the people who had built new houses and settled on the Hillingdon estate — the kind whose drawing-rooms were big enough to use as ballrooms. Besides, they were either too young to have sons and daughters of an age to go to grown-up dances, or elderly couples whose children had long ago left home.

I don't remember meeting anyone in my own age-group while we lived at Three Trees, and the only friend of Bill's whom he ever asked there for the holidays was a boy of his own age, Alexander 'Sandy' Napier; the only child of parents so elderly that they had given up all ideas of having a family when Sandy's arrival took them completely by surprise. Thereafter they had treated him more as though they were his grandparents than his parents — and Victorian grandparents at that. They never seemed to know quite what to do with him, and Sandy began to look on us as his family: an attitude that we reciprocated. He remained an honorary brother for the rest of his days, which I suppose is the reason why neither Bets nor I ever fell in love with him; for he was the dead ringer for that one-time Prince Charming, Edward VIII, Duke of Windsor. So much so that when immediately after the Abdication the new Duke went into hiding, Sandy — who had been posted to Peshawar as Deputy Commissioner — caused a terrific sensation by arriving in that city, driving his very ancient Rolls-Royce. Half the onlookers instantly leapt to the conclusion that this was their ex-King Emperor, who must have decided to take refuge among them. The excitement was intense!

However, all that is by the way, and I merely introduce Sandy at this point because he was to play a large part in our lives.

Apart from Sandy, and the two or three youths who, outnumbered ten to one by young women, were studying art at the Studio in Park Walk, I can't remember meeting any young men during my time at Three Trees. There were a few married ones of course, and perhaps a dozen or so boys ranging from six months to eight or nine years old. But it has to be remembered that the male population of Great Britain had been drastically reduced by the slaughter of the First World War, which had landed the United Kingdom with no less than three million of what the newspapers ungallantly referred to as 'surplus women'. Three million women who would never have a husband, never have a white wedding, a honeymoon or a baby, and never be a grandmother. For it was still a marriage-or-nothing time for us.

With post-war Britain still suffering from a staggering shortage of marriageable men, it was becoming all too clear to me that, short of a miracle, I was bound to join the ranks of those three million surplus if I didn't make a move to escape from my present cosy little rut in the fairly near future. Brother Bill was obviously going to be of no help. And anyway he would soon be heading for India to join a mountain battery stationed on the North-West Frontier — having taken his passing out exams and scraped into the Gunners by the narrowest of margins. Bets, I thought, would probably make it to the altar, since she was far better equipped to be popular with young men than I was.

Bets was a good artist and, if she had only stuck to it, would have been a really good pianist. As it was she could vamp any dance tune, and there are few more popular social assets than that. She was also a good tennis-player, a more than adequate rider who could (if Tacklow had been able to run to keeping a horse, which he couldn't) have developed into an excellent one; and she could both dance and sing. I always thought she would end up in musical comedy, beginning in the chorus and graduating to be a star. I still think she might have done so if things had turned out differently. And if she had been a different kind of person; one with more determination and a harder streak in her character. But there is no steel in Bets's make-up. She had, and still has, an almost pathological fear of rows and loud angry voices, and she would do anything to avoid them; anything at all. Nevertheless I still believe that if we had stayed on at Three Trees she would have found her way into musical comedy and ended up famous. As for me, that miracle I needed turned up after all, in the shape of a letter from the India Office asking Tacklow to return to India and take on the job of revising Aitcheson's Treaties, which were in dire need of an overhaul, having been made way back in the last century, between the British and the rulers of a number of India's Princely States.

Tacklow was happy at Three Trees. His editorial work was interesting and he enjoyed our daily walks through the park, to and from the station, and our lunch-times at the Kardomah. He liked strolling round the garden attended by Hillingdon Chips and her three cowboy kittens, now grown into large and prosperous cats — though still inclined to wear their stetsons well over one eye and be quick on the draw. He liked keeping an eye on the house and seeing that broken gutters were mended before they leaked, and that cracked panes of glass were replaced quickly. Ordinary, everyday things of that sort which he termed 'pottering about'. I vividly remember the day on which he decided to do a bit of pottering in the attic, because I happened to be in bed with a bad cold when he incautiously put a foot on the lath-and-plaster instead of keeping to the beams, and the next second a large chunk of ceiling hit me on the head, nearly laying me out cold. My room dissolved into a maelstrom of dust and plaster, and looking up groggily, I discerned my beloved parent's left leg waving wildly from a hole above me. It took the united efforts of his family to extract him because none of us could stop laughing.

No, I do not think Tacklow wanted to go back to India. But he thought *we* wanted to. And how right he was. Mother had never, to my knowledge, complained. But he must have realized that she could not help missing the gaiety of India; all the parties and dances and shooting-camps, 'the folly and the fun'. And then there were Bets and myself. He knew that the job would not take him away for long: only a little more than a year — if that. But he had already been parted from his children for too long, and neither his wife nor his daughters took kindly to the idea of losing him for another year. I do not think that that last consideration weighed with him as much as one might have expected, for after all, a year was only a year. What did count with him, I suspect, was a combination of three things: Mother's return from that ball at Woolwich, looking as pretty and sparkling as though she had just emerged from a dip in the Fountain of Youth; and by contrast, the way she looked after a hard day's housework when nothing had gone right and she had scalded her hand with boiling water, scorched the front of a newly washed shirt with a too hot iron and burnt the stew: one of *those* days. Then there was the sour aftermath of the General Strike. That too played its part. And finally, the realization that his elder daughter was no longer a child but a young woman, and that the younger one would soon be leaving school. What was he going to do about them?

In his father's day, and his grandfather's, the girls would have been looking forward to 'coming out' with all the fun and festivity that that entailed. But in the post-war world, and on his India service pension, he could neither afford to launch them on a London Season or send them to finishing-schools in France. And who was there for them to marry? His son, whom he barely knew, never brought any of his friends to Three Trees — with the exception of young Sandy who had by now become more or less adopted into the family. And though Bill himself had been invited to débutante dances in country houses and in London (sometimes by people he did not even know!) he had never been asked to take his elder sister along, and as yet she had been invited to few parties and no dances. Anyway, Bill would soon be in Rawalpindi with his Battery ...

Tacklow had always known how Bets and I felt about India, and though he would have preferred to stay on in Three Trees and hope one day to be able to buy it, he decided to accept the job of revising Aitcheson's Treaties and go back there. But not alone. He would take all three of us out with him.

To Bets and myself, and to Mother too, it was like winning the Calcutta Sweep or being given the most marvellous present in the world. I remember wanting to cry and then wanting to run out onto the lawn and scream for joy ... to stick flowers in my hair and dance bare-foot between the trees in the park. It was too good to be true! I remember Mother flinging her arms about Tacklow's neck and bursting into tears while Bets and I hugged each other and any outlying portions of him that we could get at, before dancing round and round the living-room like a pair of demented March hares. That was a truly unforgettable day, 'a day to be marked with a white stone' . . .

Since the revising of Aitcheson's Treaties was only a temporary assignment, the India Office was prepared to pay Tacklow's fare and travelling expenses, but not ours. So he made a last visit to Upton House to see his father and ask for a loan (not an interest-free one either!) to pay for those three extra passages. He might have known that he'd get a dusty answer. Once again the sum was a very modest one, since even in the 1930s one could get a return ticket from England to India for as little as £40, 'tourist class'. And as we were still in the Twenties, the sum required was probably no more than £200 — certainly not more than £300 — and it would have saved Tacklow from having to commute part of his pension; which was the only other way he could raise the extra money. However, my miserly old grandfather turned him down flat; not because he hadn't the money and so couldn't afford it — no, no; he wouldn't have liked anyone to think *that*. But 'as a matter of principle'.

It had been a faint chance, but worth taking. And left with no option, Tacklow duly commuted £100 a year of his pension. He could have done with that extra hundred a year in the days to come, but it paid for our passages and left quite a bit over. Poor Tacklow — darling Tacklow! I have one of his account books in which he wrote down every single one of the pennies he had to count with such care, written in the microscopic handwriting that he had developed because it helped him in decoding ciphers. The sums are so small. And so meticulously listed, down to the last farthing. He really needed to keep track of every penny, for now that he had commuted part of his pension he was left, after tax, with exactly £700 a year for the four of us to live on. This was something that I only discovered much later, because he never talked about money: a legacy from his Victorian youth and childhood I suppose, when men did not talk about money to women and it was considered vulgar to mention it in general conversation.

I don't think even Mother knew how little we had to live on, because he paid all the bills, dealt with all matters of finance and 'managed' somehow. But it must at times have been very difficult, for he never said 'no' unless it was impossible to say 'yes'; and he was incurably generous. He would never lend money to a friend because he held that to do so might lead to losing their friendship and it was always better to give it (if it was there to give) and keep one's friends.

Once, long ago, he had made that mistake when a friend and fellow officer in dire need asked him for a loan. He had instantly cashed in his life insurance — the only savings he had — and handed it over. The recipient, hysterical with relief and gratitude, promised that it would be repaid within a matter of months. It never was. His friend began to avoid him, and shortly afterwards left for England, where he did very well for himself. Some years later, meeting Tacklow by chance in London, he cut him dead.

✳ In the late autumn of that year, AD 1927 of blessed memory, we made ready to sail for Calcutta on the S.S. 'City of London'. Oh joy, oh rapture! We were actually going back to India! I was going home — home — *home!* Only one fly sullied the pure ointment of my joy. My weight.

One of the things that I hoped to find in that much-loved country was Love — conjugal love, naturally. (In those days one took that for granted, though nowadays there would appear to be more options floating around.) I didn't much care who the 'Right Man' for me turned out to be, provided that (a) I could take one look at him and think '*That's* the one!' — and fall in love on sight as Tacklow had done on the platform of Tientsin's railway station. That (b) when (not 'if', you note!) he asked me to marry him, I could reply: 'I'll be ready in five minutes — no, make it three!' And finally (c) that the Someone to Watch Over Me (hopefully for ever) should be in some India service. Tinker, Tailor, Soldier, Sailor, Rich man, Poor man … provided his work lay in India so that I could live there for at least the next thirty years, I couldn't care less.

You may wonder why I didn't come up with the obvious answer: marry an Indian and stay for good. But at that time attitudes and customs that by now have softened to an extent that would have been undreamt of in the first quarter of the twentieth century were still set hard in ancient moulds, so that that particular solution simply did not enter my calculations. Admittedly I had often thought how pleasant it would be to be able to marry into one of the Indian families whose children had been my friends and playmates, and be accepted into their close-knit, loving, bickering, clannish family circle. But I knew only too well that the very idea of an *Angrezi* daughter-in-law would have horrified the parents of any of the Indian children I knew; while as for their grandparents — ! To the older generation I would always be a casteless person. Or a *Kafir,* since even the families of my Muslim friends, who were not bothered by caste, would not have cared for the connection.

Possibly, and unfairly, the problems arising from a mixed marriage would have seemed less if it was the husband who was the Westerner and the wife an Indian. Yet even now Western women who marry Eastern men are very rarely ones who have been born and spent their formative years in the East, and who spoke their husband's tongue before their own. Which could be because the native-born knew too much? You cannot have been a child in India, playing with Indian children, talking, thinking, squabbling and making up in their language, not yours, without becoming as aware as they are of the number and importance of religious and social rules that order their lives from birth to death. Taboos that from being handed down by so many successive generations have become, to them, as much a part of their lives as breathing; but which to you, because you are not of their blood, are fatally easy to infringe, however well intentioned you may be.

Much later, I came across several very happy and successful marriages between Western men and Asian women — who make marvellous wives! But not one, the other way round, that has lasted. By the law of averages there must be hundreds that are flourishing; but I am speaking only of those I know. Being native-born, I knew far too much about Indian attitudes to flatter myself by thinking that I could ever make an acceptable or a satisfactory Indian wife. And I also knew that India is a land in which the male is still always in the right. Even though in public its womenfolk may say differently, in private (though they will condole with you) a wife who fails to give her husband a son is still regarded as having let the side down; in addition to giving the poor fellow a valid reason — should he happen to need one — for discarding her and acquiring a newer and younger model. Which has been known to happen; though time changes all things and the future was to see any number of shifts in public opinion that would once have been unthinkable. But as far as this book is concerned I am, for the moment, back in the England of the 1920s. Still gazing mournfully at the reflection of my over-generous contours, mercilessly displayed in one of those hideous Twenties bathing-suits in a looking-glass at

Three Trees, and thinking what a pity it is that I wasn't born in the days of Rubens or Titian when walloping goddesses and roly-poly nymphs were the fashion.

Unfortunately, never at any previous time had actual thinness, as opposed to slimness, been so fashionable or so highly prized by women as in the decade following the end of the First World War, when suddenly, and for the first time in recorded history, the female of the species discarded long skirts (and with them bosoms, waists and hips), cropped their hair short like boys and strove to look as much like Peter Pan as possible. And but for the systematic stuffing I had received at the hands of well-meaning adults, I too might have rejoiced in the general shape of a stick insect — which had now become the accepted ideal of the 'female form divine', and still is — and been able to face the future with a reasonable amount of confidence.

As it was I had none. When at the early age of fourteen — probably as a result of all this forced feeding — I developed a Dolly Parton bust and begged to be given a proper brassière in order to avoid the embarrassment of pounding down the hockey field or the cricket pitch (how I detested those compulsory games!) with these newly acquired appendages bouncing up and down like marker-buoys in a choppy sea, I was curtly informed that I was far too young for such an adult garment, and made to wear instead a ghastly thing called a 'liberty bodice'. This object merely flattened me down as firmly as the wide bandages that Chinese and Japanese women used to tie tightly about their bodies, from armpits to hips, in order to acquire the pencil-shaped figure that is considered ideal in the Orient — and which enables them to look so enchanting in a *chongsam* or an *obi*: items of attire that, when worn by the possessor of a pair of Western bosoms encased in uplift bras, look anything but attractive.

Alas, those liberty bodices effectively removed my chances of acquiring any natural uplift in later life. Frankly, I drooped (and looked awful in a bathing-suit). And what embittered me further was that anything I asked for, my elders, headed by Aunt Bee, refused to grant me on the grounds that I was 'far too young'. Yet when I finally became old enough to qualify for such things as proper 'bras', high heels, court shoes in place of strapped ones, long evening dresses, lipstick, face-powder, costume jewellery, or permission to stay up late in order to go to a dinner-party or a dance, they were also immediately

437

granted to Bets; this time on the grounds that 'it isn't fair on poor little Bets that you should have them and she should not'! So Bets, my junior by two years, graduated to a bra on the same day as I did: even though she did not need one, being the possessor of an enviable shape. It is no thanks to Aunt Bee, or to Mother either, that I did not grow up to dislike and resent my young sister.

I resented this favouritism all right. Bitterly! But I had the sense to realize that it wasn't Bets's fault, and to put the blame where it belonged. So we remained the best of friends; even when I realized that she would always be more popular than I, since she possessed many more social assets and was always gay, easy-going and good-tempered. Everyone always liked Bets, so I saw nothing odd in the fact that she was Mother's favourite daughter; she was, after all, the baby of the family. And I had Tacklow. Nevertheless I resented those extra years that I had to wait before I was allowed to wear and do grown-up things, only to see Bets get them the minute I did. It not only took the gilt off them, but was to mean, when we finally got back to India, that word got around that Mollie Kaye couldn't be asked out to a party unless her school-age sister was invited too. So hostesses who did not want an extra two girls (and two more men to partner them) stopped asking me out, and I missed a lot of fun. Which was initially Bee's fault, but later on Mother's ...

Poor Mother ... poor, silly old darling! She is dead now. She died just two months after her ninety-seventh birthday, while I was working on the first draft of this book, and I could not feel sad for her, because she had so *hated* being old. She could not and would not come to terms with it. The fact that she could no longer do things that she wanted to do, or go where she wanted to go (usually somewhere on the far side of the world), irked her unbearably, and someone had to be blamed for it. Somehow it was somebody else's fault: the doctor's, for one. If he knew his job he would give her something that would 'cure her'! If 'you children' (Bets and myself — both grandmothers!) had any consideration for her wishes, we would allow her to go out to India or South Africa for the winter months instead of 'forcing her' to stay and freeze in England.

It was only at the very end, when she was almost seven weeks into her ninety-eighth year and another autumn had begun — an Indian Summer of an autumn with leaves turning gold in the windless, golden days — that I got tired of being blamed for preventing her from leaving, swallow-like, for the warm south, when all I had done was to point out the difficulties that would face her if she tried to go jaunting off to Jaipur or Cape Province or wherever, now that she was so lame. Besides, thanks to the success of *The Far Pavilions,* I had, as she knew, been able to put a large sum of money into her bank account; large enough to allow her to do almost anything (within reason!) she happened to feel like doing. So now, for the first time, I pointed out that she only had to pick up her telephone and ask for the village taxi to collect her and take her down to her nearest travel agents — who by this time knew her well — and book herself a flight to the sun; why not do that?

I hoped that this would make her face facts at last and realize that she was not the only member of her generation who was growing old. She had already outlived so many friends whom she used to visit in India and the Seychelles; in Ceylon, Singapore, Canada, Africa and America — not to mention England, Ireland, Scotland and Wales! And those few who remained were now too old themselves to cope with a house-guest who was only four years short of her century and had, at ninety-two, fallen and smashed her hip, and so could no longer climb stairs; though she nipped around pretty briskly with the aid of a stick, and *detested* being helped! What I did not tell her was that several of these friends, while continuing to write to her to ask when she was coming to stay with them again, had at the same time written privately to Bets or myself to say: '*Please* don't let Daisy come out here again! We love her dearly but we cannot cope any longer with the responsibility of having her as a house-guest; she is so frail, and so obstinate — she still thinks she can do anything and everything, and she won't do what she's told. Please don't let her know we have written to you, but do, *do* discourage her from coming out, because it is all we can do to look after ourselves these days.'

I wish I had realized that when, confronted with the discovery that no one was going to prevent her from making the attempt, she would have to stop pretending, and face the inescapable fact that her travelling days were over. Because once she had accepted that never again would she be able to pack her bags and set off across the sea towards the sunrise, she metaphorically turned her face to the wall and stopped living. It was as simple as that . . .

Yet she herself had said, only a few days before she left us on her last journey, that she had had a wonderful life and would not have exchanged it for anyone else's. It's quite something to be able to say that. And at the end God was very good to her, for during her last three days she thought she was back in Kashmir on a houseboat on the Dal Lake, and that the *manji,* the owner, kept turning his boat around. Each morning and once in the evening, she said: 'Why has my bed been moved? It was on the other side last night. ... Oh, how silly of me; of course, Kadera* must have told them to turn the boat the other way; he knows that I sometimes like to look at a different view.'

How lovely just to drift off to sleep, convinced that she was in one of the most beautiful places in this still beautiful world, and knowing that Tacklow would be there waiting for her when she woke up.

---

* Her Kashmiri bearer, Kadera-lone, who had been with her for more than thirty years.

Chapter 27

~~❊~~

Far to Southward they wheel and glance
The million molten spears of morn —
The spears of our deliverance
That shine on the house where we were born.

Kipling, 'Song of the Wise Children'

Once again I will go back in time to a much earlier autumn. To the fall of 1927, when Mother was still young enough to be every bit as happy and excited as Bets and myself at the prospect of returning to India. Happier, in fact; since she had never known what it was like to be a desperately self-conscious teenager embarrassed by her shape and terrified of being a social flop!

However, a most unexpected (and while it lasted, thoroughly unpleasant) circumstance was about to come to my rescue. Seasickness, of all undignified things. Good old *mal de mer*. Once safely embarked for India, I proved to be such a bad sailor that I spent a large part of that longed-for voyage with my head over a basin, and though I went on board looking like Nellie the Elephant, by the time I landed in Calcutta I was, if not exactly a sylph, at least a tolerably attractive member of the human race. But I cannot recommend the treatment.

To begin with, all had been well, for though the Channel was once again appallingly rough, this time it did not bother me in the least; not even when, during the night, the S.S. 'City of London' turned the corner of Spain. . . .

By morning the wind had risen to gale force and far more than half the passengers had not been able to leave their bunks; Mother and Bets among them. I, however, was feeling on top of the world as I blithely accompanied Tacklow down to the almost deserted dining saloon and grandly ordered myself an Upton House-sized breakfast, starting — shall I ever forget? — with porridge. It came; and I had begun to pour cream on it when the only other passenger out of the four who last night had made up our table of eight at dinner, leant forward and inquired in jocular tones: 'Have you just eaten that, or are you going to?'

Unfortunately I had not heard that hoary old traveller's joke before, and it took me a full fifteen seconds to work it out. When I did, I looked down at the bowl of porridge ... and in the next moment I was on my feet and stumbling away between the wildly tilting tables and the empty, storm-chained chairs, making for the two-berth cabin I shared with Bets, where I remained, flat on my back in my bunk and wishing I could die, for the rest of that week.

Even with my previous experience of seasickness I could not have believed that it was possible to feel so ill and still remain alive. Our cabin stewardess and the ship's doctor evidently agreed, for when the ship reached Gibraltar and some VIP who had only been travelling as far as the Rock vacated his luxury cabin, they persuaded the Captain to have me moved into it. Which is how I came to occupy for the rest of that voyage the kind of shipboard accommodation that is normally reserved for Viceroys or millionaires, instead of a cramped little inside cabin on B deck. I didn't even have to lie on a bunk, since the VIP suite had a proper bed — and proper windows too, that looked out onto its own private bit of deck. Not portholes.

I was much impressed and only wished that I could have enjoyed it more. But sadly, I continued to be seasick on and off for most of the rest of that trip, because instead of steaming through the Straits of Gibraltar into a calm blue Mediterranean, we found ourselves sailing into more foul weather. This stayed with us all the way to Naples, where, praise be, we stopped for two blessed days and saw the sun come out for the first time since we left England.

It was heaven to be on dry land again! The sun blazed down and we were met by a strong smell of drains and, just outside the dock gates, the reek of a dead sheep that lay in the road; cheerfully ignored by one and all and smelling even stronger than the garlic that our enthusiastic guide breathed all over us with every word he spoke.

We had not wanted a guide, but there were such hordes of them, and they were so clamorous and persistent, that in the end Tacklow decided that it was better to be accompanied by one rather than followed by an importunate mob. And how right he was, for no sooner had he selected one of them than the winner turned like a tiger on his rivals, chasing them away with a torrent of shrill invective that Tacklow refused to translate. We didn't get much out of our so-called guide except at second hand, for as soon as he found that Tacklow could speak Italian he embraced him as a brother and thereafter abandoned his wonderfully fractured English in favour of his own tongue — the two of them chatting happily away for the rest of our time in Naples.

In those days the hillside to the west of the city, which is now a solid mass of concrete high-rise flats, was a mass of green trees; a truly lovely spot from where one could look down on Naples and see, across the beautiful bay, a thin plume of smoke rising up into the clear blue air from the crater of Vesuvius. We drove to Pompeii in an open horse-drawn carriage, and I remember our guide taking Tacklow aside and surreptitiously hurrying him into one of the excavated houses where women tourists were not permitted because it had once been an expensive brothel. Tacklow said there were a lot of rather racy frescoes on the walls but refused to elaborate.

The sun continued to shine for most of the following day, but towards evening ominous black clouds began to pile up over the sea, and shortly after sundown we sailed out of the Bay of Naples in the most spectacular thunderstorm I had ever seen; our way lit by furious, blazing flashes of lightning and the sort of noise that one associates with the last act of *The Ring,* when Valhalla is burning and the drums and brass in the orchestra are being assisted to raise the roof by a bevy of stage-hands flapping sheets of tin in the wings.

I watched on deck until we were clear of the harbour, and was then forced to retreat to my VIP cabin with another attack of seasickness. This one lasted until we reached Malta, which I remember as a beautiful, pale-gold island whose capital, Valetta of the Knights of St John of Jerusalem, looked as though it were made of frozen lace. It was here, walking through its narrow streets in the warm moonlight, that I caught the first authentic, heart-stirring whiff of the East ... jasmine, orange-blossom and spices and the scent of sun-baked dust. And heard, softened by distance, men's voices (Highlanders from some Scottish regiment on garrison duty on Malta, perhaps?) singing 'The Skye Boat Song'. I remembered that night many years later, and described it in a chapter of *Shadow of the Moon* which was cut from the original edition, but replaced in a subsequent reprint.

The S.S. 'City of London' stopped to coal by night off Alexandria. A noisy, messy business; the hot flare of torches accompanied by the chanting of the coalers and clouds of coal-dust that settled in a black film on the ship and the oily sea. By morning the decks were clean again, and ahead of us, lifting up out of a satin sea like an old, familiar friend who has hardly altered at all after a long period of separation, lay Port Said, friendly and welcoming. Here once more were the 'gully-gully' men — surely the same ones we had seen twice before? The same cheerful, noisy, grinning little boys who bobbed about in the water surrounding the ship and dived for the coins that passengers tossed overboard. The same sellers of rugs and carpets and Turkish Delight. And, once ashore, the familiar, crowded aisles of Simon Artz's shop where Bets and I gleefully bought ourselves new topis to replace those so much smaller ones that, close on nine long years ago, we had flung overboard as we sailed out of Port Said and headed for England, wondering tearfully if we should ever see India again.

The big, white-painted Victorian hotel on the edge of the sands was just as we remembered it, and once again we lunched in its airy dining-room where all the windows stood wide open to catch the warm sea breeze that riffled through the palms and bougainvillaeas. Even the menu seemed the same — as did the lines of bathing-huts out on the hot sands by the water's edge and those stranded blue jellyfish along the shore. Once again we saw the streak of flame and the puff of white smoke as the midday gun was fired, and once again we waited, fascinated, to hear the boom that lagged so far behind the flash and provided a practical demonstration of the relative speeds of light and sound. To our great disappointment the 'City of London' left after dark, so we passed through the first part of the Suez Canal during the night, and after anchoring for a time in the Bitter Lakes to let the westward-bound traffic go through, reached the Gulf of Suez in the evening, where we went ashore in a Canal Company launch to dine in Port Tewfik at the French Club with an official of the Company who was an old friend of Tacklow's.

In those days many French officials of the Suez Canal Company had houses there, at the eastern end of the Canal. And though tiny Port Tewfik appeared to consist of a single tree-shaded street, lined on one side by gardens and on the other by the Canal itself, while beyond it on the far bank lay nothing but desert, it was one of the prettiest places you could imagine. A two-by-four flower-scented oasis of green in a waste of blinding sand, rock and salt water. After dinner we strolled back in the moonlight down the long avenue of trees that ends on a point where a crouching lion, carved in stone, stands as a memorial to all those men of the Indian Army who during the First World War lost their lives fighting in the Middle East. Here, sitting on the warm sandstone of the low surrounding wall, we looked out across the Gulf of Suez while our host told us fascinating tales of the early days of the Canal Company. The moonlight and the tree shadows made lacy patterns on the white dust, *sable on argent*, as he talked, and I remember how sweet the air was with the scent of night-flowering stock and tobacco plants, and that across the shimmering expanse of the Gulf we could see a spangle of lights that were the town of Suez and the nearer lights of ships lying at anchor; one of them the 'City of London'. I was almost half-way home — !

The Red Sea lived up to its name. The temperature must have been somewhere up in the nineties and even my VIP cabin was red-hot, for although there was a brisk wind — enough to curdle the sea with white horses — it was a 'following wind'. The ship dipped and bucked to it and I was seasick again; but by the time we reached Port Sudan the wind had died and we docked in a flat calm sea. I don't know why we put in at Port Sudan. It is not a place that passenger-liners normally visit and I have never been there since. It was a hot, sandy, treeless and unattractive-looking place, but it had one thing to its credit that ought to have made it a star tourist attraction — and for all I know, may have done so by now. About a mile out from the shore there was a sunken reef, that we were taken out to in a glass-bottomed boat from which we could look down at the coral and the underwater life of the Red Sea.

It was a fantastically beautiful sight. Better by far than anything I have ever seen since. Better even than the Great Barrier Reef. The water was glass-clear and the blazing sunlight, slanting through it, lit up the reef as vividly as though it had been a stage in the glare of footlights, spotlights and floodlights, so that you could see every tinge and tint of colour in the corals and sea anemones, the seaweeds and sea creatures below you. It was like some fabulous fairy-tale garden out of the Arabian Nights, in which the trees were all fashioned from different corals and the birds were jewelled and enamelled fishes that

445

flitted through the branching coral and hovered over flowerbeds of rose quartz, topaz and aquamarine anemones.

'Oh, they must have been put out here on purpose!' cried Mother as a portly, turquoise-blue parrot fish swam majestically through a crowd of tiny triangular orange-and-black striped 'football' fishes. 'They *can't* have come here by chance! Those tour people must have put them here.' It was a nice thought — considering that we were almost a mile off shore and surrounded by the glittering expanse of the Red Sea — and it conjured up a pleasing picture of a squad of Middle-Eastern entrepreneurs emptying bucketfuls of tropical fish into the ocean in the hope that they would stay put where dumped. Dear Mother!

We could have spent hours there, getting badly sunburnt as we gazed and gazed, gasping and exclaiming at the lovely sight. But the 'City of London' was only making a very short stop and we had to return. Aden next: the port that to all Anglo-Indians is fixed in their memory like a folk-legend of Empire. Kipling described it in one of his Barrack-room Ballads as 'Old Aden like a barrick stove that no one's lit for years and years', and in its honour a Scotsman composed a famous pipe melody; one that is still played when the pipers march out at the head of Scottish regiments, cloaks swaying and kilts a'swing to the skirl of 'The Barren Rocks of Aden'. We ate lunch in a hotel on the hill above the town and took another brief, uneasy look at what we were again told were the dried remains of a mermaid — a real one! (Well, all I can say is that she must have been a very old and unalluring one!) Then back on board and out into the Indian Ocean at last.

Onto that dark, unforgettable, sapphire-blue sea whose water is so clear that you can see the foam bubbles sinking down through it for long seconds like pale-blue marbles, and watch the floating jellyfish, or a school of dolphins at play a yard or two below the surface, effortlessly keeping pace with the slicing bow, while flights of flying fish take off from the top of every wave to skitter away like a handful of winged quicksilver. Sometimes we would see basking sharks; or whales spouting. And always at night the foam was brilliant with phosphorus and the star patterns overhead changed their stations and became far brighter than they had been on even the clearest nights in England. Here again, above me, were the old familiar constellations that Tacklow had first pointed out and named for me on the Ridge at Simla and the flat roof of Curzon House in Delhi. And soon, very soon, I would see the Southern Cross lift up above the horizon to blaze in that enormous sky. Yes, I was nearly home.

Oh, those long sea voyages eastward! How wonderful they were. And how much do travellers in this hurrying, scurrying age miss as their jet planes whisk them in a single night from London to India without their seeing anything but blackness or a sea of clouds. (That was Cyprus, that was ... there goes Arabia!) How fortunate I was to have lived in a time when one travelled by train and ship instead of through the air, and could look and look and look. The 'City of London' must, I think, have made straight from Aden to Ceylon, since I cannot remember — and will not believe I could have forgotten — stopping at either Karachi or Bombay; especially Bombay. So presumably the City Line ships, being bound for Calcutta, took the shortest route across the Indian Ocean and made their next landfall at Colombo.

I had been assured that once we were clear of the Gulf of Aden I would be free from seasickness at last. And on first sight the Indian Ocean seemed to bear this out, for it was as smooth as the proverbial mill pond and not a breath of wind stirred. But there had been a great storm somewhere far to the southward, and rumours of it reached up across the equator in the form of a long, smooth swell that was invisible to the eye until you had some part of the ship to measure it by. Prone once more in my cabin I could see the dressing-gown hanging on my door swing slowly out towards me as the ship rolled lazily to the swell, and watch it return as slowly as the 'City of London' slid gently into the trough. From the deck, if you watched the horizon line it would be well above the deck rail one minute, and a minute later it would sink gently below it; yet always so slowly that you were almost unaware of any movement. After a day or two I was able to appear in the dining-saloon and eat a carefully chosen meal (no more porridge; or anything of the same consistency, such as thick soup or stew), always provided I kept my gaze well away from the portholes, beyond which the horizon of that deceptively calm sea rose and fell with the regularity of a soundless metronome.

When the swell diminished Bets and I, true to form, took a hand in getting up an impromptu cabaret show which was performed the night before we reached Ceylon and docked at Colombo. I can only remember the two items that Bets and I thought up and arranged. Costumes being difficult to come by, we recruited a chorus line of six girls whom we dressed in pyjamas and armed with pillows to do a 'pillow-fight dance' which ended with the entrance of the Matron (the tallest girl on the ship) and the dancers miming a hasty leap into bed and pretending to be sound asleep. In the second turn we all wore navy-blue skirts, with 'tropical-white' uniform jackets and peaked caps borrowed from the ship's officers, and sang and danced to 'All the Nice Girls Love a Sailor' — shades of the children's cabaret show when homeward-bound on the old 'Ormond'! And now we were on our way back again. It seemed a fitting curtain-raiser to our return to India, and I am happy to say that both items received standing ovations from an uncritical and possibly over-enthusiastic audience.

Ceylon might almost have been India. Coconut palms bowing to the trade winds. Blue seas crashing in lines of foam-frilled breakers on long white beaches. Gold-mohur, frangipani and jacaranda trees, and the lovely sight and heavenly scent of familiar flowers; jasmine, bougainvillaea, orange-blossoms, hibiscus. Bazaars full of dark-skinned, gaily clad crowds, and the trees full of crows and parrots and little chittering *galaries*.

We had friends in Colombo; one of them a schoolmate who had gone out to join her parents and was already engaged to be married — a piece of news bringing a whiff of romance that was headier than the scent of flowers. Norah (not her real name) was both stocky and plain. Yet here she was, almost visibly exuding joy and confidence, wearing a diamond on the correct finger and excitedly planning her trousseau. Well, if *her,* there was surely hope for me? It was an intoxicating thought; and going into dinner that night in the long dining-room of the Galleface Hotel, where a band was playing dance music on the terrace outside, I was pleasantly aware of the appraising gaze of a large number of apparently unattached men who took note of us as we made our way to our table. And charmed to see that they outnumbered the women present by at least four to one.

I had always been nuts about Romance. I used to think about it a lot and wonder what it was like to *really* fall in love. I couldn't wait to do so. But despite the success of the cabaret turns, my morale had sunk well below sea-level by the time we reached Ceylon, for I had made the lowering discovery that I was about the only girl on the 'City of London' (except for Bets, who was too young) who hadn't collected an admirer or fallen in love with someone, however temporarily, in the course of the voyage. It did not augur well for the future, and I had been forced to the reluctant conclusion that Romance was not for me and I had better face the fact now, and resign myself to ending up a spinster. But twenty-four hours in that enchanting island, aided by the romantic music of a dance band playing under a sky full of stars, the interested glances of the numerous men who were dining at the Galleface that night, and above all, the personable young tea-planter to whom my plain, chunky, hockey-playing ex-schoolmate had become engaged, had made me feel that there was hope for me yet, and I left Ceylon feeling a good deal happier and far less pessimistic about myself and the future.

Our last-but-one port of call was Madras, which stays in my mind as white lines of surf breaking on a long low shore, and clouds of large black-and-scarlet butterflies lilting through the hot, salty air above the jetty where the liner docked. Those butterflies were proof that I had indeed come home, for they were old friends; the same as the ones who used to haunt the poinsettia hedges at Narora. It was wonderful to see them again, and as I stepped off the gangplank and onto the dock I felt like going down on my knees and kissing the ground — as Pope John does when he travels abroad. I could have cried from sheer happiness.

Several Indian friends of Tacklow's, hearing of his return, were on the dock to meet him, and in the charming fashion of their country they hung garlands of flowers, and elaborate necklaces of tinsel-ribbon decorated with gold-embroidered satin medallions, about his neck before embracing him. I kept one of those glittering necklaces, and over half a century later we used it in the filming of *The Far Pavilions*. I still have it. A few days later, after anchoring for a night at the Sandheads that lie several miles out at sea opposite the mouth of the Hoogly River, the S.S. 'City of London' took up a pilot and started on the last lap of the voyage up the river to Calcutta.

I suppose Bets and I ate something that day, but if so I don't remember doing so. As far as I can recall we spent all our time on deck watching India go by, afraid to miss any of the familiar sights; the palm-thatched huts, the broom-stick palms, the groves of trees, the water buffaloes and the paddy birds; and the people — the people!

The Hoogly is one of the most treacherous rivers in the world, for it channels most of the silt of the great Ganges Delta and is therefore full of sandbanks that change their position from day to day according to the whim of the currents. And because it has claimed more ships than any other river, a Hoogly pilot can command very large sums for his services. Yet even now, with all the modern aids that the pilots have at their disposal, a ship can be lost to the sands, and as we edged up the river that day we passed the half-submerged wreck of a passenger-ship that had run aground with the loss of many lives only a couple of days previously on an unseen shoal. Her funnels, mast and bridge, and part of her upper desk, were still above the water, and the thick, muddy currents swirled hungrily around and through them. But what the quicksands catch they keep. The Hoogly has been a graveyard for ships for hundreds of years, and one of the 'City of London's' officers told me that by next day there would be nothing visible of that ship but the wreck buoys and, possibly for a day longer, the tip of the tallest mast. No more.

Towards evening we landed at Calcutta's Garden Reach where we were met by Sir Charles and Lady Teggart — friends of my parents with whom we would be staying for a week — and a great many of Tacklow and Mother's Indian friends who had come down to welcome them back. Almost all the latter brought garlands: so many of them that when Tacklow entered the Teggarts' car he was almost hidden by tinsel and flowers. There were garlands for Bets and myself too; one each, made of jasmine blossoms. It was a wonderful homecoming . . .

Years later I was to read in a book called *Eleven Leopards,* by Norah Burke, who loved India as much as I do, a paragraph she wrote about her own return to that country after many years. Here it is:

'Was it indeed really India again after all these years? Yes! it was India . . . My heart moved as does the heart of anyone who has ever lived there. Did we British bleed India for what we could carry away? Or did our men give their health — their lives for her? Did we help and love her, bring her out of cruel ignorance — famine? Did we educate her children, tend her sick, guard her frontiers, irrigate her fields, save her forests? Well, whatever else we did, we loved her.'

Yes, very many of us truly loved her. We still do.

~❊❅❊~

Appendix

Grandfather's Passing-Out Certificate from the East India Company College, Addiscombe (later, Haileybury).

JANUARY 6, 1888.
THE TIMES, FRIDAY

COMMISSIONS IN THE ARMY.

The undermentioned gentlemen are declared by the Civil Service Commissioners to be the successful candidates at the examination held on November 30 1887, and following days for Cadetships in the Royal Military College, Sandhurst :—

I.—For CAVALRY CADETSHIPS.

Name.	Marks	Name.	Marks
Wade, Alexander P.C.R.	8,987	Morris, Robert Lee	7,088
Hulse, Harold Hatton	7,432	Murray, Walter Graham	6,852
Harrison, John Collinson	7,340	Belk, William	6,648
Tancred, Thomas Selby	7,245	Stapylton, Miles John	6,846
Church, Bernard Elliot	7,244	Pitman, Thomas Tait	6,846
Burnett, Charles Kenyon	7,216	Simpson, Osmond Beckett	6,649
Hodgson, Henry West	7,133	Lloyd, John Herbert	6,608
Lascelles, William Frank	7,110		

II.—For INFANTRY CADETSHIPS.

Name.	Marks.	Name.	Marks.
Kaye, Cecil	10,328	Smith, Frederic Vincent	7,470
Cruddas, Hugh Wilson	9,964	Gardiner, George F.	7,435
Bonham, Walter Floyd	9,130	Stephens, Reginald B.	7,423
Paul, Robert Sears	8,974	Prothero, Frake Lewis	7,404
Hobkirk, Stuart W. T.	8,915	Murray, Edward R. B.	7,396
Casement, Joshua B.	8,786	Hope, John Augustus	7,373
Elsmie, Alex. M. S.	8,722	Buckle, Matthew F.	7,344
Wade, Thomas S. H.	8,627	Anderson, Charles K.	7,330
Church, Arthur J. B.	8,512	Crowther, John Ernest	7,327
Readon, Arthur Eyre	8,465	Orde-Powlett, W. G. A.	7,299
Tayler, William F. C.	8,279	Russell, Henry de Winton	7,297
Bossuquet, James T. I.	8,273	Seccombe, Archibald K.	7,292
Carleton, Henry Anthony	8,271	Tilney, William Arthur	7,291
Bunbury, William C. H.	8,259	Goode, Stuart	7,277
Malcolm, Neill	8,232	Raymond, Harry Elliott	7,277
Molyneux - Montgomerie, G. F.	8,149	peck, John Herbert	7,232
West, George W. M.	8,102	Macaraiu, Lauris Hugh	7,214
Cowan, James W. A.	8,094	Phillips, Frank Truscott	7,202
Montresor, Reginald T.	8,061	Blair, Arthur Kennedy	7,201
Ashworth, Guy Charles	8,038	Bell, Cyril Walter Bowdler	7,197
Baker, Edward H. B.	8,036	Morris, Reginald Yates	7,158
Clarke, John L. J.	8,022	Marshall, Kenneth F.C.	7,134
Powell, Harold Haines	8,008	Padelia, George Evan	7,120
Thesiger, George H.	8,000	Andrew, Frederic A.	7,119
Blumberg, Herbert E.	7,997	Drace, Godfrey	7,101
Blunt, Conrad K. G.	7,924	Legge, William Kaye	7,099
Bethune, Hector	7,895	Hewlett, Gervase Gillham	7,061
Hornby, Montague L.	7,869	Maxwell, Lawrence L.	7,032
Marshall, George	7,851	Campbell, Arthur G. J.	7,030
Coddington, Henry B. O.	7,822	Christie, Edgar Jescapp	7,016
Stevens, John L. C.	7,807	Bayshawe, Leonard A.	7,009
Kingston, Lucius A.	7,804	Harding, Maynard F.	6,982
Browne, Harold M.	7,803	Grey, Ralph Henry	6,973
Crofts, Leonard M.	7,717	Burton, Richard Watkins	6,970
Dickson, Harry Wilfrid	7,710	Nuttall, Mansfield Elliott	6,969
Maclachlan, Thomas R.	7,703	Pearce-Serocold, Eric	6,964
Tew, Harold Stuart	7,700	Clarke, Charles H. B.	6,942
Brand, Herbert	7,693	Keyworth, Walter	6,936
Stewart, Charles Edward	7,570	Watson, Arthur	6,929
Begbie, George Edward	7,547	Cottingham, Charles S.	5,913
Douglas, Walter Biney	7,542	Ovens, Robert M.	6,900
Cowell, Albert V. J.	7,539	Hill, Edward Roden	6,895
Tennant, Edward	7,505	Taylor, Frank P. S.	6,895
Egerton, William Francis	7,503	Munn, Reginald George	6,874
Howlett, Frederick Percy	3,494	Bloxam, Francis Lynch	6,866
Young, Walter Herbert	7,494	Murray, Fergus	6,861
Cassels, Gilbert Robert	7,414	Stubbs, Arthur Kennedy	6,638

Subjoined is a list of Gentlemen Cadets of the Senior Division who passed the qualifying examination at the Royal Military College in December for Commissions in the Cavalry and Infantry :—

PASSED WITH HONOURS.

	Marks.		Marks.
Paul, E. S.	2,651	Clarkson, B. St. J.	2,020
Sothecole, F. R.	2,473	Bull, E. R.	2,013
Cowan, J. W. A.	2,448	Maclachlan, T. R.	2,013
Campbell, D. G. M.	2,394	Orde-Powlett, W. G. A.	2,007
Lee, A. W. H.	2,374	Maclean, H. L. B.	2,005
Hope, J. A.	2,352	Simpson, O. B.	2,004
Tayler, W. F. C.	2,344	Collies, W. F.	2,003
Cruddas, H. W.	2,338	Tilney, W. A.	2,000
Payn, D. R.	2,325	Maxwell, L. L.	1,999
Tennant, E.	2,325	Bell, B.	1,998
Buckle, M. F.	2,319	Price, G. D.	1,996
Hornby, M. L.	2,315	Alexander, H. S.	1,984
Stevens, J. L. C.	2,312	Norris, P. B.	1,982
Saville, R. C.	2,306	Barchard, A. E.	1,977
Bunbury, W. C. H.	2,292	Young, W. H.	1,975
Kaye, C.	2,290	Pearce-Serocold, E.	1,974
Liversay, C. S.	2,287	Anderson, C. K.	1,970
Rogers, F. W. S.	2,284	Burton, R. W.	1,968
Murray, F.	2,277	Montresor, R. T.	1,967
Elsmie, A. M. S.	2,274	Lloyd, G. H.	1,965
Hutt, W. L.	2,285	Grey, R. H.	1,936
Fowell, H. H.	2,263	Levis, L. J. G.	1,953
Marshall, G.	2,258	Hanmer, L. A. G.	1,944
Douglas, W. B.	2,257	Prothero, F. L.	1,943
Casement, J. B.	2,251	Baker, E. H. B.	1,940
Bethune, H.	2,249	Brand, H.	1,940
Clarke, J. L. J.	2,245	Francis, C. G.	1,937
Seccombe, A. K.	2,240	Carleton, H. D.	1,935
Carter, E. E.	2,230	Begbie, G. E.	1,925
Hodgson, H. W.	2,225	Ewart, C. G. E.	1,925
Malcolm, N.	2,222	Watson, A.	1,922
Stevens, B. F.	2,221	Christie, E. J.	1,921
Legge, W. K.	2,219	Byers, C. B.	1,320
Mears, A.	2,217	Dundas, F. C.	1,920
Crofts, L. M.	2,215	Keyworth, W.	1,915
Gough, H. de la P.	2,215	Berdoe, G. A.	1,910
Coddington, H. B. O.	2,213	Carlyon, L. K.	1,904
Hewlett, G. G.	2,212	Clark, C. H. B.	1,902
Campbell, A. C. J.	2,209	Smith, F. V.	1,900
Cowell, A. V. J.	2,209	Howlett, F. P.	1,899
Burnett, C. K.	2,190	M'Gavin, L. H.	1,899
Morris, R. Y.	2,189	Kingston, L. A.	1,893
Dickson, H. W.	2,173	Young, M. G.	1,892
Pearson, R. P.	2,173	Cottingham, C. S.	1,839
Stubbs, A. K.	2,173	Hamilton, W. M. F.	1,889
West, G. W. M.	2,162	Lowndes, M.	1,884
Taw, H. S.	2,157	Raymond, H. E.	1,881
Bosanquet, J. T. I.	2,156	Church, B. E.	1,876
Molyneux-Montgomerie, G. F.	2,156	Beadon, A. E.	1,871
		Lynch-Blosse, F.	1,868
Firie, A. M.	2,153	Hill, W. A.	1,861
Munn, R. G.	2,151	Barton, F. R.	1,851
Drage, G.	2,151	Wade, T. S. H.	1,850
Dowdall, T. P.	2,150	Gardiner, W. A.	1,847
Taylor, F. P. S.	2,149	Dwyer, A. G.	1,836
Thomas, A. D.	2,147	Goode, S.	1,822
Hobkirk, S. W. T.	2,145	Hughes, E. M.	1,816
Falconlcjus, W. C.	2,130	Nuttall, M. E.	1,816
Gardiner, G. F.	2,125	Morris, R. L.	1,809
Plowden, T. C.	2,120	Marshall, R. T.	1,808
Drewe-Read, R. O.	2,114	Stapylton, M. J.	1,797
Ovens, R. M.	2,110	Marshall, K. F. C.	1,757
Fitz-Roy, Hon. E. A.	2,109	Clery, C. B. L.	1,786
Armstrong, E. E.	2,106	Church, A. J. B.	1,785
Travers, E. R.	2,097	Peck, J. H.	1,761
Loring, W. L.	2,093	Murray, W.G.	1,756
Thesiger, G. H.	2,092	Blair, A. K.	1,753
Stephens, R. B.	2,089	Lascelles, W. F.	1,742
Andrew, F. A.	2,086	Harrison, J. C.	1,738
Ryder, F. J.	2,068	Cassels, O. E.	1,734
Davies, N. P.	2,072	Ashworth, G. C.	1,727
Hardy, F. P. A.	2,070	Gosset, A. B.	1,720
Da Costa, O. M.' J.	2,061	Moffitt, G.	1,712
Grant-Duff, A.	2,059	Tancred, T. S.	1,651
Browne, H. M.	2,058	Bannerman, W. P.	1,680
Hales, R. H.	2,057	Bonham, W. F.	1,673
Egerton, W. F.	2,055	Warren-Swettenham, T. R. E. W.	1,669
Blunt, C. R. G.	2,054		
Trottwey, T. L.	2,051	Carleton, H. A.	1,643
Stewart, C. E.	2,041	Keene, H. L. R.	1,639
Pitman, T. T.	2,043	Macdonald, P. C. E.	1,639
Belk, W.	2,035	Osborne, A. de V.	1,629
Block, E. N. L.	2,033	Barlow, C. W.	1,553
Geoghegan, F. E.	2,027		

Left: The Times listing of entrants into the Royal Military College, Sandhurst, 6 January 1888.

Right: Listing of cadets passing out of the Royal Military College, Sandhurst, 6 March 1889.

453

I am so proud of *The Times of India*'s valedictory column written on Tacklow's retirement that I reproduce some of it here. Since it was written before the publication of the Honours List, he is referred to as Colonel Kaye.

Intelligence Department people are shy birds which prefer as a rule to avoid the glare of the limelight. Obviously, their work necessitates such habits. Yet it is a pity, for more reasons than one, that the general public is given so little opportunity of realizing the magnitude and the importance of the services that they perform for the State. In a few days' time there will leave India, perhaps for ever, a man whose recollections, if they were to be published, would reveal more than the autobiographies of many Viceroys. Yet his work had been little known, and his Department too frequently labours under a sinister reputation which it has done nothing to deserve. Colonel Cecil Kaye, the Director of the Central Intelligence Bureau of the Government of India, has held charge of this important office for five years, after ... succeeding Sir Charles Cleveland. The policy of appointing a soldier to control what was primarily a police department was much criticized at the time ... Colonel Kaye, who has a distinguished military career, came to the forefront of the cipher experts during the war. He held the post of Deputy Chief Censor, and discharged that most exacting and delicate of duties in a manner which proved his possession of rare tact and good humour. The same qualities have marked his administration of the Intelligence Bureau ... Colonel Kaye will long be remembered at the headquarters of the Government of India for his kindness, his good humour and his absolute straightness. Never has there been a more disinterested servant of the public, or one more free from suspicion of utilizing a position of great confidence for any other purpose than the general good.

Visit Penguin on the Internet
and browse at your leisure

- ◆ preview sample extracts of our forthcoming books
- ◆ read about your favourite authors
- ◆ investigate over 10,000 titles
- ◆ enter one of our literary quizzes
- ◆ win some fantastic prizes in our competitions
- ◆ e-mail us with your comments and book reviews
- ◆ instantly order any Penguin book

and masses more!

'*To be recommended without reservation ... a rich and rewarding on-line experience*' – Internet Magazine

www.penguin.co.uk

READ MORE IN PENGUIN

In every corner of the world, on every subject under the sun, Penguin represents quality and variety – the very best in publishing today.

For complete information about books available from Penguin – including Puffins, Penguin Classics and Arkana – and how to order them, write to us at the appropriate address below. Please note that for copyright reasons the selection of books varies from country to country.

In the United Kingdom: Please write to *Dept. EP, Penguin Books Ltd, Bath Road, Harmondsworth, West Drayton, Middlesex UB7 ODA*

In the United States: Please write to *Consumer Sales, Penguin Putnam Inc., P.O. Box 12289 Dept. B, Newark, New Jersey 07101-5289.* VISA and MasterCard holders call 1-800-788-6262 to order Penguin titles

In Canada: Please write to *Penguin Books Canada Ltd, 10 Alcorn Avenue, Suite 300, Toronto, Ontario M4V 3B2*

In Australia: Please write to *Penguin Books Australia Ltd, P.O. Box 257, Ringwood, Victoria 3134*

In New Zealand: Please write to *Penguin Books (NZ) Ltd, Private Bag 102902, North Shore Mail Centre, Auckland 10*

In India: Please write to *Penguin Books India Pvt Ltd, 11 Community Centre, Panchsheel Park, New Delhi 110017*

In the Netherlands: Please write to *Penguin Books Netherlands bv, Postbus 3507, NL-1001 AH Amsterdam*

In Germany: Please write to *Penguin Books Deutschland GmbH, Metzlerstrasse 26, 60594 Frankfurt am Main*

In Spain: Please write to *Penguin Books S. A., Bravo Murillo 19, 1° B, 28015 Madrid*

In Italy: Please write to *Penguin Italia s.r.l., Via Benedetto Croce 2, 20094 Corsico, Milano*

In France: Please write to *Penguin France, Le Carré Wilson, 62 rue Benjamin Baillaud, 31500 Toulouse*

In Japan: Please write to *Penguin Books Japan Ltd, Kaneko Building, 2-3-25 Koraku, Bunkyo-Ku, Tokyo 112*

In South Africa: Please write to *Penguin Books South Africa (Pty) Ltd, Private Bag X14, Parkview, 2122 Johannesburg*

BY THE SAME AUTHOR

House of Shade

An omnibus edition comprising:

Death in Zanzibar

To Dany Ashton it seems like the offer of the holiday of a lifetime when her stepfather invites her to stay on the exotic 'Isle of Cloves'. But even before her plane takes off Dany's delight has faded as she finds herself at the centre of a frightening mystery. On her arrival at Kivulimi, the 'House of Shade', her unease turns to terror when she realizes that among the houseguests is a dangerous and ruthless murderer. Dany doesn't know whom to trust . . .

Death in Kashmir

When young Sarah Parrish takes a skiing holiday in Gulmarg, a resort high above the fabled vale of Kashmir, she anticipates an amusing but uneventful stay. But the discovery of the grotesque corpse of grey-haired, sociable Mrs Matthews casts a dark shadow over the party. On learning the real truth about her death, Sarah is plunged into a deadly intrigue of secret messages, mysterious rendez-vous – and murder.

Death in the Andamans

The enchanting islands in the Indian Ocean beckoned irresistibly . . .

Though Copper Randal soon discovers that paradise has a darker side. A sense of foreboding hangs in the hot stillness among the mango trees and coconut palms. But neither she, nor her friend Valerie, stepdaughter of the Islands' Chief Commissioner, could have anticipated the sinister climax to the picnic after the hurricane struck . . .

BY THE SAME AUTHOR

The second volume of M. M. Kaye's autobiography:

Golden Afternoon

Returning from an English boarding-school to India in 1927, Mollie Kaye plunges into the glories – and embarrassments – of the Delhi season. But more than the social life of the Raj, she rediscovers her love for the country – the magic paradise of Kashmir, the sun-scorched plains of Rajputana, the teeming life of the markets and the complexities of high-caste life. Spiced with humour, incident and her trenchant views of the world, both then and now, *Golden Afternoon* is suffused above all with the enchantment that is India.

'A memoir that breathes an elixir of youthful rapture and abandonment ... the exotic sights and sounds and the ravishing and dramatic landscapes are described with irresistible tenderness and nostalgia' Elizabeth Buchan, *Mail on Sunday*

Her novels:

The Far Pavilions

'A *Gone with the Wind* of the North-West Frontier' *The Times*

The Far Pavilions is a story about an Englishman – Ashton Pelham-Martyn – brought up as a Hindu. It is the story of his passionate, but dangerous, love for Juli, an Indian princess. It is the story of divided loyalties, of friendship that endures till death, of high adventure and of the clash between East and West.

'Rip-roaring, heart-tugging, flag-flying, hair-raising, hoof-beating ... the very presence of India' *The Times*

Shadow of the Moon

When India bursts into flaming hatred and bitter bloodshed during the dark days of the Mutiny, Captain Alex Randall and his superior's wife, the lovely raven-haired Winter de Ballesteros, are thrown unwillingly together in the struggle for survival.

'A closely interwoven story of love and war whose descriptive prose is so evocative that you can actually see and – much more – smell India as the country assaults you from the page' *Sunday Telegraph*